AUSTRALIAN SCHOLARLY PUBLISHING
MELBOURNE & GALWAY

© Martin Hess 2025

First published 2025 by
Australian Scholarly Publishing
7 Lt Lothian St North
North Melbourne, Vic 3051
tel: 61 3 93296963
www.scholarly.com

ISBN 978-1-923267-17-6

ALL RIGHTS RESERVED

Cover Design: Amelia Walker

Diplomacy

The purpose of diplomacy is to strengthen the state, nation, or organization it serves in relation to others by advancing the interests in its charge. To this end, diplomatic activity endeavours to maximize a group's advantages *without the risk and expense of using force and preferably without causing resentment.*

[https://www.britannica.com/topic/diplomacy]

Politics

The activities of the government, members of law-making organizations, or *people who try to influence the way a country is governed.*

[https://dictionary.cambridge.org/dictionary]

Contents

Foreword   ix
Abbreviations   xii

Introduction   1

Overview   32

Part I
The Cold War and the Great Peace 1964–1998   35

Part II
Democracy, Violence and the New Security Paradigm 1999–2007   59

Part III
Capacity-building and the New Security Paradigm 2003–2014   127

Part IV
Applying The Rule of Law in Challenging Environments 2007–2014   175

Part V
Australian Security and Sovereignty in the Asian Century 2014–2024   215

Conclusion   247

Appendices

  1: Police Capacity Development   256
  2: Peel's Nine Principles   257
  3: Roles of the Military and the Civilian Police   260
  4: John Martinkus on Prabowo Subianto   262
  5: International Deployment Group   263
  6: Melanesian Wantok system   265
  7: Legal and Funding Parameters UN SDG International Human Rights Law (IHL) and ODA   266
  8: INTERPOL   269
  9: Xi Jinping and Vladimir Putin as Autocratic Leaders   273
  10: Thin Lines   275

Notes   277

References   300

Foreword

In ancient Athens, the lawgiver Solon was questioned as to what the best policed city was. According to Sir Alfred Zimmern, he replied 'the city…where all citizens, whether they have suffered injury or not, equally pursue and punish injustice'. Solon's somewhat utopian remark points to the wisdom of another ancient observation, namely the cynical comment recorded by Thucydides that hope is by its nature an expensive commodity. Many centuries were to pass before the evolution of the modern state set the scene for the development of anything like modern policing. Indeed, the very word 'police' long had a broader connotation than it currently bears, referring to the entirety of civil administration, or the public order of a town. Of course, monarchs in more absolutist times took steps to build agencies that would protect their security and status: in the challenging world of the 16th century, Queen Elizabeth I of England depended heavily on the work of her intelligence chief Sir Francis Walsingham (1532–90). Yet while Walsingham headed what now might be called a 'secret police', this fell far short of being anything like a modern community police force.

With the consolidation of the modern state, and particularly with the expansion of the bureaucratic capacities of the state, this began to change. Historically, two different broad mechanisms had come into play to try to secure a degree of social stability. Armed forces, particularly armies and navies, existed to repel external threats, while norms of behaviour played a role in sustaining basic social units. But between the territorial state on the one hand, and the family and basic community units on the other, lay a broad realm, best described as civil society, the stability of which depended upon something rather different: the development of laws that would proscribe certain forms of disruptive behaviour; and the establishment of agencies that would give effect to such laws. One of the key agencies of this kind was a police force, and its ability to function as a legitimate agency with popular support depended upon the force itself being subject to the law. This was not an entirely new idea: in the 13th century, Henry of Bracton had written that 'the king must be under God and the law' (*rex debet esse sub Deo et lege*). It was, however, an idea that resonated more vibrantly in the 19th century as Great Britain and its colonies were increasingly influenced by liberal and then democratic ideas, of which the political ideal of the rule of law was one of the most important.

These developments formed part of the context of the emergence of community policing, which Dr Hess describes so vividly in this book, and as a very experienced police officer himself he is remarkably well qualified to identify what the key elements of effective community policing might be. But this book goes much further, and sheds a great deal of light on a form of Australian international engagement that has received much less attention than it deserves. In many parts of the world, state and society are disrupted rather than stable, and since disrupted states have the potential to pose threats to international peace and security, they have long been the focus of international attention. One mechanism for addressing such problems of disruption has been international policing or police assistance. This has a long history, going back at least to the 1854 establishment of the Shanghai Municipal Police to provide policing services for the Shanghai International Settlement, itself a creature of the 19th century system of capitulations in China. More recently, peacekeeping under the auspices of the United Nations has very often had an important or critical police dimension, since in territories where peacekeeping is required, both the rule of law and police capacity to give it effect have typically been victims of the turbulence that gave rise to the need for peacekeeping in the first place.

This brings us to the nub of Dr Hess's important study. Australian police have long been respected contributors to this kind of activity, and the book provides a masterly survey of the forms of engagement that this has historically involved, and of the theatres of operation to which Australian police have been deployed. Dr Hess's own field experiences in Cyprus, East Timor and Afghanistan illuminate these engagements, but they by no means exhaust the range of venues in which Australian police have contributed constructively. The book provides a comprehensive overview of these contributions. This is not only instructive in itself, but it also helps redress an observable tendency amongst analysts to neglect policing in favour of large-scale military deployments such as INTERFET in East Timor in 1999 – despite the critical role that unarmed police had played in the UNAMET mission leading to the 'popular consultation' on 30 August 1999 that saw 78.5 per cent of voters opt for independence rather than mere autonomy within Indonesia, something followed by viciously violent militia attacks on vulnerable communities. The UN Security Council in Resolution 2185 of 20 November 2014 confirmed the importance of such policing by resolving 'to include, as appropriate, policing as an integral part of the mandates of United Nations peacekeeping operations and special political missions, and to give clear, credible, and achievable mandates for policing-related activities, matched by appropriate resources'. In addition to engaging in peace operations in a strict sense, Australian police have also contributed to very important missions where Australians have been exposed to criminal attack beyond Australia's shores. The two most famous examples flowed from the 2002 Bali bombings, in the aftermath of which there was significant and effective cooperation between the Australian Federal Police and the Indonesian police (POLRI), and the shooting-down over Ukraine in July 2014 of Malaysian Airlines flight MH17 by Russian-backed separatists. Such operations, underpinned by the consent of sovereign states, involve high levels of cooperation which themselves depend on a great deal of on-the-ground diplomacy.

Not all of these missions have led to happy outcomes. In Afghanistan, the main backer of the Afghan Republic, namely the United States, grew bored with its involvement and went behind the Republic's back to cut an exit deal for the U.S. with the Taliban enemy, spuriously dressed up as a peace agreement. The outcome was predictably grim. But in Cyprus, a police presence has significantly contributed at least to conflict refrigeration, if not conflict resolution, and for many Cypriots this has been a better outcome than some imaginable alternatives. And in the new Democratic Republic of Timor-Leste, not only has democracy flourished, but the Australian police who served so bravely in 1999 are remembered with the greatest affection, and honoured by the Timorese whose hopes for a better future were significantly advanced by the police deployment. In the wider swathe of history, there may be no higher reward than the gratitude that these ordinary people continue to feel for the honourable and selfless way in which the Australian police, deployed into a situation of acute danger, courageously discharged their tasks.

William Maley
Emeritus Professor of Diplomacy
The Australian National University

Abbreviations

AAPP	Assisting Australian Police Personnel (PNG ECP)
ABC	Australian Broadcasting Corporation
ACT	Australian Capital Territory
ADF	Australian Defence Force
AEST	Australian Eastern Standard Time
AFP	Australian Federal Police
AGD	Attorney-General's Department
AIPM	Australian Institute of Police Management
ALP	Australian Labor Party
ANP	Afghan National Police
ANZPAA	Australia–New Zealand Policing Advisory Agency
APEC	Asia-Pacific Economic Cooperation
APS	Australian Protective Service
ASEAN	Association of South East Asian Nations
ASEANAPOL	ASEAN Police Forum
ASIC	Australian Securities and Investment Commission
ASIO	Australian Security Intelligence Organisation
ASPI	Australian Strategic Policy Institute
ATO	Australian Taxation Office
BBC	British Broadcasting Corporation
BRIMOB	Indonesian Police Mobile Brigade
CIA	Central Intelligence Agency (US)
CIS	Commonwealth Investigation Service
CJIATF-N	Combined Joint Inter Agency Task Force (Nexus) (Afghanistan)
CNPA	Counter Narcotics Police Afghanistan
CPP	Close Personal Protection
CRS	Creditor Reporting System (OECD)
CSP	Cyber Safety Pasifika (Pacific)
CSTC-A	Combined Security Transition Command-Afghanistan

DAC	Development Assistance Committee (OECD)
DFAT	Department of Foreign Affairs and Trade
DIBP	Department of Immigration and Border Protection
DVI	Disaster Victim Identification
ECP	Enhanced Cooperation Program (PNG)
EU	European Union
EUROJUST	European Union Justice grouping
EUROPOL	European Union Police forum
FBI	Federal Bureau of Investigations (US)
FDD	Focused District Development (Afghanistan)
FFOV	Families Free Of Violence (Tonga)
FILO	Family Investigations Liaison Officer (AFP)
FRELIMO	Frente da Liberacao de Mocambique
GIRoA	Government of the Islamic Republic of Afghanistan
HMAS	His/Her Majesty's Australian Ship
HMS	His/Her Majesty's Ship
IDG	International Deployment Group (AFP)
IDP	Internally displaced person
IED	Improvised explosive device
IHL	International Humanitarian Law
INP	Indonesian National Police (see also POLRI)
INTERFET	International Force East Timor
INTERPOL	International Police Organisation
IRA	Irish Republican Army
IOCC	Interagency Operations Coordination Centre (Afghanistan)
ISAF	International Security Assistance Force (Afghanistan)
JCLEC	Jakarta Centre for Law Enforcement Cooperation
JIATF-W	Joint Inter Agency Task Force-West (US)
KAF	Kandahar Airfield (Afghanistan)
KC	King's Counsel
MEF	Malaitan Eagle Front (Solomon Islands)
MOSC	Management of Serious Crime (AFP)
MSG	Melanesian Spearhead Group (Pacific)

N-APP	Nauru
NATO	North Atlantic Treaty Organisation
ODA	Official Development Assistance
OECD	Organisation for Economic Cooperation and Development
OEF	Operation Enduring Freedom (US–Afghanistan)
OMLT	Operational Monitoring Liaison Team (Afghanistan)
ONUMOZ	UN Mission Mozambique
ORG	Operations Response Group (AFP)
OSCE	Organisation for Security and Cooperation in Europe
PCLEC	Pacific Community for Law Enforcement Community
PFP	Pacific Faculty of Policing (AIPM)
PFWG	Pacific Forensics Working Group
PICP	Pacific Islands Chiefs of Police
PIF	Pacific Islands Forum
PNG	Papua New Guinea
PNG-APP	Papua New Guinea-Australian Police Partnership
POLRI	Police Republic of Indonesia (see also INP)
POM	Public order management
POMLT	Police Operational Mentoring Liaison Team (Afghanistan)
PPDP	Pacific Police Development Program (AFP)
PPDP-R	Pacific Police Development Program-Regional (AFP)
PPF	Participating Police Force (Solomon Islands)
PRC	People's Republic of China
PRK	People's Republic of Kampuchea (Cambodia)
PRPI	Pacific Regional Policing Initiative
PPPP	Pacific Police Partnerships Program
PPTAG	Pacific Police Training Advisory Group (AFP)
PTC	Provincial Training Centre (Uruzgan Province-Afghanistan)
PTCCC	Pacific Transnational Crime Co-Ordination Centre (Samoa)
PTCN	Pacific Transnational Crime Network
QC	Queen's Counsel

RAMSI	Regional Assistance Mission Solomon Islands (now RAPPP)
RAPPP	RSIPF–AFP Partnership Program
RC(S)	Regional Command (South)(Afghanistan)
RENAMO	Resistencia Nacional Mocambiquana
RN	Royal Navy
RPNGC	Royal Papua New Guinea Constabulary
RSIP	Royal Solomon Islands Police
RSIPF	Royal Solomon Islands Police Force
SAPP	Samoa Australian Police Partnership
SCIF	Secure Compartmentalised Intelligence Facility
SLOC	Sea Line of Communication
SOCA	Serious Organised Crime Agency (UK)
SSR	Security Sector Reform
TAPP	Tonga Australia Police Program
TCU	Transnational Crime Unit
TK	Tarin Kot (Afghanistan)
TLPDP	Timor Leste Police Development Program
TNI	Tentara Nasional Indonesia (Indonesian military)
TPDP	Tonga Police Development Program (now TAPP)
UN	United Nations
UNAMET	United Nations Mission East Timor
UNBRO	United Nations Border Relief Organisation (Thailand-Cambodia)
UNBZ	United Nations Buffer Zone (Cyprus)
UNCIVPOL	United Nations Civilian Police (later UNPOL)
UNFICYP	United Nations Force in Cyprus
UNMIS	United Nations Mission in Sudan
UNMISS	United Nations Mission in South Sudan
UNMIT	United Nations Mission in Timor
UNPOL	United Nations Police
UNSC	United Nations Security Council
UNSCR	United Nations Security Council Resolution
UNTAC	United Nations Transitional Authority Cambodia

UNTAET	United Nations Transitional Authority East Timor
US	United States
USSR	United Soviet Socialist Republics (Soviet Union)
VAP JP	Vanuatu–Australia Police and Justice Program
VAPP	Vanuatu–Australia Police Program (now VAP JP)
WAN	Women's Advisory Network (Pacific)
ZOPFAN	Zone of Peace, Freedom and Neutrality (ASEAN)

Introduction

As we approach the end of the first quarter of a century of the third millennium, global affairs appear to be at an inflection point. There is now a level of strategic competition between liberal democracy and autocracy. At present, the battleground is largely within the hearts and minds of the voting public in democratic nations. Not so in autocratic nations, where the choice is generally limited to the prevailing power and often based on religious or political ideology. There are some who believe we are in the foothills of a third world war, featuring the actual or perceived decline of the West, the emergence of a new coalescence of autocratic powers, including China, North Korea, Iran and Russia, two of which are existing nuclear powers and the other two aspirants to a nuclear arsenal. It is important to bear in mind the maxim attributed to Albert Einstein upon the advent of nuclear weapons. In March 1947, reports appeared about an exchange that Einstein reportedly had with a group of friends at a dinner party:

> Professor Albert Einstein was asked by friends at a dinner party what new weapons might be employed in World War III. Appalled at the implications, he shook his head. After several minutes of meditation, he said. 'I don't know what weapons might be used in World War III. But there isn't any doubt what weapons will be used in World War IV.' 'And what are those?' a guest asked. 'Stone spears', said Einstein.[1]

If the strategic competition between two nuclear powers, the United States (US) and the People's Republic of China (PRC), escalates into open warfare, then the potential for further escalation and global devastation is profound, particularly when the formal alliances involving other nuclear powers, or potential nuclear powers, are taken into account. These include the United Kingdom, France, Russia, Israel, India and Pakistan, and North Korea and Iran as aspirants to join the nuclear group.

The stakes are very high and the consequences of conflict catastrophic. This is a time when preventative diplomacy in all its forms should take the highest priority, including police diplomacy.

This book is about Australian police diplomacy over the past sixty years, from the first Commonwealth Police deployment to the troubled Mediterranean island of Cyprus in 1964 to contemporary Australian Federal Police (AFP) placements in the South West Pacific and the AFP International Network in 2024.

There are many books written on military interventions and on diplomacy. The reason for this book includes a need to fill a significant gap in the narrative about Australia's regional and international police engagement over such a lengthy period, not through an operational lens but through a diplomatic one. Police are generally regarded as security-sector actors, but rarely in a field dominated by military thinkers as justice-sector actors. As a result policing is often aligned more with military activities, but in fact international policing is more akin to diplomacy, and the individual qualities of police themselves more closely align with diplomats than soldiers. For this reason, international police engagement is often misunderstood and is certainly under-represented in the literature.

This examination and review of the sixty years of Australian police diplomacy seeks to rectify this misunderstanding and emphasise its importance on a regional and perhaps global scale.

This book demonstrates some of the outcomes Australian police diplomacy has achieved in the past and can potentially achieve in the future and argues that it is an important part of the global effort to deal with highly volatile political conflict in as diplomatic a manner as possible.

Most nations have two broad vectors for international engagement: Left of Arc, traditional diplomacy, dealing with trade and aid, known as soft diplomacy; Right of Arc, military engagement, including the use of force, known as hard diplomacy. This book refers to police diplomacy as a form of 'firm' diplomacy, as it sits between 'soft' traditional diplomacy and 'hard' military force. The distinctive aspect of policing is that, unlike traditional diplomacy and military intervention, which are usually aimed at defeating or outwitting the opposition, policing efforts in the pursuit of justice-based outcomes are usually enhanced through cooperative engagement with international counterparts because their common challenge is aimed at addressing crime and criminal behaviour. This is one of the reasons police diplomacy should be considered as operating on its own diplomatic track.

The book argues that police at an individual level share many traits with diplomats, and institutionally, when deployed, have engaged in activities that have had positive diplomatic outcomes for Australia's national interests, including regional and global security and stability which underwrite peace and prosperity, and for the international 'good' these bring, a very important part of international good citizenship.

Police serve the interests of both security and justice, both of which are essential for a cohesive society. Security and justice are not mutually exclusive concepts, but form part of a continuum. The manner in which policing is conducted is largely reflective of both the extant political system and the values and social mores of the general population. As such police, and the manner in which policing is done in terms of things like the use of force and intrusion, the policing of dissent, and the degree of police autonomy and accountability for their actions, are reasonably reliable indicators of social cohesion, from which predictions relating to social breakdown and state fragility can be made and ideally avoided. It must also be recognised that policing does not take place in a vacuum, but is one of a broader four-part criminal justice system comprising a legislature, the police, a judiciary and a corrections system, all of which are inter-dependent, but which operate independently of each other.

In the South West Pacific, policing and justice has emerged as a key battleground in the contest for influence in the Pacific region, with the basic alternatives being the Western concept of liberal-democratic policing and the more autocratic approach to law and justice, which can run the risk of transitioning into regime-protection policing, thus entrenching compliant political elites.

Many Pacific nations have no military forces, and so police play an outsized role in security and stability, as well as justice. In this context, the AFP seeks to retain its status as the 'partner of choice' for Pacific police organisations and to encourage a liberal-democratic model of policing based on accountability and the rule of law. This strategic engagement can amplify the AFP's impact and influence in the Pacific, and by extension the way in which Australia and the West generally is regarded.

It should be noted that these efforts are at risk of being politicised at the local level as Pacific Island nations exercise their national sovereignty and are tempted or coerced to turn to other more autocratic security partners and providers such as the PRC. In an era where some posit that we are in the foothills of a third world war, diplomatic efforts aimed at preventing such an eventuality or, in a worst-case scenario, being well positioned to respond appropriately, should be a high priority. There is even a prospect of policing, operating on its own diplomatic track, being well positioned to offer a discrete diplomatic back-channel between trusted law enforcement partners in times of political and strategic volatility, including between potential belligerents.

Two questions should be borne in mind when reading this book. The first relates to Defence and the use of military force and the second to the reason for diplomacy. The Australian Defence Force works for the Australian Department of Defence. A central question to keep in mind throughout the book is this: What are we as a nation, government or community defending, and what are we defending against? Australian diplomats work for the Department of Foreign Affairs and Trade. A second consideration for the reader is to query not what diplomacy is but why is diplomacy done?

My own thoughts are that we are not only defending our territorial integrity, maritime approaches, trade routes and national sovereignty. We are also defending our liberal-democratic principles and values which are the foundation for our contemporary security stability, peace and prosperity. At the core of this is adherence to the rule of law and respect for justice-based outcomes. Unfortunately, given some regional and global developments, with the recent rise of more influence by authoritarian powers, none of these aims can be taken for granted. Viewed through this prism, my response to the second question is that diplomacy is done in furtherance of security stability, peace and prosperity and this is achieved through pursuit of national interests directly, and also indirectly through the pursuit of international good citizenship. This creates an environment in which the rule of law and the pursuit of justice-based outcomes can take place without undue interference from malign actors. Effective policing is integral to this pursuit and Australia and Australian police have played a significant role in these efforts domestically and over the past sixty years internationally, as global strategic circumstances have evolved.

Bearing these concepts in mind will assist the reader to understand and gain an appreciation of the significant role Australian police have played, and continue to play, on the international stage. Australian police serve both the national interest and international good citizenship as they work to enhance the rule of law and, in an operational sense, pursue justice-based outcomes in an environment which appears to be becoming increasingly lawless.

My reason for writing this book is to serve four purposes. Firstly, to explain that diplomacy in the modern era is not confined to official diplomats, and that police can play a very effective diplomatic role. Secondly, to highlight that international police missions, operations and programs can encourage a less politicised diplomatic track than traditional diplomacy or military intervention. Thirdly, to provide a note of caution that, as effective as these international police activities may be at promoting liberal-democracy, they are still subject to political influence and are subject to increased pressure from influential but less-than-liberal-democratic quarters. Finally, to suggest that the AFP has a degree of experience-based credibility as a legitimate voice to make a meaningful contribution to any reforms of supra-national bodies such as the United Nations in their approach to policing, justice and the broader concept of the rule of law.

The essential message of this book is that the AFP has a high degree of credibility and is an extremely flexible, versatile and agile actor in many ways, and is well-suited to adapt to situations, circumstances and environments with 'unique' characteristics. I argue that because of these characteristics, 'firm' international policing should be considered as a different and distinct diplomatic 'track' to traditional 'soft' track 1 diplomacy, non-government track 2 diplomacy and 'hard' military intervention.

The over-arching narrative of this book is that the AFP has demonstrated a rare agility and ability to respond to emerging international demands and evolving challenges within the rules-based international order in which Australia and its likeminded partners place much value. This has aided in building a network of trusted police partners which helps to maintain security and stability in time of peace with the potential to provide an effective and discrete diplomatic back-channel in times of rising tensions, even with potential belligerents.

This book provides an opportunity to review and contextualise through a diplomatic lens the activities of Australian international police activities during some of the most momentous events in post-1945 world history. These events include the rise and demise of the Cold War; the rise of global Islamic jihadism; the global adoption of the means of mass communication via the internet; the expansion of global trade, including the trade in illicit substances; the mass movement of people globally, through both legitimate and illegitimate means, the prevalence of intra-state rather than inter-state conflict and the contemporary rise of autocratic powers such as the People's Republic of China, the Russian Federation and others as adversarial, competitive peers to the US-led Western alliance. All of these have had implications for police and how policing is done, particularly in Australia's immediate region, the Indian Ocean, Southeast Asia and the South West Pacific, often referred to as the Indo-Pacific region.

The Commonwealth of Australia has in its relatively short history achieved much in the shaping and furtherance of the international rules-based order and the observance of human rights. The Australian Federal Police in its even shorter existence has a proud history in effective police diplomacy in support of these noble endeavours. This book is written to explain the significance of this history.

Police as Social Barometers

Police, because they are drawn from the community they serve, provide a very reliable barometer of societal health. In their domestic duties, police work twenty-four hours a day, seven days a week, all public holidays. They are always there, speaking to members of the public, entering people's homes and private businesses, dealing with motorists, investigating crimes, consoling victims, responding to emergencies, giving evidence in court and lending a hand when required. All Australian police conduct their duties armed, yet incidents of police shootings are rare and make national news. This is one indication of the degree of public consent in the liberal-democratic society, as per the principles laid down in 1829 London with the establishment of the London Metropolitan Police (often known as the London Met). These were adopted and adapted to local circumstances in many parts of the British Empire, including the Australian colonies, which became states upon federation in 1901. These principles encourage community consent to the police and their actions by minimising force and intrusion, to be used as a last resort, and by moderate policing of public dissent as an alternative to military force and repressive legislation. This moderation is a deliberate pillar of the benign nature of British-based liberal-democratic forms of government. [See Appendix 2: Peel's Nine Principles of Policing].

Although it is rare for Australian police, when deployed internationally, to be armed or to exercise executive policing powers,[2] they should nonetheless carry these consent-based principles with them.

What is Police Diplomacy?

Daryl Copeland in his 2009 book *Guerrilla Diplomacy* lists the qualities of 'new' diplomats. They include:

> autonomy, agility, acuity, and resilience; the ability to generate and use intelligence; personal and situational sensitivity; local knowledge, cultural awareness and linguistic and communication skills; irregular representational capabilities and characteristics; an affinity for collaboration and teamwork; functionality in conflict situations; connectedness to the global political economy of knowledge; the capacity, enhanced by science & technology act with suppleness and a catalytic and transformational orientation.[3]

Further, it has been said that the qualities of a diplomat include 'a quick mind, a hard head, a strong stomach, a warm smile and a cold eye'.[4] It is asserted that police, official diplomats or not, display all the above characteristics as a normal part of their daily duties dealing with crises, crime, criminals, witnesses and victims with humanity, compassion, impartiality and objectivity. That is the very essence of the Peelian policing model.

As policing is a people-based endeavour, these qualities should be shared by police both at the individual level and at the institutional level. They are also characteristics that are shared to varying degrees by police counterparts worldwide, even in autocratic political systems, although there are many reasons to dispute this assertion.

Broadly speaking, traditional diplomacy is the conduct of relations between nation-states using peaceful means. It is advanced that police diplomacy exists on its own diplomatic track and has its own strengths, weaknesses and risks; it is a distinct form of diplomacy. It complements, rather than displaces, other diplomatic efforts, including the more traditional track 1 or transactional form. It also certainly does not seek to displace or replace military force as an effective option, but it does offer an alternative.

Police can be deployed internationally for operational, development, stability or strategic purposes and can build resilience and provide influence in international relationships. As such, effective international police engagement is an increasingly important part of Australia's response to crime, instability and geopolitics in our region. When deployed internationally, police can be highly effective diplomats because of their crime-fighting mission and the sense of solidarity they must share with their foreign counterparts as members of a global policing effort.

Police diplomacy is less susceptible to political interference than traditional diplomacy because of the relative independence of policing agencies working across borders in pursuit of common interests. It is this independence of police agencies that helps to protect their international partnerships from political tensions between states, but they are not immune.

Australia's sixty years of international police engagement had some notable diplomatic impacts. These include long-term institutional partnerships between national policing agencies and the establishment of strong and resilient platforms for cooperation that are sometimes absent from transactional forms of traditional diplomacy. The AFP has a demonstrated and highly credible capacity for shaping and potential to shape decision-making at the highest levels of government and supra-national levels of policy development and operational outcomes. This includes the UN and International Police organisation such as INTERPOL, as well as regional policing and justice bodies in the Indo-Pacific region, notably the Association of Southeast Asian Nations Police (ASEANAPOL) and the Pacific Islands Chiefs of Police (PICP) forums. The AFP has played a highly credible and influential role in all of these and more.

'Firm' Police Diplomacy Between Traditional 'Soft' Diplomacy and 'Hard' Military Intervention

It is important to ask not what diplomacy is but why it is done. One of the primary objectives of traditional diplomacy is to maintain cordial relations between nation-states. In terms of police diplomacy, the nature of police as both security and justice actors places them between traditional 'soft' diplomacy and the 'hard' diplomacy of military intervention, the purpose of which should be to seek victory and, by doing so, achieve a better peace, namely a post-conflict situation which is an improvement on the pre-conflict situation. Peace, in this case, is described as not just the absence of conflict, but the presence of justice.

The 17th century Dutch philosopher Baruch Spinoza, in a rejection of Hobbes definition of peace as the 'absence of war', is quoted as stating that *peace is not an absence of war, it is a virtue, a state of mind, a disposition for benevolence, confidence, justice.* The eminent physicist and a leading thinker of his age, Albert Einstein is often quoted as stating *peace is not merely the absence of war but the presence of justice, of law, of order - in short, of government.* George Washington stated that *the due administration of justice is the firmest pillar of good government.*[5] Combined, these quotes from three eminent thinkers can be summarised as: *'peace is not just the absence of conflict, but the presence of justice, which is the firmest pillar of good government.'* It is this portmanteaux statement which forms the basis of my belief that policing, as part of a broader justice effort, is a major component in conflict prevention and de-escalation in situations short of actual and open military conflict.

The role effective policing can play in this regard has often been overlooked or assumed to occur naturally. This is a mistake. Police and policing do not operate in a vacuum; they are vital components of a basic four-part criminal justice system involving the legislature (those who pass the laws), the police (those who enforce the laws within the general public), the judiciary (those who interpret the actions of the police and the behaviours of members of the general public charged with criminal offences) and the corrections system (those who are responsible for those determined by the judiciary to be guilty of committing crimes).

The primary roles of the police element within this system are to prevent crime, detect offences, bring offenders to justice, protect life and property and maintain public order. Various criminal justice systems combine some of these actions, but these are the basic components of any criminal justice system and policing approach. How the police deal with the use of force, intrusion and the maintenance of public order in the face of public and political dissent are areas where significant differences exist between different political systems ranging from the autocratic to the liberal-democratic. Australian police diplomacy, then, is a relatively benign projection of Australian liberal-democratic values and principles as a middle power which respects the international rules-based order and seeks justice-based outcomes. Used effectively Australian police diplomacy can also act as part of a preventative strategy and act as a back channel in the face of rising regional and global tensions. Australian police diplomacy is a form of 'firm' diplomacy and has served both the national interest and international good citizenship.

Police and Peacekeeping: Some Concepts Clarified

International police engagements are often referred to by the generic term 'peacekeeping'. One of the oddities of police peacekeeping is that very few people recognise it, let alone understand it. There are many reasons for this. Even within police organisations themselves, activities such as international 'peacekeeping' are regarded with a degree of disdain, as the core business of police is domestic crime-fighting. Caught between political ideologies and organisational misunderstanding, police peacekeepers operate in a space surrounded by metaphorical force fields exuded by 'diplomats', 'war-fighters', 'crime-fighters' and political ideologies that simply do not understand or appreciate the actual and potential role that effective international police engagement can play, and has played, in promoting a better peace. The AFP, in its relatively short history, has made significant contributions to diplomatic and justice-based outcomes, regionally and globally.

A further complication is that 'police peacekeeping' contains the word 'peace'. It must be clearly stated that the environments the AFP deploy to are not always benign or peaceful. In some cases, police operate unarmed in small groups in highly volatile and dangerous environments. In many cases, there is no peace to keep as various factions compete for ascendency and, ultimately, power.

The term 'peacekeeping' covers a very diverse range of activities, ranging from traditional peacekeeping between belligerent parties, training, advisory and mentoring roles, to police capacity development. AFP deployments to places such as Cyprus (UNFICYP), Mozambique (ONUMOZ), Cambodia (UNTAC), Haiti, East Timor/Timor-Leste (UNAMET, UNTAET, UNMISET, UNMIT and TLTDP), the Solomon Islands (RAMSI and RAPPP), Papua New Guinea (PNG-APP) as well as various missions to the South West Pacific and further afield to places such as Afghanistan. The primary focus of these sorts of activities is related essentially to one of the two main reasons for such international police engagement: international good citizenship. Most of these missions either fall directly under the purview of the UN or have UN approval. The other main reason for international police engagement is to serve the national interest. This is the aspect that underlies more operational policing engagements in the international space. These activities generally fall to the AFP International Network, which conducts activities more related to liaison and police-to-police cooperation on criminal matters, and include responses to mass-casualty events such as the bombings in Bali in 2002 and the downing of Malaysian Airlines MH17 in 2014.

Geography and History

The AFP is unique as an international police organisation. Australia is an English-speaking British-based constitutional monarchy practising consent-based liberal-democratic policing adopted from Britain in Australia's 19th-century colonial period and adapted to suit the local environment and local circumstances. This is a consequence of history. Australia's former British colonies were practising responsible and representative government well before federation in 1901. Australia's government is a federated model, and the AFP is the police entity that operates at the national level and is therefore the face of Australia's international policing.

Australia also exists in a volatile and diverse region in terms of geography and geopolitics. There is thus a unique regional imperative for a more prominent international policing presence than is standard for Western democratic countries in Western Europe and North America. This is a consequence of geography.

Left and Right of Arc

This book refers to police diplomacy as a form of firm diplomacy, as it sits between soft traditional diplomacy and hard military force. The unique aspect of policing is that, unlike traditional diplomacy and military intervention, policing is usually enhanced through cooperative engagement with its international counterparts, because their common challenge is reducing crime and criminal behaviour. This is one of the reasons police diplomacy should be considered as operating on its own diplomatic track.

The concept of 'firm' police diplomacy is explained as activities which involve executive policing activities such as investigation, search, seizure, arrest, prosecution, and judicial outcomes such as imprisonment. Traditional diplomats do not engage in such activities, and these are not activities with which the military generally engages, although this is not unknown. In circumstances where Australian police deployed internationally are not authorised to perform an executive policing function, in capacity-development missions and programs, significant effort is devoted to implementing processes and procedures in the host nation police, to conduct themselves in accordance with similar principles as Australian police, largely influenced by the Peelian approach to policing. It must be stressed that this is not always immediately successful.

Intra-state v Inter-state Conflict and Instability

Recent experience demonstrates that it is internal, intra-state conflict rather than inter-state, state-on-state conflict that creates instability. Most security, emergency and enforcement actors in the Pacific are police rather than military. There are only three militaries in the SW Pacific: in PNG, Tonga and Fiji. All have direct and strong links with both the Australian and New Zealand militaries.

Operations and Missions

At this early point, it is important to explain the distinction between police operations and police missions, which have been renamed 'partnership programs' to reflect the increasingly significant peer-to-peer nature of AFP engagement in the Pacific. Nonetheless, the distinction between police operations and police missions or partnership programs needs to be made because they are two distinct activities.

As the name suggests, police operations generally focus on justice-based outcomes and generally feature an element of Australian domestic-related criminality. In the case of the AFP, these have included the response to mass casualty events such as the responses to the terrorist bombing attacks in Bali in 2002 and the downing of Malaysian Airlines flight MH17 in eastern Ukraine in 2014, both of which involved significant Australian casualties. Police activities in both of these responses involved evidence collection, witness statements and a host of other activities directly related to and focused on a justice-based outcome, namely, to hold those responsible to account through the rule of law.

Both police operations and police missions and partnership programs involve significant levels of international cooperation, including working with the host nation's police. In some cases, the host nation's police do not exist or cannot function in an effective way, hence the need for international police assistance.

Policing respects jurisdictional sovereignty. It is a pursuit usually restricted to an identifiable geographic jurisdiction where the police exercise normal executive powers associated with law enforcement, such as the use of force and intrusion. It is important to note that even if police are operating in another jurisdiction, it is rare that international police exercise executive police powers. The respect for jurisdictional sovereignty is an extremely important element of policing. A direct extension of this is that police do not deploy on either international programs, missions or operations without the express permission of the host nation government, or the authority from a mandate of a UN Security Council Resolution, or both. This distinguishes police from military expeditionary forces, which by definition have both the capacity and function to breach another nation's sovereignty and sovereign jurisdiction, based on the authority of their own government or collation of governments, ideally with the authority of the United Nations.

Firm Diplomacy

In September 2003, Professor Hugh White wrote an article in the *Sydney Morning Herald* mentioning 'firm power' in international affairs, which sits between the traditional 'hard power' of military intervention and the 'soft power' of trade, aid and normal diplomatic links. This 'firm power' is tougher than aid but softer than military intervention, and it is provided by justice sector actors such as police, prison officers, judges and governance actors such as auditors.

This book is not about police power *per se*, but it is about police prestige as a form of firm diplomacy offered by Australian international police engagement. The reason is that power implies strength and an imperative to use that strength to overcome an adversary. The principle behind the use of power is straightforward: to be more powerful, one must be bigger, stronger, faster, more agile and better equipped than one's adversary. While there are elements of this in policing, the use of power or force are last resorts for liberal-democratic police, whose general stance is a preference for other less confrontational forms of conflict resolution, such as negotiation and reconciliation, and of course justice. These require empathy, understanding and a willingness to cooperate, collaborate and compromise, as well as effective use of intelligence, which are characteristics more closely aligned to 'soft' diplomacy than 'hard' military activities. This book, therefore, builds on Professor White's notion of firmness, but instead of focusing on 'firm power', the book considers the actions of the AFP in the international arena through the prism of 'firm diplomacy'. This is discussed in the context of examples in later chapters over a 60-year period where the AFP was deployed internationally, sometimes in lieu of the military. I argue that police at an individual level share many traits with diplomats, and institutionally when deployed have engaged in activities that have had positive diplomatic outcomes for Australia's national interests, including regional and global security, peace and prosperity, and for the international good these bring. It is also important to acknowledge at this stage that police do not act in isolation but are an important component of a broader justice system. On the notion of peace, it is worthwhile to remember the maxim that 'peace is not just the absence of conflict, but the presence of justice'. Integral as police are to the functioning of an effective justice sector, the other components – the legislature, the judiciary and the corrections system – are of equal importance.

National Sovereignty

In relation to the notion of national sovereignty, it is also important to acknowledge that the United Nations Declaration on the Principles of International Law decrees that:

> No state or group of states has the right to intervene directly or indirectly, for any reason whatsoever, in the internal or external affairs of any other State. Consequently, armed intervention and all other forms of interference or attempted threats against the personality of the State or against its political, economic or cultural elements are in violation of international law.

The Australian Government and its police respect national jurisdictional sovereignty and, therefore, do not deploy internationally without either an express invitation from the host government or an international mandate from the UN. This is the context in which Australian police 'firm diplomacy' will be discussed.

Diplomacy can mean many things simultaneously. The AFP has deployed its members in the pursuit of peace, stability, security and justice; in themselves, these are among the worthiest ideals of diplomacy.

I propose that the understanding of what diplomacy can be, why diplomacy is done and why it is increasingly important in the era of globalisation and the rise of global authoritarianism should be reviewed, and that the proposition of a separate police diplomatic Track be given serious consideration.

The notion of policing and diplomacy are not necessarily natural partners. This is because policing is generally viewed through a domestic prism and diplomacy through an international one. These traditional paradigms are changing primarily due to a rapidly changing policing and political environment, both domestically and internationally. Historically, the traditional modes of international engagement are by state-to-state diplomacy and, when required, by defence or military forces to further government objectives or the defence of national interests. There is now an increased impetus to add policing to this suite of options.

Liberal-democratic policing is somewhat unique in the Indo-Asia-Pacific region. It has faced serious stability and security challenges because regional democracy has developed only recently in each nation, in the post-colonial period. The AFP is a significant international participant operating in areas where traditional regional defence capabilities or traditional regional diplomatic actors do not share a liberal-diplomatic history. In that sense, the AFP as an international police participant lies between traditional diplomacy and traditional defence and, as such, is very much a part of a new form of diplomacy, and its activities constitute 'diplomacy by default'.

The Police and Politics

In his book *The Politics of the Police*, Robert Reiner, an esteemed British expert on police and policing in the British context, quotes Frederick William Maitland, the author of *Justice and Police*, 1885. Maitland posits that the group of words 'police, policy, polity, politics, politic, political, politician is a good example of delicate distinctions'.[6] This is as true and relevant in the contemporary environment as it was in 1885.

Despite a strong inclination to keep discussion related to daily politics to a minimum in this book, the policies upon which Australian police activities are based and their outcomes are inherently political. Because the police are publicly funded, they are inevitably connected to government policy and, as such, could be said to be 'political'. In British-based legal systems, police endeavour to remain aloof from the politics of the day and maintain a posture of political impartiality and operational objectivity by serving the law, rather than the government. This tends to underwrite their institutional legitimacy in the eyes of the public and, thereby, the required trust in the consent-based policing model. It is public *consent* rather than *coercion* or police *prestige* rather than police *power* which underpins this model. Australia is a constitutional monarchy, and the mechanism by which political impartiality and operational objectivity are achieved, is by having the police, and in fact, all participants in the criminal justice system—the legislature, the judiciary and corrections officers—swear an oath to the Crown rather than to other entities such as the Constitution, the 'people' or the government of the day. The Crown is an institution whose antecedents date from centuries of refinement, which underpins the legitimacy of those who represent it when dealing with fellow citizens whose rights and liberties are protected under the laws enacted in the name of the Crown. This brings with it certain expectations and responsibilities relating to both police behaviours and misdeeds. The prominence of the Crown on police uniforms is a constant reminder of this. It is a visible representation that rights should not be abused, freedoms should be protected by force of law, and any abuses should be addressed through specifically designed accountability mechanisms. It is the police who physically carry out law enforcement in accordance with well-established values, principles and approaches, which will be further discussed. The Crown is as much a symbol of accountability as it is a symbol of authority. It is a visible representation of the liberal-democratic social contract.⁷ There is also a difference between law enforcement in the strictest sense and the broader concept of policing, which encompasses enforcement of the law, as well as a host of other community-based engagements, often aimed at preventing crime and early intervention, before the law has to be enforced. In many ways, the deployment of the AFP internationally, especially to missions and programs, is more related to the latter pursuit of preventative policing than to law enforcement because this sort of executive policing or enforcement has been relatively rare in the AFP's international engagement.

Policing worldwide balances the two competing priorities of respecting the individual's right to go about their business and the broader community's expectations of safety and security. This is a fine balance and the police do not always get it right, especially in a community which consists of sub-communities with competing and sometimes contradictory objectives. The policing of protest and dissent by liberal-democratic police agencies throughout the Western world is under increased scrutiny and has sometimes been the subject of complaint from one or other party to the matter in dispute.

The distinction between liberal-democratic policing and more authoritarian approaches is an important one to make. The way policing is done, especially related to the use of force and intrusion, and the way police are held accountable for their actions are effective indicators of the degree of 'liberality' of any jurisdiction.

The notion of a liberal-democratic social contract is a common understanding between the 'Five-Eyes' communities of Australia, New Zealand, Canada, Britain and the U.S. Ironically, despite its historical colonial ties to Britain, it is each state's relationship with the latter, arguably the most influential republic in history, that is the cornerstone of this community of most-trusted international partners. The U.S., although a republic, shares British common law antecedents with the other members as a legacy of its own British colonial heritage. It should however, be noted that the American War of Independence took place over half a century before the Peelian principles were developed, and as such, policing in the United States has had less influence from that model than countries like Australia, New Zealand and Canada.

There is no doubt that policing in the United States is fragmented and is far more forceful that these countries. Nonetheless, police in all of these countries derive their authority from the community they serve.

In a paper written under the auspices of the International Centre for Criminal Law Reform and Criminal Justice Policy, the United Nations Interregional Crime and Justice Research Institute, the Centre for International Crime Prevention, the Austrian Study Center for Peace and

Conflict Resolution and the Department of Justice of Canada, Duncan Chappell and John Evans put forward the following:

> ...police derive and exercise their extensive powers and functions on behalf of the entire community. Consensus rather than conflict is the preferred mode and style of law enforcement. In contrast, non-democratic societies more frequently use police to impose the dictates of the ruling elite upon the masses. Their function is largely one of exercising control over the population rather than serving the needs of the broader community. These competing models of policing undoubtedly represent extremes...The police regulate the freedoms that are essential to democracy—immunity from arbitrary arrest, detention, and exile, the ability to speak, write, demonstrate, and form associations.[8]

With a resurgent China, we are witnessing the initial stages of the erosion of these assumed rights in the Indo-Asia-Pacific region. The importance of this in Australia's immediate region, and its potential effect on liberal-democratic policing, even in the Australian domestic environment, is discussed towards the end of the book.

Law and Policy

This book is concerned with AFP engagement with a rapidly changing international stage over the past sixty years. The distinction between law and policy, therefore, needs to be made early in this discussion. The AFP is essentially a domestic crime agency tasked with addressing nationally and internationally related criminal activity. This is done in accordance with legislation as a sovereign police force operating within its own exclusive national jurisdiction in partnership with its state and territory counterparts. Despite this international imperative, the AFP has many international aspects related to its own persona as Australia's national police force. The AFP engages internationally in four broad ways: 1) via 'boots on the ground' deployments related to peacekeeping or police capacity development, 2) via crisis response in which Australia has an interest, 3) via a highly effective international police liaison officer network and 4) via participation in various regional and international police forums.

The AFP respects the notion of sovereign jurisdictions. When the AFP deploys internationally, particularly in 'boots on the ground' deployments, it does so in accordance with international law, as applied in Australian Government policy, to another nation's sovereign jurisdiction. It bears repeating that police never deploy without an international authority in the form of a UN mandate or an express invitation from the host government of the nation concerned. When, how and why these are negotiated is the preserve of official diplomats as part of traditional

Track I diplomacy. This book examines how the AFP has deployed under both UN mandates and host government invitations over the period of its existence and before. This respect for national sovereignty means that when the AFP does deploy to another national jurisdiction, certain legal requirements must be met. Prominent among these is the concept of diplomatic privileges and immunities.

Diplomatic Immunity

Diplomatic immunity is a principle of international law that provides immunity from host nation legal processes for certain foreign government officials. It has its origins in ancient culture, where messengers were protected and were permitted to travel from tribe to tribe without fear of interference. In contemporary terms, this protects modern diplomatic communication channels, which allows certain foreign government representatives to conduct their duties with freedom, independence and security. Under the Vienna Convention on Diplomatic Relations of 1961 and the Vienna Convention on Consular Relations of 1963, this is a globally accepted concept; thus, all nominated diplomats enjoy the same immunity from host nation legal processes. The conventions provide immunity to persons according to their rank in a diplomatic mission or consular post according to the need for immunity in performing their duties.

Diplomatic privileges and immunities guarantee that diplomatic agents or members of their immediate family:

- may not be arrested or detained
- may not have their residences entered and searched
- may not be subpoenaed as witnesses
- may not be prosecuted.

Those of lower diplomatic status may not enjoy full immunity but may only be immune from legal action in relation to duties performed in an official capacity. Diplomatic immunity can be waived by the diplomat's own government, and action may be taken by that government for any abuses.

It is also possible for the host country to declare any member of the diplomatic staff of a mission persona non grata (or unwanted person). This may occur at any time without explanation. The home country would normally recall the person or persons under these circumstances.[9]

As mentioned above, the AFP has four broad areas in which it engages internationally. The first is the international liaison network, whose members perform duties involving the exchange of criminal information with the countries to which the member is accredited. These members generally reside in their nation's embassy or high commission in a capital city and usually enjoy full diplomatic privileges and immunities. They travel on diplomatic passports.

The second involves members deployed on missions such as UN peacekeeping or regional police capacity development missions and programs. These members do not usually enjoy diplomatic privileges and immunities but do travel on green official passports that provide a degree of limited protection for matters directly related to official duties.

The third involves members who may deploy in response to emergency situations such as the bombings in Bali in 2002, the Boxing Day Indian Ocean tsunami in 2004 and the response to the downing of Malaysian Airlines MH17 in eastern Ukraine in 2014. These members generally travel on green official passports.

The fourth broad circumstance is attending global or regional police forums such as the Pacific islands Chiefs of Police (PICP) forum, the ASEANAPOL forum, the European Union Police (EUROPOL) forum and the INTERPOL forum. Members of the international liaison network, who are permanently stationed in these organisations, normally enjoy full diplomatic privileges and immunities. Those participating in such forums from Australia generally travel on green official passports.

Diplomatic status has not generally been a concern to deployed AFP members, as the AFP outlines some very strict behavioural guidelines expected of their members, including several related to security, information protection, appropriate cultural behaviours, alcohol consumption and fraternisation, especially with host nation nationals. These are rigidly enforced, and any breaches are usually met with immediate repatriation and internal disciplinary action, and can result in dismissal.

Executive Policing: The Legal Power to Use Force and Intrusion to Enforce the Law

There have been circumstances where the AFP has been deployed in an active policing capacity; namely, AFP members (among others) have been required to enforce the domestic laws of the jurisdiction concerned, and to do so, they have been armed as they would be when performing such duties in Australia. In such cases, the relevant use of force posture remains the same as that in Australia under the AFP Commissioner's Order 3. This order follows Peelian policing notions of self-defence or the defence of a third person and requires that any force used must be minimal, used as a last resort and be legal, reasonable, necessary and proportionate to the threat posed. Further, the use of lethal force must only be in self-defence or the defence of a third person at risk of death or serious injury. The AFP has only deployed in an executive policing capacity on rare occasions, including in Cyprus in the very early days, in Timor-Leste with the UNTAET mission, in the early days of the RAMSI deployment to the Solomon Islands and in the Enhanced Cooperation Program (ECP) in PNG in 2005.

The ECP in PNG encountered several challenges relating to immunity. In recognition of the highly litigious nature of the Papua New Guinea community, a number of immunities relating to prosecution were sought and granted with the approval of the PNG Government. This, however, was successfully challenged by the Governor of Morobe Province in the PNG Supreme Court, and the ECP was withdrawn. This is further discussed in the chapter on PNG.

The Police and the Military

The U.S. scholars David Bayley and Robert Perito, in their book *The Police in War: Fighting Insurgency, Terrorism and Violent Crime*, identify the distinction between the different roles police play from their military counterparts, which is best summarised by the statement that police are not 'little soldiers'. Bayley and Perito refer to non-permissive environments and advocate the development of core policing as an element of counter-insurgency, but they indicate that it is easier for the military to consider police as part of a security force because it fits within a military set of parameters:

> Because the military, both foreign and local, is uncomfortable fighting unconventional wars, the great temptation is generally to substitute police for military units. Furthermore, it is easier to train local police as 'little soldiers' than as 'professional, accountable, public-safety-oriented police'…Initial training for police is often as counterinsurgency, not as 'serve and protect' police…Core policing comes first, not last, in forging a new police force. If offensive counterforce is required, it should be done by the military…police contribute to counterinsurgency by winning the allegiance of the population; the military contributes to counterinsurgency by eliminating immediate threats of violence.[10]

This is easier said than done, particularly in a contested environment, without resorting to forceful and intrusive policing methods that are inimical to consent-based liberal-democratic policing, in which the consent of the community underpins police legitimacy. The AFP's experience in Afghanistan between 2007 and 2014 runs counter to the premise that 'serve and protect' police are effective in a highly contested, violent and non-permissive environment, such as an active insurgency. This is particularly important when the host nation police themselves are corrupt, partisan, factionalised or otherwise compromised, as was the case in large parts of southern Afghanistan in the period the AFP deployed there.

A popular misconception, also held by some military commentators, is that police are, in fact, 'little soldiers' and are therefore 'interoperable' with their military counterparts. This may be the case in limited circumstances, particularly in relation to public order management or even in violent extremist situations, where high-end policing mandates and capabilities meet low-end military mandates and capabilities. What is overlooked in such considerations, however, is that the suite of skills and approaches brought by police to an increasingly complex set of problems is more than merely security-related; it involves values, principles and approaches more akin to their diplomatic or justice sector colleagues than to their military ones. In terms of post-conflict transition, the police play a vital role in progressing from the disruption created by conflict to a stable environment from which sustainable peace can have a reasonable chance of being maintained. The police span the 'security-justice continuum' between military 'peace-making' and police 'peace-keeping'. Broadly stated by Briton Paul Sieghart in a complaint about excessive use of force by the London Metropolitan Police in 1978, in a Commonwealth country like Australia, 'the job of a soldier is to kill the Queen's enemies in wartime; that of a policeman to protect the Queen's subjects in peacetime'.[11] Due to varied circumstances, the international has merged with the domestic. As a result, the distinction between an external and internal threat is no longer as clear as it once was, and exactly who is the 'enemy' and how they are affecting the 'peace' is no longer the exclusive preserve of either the military or the police. Militaries are becoming increasingly involved in domestic security, and policing is now a global pursuit, particularly in relation to transnational and serious organised crime, violent extremism, politically-motivated violence and the movement of illicit material. Policing is becoming more forceful and intrusive, and militaries are learning to conduct duties that are not directly related to warfare.

The traditional broad divisions between police and military roles and responsibilities are further explained in Appendix 3.

In response to an increasingly violent criminal environment, these traditional roles and responsibilities between police and military are becoming increasingly blurred as law enforcement activities adopt more forceful and intrusive postures and draw more on military-style techniques and equipment in the face of a more challenging criminal environment. For example, police throughout Australia are now expected to react in an offensive sense to incidents involving active armed shooters, namely they are expected to locate and eliminate the threat to the general public posed by such an offender. It should be borne in mind that police are generally lightly armed and armed offenders of this nature have traditionally been well-prepared and well-armed with more powerful weapons. The previous methodology was to cordon and contain and await better armed specialist police. This is no longer an acceptable approach. This puts police in what can only be described as an asymmetric military-style combat environment. This is just one example of the changing criminal threat environment faced by police.

Cooperation, Competition and Coercion

Some mention should be made of the scale of cooperation and competition engaged in between elements such as foreign diplomatic services and military forces and how they apply to police. The basic premise is that both foreign diplomatic services and military forces are more inclined to be in competition with their foreign counterparts and adversaries, either seeking advantage or leverage in the case of foreign diplomatic services or, in the case of the military, seeking to out-manoeuvre or defeat their adversary. These activities are, by definition, competitive. Police and policing, conversely, are more inclined to engage in more cooperative and even collaborative behaviour and are unquestionably more effective when they deal in this way with their foreign counterparts. The reason for this is relatively straightforward: the common objective of police, policing and justice is to address crime and criminal behaviour. How does this mesh with our perceptions of diplomacy?

Track I and Track II Diplomacy

The essence of this book considers police and policing as acting between the 'tracks' laid down by conventional ideas of diplomacy. Track I diplomacy involves traditional diplomacy between official government representatives of nation-states engaging in a formalised setting, and Track II diplomacy involves relationships between non-government organisations and individuals to further diplomatic objectives. The goal of both Track I and Track II diplomacy is ultimately to restore or preserve sustainable peace, stability and ongoing prosperity. As relative newcomers to the international environment, the police fall somewhere between these two 'tracks' but make significant contributions to the service of security, stability, peace and prosperity, and effective international policing engagement deserves to be regarded as operating on its own diplomatic track.

As a government agency, the AFP represents the Australian Government, but only in an official diplomatic sense through AFP Liaison Officers, who are accorded official diplomatic status, privileges and immunities. The Department of Foreign Affairs and Trade (DFAT) is prioritised at all times in Australia's international engagement, and the police form another effective facet of that primacy. The AFP, however, is a government agency; as such, its advisors, trainers, peacekeepers and other responders—such as search and rescue and disaster victim identification members, whose efforts cover the bulk of this book—are not afforded diplomatic status like their liaison officer counterparts and fall outside the accepted notion of Track II diplomacy, which concerns only non-government actors. Nonetheless, while not being officially regarded as 'diplomatic' actors in the narrow sense, the actions and outcomes of these AFP members, when engaged internationally, are increasingly diplomatic in nature, influence and impact. To that extent, traditional theory is perhaps anachronistic and requires a review to encompass the increasingly globalised world and the contemporary actors within it, including the police, and the malign non-state actors they pursue.

International circumstances are no longer confined to government-to-government relationships in the form we have become accustomed to. Due to the unprecedented globalisation of people and materials and instantaneous communication, people-to-people relationships across the globe are now a reality. This phenomenon also includes non-traditional threats and challenges to peace, prosperity, public confidence, social cohesion and, in some cases, national sovereignty, which can only be addressed by the combined and coordinated efforts of all elements of the state in 'joined-up government'.

The relationship between 'firm' police and 'hard' military diplomacy is reasonably well understood, at least conceptually, in Australian security circles, and deals primarily with inter-agency 'complementarity' in an operational sense and 'transition and transfer' in an intervention sense. The former generally relies on guidelines and protocols, and the latter requires certain preconditions relating to 'permissiveness'. This will be discussed in the section on Afghanistan and the response to the MH17 tragedy in Ukraine. The police–military relationship is usually discussed in the context of the security aspect of policing, such as public order or the enforcement of the law by use or threat of force. The most important thing to bear in mind in this context is the police and the military are not interchangeable but are complementary. They have well-established roles in society; however, given the emerging nature of some of the threats and challenges to be addressed, the traditionally distinct lines of demarcation between what was once traditional military and traditional criminal lines of authority and effort are also becoming increasingly blurred. This is well understood, and adjustments are being made in this regard in all Western liberal democracies, including Australia, as police adopt a slightly more militarised posture and the military becomes more engaged in constabulary- and domestic response-type duties. Increasingly, police are calling upon military capacity or niche capabilities to supplement their own limited resources and capabilities. Perception is important in this regard. The spectacle of joint police and military patrols on the streets of major European cities after major terrorist incidents are measures designed to reassure the public in addition to being response and deterrence capabilities. In a different threat environment, they may well be perceived as oppressive and intrusive. Perceptions in this regard are very much contextual.

There has also been an observable trend in the post-Cold War decades: the nature of conflict itself has changed from predominantly inter-state conflict between sovereign states to predominantly intra-state conflict or conflict within established national boundaries.[12] The dynamics underlying such asymmetric conflict are different and are related less to the interests of states themselves and more to the competing interests of groups and individuals within. They include fissures emerging from culture, ethnicity, ideology, income or wealth disparity, resource competition, historical animosities and crime. These are difficult to address by 'hard' or military power alone and require supplementation by other actors, including police and justice sector actors. This has become increasingly understood in Australia in large part by virtue of the contemporary involvement of the AFP in regional police interventions and community-based police development efforts, particularly over the first twenty-five years of the millennium.

Less understood is the relationship between 'firm' and 'soft' or traditional diplomacy, which, in a policing sense, often relates to 'international good citizenship' engagements, such as traditional peacekeeping, police capacity development, training and advising projects and humanitarian-focused foreign aid projects, often funded by Official Development Assistance (ODA), in accordance with extant Australian foreign policy positions. In an international policing sense, this is a partially flawed funding model, as there are both development and operational outcomes from police interventions, and the line between them is not easily discerned. In a similar vein to international relations and both Track I and II diplomacy, the ODA formula, and its applicability to international police engagements, needs to be revisited.

Transition

Ideally, the goal of peace operations should be to transition from an international military-led guarantee of safety and security to a democratic host nation–led society under the rule of law that can stand alone with little or no international assistance. It is only under the latter that economic development and community harmony, which are usually associated with such development, are made possible. Effective and accountable host nation police primacy and responsive policing have vital roles to play in this process, and they are the hallmarks of true state sovereignty. Interventions by international police can play a significant role in these sorts of transitions, and the AFP has a demonstrated history of successful, sizeable interventions in Timor-Leste and the Solomon Islands, both of which will be discussed in detail in this book.

International policing should, therefore, be considered a form of 'firm' diplomacy, namely 'police diplomacy', which includes aspects of international police activity designed to use 'police-to-police' and 'police-to-community' linkages more broadly to build upon common ground when more traditional approaches may find barriers. Such common ground includes a mutual desire, and indeed a duty, to prevent and respond to crimes common to all societies, such as violent extremism, organised criminal activities, child exploitation, narcotics and cybercrime, to name a few. It is this distinctive feature of police relationships that distinguishes them from more traditional international relationships such as traditional diplomatic or, even more so, military relationships, which, at their very core, often rely on seeking advantage over their international counterparts. It is in this aspect of 'advantage' that police differ from both traditional diplomats and military actors. Police perform better when they cooperate rather than compete to the mutual benefit of their respective citizens. In fact, police are at their most effective when that cooperation and collaboration is maximised, and competition minimised. The AFP's international experience demonstrates this. In that sense, operational policing support and police capacity development missions nest seamlessly into the strategy to protect the Australian community from crime by first addressing crime as close to its source as possible and second by helping our neighbours develop their own capabilities, safety, security and eventual peace and prosperity. This inevitably involves police development defined by the AFP as:

> the support provided to police in post-conflict and developing nations to build their capacity to provide sustainable and quality policing to their citizens. This support develops the operational capacity, enabling services and leadership that police services require to be accountable to their citizens and to build and maintain the legitimacy required to support the delivery of the rule of law.[13] [14]

One aspect that is often overlooked in discussions relating to police development and assistance is a return to a state of stability. Such a state enhances the rapid transfer of criminal information and intelligence between trusted policing partners, which in the contemporary criminal environment is of vital importance. This form of police-to-police relationship is the basis upon which the AFP has operated domestically with its whole-of-government counterparts, including with each state and territory police agency and internationally as part of a global international police liaison officer network.

Context

When the AFP was established in 1979, it adopted the Peelian policing model which had been extant in all Australian state jurisdictions inherited from their individual colonial pasts in the second half of the 19th century, after a troubled period of conflict with Indigenous inhabitants. A combination of UN-inspired post-colonialism and Cold War dynamics in Australia's near north created a situation where Australian police were deployed in 1964 as a part of a UN peacekeeping mission in Cyprus in the eastern Mediterranean known as the United Nations Force in Cyprus (UNFICYP) in lieu of the Australian military. This was the beginning of a continuous 53-year presence with UNFICYP, during which the AFP was established in 1979 and deployed members to other UN missions, including United Nations Mission in East Timor (UNAMET) to East Timor in 1999, once again in lieu of the Australian military.

A series of events between 1999 and 2002 created a new security paradigm in which Australia and the AFP became prominent in foreign policy considerations, particularly in the South West Pacific through the AFP's International Deployment Group (IDG) and Southeast Asia through the AFP's International Liaison Officer Network. The book contextualises decisions concerning international engagement by the AFP within global, regional and domestic environments and circumstances throughout the first two decades of the third millennium, including those of Australia's major security guarantor, the U.S. This includes the resurgence of both China and the Russian Federation as global competitors to dominance by the U.S.-led 'Western alliance'.

It also includes the rise of global ideologically inspired violent extremism within the rapid and unprecedented global connectivity in both technological and demographic terms, both of which are enduring features of the contemporary international environment and have implications for police and policing and, by definition, social cohesion, the social contract and the community trust that underpins them.

The book discusses the AFP's involvement with the UN in Cyprus, Cambodia, Mozambique, the Thai–Cambodian border and briefly with Somalia, as well as some non-UN missions in Haiti and Bougainville. The overall observation made in relation to these missions is that they were primarily related to international good citizenship with very little connection with regional or domestic considerations or the national interest. These missions did, however, consolidate the role of the AFP as an international actor, albeit for missions distant from Australia both in geographic and political terms.

This changed in 1999 when an AFP-led deployment to East Timor with the UN (UNAMET) had considerable and competing domestic, regional and international implications. This mission, and the subsequent Australian-led military mission known as INTERFET, was of particular significance to the relationship between Australia and Indonesia. It should be noted that Indonesia is the largest Muslim-populated nation in the world, and in the context of a growing level of violent Islamic-inspired extremism, particularly the attacks on the World Trade Centre and the Pentagon on 11 September 2001, the peer-to-peer police relationships between the AFP and its Indonesian counterparts played an extremely important role at a crucially sensitive time for both Australian and Indonesia. A bombing attack on the Indonesia island of Bali in 2002, discussed in detail in a section of the book, reset the police-to-police relationship between the AFP and the Indonesian National Police, which continues to prosper, and demonstrates just how effective a professional police-to-police relationship can be in terms of mending diplomatic fences.

In 2003, the AFP led the security element of a multilateral regional intervention in the Solomon Islands in the RAMSI, which also concluded in 2017 after fourteen years. In a similar vein to the intervention in East Timor (now Timor-Leste), the Solomon Islands intervention provides an example of a successful transition from an international guarantee of safety and security to a guarantee provided by the host nation police, which is one of the hallmarks of national sovereignty.

The successes in Timor-Leste and the Solomon Islands and a number of political developments arising from a military coup in Fiji in 2006, including the rise of the Melanesian Spearhead Group (MSG) and its 'Look North' posture, resulted in the AFP enhancing its IDG and developing a program known as the Pacific Police Development Program (PPDP) with involvement in PNG and in the Polynesian nations of Tonga and Samoa, as well as Vanuatu. The PPDP also has a regional extension known as the PPDP-Region (PPDP-R) that provides police advice to the vast but sparsely populated island nations of Micronesia.

These successes in the Pacific have been built upon and have now developed into Pacific Police Partnership Programs. This reflects the more mature police peer-to-peer approach to AFP engagement in the South West Pacific region.

Several concepts have been discussed and clarified in this introductory section of the book. These include that police are not 'little soldiers', that peace is not just the absence of conflict but the presence of justice, that 'peacekeeping' environments may not be peaceful, and, in some circumstances, there may not be a 'peace to keep'. In terms of diplomacy, it has been discussed that international police engagement is highly respective of national jurisdictions and that most international police engagement does not involve the exercise of police powers on the part of the internationally deployed police. Despite this, internationally deployed police do engage with their host nation counterparts who exercise those police powers in their own jurisdiction. It is this aspect of international police engagement that constitutes the 'firm' aspect of international policing, which falls between traditional 'soft' diplomacy and 'hard' diplomacy in the form of military intervention. International police engagement also falls between Track I (official government) diplomacy and Track II (non-government) diplomacy. Rather than trying to define diplomacy and determine what it is, it is perhaps more fruitful to consider the way diplomacy is done. Seen in this light are the two primary drivers of foreign policy: first, to serve the national interest and second, to engage in international good citizenship. It can be seen that effective international police engagements, and the broader pursuit of justice-based outcomes, can serve both.

Seen through this prism, sixty years of international police engagements are, in fact, a distinctive form of 'diplomacy by default' deserving of its own 'firm' diplomatic track.

The Peelian principles upon which Australian policing is based have endured for almost two centuries, but they are under considerable pressure in a more complex globalised world. This is the subject for discussion in the final section of the book, which reviews the past sixty years and projects into the future with a particular focus on policing in the Indo-Pacific region in light of the rise of a more autocratic approach to policing influenced by the PRC.

Prior to a discussion of the actual missions and operations, it is important to discuss the origins of the AFP and outline a brief history of why the AFP engaged as Australia's international police representative body. This is important because the AFP conducts itself according to the principles of community policing by consent. These were adopted by the AFP when it was established in 1979.

The Australian Federal Police 1979

As a result of a fatal bombing targeting the Commonwealth Heads of Government Meeting (CHOGM) outside the Hilton Hotel in Sydney in

February 1978, there were calls for a national policing agency. A former London Metropolitan Police Commissioner, Sir Robert Mark was called upon to oversight this. [15] The AFP was formed on 19 October 1979 under the *Australian Federal Police Act 1979* after the merging of the former Commonwealth Police and the Australian Capital Territory Police. In November 1979, the Federal Narcotics Bureau was transferred to the new agency. In 1984, the protective service component of the AFP was separated and formed the Australian Protective Service (APS), governed by the Attorney-General's Department. The APS was transferred back to the AFP twenty years later in 2004.

The AFP enforces federal law and protects federal and national interests from crime in Australia and overseas. The AFP is Australia's international law enforcement and policing representative and is the chief advisor on policing issues to the Australian Government. Traditionally, the types of crime addressed by the AFP revolved around narcotics importations and fraud committed against the Commonwealth. These duties also involved the emergence of organised crime, particularly those with an international aspect. At this time, Southeast Asia was the major transit region for heroin coming from the 'Golden Triangle' in the border area between Laos, Thailand and Myanmar. The illicit drug trade, along with many other criminal activities, is now a global phenomenon which requires a globalised response.

As a result, the AFP maintains an International Liaison Officers Network to act as an effective operational and criminal intelligence interface between Australian law enforcement and host nation police in nations with policies addressing crime as close to its source as possible. Particular emphasis is placed on drug source and trans-shipment countries, especially in Southeast Asia. In addition to these duties, the AFP inherited the international aspect of Australian policing from its predecessor, the Commonwealth Police, including the UN service in Cyprus, which in 1979 had been operating for fifteen years. This was the vanguard of a proud history of Australian international 'boots on the ground' policing, primarily but not universally with the UN. The international aspect of the AFP continues and falls under the International Command portfolio.

Peelian Policing Principles and the Australian Federal Police

Noteworthy is the fact that the Peelian approach to policing had been extant in the Australian colonial police forces, which took some time before it was universally adopted. In his report, Sir Robert Mark directly encouraged this approach based on his own experiences in the London Met. The significance of the Mark Report as a foundation document for the AFP is manifold. Its primary significance, however, is that the adoption of Peelian approaches to policing should be adopted at a national level when alternative approaches involving more intrusive or forceful methods could well have prevailed. The primary features are (1) separation from political control, (2) accountability, (3) public consent and (4) the minimum use of force.

The report also draws a distinction between administration and operations, which creates a situation where operations should be impartial and free from parliamentary interference, the antithesis of political impartiality. The rationale is that any community perception that operational police decisions have been subject to political influence tends to result in damage to the reputation and status of the force that underpins public confidence and trust. Institutionally and individually, police should consciously and unconsciously monitor, regulate and enforce the social contract between the community and its government—between the government and the governed—and strict impartiality is an essential aspect of this.

This is the essence of liberal-democratic consent-based policing where, as an institutional representative of both the community and its government, the police should represent the government by consent rather than by coercion and rely on prestige rather than power to achieve its objectives. The significance of this for police is that the community generally resolves its own disputes and settles its own affairs, which frees up police resources to address more serious issues.

It is the Peelian values-based principles and approaches that all members of the AFP carry with them in the execution of their duties both domestically and internationally. The AFP has also developed its own overtly stated values. They are fairness, accountability, trust, integrity, commitment, excellence and respect.[16] Whether these values, principles and approaches can be successfully transferred to other police agencies the AFP deals with as part of its international mandate is part of the discussion of police diplomacy. A related issue of globalised policing is how these values, principles and approaches can be sustained in the continual, moveable balance between the preservation of individual rights and freedoms and collective security, domestically and internationally. These are not without their challenges, as discussed in the following chapters. One particular challenge for police operating internationally is that many areas that require international intervention are undergoing such extreme civil disorder that a consent-based liberal-democratic policing posture is impossible, and it is only by more forceful and intrusive means that order can be restored, laws enforced, and justice done.

Authority and Accountability: Systems and Circumstances

The relationship between the Crown and the police, via their respective oaths of 'law and justice in mercy' (the Coronation Oath) and applied objectively and impartially 'without fear, favour, affection or ill-will' (the Police Oath), provides a solid foundation upon which to build a consent-based model of policing. This, in turn, is essential to legitimacy, which underpins sustainable peace and stability. It is a robust and elegant mechanism that balances both authority and accountability.

Not all policing approaches adopt this finely tuned and flexible balance between respecting the rights of individual citizens and the expectations of the broader community in relation to safety and security. Authoritarian and totalitarian policing systems tend to serve the political elites at the expense of the rights and freedoms of ordinary citizens. They are very effective at meeting security criteria but generally at the expense of individual rights via both force and intrusion; authority is maximised, but accountability is minimised. Dissent is discouraged, often by force.

Recent examples of this sort of policing come from the former Soviet Eastern Bloc (Warsaw Pact) communist countries and existing communist countries such as the totalitarian Democratic People's Republic of Korea (North Korea) and the PRC under the authority of the Chinese Communist Party. Of course, there are totalitarian and authoritarian models from Europe's recent past, notably in the 1940s in Germany and Italy. All of these models prioritise the state, and usually the party in power, over the liberty of the citizenry.

The European policing model, the 'gendarmerie' model, adopted in most of continental Europe, is forceful and intrusive but not to the extremes of authoritarian or totalitarian policing approaches. In fact, it was the repugnance at the French paramilitary policing model during the French Revolution and Napoleonic periods that shaped British political attitudes in the early 19th century and led to the establishment of the London Met in 1829 as a specific non-military institution that relied almost exclusively upon cooperation from the public and adopted a posture of minimal use of force. Prior to the adoption of this model, policing in the Australian colonies had been ad hoc and was often based on functional lines, such as the goldfields police, mounted police and water police, rather than territorial lines. The transition from the rudimentary and often brutal policing in the Australian colonies to the Peelian model, was not always easy and many troubling aspects of the period of Australia's history remain. This is worthy of an entirely separate study.

That said, however, it was the centralising of policing within identifiable sovereign colonial jurisdictions in an accountable and well-functioning judicial system that formed the foundations upon which contemporary Australian liberal-democratic policing rests.

Liberal-democratic policing in the context of this book has a number of distinctive features and principles, including police primacy, namely the principle that sworn police retain a monopoly on the use of force, including armed force, within a given jurisdiction; that the use of force is a last resort used in self-defence or in defence of a third party at risk of death or serious injury; that force is minimised and that it is legal, reasonable, necessary and proportionate to the threat posed; and that all actions by police are accountable at both the institutional and individual level through a functioning judicial system and an open and transparent media. These are essential elements in a functioning liberal-democratic policing approach, as they tend towards broad acceptance by the majority of the community being policed.

The central role played by the Crown in these arrangements also needs to be recognised as an institution that occupies space that could potentially become politicised; this has a high potential to affect impartiality and objectivity, as it risks compromising the apolitical nature of the administration of justice and, thus, undermine its legitimacy. It is noteworthy that even in British-based liberal democracies, parliamentarians do not swear an oath to act 'without fear, favour, affection or ill-will', yet it is parliamentarians whose policies shape the way in which services, including police, direct and conduct their activities, particularly when they are involved in hostile environments. It is politicians who formulate the policy settings under which police deploy internationally to missions and programs. In this sense they serve the national interest by engaging in good international citizenship. On the other hand, when police deploy to the International Network, they serve the national interest directly and adhere more closely to the rule and application of criminal law to advance and protect that national interest and the Australian community. In both cases, the individual police are expected to adhere to their oath and perform their duties 'without fear, favour, affection or ill-will.'

Overview

With the above quotes and sentiments in mind, this book considers selected areas of international engagement by the Australian Federal Police (AFP) and, in the case of Cyprus, one of its predecessor organisations, the Commonwealth Police, over the 60-year period from 1964 to 2024. This is book is written with a view to providing a historical record within the prevailing strategic context, particularly in relation to contemporary engagement in the Indo-Pacific. Despite a strong inclination to keep discussion of domestic politics to a minimum, political discussion is not only necessary but integral to the concept of 'police diplomacy' because the deployment of police offshore is, of course, a political decision. This is arguably more political than decisions to deploy the military because, unlike military forces, retained for that exact reason, police are primarily domestically focused, and any police deployment offshore runs the risk of the general public asking uncomfortable questions of government about domestic priorities, especially in the light of an escalating crime rate.

For the purposes of this book, reflecting the evolving nature of international affairs, the 60-year period is divided into five mostly chronological Parts, although there is some blurring of the lines between these broad Parts:

Part I: The Cold War and the Great Peace 1964–1998
   Cyprus, Cambodia, Mozambique, Haiti and Bougainville

Part II: Democracy, Violence and the New Security Paradigm 1999–2007
   East Timor and Indonesia

Part III: Capacity-building and the New Security Paradigm 2003–2014
   The Solomon Islands, the South West Pacific and Papua New Guinea

Part IV: Applying The Rule of Law in Challenging Environments Further Afield 2007–2014
   Afghanistan and Ukraine

Part V: Australian Security and Sovereignty in the Asian Century 2014–2024
   China and Australia's northern approaches

The first Part, The Cold War and the Great Peace, commences in 1964 with the first deployment to Cyprus and concludes in 1998. The Cold War started in 1945 and ended in 1990 with the collapse of Soviet communism following the fall of the Berlin Wall in 1989. The 'Great Peace' is a phrase sometimes used ironically by members of the Australian military to describe the period between the Australian withdrawal from South Vietnam in 1973 and the deployment of the Australian Defence Force (ADF) to the International Force East Timor (INTERFET) mission in East Timor in 1999. During this period, the ADF participated in a number of United Nations (UN) peacekeeping missions and the Australian Federal Police was also active with UN service during this period.[1]

In addition to Cyprus, this period includes AFP deployments to Cambodia, Mozambique, Haiti and Bougainville, which were almost exclusively focused on international good citizenship as their primary basis. Most were UN missions and were in places either far away or so remote from domestic affairs that the impact on domestic politics was negligible. Most of these deployments fall under the broad description of 'peacekeeping', including classical or traditional peacekeeping, namely maintaining a status quo ceasefire as in Cyprus, but also included assistance with elections in post-conflict environments as in Cambodia, and Mozambique and the restoration of stability as in Haiti and Bougainville.

This changed in late 1998 and throughout 1999 to 2002 with a series of crises and events in East Timor, just a two-hour flight from Darwin, and follow-on missions provided a pretext for al Qaeda affiliates in Indonesia to specifically target Australians as legitimate targets. The East Timor missions were based on international good citizenship via a UN-sponsored ballot but resulted in some very serious challenges to Australia's national interest via mass murder in East Timor, a military deployment to restore order and a mass casualty event in Bali in 2002, which resulted in over 200 casualties including eighty-eight Australians. This second Part, Democracy, Violence and the New Security Paradigm, relates primarily to the AFP response to a call for assistance during a UN-sponsored ballot in East Timor, some follow-on missions in Timor and the rise in regional Islamic jihadism, culminating in the Bali bombings in 2002.

Part III discusses the establishment of the initial peace-making and capacity-building Regional Assistance Mission to the Solomon Islands (RAMSI), which was exclusively focused on international good citizenship. RAMSI heralded the call for further international good citizenship–based missions in the South West Pacific, including in Papua New Guinea (PNG), where the lines between international good citizenship and the national interest merge. For an explanation of capacity development as practised by the AFP, please see Appendix 1.

The fourth Part, Applying The Rule of Law in Challenging Environments, examines the AFP's involvement in two very challenging missions and operations from 2007 to 2014, each with its own characteristics and each combining international good citizenship with the national interest. The two events discussed are Afghanistan, 2007–14 and the AFP response to the shooting down of Malaysian Airlines flight MH17 in Ukraine in 2014.

The fifth and final Part, from 2013 to 2024 and onwards, titled Australian Security and Sovereignty in the Asian Century, encompasses the regional impact of the rise of a more assertive People's Republic of China on Australia's long-term sovereignty and future as a liberal democracy through a policing lens. Discussion of this period ends mid-phase, which some contend positions us in the foothills of a major global conflict and poses the uncomfortable question of what police and policing will look like in the Indo-Pacific, and even domestically in Australia, in a region dominated by an autocratic rather than a democratic power.

These Parts are not distinct phases and are not lineal. They were not centrally planned as the AFP deployed in response to emerging challenges, on occasion, because more traditional diplomatic or military options were not possible or effective. For this reason there is no over-arching narrative other than to illustrate that the AFP and its members have always answered the call to deploy often at very short notice and often to challenging circumstances and environments, with limited visibility or support. There is considerable blurring of the lines between these Parts because many of these missions and operations occurred contemporaneously. The diplomatic impact of these missions and operations is rarely if ever discussed. The intent of this book is to address this.

Whilst traditional notions of 'policing' and 'diplomacy' may not automatically sit as natural partners, as has been previously discussed, international relationships, engagement and discourse are changing. We now talk of ping-pong diplomacy, gunboat diplomacy, public diplomacy, cowboy diplomacy, dollar diplomacy, big stick diplomacy, defence diplomacy, missionary diplomacy, science diplomacy, sport diplomacy and others. The obvious question is: why not police diplomacy?

Part I

The Cold War and the Great Peace 1964–1998

Cyprus, Cambodia, Mozambique, Haiti and Bougainville

United Nations Force in Cyprus: Police – 'Accidental Peacekeeper'   37
United Nations Force in Cyprus 1964–2017   39
United Nations – Cambodia   44
U.S. Bombing and Khmer Rouge   45
United Nations Transitional Authority (UNTAC)   49
Cambodia 1992–1993   49
AFP in Cambodia   49
Other AFP Missions 1989–2003   51
United Nations Border Relief Organisation (UNBRO) 1989   52
Mozambique: ONUMOZ, 1994   52
Somalia 1993   55
Haiti: Operation Uphold Democracy 1994–1995   56
Bougainville 1997–2003   56

This chapter discusses the way in which the AFP was initially positioned as a contributor to international policing and diplomacy through peacekeeping deployments. The AFP has shown itself to be capable and ready to respond effectively to extant and emerging challenges at the request of the Australian Government. In 1964, the Commonwealth Police,[1] one of the three agencies which amalgamated in 1979 to form the AFP, responded to the call from the international community to deal with the outbreak of violent hostilities in Cyprus as a civilian police contribution to the United Nations Force in Cyprus (UNFICYP). This mission provided the foundation upon which further AFP deployments were based, including Cambodia, the United Nations Transition Authority Cambodia (UNTAC) in 1992, Mozambique, the United Nations Mission in Mozambique (ONUMOZ) in 1992 and Haiti in 1994.

United Nations Force in Cyprus:
Police – the 'Accidental Peacekeeper'

Sometimes, even in a heavily 'militarised' environment, an effective civilian police presence can offer an alternative to an exclusively military solution to what are often community-based problems. This is particularly important in situations where ingrained ethnic hatreds, strongly held beliefs and sheer stubbornness combine to create highly volatile situations where accidental or deliberate misunderstandings can escalate quickly. The situation in Cyprus was one of these.

Involvement in Cyprus spanning more than fifty years of international Australian policing began in 1964 when police were deployed in lieu of Australian troops due to more pressing regional priorities in the post-colonial era when wars of 'national liberation' were conflated with aggressive and expansionist Cold War international communism. The strategic genesis of this deployment lies almost a decade earlier in the 1950s and arose from what became known as the Suez Crisis, which was caused by the nationalisation of the Suez Canal by Egypt and precipitous military action by Britain and France in conjunction with Israel, which failed and resulted in Egypt taking full control of the canal. The ability of Britain to maintain its military commitments in the Persian Gulf and Southeast Asia was diminished. The Suez Crisis also created a major rift between the foreign policies of Britain and its major ally, the U.S., and ultimately resulted in Britain's 'East of Suez' policy in the 1970s, whereby British military forces east of the Suez Canal would be withdrawn.

As one of Australia's security guarantors in the Southeast Asian region, this created an even more serious re-think of Australian foreign and defence policy in the region, which had taken a battering with the fall of Singapore to Imperial Japanese Forces in February 1942 and Indian independence in 1947. The nascent nationalist, post-colonial independence movements, often conflated with expansionist communist aggression in Indo-China and Southeast Asia, resulted in Australian military forces becoming involved in conflict alongside British military forces in Malaya[2] and North Borneo in the 1960s, which resulted in the creation of the sovereign nation of Malaysia, later Singapore, and later alongside U.S. military forces in Indo-China, specifically Vietnam. This re-focused Australia in its interaction with the Southeast Asian region as it sought trading partners to replace Britain as a destination for Australian agricultural and mineral exports, as stated by Kwan:

> As Britain gained entry to the European Economic Community and withdrew from most of its defence commitments east of Suez, trade, investment and defence ties with the United States and Japan became more important to Australia. Its citizens found their traditional easy access to Britain increasingly difficult after restrictive British laws in 1962 and 1968.[3]

Britain's courtship of the European Common Market, later the European Union, caused a re-prioritisation of Australian trade efforts into East Asia and Southeast Asia. Japan became a major trading partner in lieu of Britain; however, this was potentially compromised by communist threats to the sea lanes to the north and south, between Australia and Japan, and to the west and east from the Straits of Malacca and the Taiwan Strait to Japan, which threatened Japan's oil supply from the Middle East. This required military involvement by Australia to bolster the U.S.'s support for Japan. As a result, when asked for a military contribution to Cyprus in 1964, the Australian Government was unwilling to provide it and cited regional priorities as outlined by Sue Thompson from the Australian Strategic Policy Institute (ASPI):

> at Britain's request, the UN Security Council took a look at the situation in Cyprus, which had steadily deteriorated since the outbreak of violence between Greek and Turkish Cypriots in December 1963. After the UN Secretary General had failed to reach an agreement with the parties, and following Turkish naval manoeuvres off the Cypriot coast, the Security Council adopted on 4 March a resolution authorising the Secretary General to create, with the consent of the Government of Cyprus, a peacekeeping force for the island. Australia chose not to contribute soldiers to the peacekeeping force, despite British attempts to convince Canberra otherwise. Australia's position was that, because of other commitments and the onset of the Confrontation between Malaysia and Indonesia just as America increased its involvement in Vietnam, Australia would be unable to consider a contribution to Cyprus.[4]

The situation in Cyprus was, and remains, classic peacekeeping. There is a ceasefire and, thus, a 'peace to keep'; there are two identifiable belligerents, who choose to use conventional military forces, and there is a combination of ethnic and religious tensions and a territorial dispute. Unlike many other missions in which the AFP eventually became involved, the nature of the dispute is between governments, which are, ironically, both members of a larger alliance, the North Atlantic Treaty Organisation (NATO). It was, and remains, a 'wicked problem', but one that involves community sentiments as much as military actors.

In the case of Australian involvement in Indo-China and Southeast Asia, one lesson learned from regional military involvement in places such as Malaya and Vietnam is that most post-1945 conflict has been 'intra-state' rather than 'inter-state'.[5] The world's militaries are still structured for inter-state conflict; thus, an exclusively military solution to these conflicts is rarely achievable and very expensive. Militaries are designed to win wars rather than keep the peace. They are not generally structured, equipped or trained to deal with community issues as they are peacemakers rather than peacekeepers.

Australian military involvement in the Vietnam War was controversial, and its ignominious end, involving acrimonious domestic politics, heralded the start of what some Australian military commentators have coined 'The Great Peace'. It was during this 'Great Peace' between the end of Australian military involvement in Vietnam in 1972 and the entry of the Australian military in East Timor with INTERFET in 1999 that the AFP continued a 'firm' international presence, including with UNFICYP in Cyprus.

The United Nations Force in Cyprus 1964–2017

Australian police became involved in contemporary UNCIVPOL[6] duties in Cyprus in 1964 when a number of state and territory police, and later Commonwealth Police, were asked to form part of UNFICYP. The intercommunal violence between Greek and Turkish Cypriots, which broke out in late 1963 following independence from Britain in 1960 in the wake of the Suez Crisis, caused the mainland nations of Greece and Turkey to become involved in the situation. The UN became involved during the intercommunal violence, and UNFICYP was established in 1964 to 'prevent a recurrence of the fighting, help maintain law and order, and promote a return to normal conditions'.[7] This is a classic peace-making, peace-building and peace-keeping approach.

The actual catalyst for the deployment of Australian police to Cyprus rather than the Australia military was a Minute sent by First Assistant Secretary Patrick Shaw to the Department of External Affairs to the Minister Sir Garfield Barwick on 20 April 1964.[8] The text of this Minute lists several reasons to deploy Australian police. These were:

1. The Allocation of Limited Resources whereby the Australian Military was too committed regionally in South East Asia. The Minute states, '…our strategic commitments in South-East Asia preclude our entering into a new commitment at this stage in an area outside our immediate strategic concern. These considerations do not apply to non-military personnel.'
2. Upholding and supporting United Nations Principles and Values where it states, '…Australia has always had, and has sought to preserve, a reputation as a leading and responsible supporter of the principles of the United Nations. Our inability to make a minimal contribution to the United Nations peacekeeping force could be represented as a lack of concern for our obligations towards the principle of collective security…'
3. The Limited Direct Australian Strategic Interests in Cyprus or the Eastern Mediterranean,. This also mentions a criterion which was reversed in 1999 when Australian Federal Police were deployed to East Timor, This criteria states: 'The Secretary-General, in selecting countries for approach for help in Cyprus has been guided by the principle frequently stated by the Secretary-General, that in any such operation countries with a specific interest should if possible, be <u>excluded</u>. Australia has much to gain by establishing this principle, and by establishing a general duty of the United Nations, to help solve distant disputes in which they are <u>not</u> strategically concerned…'
4. Commonwealth Member Obligation to Attempt to Remedy Any Breakdown on Constitutional Government in a Commonwealth Country. The Minute states, '…we have some obligation to demonstrate that we as a senior member of the Commonwealth regard trouble in another Commonwealth country as a matter of concern to us…. any breakdown of constitutional government in a Commonwealth country is something we should wish to see remedied…'

These are all sound reasons for the deployment of the first Australian police to Cyprus later in 1964 which was the basis for over fifty years in that mission and which provided the foundation for sixty years of AFP missions, operations and programs, some of which are still current at the time if writing in 2024.

As Chappell and Evans identify, the involvement of a civilian police component has its origins in an earlier mission in the Congo (ONUC). One of its former military commanders, Brigadier Sean McEown, the Chief of the Irish Army, considered the police to be a better alternative to the UN military to encourage meaningful negotiation and liaison between the communities and their representative police agencies. In this regard:

the role and function of CIVPOL must be seen as part of a continuum from preventative diplomacy to post conflict peacebuilding. That continuum may be divided into three stages, beginning with CIVPOL's participation in conflict resolution through helping to build confidence between former combatants.[9]

This can often be a lengthy process. A coup d'état in Cyprus in July 1974 by Greek and Greek Cypriot elements, favouring 'enosis' (unification) with mainland Greece, caused consternation in mainland Turkey. The Turks then 'intervened' militarily from the north and pushed the retreating Greeks and Greek Cypriots back towards the south. The UN Security Council immediately called for a ceasefire, and a conference was arranged between Greece, Turkey and the UK – the erstwhile colonial power – in Geneva in August 1974.

These talks subsequently broke down, and the Turkish forces pressed on with their 'intervention'. They eventually ceased their southward thrust on 16 August 1974, having gained ground to the middle of the capital Nicosia and to the northern outskirts of Nicosia International airport, which also happened to be a Royal Air Force (RAF) base. Anecdotal information suggests that the British commander alerted the Turkish commander to the existence of the RAF base, two British Sovereign Base Areas on the south coast, a Royal Navy Base at Limassol and an RAF Base at Dhekalia. In addition, the proximity and readiness of the British Army in Germany, a mere four hours away, may have been a highly persuasive factor in the decision by the Turkish military to halt its advance.

The ceasefire lines were drawn in August 1974 to form the northern and southern perimeters of what became the United Nations Buffer Zone (UNBZ), which runs east–west along almost the entire length of the island. The UNBZ is still in existence, and it divides the Turkish-held northern third from the Greek Cypriot–held southern two-thirds. The UNBZ passes through the middle of Nicosia, where it is in some parts a mere two metres wide. On the northern, or Turkish, side of the ceasefire lines, there are still troops dug in fortifications, fully armed and ready to mobilise at a moment's notice. After many years of very limited and restricted connectivity between the Turkish Cypriot north and the Greek Cypriot south, there are now a number of crossing points between the north and the south, including in Nicosia itself. There are fortifications on the southern or Greek side; however, they are rarely fully manned. Essentially, both sides merely agreed to apply their safety catches and take their fingers off their triggers, but all else remains as it was in 1974.

The areas between the two ceasefire lines are patrolled by the UN, both military and UNCIVPOL, who, for all intents and purposes, are the actual civilian authority in the UNBZ. The UNCIVPOL in Cyprus are unarmed, which is a deliberate policy to encourage community engagement and a feature that resonated in a later mission in East Timor in 1999. The UNCIVPOL, however, are unable to enforce the law as they would in a domestic sense primarily because of a reluctance to charge offenders criminally to appear before a court in either the north or the south of the island. UNCIVPOL in UNFICYP initially deployed in an armed capacity for self-protection, but after the first few years, following the establishment of a relatively peaceful environment, UNCIVPOL deployed unarmed. This experience was to inform later decisions on this subject, particularly in East Timor with UNAMET in 1999.

With the inter-communal violence and the Turkish 'intervention' in 1974, a major refugee problem ensued: an excess of 200,000 people required assistance due to dislocation. Members from each community were permitted, under UNCIVPOL supervision and escort, to cross the UNBZ to be reunited with their families. In February 1975, the Turkish Cypriot leadership unilaterally announced the formation of the 'Turkish Federated State of Cyprus', which was renamed by the same authorities in November 1983 as the 'Turkish Republic of Northern Cyprus'.

The UN has never recognised Turkish sovereignty in this northern part of Cyprus; however, the reality is that the Turkish military is well entrenched there. In pragmatic terms, the Turks believe they have a right to the entire island due primarily to geographic proximity; a notion that conflicts with the Greek claim of sovereignty, which, among other things, includes the assertion that the Ancient Greek goddess Aphrodite was born on the island of Cyprus.

The British have two sovereign bases in the southern part of the island, negotiated with the Cypriots before partition when Britain ceded independence in 1960. These bases, one RAF base (Dhekalia) and one Royal Navy base (Limassol), form an integral part of the British strategy in the Mediterranean, along with similar installations in Malta and Gibraltar. From this combination of bases, the British can respond to issues arising in the Mediterranean, Middle East and Suez Canal, a vital sea-lane for fuel supplies to Europe and the Black Sea and the egress point for Russia into the Mediterranean. As part of NATO, the U.S. has bases within mainland Turkey itself that form a forward 'foothold' for any intelligence or military activity involving the former USSR, now the Russian Federation, and the more hostile nations within the volatile Middle Eastern region.

This has created a situation whereby neither the U.S. nor the UK has been inclined to apply military force, or the threat of such, to force Turkey off the island of Cyprus. This situation is complicated further by the fact that both Greece and Turkey are members of NATO. Greece and Cyprus are both members of the EU, and Turkey is actively seeking membership to the EU. Cyprus, therefore, remains at a stalemate while each of the parties remain intractable.

When Turkey 'intervened' in 1974, many Cypriots from both communities left Cyprus and sought more tranquil lives elsewhere, including Australia. Both communities formed lobby groups that had an influence on both major Australian political parties. The Cyprus issue, thus, became loosely linked with Australian domestic politics, and whenever the withdrawal of Australian police was raised, the Greek Cypriot lobby group would oppose it, and the matter would drop from the agenda. This changed, however, in 2007 with the election of the Rudd/Gillard/Rudd Government and the Abbott/Turnbull Government in 2013, which put financial pressure on the AFP, which consequently sought to cease its contribution to UNFICYP and withdrew mid-2017 after fifty-three years of continuous service.

The AFP was in Cyprus for over fifty years and had built up a level of trust among members of both communities. Australian police have traditionally been understood as 'honest brokers' in this difficult situation, as Australia, unlike the former colonial power Britain, had no agenda in relation to the future of Cyprus. This had many positive by-products, not the least of which was the willingness of members of both communities to approach unarmed Australian police to provide information they would often be unwilling to provide to members of other UN contingents.

Cypriots from both communities who have lived outside Cyprus and have returned are far more approachable than those who have remained on the island. It is an enduring contact between these people and trusted UN members that helps to diffuse potentially volatile situations, and it may eventually break down the intractability that persists on both sides of the UNBZ. Noteworthy is the open invitation made by the Cypriot community of Darwin to the Federal and Northern Territory governments to use their club facilities in Darwin to assist in the post-evacuation procedure for the refugees from East Timor in September 1999 following the outbreak of violence following a UN-sponsored ballot.

The AFP was also heavily invested in that mission, and much of the posture adopted by the AFP in East Timor in 1999 was informed by their experiences in Cyprus and elsewhere, including Bougainville, Mozambique, Haiti and Cambodia. When deployed to Cyprus in 1964, the Commonwealth Police was among one of the first civilian police forces to deploy into a disrupted state. As such, it set a precedent for other UN missions, including some that involved the AFP. This was a major shift in thinking away from military dominance of this sort of intervention towards a more 'civilianised' approach involving civilian police as well as military forces. This has taken some time to be recognised by military forces, including in Australia; however, it was recognised early by the British military or at least by one of its more senior and experienced officers. As a former senior member of the AFP, Adrian Whiddett wrote of a former British Chief of Staff to UNFICYP, Brigadier Michael Harbottle:

> the decision to raise a small multinational civilian police component to form part of the UN Peace-keeping Force in Cyprus (UNFICYP) was a novel and experimental departure from usual practice, acknowledging that, as useful as the military are, they are limited in dealing with a usually resentful citizenry. Harbottle, a former Brigadier and Chief of Staff of UNFICYP from June 1966 to August 1968, came to realise that the insinuation of impartial civilian police into what now is a largely civil situation was indeed one of the 'unqualified successes' of the UN action in Cyprus.

The UN is still there patrolling the UNBZ that separates the two communities. Turkish soldiers are still dug in on the northern perimeter of the buffer zone. Britain still maintains its sovereign bases. The AFP, after fifty-three years patrolling the UNBZ, engaging with the communities on both sides and conducting humanitarian patrols, lowered the Australian National Flag in Nicosia in 2017 and concluded its involvement in UNFICYP, but the experience-based lessons learned there formed the basis for future 'boots on the ground' missions for half a century.

United Nations – Cambodia

Closer to home, in the Indo-China region, the involvement of Australians in the post–Pol Pot era in Cambodia under the leadership of the UN, UNTAC, had some Australian domestic political implications due to the intimate involvement of the then Australian Foreign Minister Gareth Evans and the leadership of UNTAC by the Australian military commander General John Sanderson. UNTAC involved a combination of Australian government elements, including the ADF and two contingents of the AFP. It was a largely successful transition from the turmoil and trauma of Pol Pot to what is now a relatively peaceful if not fully democratic country, and it was a feather in the caps of both Gareth Evans and General Sanderson. Sadly, the influence of the PRC in Cambodia has seen it move more towards authoritarianism.

U.S. Bombing and the Khmer Rouge

The genesis of the situation in Cambodia lay in the conflation of its French post-colonial past and its proximity to Vietnam, which, during the 1960s and 1970s, became engaged in a war with the U.S. as part of the Cold War. Cambodia had been plunged into the U.S. war in Indo-China in 1969 when U.S. President Nixon began a secret bombing campaign, codenamed Operation Menu, to attempt to destroy a Vietnamese communist headquarters that the U.S. claimed had been operating inside Cambodia along the border with Vietnam since 1964 in violation of Cambodian neutrality. The North Vietnamese were operating with the approval of Cambodia's leader Prince Norodom Sihanouk. Sihanouk tried to maintain neutrality; however, '[in] return for a North Vietnamese pledge to respect Cambodia's frontiers, he allowed Vietnamese communists to operate covertly from bases inside eastern Cambodia'.[10]

For over a decade, from 1979, the conflict over Cambodia became the dominant political and security problem in Southeast Asia. Within Cambodia, the Vietnamese-sponsored regime, the People's Republic of Kampuchea (PRK), whose dominant leader was Hun Sen, attempted to promote economic reconstruction and its own political consolidation. Vietnam and the PRK regime faced armed opposition from three Cambodian resistance movements operating on and near the Thai border: the ousted Khmer Rouge (referred to widely as the 'Pol Pot regime' after its leading figure),[11] the royalist FUNCINPEC (the National United Front for an Independent, Neutral, Peaceful and Cooperative Cambodia) led by Prince Norodom Sihanouk and the republican Khmer People's National Liberation Front led by Son Sann.

Vietnam and the PRK also faced opposition from the Association of Southeast Asia (ASEAN)[12], which refused to accept the PRK regime's legitimacy and worked to deny acceptance of the regime internationally and mobilise support for Vietnam's withdrawal. A key avenue for ASEAN's diplomacy was the sponsorship of a resolution in the UN General Assembly calling for an immediate ceasefire and the withdrawal of Vietnam's forces. The first such resolution was adopted on 14 November 1979, and ASEAN continued to gain large majorities in support of similar resolutions for the next decade.

This created a significant dilemma for Australian foreign policy. Abhorrent as it was, the Khmer Rouge was seen as the internationally recognised government of Cambodia and Vietnam as an 'invader'. Responding to domestic concerns in relation to the excesses of the Khmer Rouge, the then Fraser government, via its Foreign Minister Andrew Peacock, announced on

14 October 1980 'that Australia had decided on a policy of "de-recognition"; he stated that "Australia cannot prolong its recognition of such a loathsome regime as that of Pol Pot."'[13]

This resulted in de facto recognition of the Vietnamese 'invaders' by Australia, which created a divergence of views between Australia and its ASEAN allies. ASEAN had as its central pillar a policy of non-interference in the affairs of other nations under the ASEAN doctrine of the Zone of Peace, Freedom and Neutrality (ZOPFAN). The unfortunate outcome was that ASEAN was providing de facto support to a genocidal regime under the Khmer Rouge in Cambodia, a situation by which an increasingly human rights–aware Australian public could not abide.

The Australian Government's change of policy on recognition had responded to domestic opinion but produced some critical reactions from ASEAN, China and the US, especially after the May 1981 announcement on recognition policy at international forums. In late May, the policy change was criticised by Singapore's Deputy Prime Minister Sinnatamby Rajaratnam as one that 'will certainly damage the foreign-policy interests of Australia, seriously question its credentials as a reliable ally of those who have taken up the Soviet challenge in Southeast Asia and bring comfort to the Vietnamese.'[14]

At the time of the ASEAN Ministerial Meeting in June 1981 in Manila, the Philippines's Foreign Minister described Australia as being 'recalcitrant' on the issue, and reservations were also reported to have been expressed by U.S. and Chinese officials. The Australian conservative government of Malcolm Fraser was replaced in 1983 by the Australian Labor Party under Prime Minister Bob Hawke, who in opposition had welcomed the Fraser government's withdrawal of diplomatic recognition of the Khmer Rouge Democratic Kampuchea. In government, Prime Minister Hawke and Foreign Minister Hayden decided to explore some options to resolve the Cambodian situation. Prime Minister Hawke wrote in his memoir:

> [O]ne of the most important initiatives of my entire prime ministership was our diplomatic effort to help bring about a lasting peace in the tragic, conflict-ridden country of Cambodia…Both Hayden and I were acutely aware of the obstacles ahead. ASEAN had arisen from the instability in Indo-China and the intrusion of the Soviet Union and China into the affairs of the region; its members remained suspicious of Vietnam and the two communist giants. The antagonism between China and Vietnam stretched back a thousand years. Cambodia itself remained sunk in conflict, with an uneasy alliance of forces arranged against the puppet Hun Sen regime. Our knowledge of and closeness to the regional players had its advantages, but understanding the

range of their conflicting interests meant that Australia's diplomacy would have to be deft in the extreme.[15]

Hayden, as Foreign Minister from March 1983-August 1988, observed:

[t]he aim was to facilitate a process of dialogue leading to a peaceful settlement of the warring inside and near the borders of Kampuchea. I regarded the proposal with some caution. There were a great number of differences between many of these parties and some had large political interests at stake. Australia strolling into this particular pastry shop and upsetting the wares so carefully if unsteadily arranged could well be disastrous.[16]

On the ground, there was a new form of stalemate. ASEAN had the strength and unity to stand behind Thailand and the Cambodian coalition in their resistance to Vietnam; on the other hand, Vietnam took comfort from the fact that the situation on the ground in Cambodia was largely in its favour despite resistance to its occupation, especially in the border areas.

The Australian approach sought a comprehensive solution based on Vietnamese acceptance of a phased troop withdrawal and an arrangement to facilitate the return of displaced Cambodians that prevented the return of the Khmer Rouge, as well as an act of self-determination in Cambodia itself, all predicated on the universal acceptance that 'Cambodia should be neutral, independent and non-aligned; and the restoration of normal relations on the part of Vietnam with China, ASEAN and the West.'[17]

By 1988, after five years of diplomatic activity, the efforts to promote dialogue over Cambodia had raised Australia's profile as a concerned regional participant but had produced few results, as the major power blocs maintained their intransigence: the Soviets backing Vietnam, the Chinese backing the Khmer Rouge and the U.S. backing ASEAN. Australia was politically isolated, as it had de-recognised the Khmer Rouge, was neutral on Vietnam and was an active supporter of ASEAN. Frost identifies that this isolation 'stood it in good stead when putting forward its peace initiative in 1989, since the country was clearly not aligned to any of the major powers in their client Cambodian factions'.[18]

In strategic geopolitical terms, the stalemate was only broken when European communism collapsed in 1991. The end of the Cold War in Europe, following a 10-year Soviet occupation and humiliating withdrawal from Afghanistan in 1989, and the fall of the Berlin Wall in the same year, brought about some profound changes globally, regionally and domestically in Australia and its region. A key catalyst internationally was the effect of President Mikhail Gorbachev's policies in the Soviet Union. Gorbachev's speech in Vladivostok in July 1986 introduced a new era of flexibility in foreign relations as the Soviet Union sought to curtail costly foreign involvements. This included the withdrawal of support provided by the Soviet Union to countries such as Vietnam.

This provided the catalyst for some more assertive action by ASEAN to resolve a long-standing regional issue. In July 1988, further negotiations occurred when ASEAN's largest member, Indonesia, hosted formal multilateral talks among the Cambodian parties along with the other ASEAN members and Vietnam and Laos:

> In July 1989...the Paris International Conference on Cambodia...met for one month and was attended by the four Cambodian factions, the six ASEAN members, the "Permanent Five" members of the UN Security Council (China, France, the Soviet Union, the United Kingdom and the United States), Vietnam, Laos, Australia, Canada, India, Zimbabwe (representing the Non-Aligned Movement) and a representative of the UN Secretary-General.[19]

Contemporaneously, the surrounding nations in the region, including Thailand, Malaysia, Singapore and even China, were in the midst of an economic boom. This gave added incentive for Cambodians to solve their differences.

The global strategic situation was also changing. The dissolving Soviet Union and Warsaw Pact ended aid to both their long-standing ally Vietnam and the PRK, while Thailand and other members of ASEAN concluded that Indo-China was more lucrative as a marketplace than as a battlefield. Several attempts were made to negotiate a peace settlement for Cambodia in the 1980s; the most successful were meetings in Jakarta brokered by India and Indonesia.

Called the Jakarta Informal Meetings (JIMs), they were attended by all four Cambodian factions, Laos, Vietnam and the ASEAN member states. This was followed by a Sino–Soviet meeting in 1988, which resulted in a thaw in relations between Vietnam and China. Further talks involving Thailand in 1989 produced a key breakthrough in the shape of Vietnam's offer to withdraw its troops and an agreement to an international peace-monitoring force.

Vietnam, facing a decline in economic and military assistance from the Soviet Union and anxious to extricate itself from Cambodia, announced its withdrawal of combat forces from Cambodia and, in September 1989, declared this process completed. Building on initial suggestions by Prince Sihanouk and U.S. Congressman Stephen Solarz, Australia suggested an enhanced role for the UN in the transitional process that had been initially proposed in November 1989:

[To avoid] the power-sharing issue that had confounded the Paris conference, and to constrain the role of the Khmer Rouge, Australia proposed that the UN be directly involved in the civil administration of Cambodia during the transitional period. A UN military presence to monitor the ceasefire, cessation of external military assistance, a UN role in organising and conducting election, and UN involvement in the transitional administrative arrangements would, it was hoped, ensure a neutral political environment conducive to free and fair general elections.[20]

A departmental task force, under the direction of Australian Foreign Minister Senator Gareth Evans, drew up a detailed set of scenarios and plans for a UN role in Cambodia, and these papers were presented to a meeting of the ASEAN members, the Cambodian parties, Vietnam and Laos in February 1990. These were then published and became known by the colour of the cover: the 'Red Book'. The issue of Cambodia was an instance where Australia and ASEAN cooperated on a major issue of security and regional concern and achieved a significant outcome.

United Nations Transitional Authority (UNTAC)

Cambodia 1992–1993

Foreign Minister Senator Gareth Evans engaged in a re-formulation of a concept originally proposed by Prince Sihanouk and enunciated by U.S. Congressman Stephen Solarz. The proposal envisaged that, instead of a quadripartite power-sharing arrangement, the UN itself would temporarily take over the administration of Cambodia, canton and demobilise the armed forces of the various parties and conduct an election, after which it would transfer power to a new Cambodian government. This was to become the UN Transitional Authority Cambodia (UNTAC).

Overshadowing the entire peace process was the question of the atrocities committed by the Khmer Rouge. The term 'auto genocide' was diluted to the unrecognisable 'no-return to the policies and practices of the past'. The compromise to restore peace to Cambodia was the withdrawal of the charges of mass murder, as no provision would be made for war crimes trials or other means of achieving justice. In 1991, the Paris Peace Accords were formally adopted by the UN in New York.

The AFP in Cambodia

Thus, the UNTAC was created by accord and in May 1992, and ten members of the AFP were dispatched to Cambodia. They were stationed at Thmar Puok and had a patrol area of 2500 square kilometres, which was home to approximately 78,000 Cambodians in a state of post-conflict shock. The infrastructure was poor, and the police, along with their international counterparts, had to construct many of their own places of accommodation and work from available materials.

The overall role of the contingent was to assist the UN in bringing peace and democratic elections, which they implemented by supervising training and controlling local police and investigating allegations of human rights abuse reported to the UN command. This created a more stable environment in which elections could be held. Part of their role was to assist in bringing an environment of calm and confidence conducive to the holding of free elections.

A second AFP contingent replaced the first in early 1993. During the deployments of both contingents, more than 200 suspected human rights violations were investigated, and over 400 local police were trained. These local Khmer police came from all political factions. Khmer police instructors went on to maintain a Khmer police training program. The command and control of UNCIVPOL in UNTAC was a system where police were deployed to districts where the contingent commander was also the police district commander for the area of operations. Police in this situation acted in concert with the military force in the district but were independently controlled. The mechanism for this was via a Memorandum of Understanding on Police/Military cooperation, which formalised a clear delineation of responsibilities to prevent the duplication of effort and resource allocation.

Australian police were fortunate to have Australian mission commanders in both contingents. Working in conjunction with Australian UNCIVPOL were five German and five Tunisian police, with six Indian and five French police in nearby locations. Australian police were being led by Australian police commanders, which created an environment conducive to success through initiative and cooperation. Anecdotal information from AFP participants from both Cambodian contingents highlights the positive aspect of Australian police being led by commanders from Australia.[21] The contingents were very small but very effective because they were under Australian command; they were empowered to take the initiative to do the 'right thing', and, most importantly, they knew what the 'right thing' was.

A former senior AFP member Adrian Whiddett comments on the good work the AFP did in Cambodia that 'its successes were laudable and quite disproportionate to its size'.[22] However, the most appropriate praise comes from the overall military Commander of UNTAC, Australian General John Sanderson, who stated:

[T]he very small AFP contingent did a remarkable job in Cambodia. Its members numbered 10 out of a total civil police force of 3600. If there had been 360 groups of that potency, I think we would have had a much more significant impact on the outcomes in Cambodia because the law is the key issue in this. While we were not the sovereign authority in Cambodia, the process of taking the law down to the grassroots and getting it implemented there…was the key process and the AFP contingent did that…[T]he contingent actually wrote the body of law, established the school and the police station and supervised the activity.[23]

It was experience on the ground by members in places such as Cambodia and other missions that built up a corporate knowledge of how such deployments should be planned, equipped, staffed and deployed.[24] This was to play an extremely important role in the near future in equally challenging circumstances in East Timor in 1999.

Other AFP Missions 1989–2003

A credible international police peacekeeping experience by the AFP in Cyprus and Cambodia provided a basis for further deployments, particularly in a UN context. The transition from 'post-colonial civil conflict' to self-determination, as illustrated in the previous chapter, is seldom a peaceful process, and in the context of Cold War dynamics and the post-Cold War 'peace dividend', these transitions were very complex. Two examples involving first the former Portuguese colony of Mozambique on the South East coast of Africa and second the Caribbean island of Haiti, a former French colony, provide illustrations of the sort of challenges such post-conflict transitions can pose. In Mozambique, a number of AFP deployed with the UN to a mission known as ONUMOZ. In Haiti, a number of AFP were deployed with a U.S.-led intervention known as 'Operation Uphold Democracy'.

One feature of both missions is that they were distant from Australia and, thus, relatively free from Australian domestic political considerations. One was a UN-led mission, and the other was a U.S.-led mission. Both missions fulfilled Australian international obligations, especially with the UN during the 'Great Peace'.

In addition, the AFP deployed in small numbers to three other locations: the Thai–Cambodian border between 1989 and 1993; Somalia in 1993 and Bougainville between 1997 and 2003. In all these deployments, AFP members brought with them a strong sense of trust-based values and principles that were applied in societies where such trust had broken down. Although small in number, their effect was generally positive. The situation in Somalia was highly contested and non-permissive, which reinforces the precept that such trust-based approaches can really only be effective if the environment is permissive and there is a peace to keep. This is a 'lesson not learned' in 2008 when the AFP was asked to contribute to police training in a highly contested environment in southern Afghanistan, where there was no peace to keep.

United Nations Border Relief Organisation (UNBRO) 1989

As a result of the post-conflict turmoil created by the war in Indo-China and the devastation visited on the long-suffering people of Cambodia, there was a mass exodus of approximately 300,000 displaced persons and refugees fleeing westward to the border area with Thailand. The UN established the UNBRO in 1989. Shortly after UNBRO was established, two AFP Superintendents deployed to Aranyaprathet in North East Thailand.

Their mission was to assist UNBRO and the Government of Thailand to improve security and protection within the camps located along the border between Cambodia and Thailand. These camps were subject to hostile action, including guerrilla attacks and artillery fire, further eroding peace, law and order. During the period the AFP Superintendents were working with UNBRO, they encountered a high level of lawlessness inside the refugee camps, a tendency they assisted in alleviating.

The AFP members assisted the newly formed Khmer police with training and equipment, the establishment of justice committees along the lines of traditional Cambodian justice as well as a central prison. A key outcome for the AFP members was the development of the criminal code and regulations for the police, judiciary and prison services.

Mozambique: ONUMOZ, 1994

In the post-war anti-colonial wave, the Portuguese government remained obdurate in its desire to retain its colonial possessions. In Mozambique, various independence movements merged in June 1962 to form the *Frente da Liberacao de Mocambique* (FRELIMO) (Mozambique Liberation Front). FRELIMO commenced military activities against the Portuguese and conducted their activities from bases inside Tanzania. A 1974 coup in Portugal, known as the Carnation Revolution, led to the signing of an agreement between the Marxist-oriented Portuguese government and their appointed government in Mozambique, which was dominated by the pro-Marxist FRELIMO movement. Mr Joaquim Chissano became Prime Minister, and independence was declared on 25 June 1975.

Mozambique borders several countries, including Tanzania, Malawi, Zimbabwe (formerly Rhodesia), South Africa and Swaziland. The prospect of a Marxist government on one of its northern borders caused a great deal of concern in South Africa, which was then under the administration of the pro-apartheid Botha government. This was also the period before the independence of Zimbabwe, which was then known as Rhodesia under the Smith government.

In 1977, FRELIMO declared its Marxist-Leninist leanings and signed aid agreements with the Soviet Union and Cuba. FRELIMO was also assisting the Zimbabwean National Liberation Front struggle in Rhodesia and the African National Congress in South Africa. The Rhodesian and South African governments commenced assistance to a group formed to oppose FRELIMO; initially called the Mozambique National Resistance, it was renamed RENAMO: *Resistencia Nacional Mocambiquana*. Eventually, Mr Marceta Dhlakama became president of RENAMO, which pursued a guerrilla war aimed at destroying the social and economic infrastructure of the country. Between 1981 and 1983, South Africa itself launched commando and air force raids inside Mozambique.

The Mozambique government, via its armed forces, the FAM, closed the land transport routes vital for Zimbabwe, which responded by sending its own troops into Mozambique to protect the transport routes. RENAMO activities created a refugee problem in neighbouring states, and a major drought between 1982 and 1984 combined with the disruption by the war caused a major shortage of food.

In 1985, the FAM was stretched and had to rely on the support of neighbouring states, including Tanzania and Zimbabwe, the latter of which had gained its independence and ousted the Smith government in March 1980. The new Zimbabwe government of Robert Mugabe was a pro-Marxist government well-disposed to the incumbent government in Mozambique. The new Zimbabwe armed forces were trained by North Koreans.

RENAMO and the Mozambique government continued fighting. Following the collapse of the Soviet Union and the fall of the Berlin Wall in 1989, in 1990, the Mozambique government altered its Marxist-orientation towards a more market-oriented, multi-party system. This attracted more favourable treatment from the West and helped to isolate RENAMO politically, as well as the White minority South African government. Both the Mozambique government and RENAMO faced exhaustion, and neither was capable of ultimate victory, which created a political impasse: a precursor to a political solution.

Peace negotiations took place between July 1991 and October 1992, and a General Peace Agreement between President Chissano and Mr Dklakama was signed in Rome. This included a joint political declaration, which committed the parties to accepting the role of the international community, and especially that of the UN, in monitoring and guaranteeing the implementation of the General Peace Agreement, in particular the ceasefire and the electoral process. In December 1992, ONUMOZ was approved by the UN Security Council with a mandate that included four distinct sets of objectives: political, military, electoral and humanitarian, with a one-year timetable, later revised and extended. ONUMOZ needed to build trust and confidence in both parties and the general Mozambican population as a whole and convince them that the process could succeed.

The collapse of Soviet communism in 1991 and the resultant reduced internationalist posture by the Soviet Union made the 1992 elections in Mozambique possible. The UN-sponsored elections in 1992 were possible because RENAMO was losing support from South Africa, and FRELIMO had dropped its Marxist policies, which made peace talks possible.

In early 1994, the AFP dispatched a contingent of sixteen officers to Mozambique to aid the civil authorities in restoring law and order to a shattered infrastructure. This contingent was replaced later in 1994 on a rotation basis, as the posting was for six months. The Australian police were under the operational command of a Chief Police Observer, or UNCIVPOL Commissioner, an Egyptian national, who reported directly to the Special Representative. The Australians were posted to various districts in Beira, Lichinga, Gurue, Tete, Nampula, Xai Xai, Inhambane and Matola.

The situation that the first contingent encountered was a serious deterioration of infrastructure, which had improved little despite the presence of the UN for several months. Australian police were instructed by the UNCIVPOL Commissioner to 'get out and get things moving'. The original concept was for the Australians to be split totally; however, negotiations between the Australian Contingent Commander and the UNCIVPOL Commissioner resulted in Australians working in pairs in the districts. They largely assumed command positions and supervisory roles.

The Australians worked alongside police from Scandinavia, Malaysia, Guinea-Bissau, India, Pakistan, Bangladesh and Egypt. Upon the arrival of the Australian police, they immediately set about restoring a command structure and establishing investigation teams. Numerous reports of multiple murders, rapes and other general criminal activity had been evident. This established an environment in which the electoral component of the mission could proceed.

A general election was held, and the entire process passed peacefully. The second contingent of Australian police returned home in late 1994.

In 1995, Mozambique, by supporting the Commonwealth of Nations in its call for an end to apartheid in South Africa, was in turn supported by the Commonwealth to join it, the first non-British colony to do so.[25] This provided several non-tangibles but important diplomatic benefits for Mozambique. It allowed access to larger and more wealthy members; it provided for direct diplomacy at the ministerial and head-of-government level, a facility available to all Commonwealth members; and it assisted in reducing Mozambique's post-conflict reliance on foreign donations by gaining access to Commonwealth-related NGOs and their expertise and goodwill. Meanwhile, further north along the eastern coast of Africa, the UN was engaged in another mission in Somalia.

Somalia 1993

In May 1993, one Superintendent, released from duties with UNBRO, was seconded to the UN Operation in Somalia (UNOSOM II) in Somalia to the post of senior police advisor to the Special Representative of the Secretary General. His task was to assess the need for police monitors and, if possible, to organise and develop a training program for a civilian police authority in Somalia. In November 1993, a second Superintendent was appointed as the director of police services and deputy director of justice in Somalia. His task was to control and direct UNCIVPOL in their task to assist in re-establishing a local Somali police force with a view to eventually restore peace, stability and law and order. Insufficient staff and indecision by the UN administration in the early stages of this mission resulted in the AFP members struggling to achieve their mission. The withdrawal of the U.S. in March 1994 resulted in the withdrawal and closure of the mission. This was a situation where there was 'no peace to keep', where any form of UN civilian policing would have been effective.

The sight, in the lounge rooms of middle-America, of the corpse of a U.S. serviceman being dragged through the streets of Mogadishu, captured graphically in the 2001 movie *Black Hawk Down*, recalled similar images portrayed during the Vietnam War. It was probably this incident that resulted in the withdrawal of U.S. troops from Somalia in March 1994. This caused a fundamental shift in U.S. policy opinion relating to UN peacekeeping duties.

> The Clinton administration issued stringent new guidelines for American participation or even support of UN peacekeeping. If these guidelines were followed strictly, the United States would never support another peacekeeping operation again. The Americans, in fact had to close their eyes to their own

guidelines in 1994 when they persuaded the Security Council to vote for a new peacekeeping venture in Haiti.[26]

Haiti: Operation Uphold Democracy 1994–1995

In 1990, the UN observed the first democratic elections in the Caribbean island nation of Haiti since a military coup had forced President Aristide into exile. Haiti's self-appointed military leader, Colonel Cedres, did not comply with a UN Agreement for the return of democracy, which resulted in the UN Security Council authorising the formation of a multi-national force to facilitate Cedres' departure and the return of Aristide. The US-led force in 'Operation Uphold Democracy' facilitated the return of the exiled president in 1994.

Part of the multi-national force included thirty Australian Civilian Police, primarily from the AFP, with three Victoria Police and two Queensland Police members. This contingent served in Haiti from October 1994 until March 1995 and was posted as a contingent, under Australian police command, to police a district surrounding the town of Jeremie. The Australian police worked alongside U.S. Special Forces.

The mission in Haiti was unique in three aspects: first, it was the first mission in which state police members had participated in an international police mission since the very early days in Cyprus; second, it was, until then, the only mission in which Australian police had been armed, at the insistence of the US, and third, it was not a UN mission, but a Chapter VII engagement. The U.S.-led mission was later taken over by a UN mission; however, by this time, the Australian police had returned to Australia. Experience gained in Mozambique, Haiti, Cambodia and Cyprus saw the AFP deployed in small numbers to the troubled island of Bougainville in 1997.

Bougainville 1997–2003

The island of Bougainville suffered seven years of conflict before a peace settlement was reached. In October 1997, peace talks were held in Burnham, New Zealand that resulted in the formation of a Truce Monitoring Group (TMG), which included four AFP members deployed to Bougainville. They were later supplemented by additional AFP members. Their role involved observation and monitoring the progress of the truce, liaison between the various factions involved in the conflict and reporting and investigating breaches of the truce.

The TMG ceased on 30 April 1998 and was replaced by the Peace Monitoring Group (PMG). AFP members of the PMG monitored and reported on the compliance of the parties and worked to rebuild trust and confidence among the communities concerned. This involved assessing and reporting on other aspects of community resilience and development, including fresh water, health and schooling. They were also involved in the location, recording and disposal of weapons, ammunition and explosives. The PMG finished in mid-2003.

The New Zealand Police continued to engage in Bougainville with a community policing program. Bougainville remains a province of PNG and conducted a referendum in relation to its political future in 2019 along the lines of the Matignon Accords, which relates to French possessions in the Pacific. This remains an outstanding matter between the people of Bougainville and the Government of Papua New Guinea.

In an article titled The Bougainville Referendum and Beyond: Institutional Options and Issues for Transition, the Melbourne University Law School stated:

> In November 2019, the people of the Autonomous Region of Bougainville in Papua New Guinea voted on whether to pursue 'greater autonomy' within Papua New Guinea or independence. The vote showed 97% of the people were in favour of independence. The outcome is subject to ratification by the Parliament of Papua New Guinea and in 2020, the governments of Bougainville and Papua New Guinea will begin consultations about the way forward.[27]

The independence of Bougainville was announced on 7 July 2021. Pending approval by the Papua New Guinea Parliament, Bougainville will become independent by the end of 2027.

Part II

Democracy, Violence and the New Security Paradigm 1999–2007

East Timor and Indonesia

East Timor 1999 62
United Nations – Resolutions 384 and 389, 1975 63
Human Rights Abuses 63
Santa Cruz Massacre 1991 64
Santa Cruz Massacre Protests Canberra 1991–1992 65
Activism 66
Blind Eye: Influence of Jakarta Lobby 66
The Election of President Habibie 68
Letter from Prime Minister Howard to President Habibie 1998:
Offer of Special Autonomy 69
Indonesian Response 70
Loss of Control Over the Process 70
Australian Response 71
Militia Warnings Pre-ballot 72
Pro-Indonesian Militia Groups 73
Militia Groups UNAMET East Timor 1999 Why, Who, How and What 74
Militia Groups East Timor 1999 75
Operation Global Clean Sweep Pre-ballot 76
United Nations Security Council Resolution 1246: 1999 77
Security Agreement Civilian Police: The Third Force 78
Decision to send Australian Federal Police to UNAMET 78
Australian Federal Police Expression of Interest 29 April-3 May 1999 79
UNAMET AFP Pre deployment Training and Deployment 81
UNAMET is Established: June 1999 82
The Security Environment 82
Indonesian Perception of Australian Partisanship 83
Armed Police? 84
Operation Global Clean Sweep: Ballot 85
The Ballot 86
Ballot Result 87
Overreaction by TNI/Militias:
Operation Global Clean Sweep: Post-Ballot 89
The UN Compound Dili 4-14 Sept 1999 90
The Casualty List and Indictments 92
The Military-Militia Connection 95
Language is Important 96
Militia Targets 97
Plausible Deniability 97
Kopassus and Secret Warfare 98
UNAMET: The Consequences 100
Follow-on UN Missions 103
UNTAET Serious Crimes Unit: Crimes Against Humanity 104
Australian–Indonesian Relationship 105
Transition – UNAMET and Global War on Terror 108
Indonesia: Counter-terrorism and AFP Liaison Network 108
The 9/11 Attacks, PM Howard 109
Indonesia 111
UNAMET, INTERFET and Global Jihad: 1999–2002 113
Islamic Extremism in Indonesia 115
The Bali Bombing 2002 116
Arrest of Amrozi 119
Domestic Response: Immediate 119
Why Police? 120
International Policing 121
Jakarta Centre for Law Enforcement Cooperation (JCLEC) 2004 122
Government and Academic Partners 122
UNAMET and Consequential UN Security Council Resolutions 123

This chapter explores the repercussions of AFP involvement in a UN-sponsored ballot in the UN Mission East Timor, known as UNAMET¹ in 1999. This was a seminal mission and, combined with a number of subsequent missions, had significant implications for Australian foreign policy in the new millennium as the world experienced a sharp rise in global Islamic jihadism which in turn had implications for a new Australian security paradigm. The involvement of the AFP in UNAMET and the subsequent Australian-led military intervention known as the International Force East Timor known as INTERFET, as well as the international reactions to the terrorist attacks on New York and Washington in 2001, changed Australian government policy. This resulted in a new foreign policy focus in which the AFP played a key role, which had implications for regional relationships and diplomatic sensitivities with Indonesia, the South West Pacific in what was known as the 'Arc of Instability'² and further afield.

At this juncture it is worth recalling the rationale for the initial deployment of police to Cyprus in 1964. On 20 April 1964, Patrick Shaw the First Assistant Secretary sent a Minute to the Minister for External Affairs outlining several reasons Australia should deploy police to Cyprus. Among the most relevant in the context of East Timor thirty-five years later in 1999, is the principle that the UN Secretary General was '…guided by the principle…that in any such operation countries with a specific interest should if possible, be <u>excluded</u>. Australia has much to gain by establishing this principle, and by establishing a general duty of the United Nations, to help solve distant disputes in which they are <u>not</u> strategically concerned.'³

This principle applied to all pre-1999 police deployments to Cyprus, Cambodia, Mozambique, Haiti and Bougainville, but was turned on its head in 1999 when a large deployment of AFP members was deployed to the troubled Indonesian province of East Timor.

A common belief is that Australia's involvement in East Timor commenced with the arrival of Australian General Peter Cosgrove on 20 September 1999. It was, in fact, the AFP, as part of UNAMET, which was the first Australian engagement in East Timor, which was then the 27th Province of the Republic of Indonesia. The UNAMET mission, tasked with securing a legitimate ballot of the East Timorese as to their political future, commenced in June 1999 and withdrew under extreme security concerns earlier in September 1999. The ballot result was an emphatic rejection of the Indonesian offer of 'special autonomy' within the Republic of Indonesia. The ballot was deferred once due to pro-Indonesian militia violence, but despite the violence, harassment and intimidation, 78.5 per cent of the population of Timor-Leste voted in favour of becoming an independent nation. The ballot result unleashed a pre-meditated campaign of violence and destruction in the immediate post-ballot period. This was led by both Indonesian security forces and Indonesian-backed militia, as part of a deliberate scorched earth campaign.

This situation became so extreme in mid-September, that an international military force was required. Approximately 70 per cent of Timor-Leste's infrastructure was destroyed by arson, between 1200 and 1600 of East Timor's population were murdered, and approximately 250,000 people were forcibly deported to a very uncertain future in camps in West Timor. Much of this violence and destruction was initially prevented by unarmed UNCIVPOL, including AFP members, but they were out-numbered, out-gunned and out-manoeuvred and they had to eventually withdraw or face certain death at the hands of the Indonesian security forces and their militia proxies.

East Timor 1999

The AFP commenced involvement in East Timor in June 1999 and has remained engaged in one capacity or another in the subsequent twenty-five years. International and Australian involvement in East Timor had its genesis in the mid-1970s arising from the Carnation Revolution in Lisbon where the new socialist government of Portugal sought to divest itself of its former colonial possessions, including what was then referred to as Portuguese Timor. The rapid withdrawal of the Portuguese administration left a post-colonial power vacuum which created some serious governance issues as competing parties fought with each other to fill the vacuum. This created the pretext for an Indonesian invasion in 1975, where Indonesian forces became involved in a prolonged and violent counter-insurgency with pro-independence forces.

Given the Cold War dynamics, the U.S. was at best ambivalent and was unofficially supportive of the Indonesian invasion for a number of reasons, including an aversion to antagonising a largely Islamic, anti-communist, oil-producing nation with control of significant sea lanes between the Pacific and Indian Oceans, including the Straits of Ombar and Wetar, important as sea transit lanes for U.S. submarines travelling from the Pacific to the Indian Oceans. Other sea lanes in Indonesian waters, such as the Sunda and Lombok Straits have also been part of specifically Australian strategic considerations as much of our trade transits through these waters to South East Asia and East Asia.

Domestically, in Australia, the 1975 invasion was treated politically with a bipartisan 'blind eye', although there was some agitation among activists. The two major domestic influences in Australia were the 'Jakarta Lobby', an informal group of academics and senior defence and foreign affairs officials who were pragmatically pro-Indonesian, and domestic political activists who were pro-East Timorese independence. There is also a line of thought that despite assurances given by President Suharto to then Prime Minister

Whitlam that Indonesia would refrain from taking military action in East Timor, in the eyes of the Indonesian President, that promise was no longer an obligation after Whitlam was dismissed on 11 November 1975.

The significance of the Indonesian invasion and occupation of East Timor in late 1975 needs to be put into context. The capital of South Vietnam, Saigon, had fallen to victorious communist forces from the north in April of that year. The Americans had largely withdrawn from active military involvement in Southeast Asia and Indo-China, and Australia, as a result, had also changed its posture from 'forward defence' to 'defence of Australia'.

United Nations – Resolutions 384 and 389, 1975

The Indonesian invasion in 1975 caused the United Nations General Assembly to pass Resolutions 384 and 389 on 12 December 1975, which deplored Indonesia's invasion and called for the immediate withdrawal of its troops.[4] The UN maintained this position consistently for more than two decades, which formed the basis for the UNAMET mission in 1999.

Human Rights Abuses

Indonesian forces almost immediately became engaged in a full-scale counter-insurgency which they met with military force, with inevitable human rights abuses. Braithwaite described the counter-insurgency as 'ruthlessly brutal with those who openly resisted it, while seeking to respect human rights, and enrol and win the hearts and minds of those who collaborated with it'.[5] Kingsbury identified how this brutal counter-insurgency resulted in up to 200,000 deaths from human rights abuses, including 'starvation caused by compulsory relocation, preventable diseases caused by a lack of otherwise available medicines, and the killing of combatants and more commonly civilians often on a scale of wholesale massacres by Indonesian soldiers'.[6]

This was matched on the Indonesian side by a high cost in blood and treasure, as highlighted by Braithwaite, who identified Indonesian estimates of between 4000 and 20,000 lives lost, which sapped the moral of the Indonesian elite, and a financial cost of between U.S. $ 1–3 million per day, which was money which could have been spent elsewhere on development projects.[7]

Despite such gross human rights abuses the Australian Government continued to turn a blind eye. It wasn't until a decade later with the release of a video taken by photo journalist Max Stahl of a massacre at the Santa Cruz Cemetery in Dili in 1991 that international activism began to take on a more influential role. Even so, the Australian Government under Prime Minister Keating continued to ignore it.

Santa Cruz Massacre 1991

In October 1991, a protest march organised by the East Timorese resistance movement marched to the Santa Cruz cemetery in the capital, Dili. During this march, a protester Sebastio Gomes was killed, and two Indonesian soldiers were allegedly stabbed. Gomes was buried in the Santa Cruz Cemetery. A protest march was organised by Xanana Gusmão, then leading the East Timorese resistance movement, to demonstrate in front of a visiting Portuguese delegation. Indonesian soldiers then opened fire on the march as they took refuge in the Santa Cruz cemetery. Braithwaite indicated that the shooting continued indiscriminately for about fifteen minutes and that the bodies were moved to trucks and removed. The estimated casualty rate was 271 dead, 382 wounded and a further 250 missing.[8]

Journalist Max Stahl filmed the entire incident and when the graphic footage and when this graphic footage was released and widely distributed by journalists it proved to be a turning point in galvanising international support for the people of East Timor. It also provided an increased momentum behind Indonesia's domestic pro-democracy movement. The impetus also helped to support a clandestine activist movement in East Timor. One graphic photo of the post-Santa Cruz massacre was of the naked body of a young girl in a cell:

> [c]overed in cuts and horrific wounds. Various profanities written in Bahasa Indonesia are written on her body, and a crucifix…drawn on her stomach. Stuck to the wall just above her head…a picture of Jesus Christ, and at her feet…a sign in Bahasa, paralleling the death of Christ on the Cross, which translates as 'If you really are God, come down and bring her back to life'.[9]

Being a member of the Catholic Church had become a form of resistance. It was well organised, reached into rural areas and provided access to an international network. As Braithwaite observed, that being a member of the Catholic Church had become a form of resistance and that '[j]oining the Church…became a private gesture of resistance to perceived Muslim invaders and an affirmation of Timorese identity'.[10]

Bi-partisan political ambivalence continued in Australia, probably due to the influence of the pro-Jakarta Lobby amongst influential government circles. This included implied denial of the incident itself. As journalist John Pilger, as quoted in Braithwaite states:

Prime Minister Paul Keating...even cast doubt on the original massacre, saying 'it isn't clear what happened'. Pilger and the solidarity movement won this contest for Western public opinion resoundingly, and Australian leaders were again seen as apologists for a crime against humanity.[11]

Santa Cruz Massacre Protests Canberra 1991–1992

In protest, in Canberra East Timorese activists and their supporters erected two hundred and seventy-one white crosses which they erected outside the Indonesian Embassy in Canberra. They had been blessed by Catholic, Anglican and Uniting Church leaders.[12]

During this press conference on 16 January 1992, held by the Minister for Foreign Affairs and Trade, Senator Gareth Evans described the protest as:

> a theatrically very effective demonstration...which although of... immense symbolic significance to the East Timorese people...was...immensely provocative to the Indonesians...and was therefore...a fairly comprehensive intrusion on the integrity...of the mission'.[13]

The Australian Federal Police, performing the role of community police in the Australian Capital Territory, were well-versed in dealing with sensitive political demonstrations and demonstrating characteristic sensitivity, and acting under direction from the ACT Government, they removed, removed the crosses and gave them to the then ACT Attorney-General Bernard Collaery, who held them in safe-keeping. They were again placed outside the Indonesian Embassy following a temporarily successful appeal by the East Timorese protesters and their supporters in the Federal Court on 17 January 1992.[14]

There then followed a series of appeals and judgements by the Federal Court over most of 1992. In 1995, a Parliamentary Inquiry was formed to investigate the rights of protest in the Parliamentary Zone.[15]

It was during this inquiry that Ms Almeida,[16] one of the East Timorese protesters, outlined the following:

> We were calling for an independent inquiry into the Dili massacre. We were calling for the Indonesian government to allow human rights organisations to go and see what was happening in East Timor, because at that time there was a blockade against foreigners going into East Timor because of the massacre. We wanted to know the truth. We knew that hundreds of people were killed, but the message we were getting was that only 19 people were killed...the people of East Timor have endured torture, killing and the raping of our women for 20 years and to us the flag represents our tyranny.

Of particular relevance to the later involvement of the AFP in East Timor, starting with UNAMET and beyond, is the very positive and respectful relationship between the protesters and the police. Ms Almeida stated:

> I have no complaints about the Australian authorities. In fact, our protests have been very peaceful outside the Indonesian Embassy. There were no arguments whatsoever with the police when we protested outside the Indonesian Embassy.

In relation to the crosses themselves, the former ACT Attorney-General Bernard Collaery identified that:

> the Christian cross had not been banned for more than 400 years...future High Court Chief Justice, Federal Justice Robert French, in a hint that even Foreign Minister Evans could not miss, expressed the view that 'it is difficult to see how the lawful placement of a reproachful and dignified symbol on public land in the vicinity of a mission would amount to a disturbance of its peace or an impairment of its dignity'.[17]

This series of protests is demonstrable of several things: the strong sense of wrong experienced by the East Timorese at the hands of the Indonesians; the mutual respect and impartiality and the positive relationship between the East Timorese protesters and the police (AFP) in Canberra,[18] and the length to which the Australian Government was prepared to go to avoid insulting the Indonesians, to the extent that Christian crosses were removed because they could be interpreted as being offensive. The latter is an indictment on the polity involved, made all the more shameful and hypocritical because they occurred under the Prime Ministership of Paul Keating who revels in his Irish Catholic heritage, as head of an Australian Labor Party which prides itself as the champion of the oppressed.

Activism

Despite this blatant hypocrisy and political obstruction, a disparate East Timorese solidarity network continued to apply pressure upon successive governments in Australia. The issue of East Timor was a 'pebble in the shoe'[19] of the Australian–Indonesian relationship, but successive Australian governments continued to ignore the situation in East Timor despite the increased reporting of obvious human rights abuses by the Indonesian military.

Blind Eye: Influence of Jakarta Lobby

The Australian position, based on pure pragmatism, was a de jure recognition of Indonesian sovereignty in East Timor, contrary to the UN position which continued to not recognise Indonesian sovereignty over East Timor.

This position was maintained by the so-called 'Jakarta Lobby', a group of academics and defence and foreign affairs officials who maintained an active interest in pursuing strong diplomatic relations with Indonesia. The existence of this group as a formal entity is very difficult to establish with any fidelity; however, the pragmatic attitude adopted by successive Australian governments of either political stripe certainly reflected advice from a:

> group of scholars and diplomats [that] included most of the big guns of their professions who specialised in Indonesian affairs [who] throughout the 1970s, 1980s and most of the 1990s…utterly outgunned the mostly more marginal intellectuals who were active in the East Timor solidarity movement. Political leaders of both major political parties in Australia liked the hard-headed political pragmatism of the pro-Indonesia network.[20]

As Australian academic James Cotton stated to ABC reporter Mark Colvin in 2004:

> whichever way you look at it, Indonesia is the key country. It's the key country strategically in geographic terms. It's the core country of the South-East Asian regional organisation, ASEAN. For two generations, managing the relationship with Indonesia has been a key concern of governments of both persuasions in Canberra.[21]

The two primary nodes of this group were:

> in Canberra at the Department of Foreign Affairs (its most important player being Richard Woolcott, former Ambassador to Indonesia)…at the Australian National University (its most senior players being the distinguished political scientist Jamie Mackie and the renowned economist Heinz Arndt).[22]

They were unified by 'the idea…that Australian diplomacy and scholarship were far too oriented to other Western nations and insufficiently to the largest Muslim population of any nation in the world'.[23]

The influence of this group of pro-Indonesian scholars and others on policy had significant implications for members of the AFP who deployed to East Timor in the second half of 1999 was potentially fatal. There were many pro-Indonesian insiders, and it seems the lives of Australian police meant little in the face of the priority placed on the Australian-Indonesian relationship. In fact, when the ADF was preparing to deploy to East Timor 'Brian Toohey, a leading Australian investigative journalist, wrote in September 1999 that a high-level Canberra official was spying for Indonesia when the Australian military was about to deploy to East Timor.'[24] Presumably, this person was also in office prior to, during and immediately following the deployment of unarmed Australian police with UNAMET. This is not a comforting thought. Whether the executive of the AFP was aware of these machinations is uncertain. What is certain is that none of this was known to the deployed AFP members.

In relation specifically to East Timor in March 1999 David Connery in his 2010 submission on crisis policy-making related to East Timor,[25] tabulates the strategic priorities of the Australian Government in Table 7 (Australia's Strategic Objectives – March to September 1999), which is reproduced in part below:

Date	Priority	Source
March 1999	• East Timor would remain a part of Indonesia. • East Timor does not disrupt Australian-Indonesian relations. • East Timor does not disrupt ADF-TNI relations. • Australia does not have large parts of the ADF deployed in East Timor.	Interview with Hugh White
March 1999	• Seek engagement with Indonesia to develop a sense of shared strategic interest. • Enhance Indonesia's self-defence capabilities and interoperability between the ADF and TNI in key areas. • In relation to an 'independent' Timor: • For East Timor not to develop close military ties with a country hostile to Australia. • For East Timor not to disrupt the territorial integrity of Indonesia.	Department of Defence (a)
March 1999	• Continued recognition of Indonesian sovereignty over East Timor. • Support for close involvement of the people of East Timor in decisions about their future. • Support for an act of self-determination…preferably following a long period of autonomy, while accepting the possibility of independence. • Reconciliation among East Timorese. • Support for a peaceful and orderly transition. • Support for the long-term development of East Timor.	DFAT (b)

The Election of President Habibie

The retirement of the autocratic Indonesian President Suharto and subsequent election of interim President Habibie in 1998 was conducted relatively peacefully. The collapse of the Suharto government in 1998 and the emergent forces of democracy in Indonesia brought the issue of East Timor once again to the international table. There had been a change of government in Canberra in 1996. The new, conservative Liberal Prime Minister John Howard, having witnessed the success of the Cambodian mission in 1993 under the ALP Foreign Minister Gareth Evans and the enlightened involvement of the Indonesian Government with the Jakarta Informal Meetings (JIMs) to facilitate the Cambodian solution, perhaps glimpsed a window of opportunity for East Timor, which was open for a fraction of a political second. Prime Minister Howard made an approach, by letter drafted by three diplomats, to President Habibie. The letter raised the issue of East Timor and after some hesitation and deliberation, President Habibie acquiesced, and arrangements were made to ascertain the intentions of the East Timorese public via a UN-conducted plebiscite.

This was not appreciated by powerful elements within the Indonesian military, as Habibie's presidency was regarded by them as transitional. Upon the announcement of the ballot, several pro-Indonesian militia groups became active within East Timor. Each was assigned to a particular area or regency and was raised, trained, armed and supported by the Indonesian Kopassus Special Forces. Before his fall from grace, General Prabowo Subianto, as head of Kopassus, had played a significant role in establishing these militia groups in East Timor.[26]

Letter from Prime Minister Howard to President Habibie 1998: Offer of Special Autonomy

It was President Habibie's reaction to the contents of Prime Minister Howard's letter of 19 December 1998 that created momentum over which the Australian Government and Prime Minister Howard lost control of subsequent Indonesian reactions, results and decisions in Jakarta. The letter was purportedly drafted by Michael Thawley (International Advisor to Prime Minister John Howard between 1996 and 1999), Peter Varghese (First Assistant Secretary of the International Division, Department of the Prime Minister and Cabinet 1998 to 1999) and John Dauth[27] (Deputy Secretary of DFAT) and discussed by Ashton Calvert (Secretary of the Department of Foreign Affairs and Trade 1998–2005). A faxed copy of the letter was hand delivered by the Australian Ambassador to Indonesia John McCarthy to the Indonesian Foreign Ministry, with the formal copy to follow. It was a letter that would have profound consequences.

The letter states inter alia:

My dear President

Your offer of autonomy for East Timor was a bold and clear-sighted step that has opened a window of opportunity both to achieve a peaceful settlement in East Timor and to resolve an issue that has long caused Indonesia difficulties in the international community. A settlement would enable you to put the issue behind you. It would make a substantial difference to Indonesia's standing in the world, with the benefits that could bring.

I want to emphasise that Australia's support for Indonesia's sovereignty is unchanged. It has been a long-standing Australian position that the interests of Australia, Indonesia and East Timor are best served by East Timor remaining part of Indonesia...It might be worth considering...a means of addressing the East Timorese desire for an act of self-determination in a manner that avoids an early and final decision on the future status of the province. One way of doing this would be to build into the autonomy package a review mechanism along the lines of the Matignon Accords in New Caledonia. The Matignon Accords[28] have enabled a compromise political solution to be implemented while deferring a referendum on the final status of New Caledonia for many years...[This] would allow time to convince the East Timorese of the benefits of autonomy within the Indonesian republic.[29]

Contrary to the popular narrative among the Indonesian military and their militia proxies during UNAMET that Australia was actively supporting the pro-independence movement, the letter contained support for Habibie's decision to offer autonomy to East Timor and reaffirmed Australia's support for East Timor to remain a part of Indonesia. The perception of a lack of impartiality held by the Indonesians about Australia and Australians posed a serious risk to AFP members who deployed as part of UNAMET. UNCIVPOL, including AFP were immediately identifiable as they wore the Australian National Flag prominently on their uniforms in accordance with UN uniform requirements. When the violence was at its height they were specifically targeted by the pro-Indonesian militia particularly after the UN ballot in late August and early September 1999.

Indonesian Response

Although the letter was carefully drafted and delivered discreetly, the letter provoked an unexpected and unwelcome reaction from President Habibie. It was intended to open the East Timor issue tactfully to address what the Indonesian Foreign Minister Alatas referred to as the 'pebble in the shoe' of the Indonesian–Australian relationship. The letter's contents, particularly the reference it contained to the Matignon Accords, angered Habibie and was misconstrued by him to be a suggestion that Indonesia was acting like a colonial power. This inference was unwelcome and probably spurred his desire to address the East Timor issue once and for all.

Loss of Control Over the Process

In late December 1998, the existence of the letter was leaked and published in the Australian media, which then became difficult to control by the

Australian Government. On 27 January 1999, following a media release by the Australian Government on 12 January 1999, President Habibie consulted with his cabinet and decided to offer East Timor 'regional autonomy plus'. If the offer of autonomy was rejected, his government would recommend that the Indonesian parliament release East Timor from Indonesia.

These events and decisions in January 1999 created some serious concerns for the Australian national security policy community. The meeting of the Strategic Policy Coordination Group on 15 January highlighted Defence's disappointment with the lack of internal consultation and provided a negative prognosis for what might happen next. Rear Admiral Peter Briggs, a participant at that meeting, recalled:

> Hugh White [Deputy Secretary for Strategy, Australian Department of Defence] was very forthright, and questioned the DFAT representatives on the process and intentions of the letter. Hugh said something like 'Do you know what the f...is going to happen?'—they were taken aback at Hugh's language and expression— 'Habibie is going to accept the offer, there will be a process of self-determination which the Indonesian military will resist, and the local militias will be the tool they will resist it with, and we will end up with the ADF [Australian Defence Force] on the ground between the Indonesians and the East Timorese. We could well end up with body bags coming back to Australia.' It was an extremely strong event.[30]

This was prophetic, but it wasn't the ADF who stood between the predatory pro-Indonesian militia, and on occasions Indonesian soldiers and police, and their prey, the rest of the East Timorese community, but unarmed AFP members, who formed the largest single national contingent of the UNCIVPOL component of UNAMET. Fortunately, there were no body bags returning to Australia, but that was more due to good luck than good management, as there were many situations in which death or serious injury at the hands of pro-Indonesian militia groups were a definite possibility. Noteworthy is the fact, as outlined by Connery, that the AFP was not part of this consultative group, leaving the major decisions to the traditional participants, Defence and DFAT.

Australian Response

The emerging situation concerning East Timor created a significant divergence of opinion between DFAT and Defence in the first half of 1999. DFAT believed that Indonesia, specifically the Indonesian National Police,[31] was responsible for security in East Timor. DFAT advocated the use of diplomacy to avoid the need to deploy an international military peacekeeping force. They did not want to convey a perception that Australia was preparing to intervene in East Timor, as it could create tension with Indonesia or allow others to assume that Australia would take the lead and 'bankroll' the process. Australian officials also feared this perception could have discouraged Indonesians and East Timorese from coming to their own compromises.

Militia Warnings Pre-ballot

The political choices for the East Timorese were becoming clearer: special autonomy and continued integration within the Indonesian republic or a formalised UN-sponsored electoral path towards full independence as offered by President Habibie. This aroused deep passions on both sides of this question, and serious breakdowns in civil order occurred, including the formation of paramilitary militia groups supporting the pro-Indonesian position, which became increasingly violent in the first half of 1999.

As Mules *et al.* explain:

> The need for some form of international intervention was underlined by the precarious state of civil order. The appearance of armed 'militias' in the territory, including Halalinitar led by Joao Tavares (former Bupati of Bobonaro), Mahidi led by Cancio Lopes de Carvalho, as well as Besih Merah Putih and Pana led to a sharp deterioration in the security of the territory. The use of militias, raised by the Interior Ministry but attached to the territorial or combat military groups, has been a long-standing practice in East Timor. Now these and other groups declared themselves in favour of integration, and were provided with additional arms so that they might terrorise the populations in their areas. Through February, attacks on civilians continued while villages emptied, and roadblocks staged by armed gangs led to beatings and murders.[32]

The militia groups were organised along Portuguese colonial regency lines, which generally coincided with UN Electoral Districts. After being initially raised by Prabowo Subianto, they were re-invigorated through the Indonesian Kopassus Special Forces and by Major General Zacky Anwar Makarim, the former head of Indonesian military intelligence. Their predilection for violence was known in some Australian intelligence and political quarters as early as February 1999. At a meeting at the Australian National University in Canberra in February 1999, discussions ensued about forward momentum concerning East Timor. As Mules et al. recount:

> At the end of the meeting (on 25 February 1999), FPDK spokesman Basilio Araujo handed Downer a letter, which he opened after the group had departed. It was addressed to him and signed by Eurico Guterres, head of the Aitarak militia group, and Cancio Carvalho, head of the Mahidi militia, on behalf of the 'Commander of the Pro-Integration Paramilitary'. The letter declared integration as 'final', claimed that the pro-integration forces fought for those

who were politically immature and vulnerable to manipulation, and contained threats to the safety of Australian diplomats and journalists in East Timor. 'It is better to sacrifice an Australian diplomat or journalist to save the lives of the 850,000 East Timorese...the pro-integration paramilitary group is... looking forward to meeting and facing any Australian hypocrites, deceivers and political mercenaries (including the East Timor pro-independence Australian peacekeeping force) on the soil of East Timor-day or night.[33]

In the meantime, the militia-led violence continued on the ground in East Timor, under the military operational name Operation Global Clean Sweep organised by the Indonesian military.

Pro-Indonesian Militia Groups

The evolving situation set the machinery of government working in Canberra. The ADF commenced planning on the understanding that they would be called to assist any likely mission or operation in East Timor. Australian intelligence sources commenced collecting, analysing and disseminating information within defence and foreign affairs circles. This involved a great deal of intelligence related to a number of militia groups raised by the Indonesian military, particularly the Indonesian Kopassus Special Forces which had infiltrated two groups known as Venus and Tribuana to train, equip and support these militia groups. In the first half of 1999, these militia groups became extremely violent, which raised deep concerns with the Australian Government. This was known to a select group in the defence and foreign affairs departments in Canberra, but not shared with other agencies such as the AFP. In fact, the AFP was specifically excluded from a number of high-level meetings concerning the deployment of AFP members into this dangerous, volatile and unpredictable situation. This has never been acknowledged by the Australian authorities, A number of recently declassified U.S. diplomatic cables copied to the U.S. Embassy in Canberra[34] provide evidence of these known relationships and their violent activities from as early as February 1999.

According to Hugh White, the estimated size of a military peacekeeping force to provide security in East Timor, was between 12,000 and 16,000 armed military peacekeepers, but that the ADF would be unable to field that number. White stated:

> It became increasingly clear in Canberra however that while TNI should retain principal responsibility for security in East Timor, a major UN PKF should be deployed before the ballot as part of the United Nations Mission in East Timor (UNAMET) to ensure that TNI behaved responsibly.

Preliminary thinking in Canberra suggested that a PKF of around 12,000 to 16,000 military personnel would be needed.[35]

The weapons carried by the militia groups included homemade firearms known as 'rakitans', machetes, knives, swords and, on occasion, semi-automatic military long arms. There were strong rumours that they were also supplied alcohol and amphetamines by the Indonesian Kopassus to increase aggression. The types of activities employed by the militia groups included threats of violence, and actual violence, denial of fuel, food, water and electricity supply, hostage situations, rock throwing, shootings and several murders of UNAMET Locally Engaged Staff. There were many other examples.

Militia Groups UNAMET East Timor 1999 Why, Who, How and What

No document on the UNAMET mission in East Timor in 1999 would be complete without a discussion of the pro-Indonesian militia groups, which were active in the province from their formation in late 1998 to the end of September 1999. This remains an area relatively under-discussed in official government circles in both Australia and Indonesia, perhaps because any such discussion necessarily involves political and personal sensitivities.

The East Timorese militia groups were based on a long-standing and legitimate military counter-insurgency function and were raised by the Indonesian military in the second half of 1998 in response to movement at the political level by the reformist Indonesian President Habibie. This legitimate structure was subverted by elements hostile to the UN ballot, particularly an informal network of Indonesian Kopassus,[36] special-forces operators, and they were thus converted into instruments of the state against their own citizens.

An Indonesian journalist, Hidayat Djajamihardja, outlines the corrosive role Kopassus played in further eroding state legitimacy in East Timor under the command of then Lieutenant General Prabowo Subianto:

An Indonesian Reporter's View:

The elite regiment Kopassus had been based semi-permanently in East Timor since 1987. The red beret commando unit had been held in high regard among Indonesians. They were said to be a good fighting regiment. However, its prestige dissipated after the Kopassus command was placed under Major General Prabowo Subianto. The red beret regiment became a notorious unit specialising in kidnapping pro-democracy activists and student leaders during the last days of Suharto's presidency.

In East Timor, Kopassus quickly became an oppressive force. The year was 1987 and the man who had that idea was (then) Colonel Prabowo.

The intention was to provide Kopassus with a training ground to 'blood' its members in counter-insurgency operations. The fate of East Timor would have been different had the President's son-in-law not suggested that Kopassus open a base in East Timor.

The Indonesian army made East Timor its own playground. They protected it from unflattering reports religiously. Each report about East Timor had to be vetted very thoroughly.[37]

Essential to an understanding of the dynamics in late 1998 and early 1999, is that Habibie was the first post-Suharto President, having assumed the role from his position as Suharto's Vice President. He, as a result, was regarded as an interim president, and thus lacking in the legitimacy required to make decisions on matters as important as the potential separation of East Timor from the Indonesian Republic. His changed policy stance on East Timor was politically risky and raised some significant voices in opposition, not the least of which was that of the military.

This had implications for the broader 'western' security alliance, in the face of two emerging challenges: the rise of violent Islamic jihadism and the ascendency of China. The Suharto era featured a very strong and influential Indonesian military, a situation supported by the 'western' alliance, including Australia, particularly during the Cold War era where South East Asia experienced a high level of violence and political volatility.

Alatas warning to Habibie involved risking…

>…the ire and opposition of three groups in society: those East Timorese who had fought so hard for integration with Indonesia, the Armed Forces, especially the veterans among them, and those who had lost husbands, sons and relatives in the armed conflict over East Timor; and the nationalists in Indonesia and by that I meant not only the members of the Indonesian nationalist parties.[38]

Militia Groups East Timor 1999

The militia groups varied in strength and consisted of active volunteers, sometimes from the military, coerced East Timorese and even criminal prisoners released from custody for this purpose. They adopted names to reflect their patriotism and ferocity. As the Table below illustrates, they were managed according to military districts (Kodim) in three broad sectors: A being the easternmost, B being the central area and C the westernmost adjoining the porous border with Indonesian West Timor.

Sector	District	Mil Dist/ Kodim	Militia
A	Lautem	1629	Team Alfa
A	Baucau	1628	Saka, Sera, Forum Komunikasi Partisan (FKP)
A	Manatuto	1631	Morok and Mahadomi (Manatuto Hatomi Otonomi – Manatuto Loves Autonomy)
A	Viqueque	1630	Makikit, 59/75 Junior
B	Dili	1627	Aitarak (Thorn)
B	Liquica	1638	Besi Merah Putih (BMP), Pana
B	Ermera	1637	Darah Integrasi, Darah Merah, Naga Merah, Team Pancasila, Aitarak
B	Ailieu	1632	Ahi
C	Cova Lima	1635	Laksaur, Mahidi
C	Oecussi	1639	Sakunar
C	Ainaro	1633	Mahidi, Laksaur
C	Manufahi	1634	Ablai
C	Bobonaro	1636	Halilintar, Dadurus Merah Putih, Firmi Merah Putih, Saka Loromonu, Armui Merah Putih, Guntur Merah Putih, Hametin Merah Putih, Harimau Merah Putih, Kaer Metin Merah Putih

Operation Global Clean Sweep Pre-ballot

The deteriorating circumstances on the ground in East Timor were becoming evident to the Defence establishment. According to Kingsbury:

> Aitarak and the other militias were supported and armed by the regional Udayana IX Military Command, based in Bali, and occasionally led in the field by (sometimes former) military intelligence officers, associated with the Satuan Tugas Intelijen (Intelligence Duty Unit-SGI) and Kopassus (Special Forces). Through what it called Operasi Sapu Jagad (Operation Global Clean Sweep), these gangs were responsible for hundreds of deaths in East Timor between January and July 1999 and caused more than 600,000 people to flee their villages, creating a serious refugee problem. Officials from the key independence organization, the Timorese National Resistance Council (CNRT) were killed, while its offices in the western part of East Timor were effectively kept closed.[39]

ABC Background Briefing program journalist, Peter Cronau, in May 2004, interviewed a number of Defence, intelligence and DFAT officials about the situation in East Timor in 1999. He stated: 'There were shootings and massacres, and Indonesia continued to fend off calls for UN peacekeepers in East Timor. And a steady trickle of leaked secret documents from Defence Intelligence Organisation, with details of the TNI backing for the violent militias, flowed to journalists.'[40] It was obvious to those responsible in Canberra that something needed to be done, and the expectation was that Australia was best placed to do it. Unfolding events were to determine who was actually going to do it, and it ended up being the AFP under a United Nations banner.

United Nations Security Council Resolution 1246: 1999

The UN was committed generally to decolonisation had never recognised Indonesian sovereignty successfully negotiated an agreement between the governments of Portugal, the former colonial power, and Indonesia, the actual occupiers of East Timor in March 1999. This had the perverse effect of the UN actually recognising Portugal's claim in preference to Indonesia's until a legitimate mechanism could be found to gauge self-determination. This set in motion a series of meetings concerning the deteriorating security that was clearly an issue in such a volatile environment. As Cotton explains:

> [O]n 12 March, UN Secretary General Kofi Annan was able to announce that all parties had agreed that a 'method of direct ballot will be used to ask the people of East Timor whether they accept or reject a proposal for autonomy, the details of which were soon to be provided by the Indonesian Government. Though it was clear that there were still some obstacles in Jakarta to be overcome...this was nevertheless a significant breakthrough. The conditions necessary for the conduct of such a vote would require a UN presence, including a role for armed forces, and the Secretary General suggested that UN personnel would be in place by June 1999...The Government's position was that in advance of any possible settlement, the use of Australian military forces as 'peacekeepers' was likely to have disastrous consequences...The opposition's view was that without a third force to prevent the violence and intimidation which was becoming commonplace in parts of the island, no ballot could hope to produce a fair and accurate result. It followed that such a force was necessary ahead of the ballot.[41]

This also place Australia in a difficult situation, whereby, in terms of Australian foreign policy, Australia, having initiated a process towards a long-term, peaceful political solution in good faith, it had largely lost control of the process by which this could possibly be achieved, both in Jakarta and in New York with the UN. The official Australian position which recognised Indonesian sovereignty over East Timor, was in direct contravention to that of the UN, which still recognised Portugal as the legitimate power. Portugal had divested itself of its colonies in 1974. Indonesia was in all respects acting as a violent and oppressive colonial power. It was a tense and complex situation.

To complicate matters further, Australia was best placed to provide the military peacekeeping force that was clearly required in the circumstances, but was not considered suitable for political reasons primarily related to the active opposition from the Indonesian military to have a foreign force, particularly Australian forces, on what it considered sovereign Indonesian territory, a point made clear at a meeting in Bali on 27 April 1999 between Indonesian President Habibie and Australian Prime Minister Howard. The ADF was also unable to deliver on the required 12,000–16,000 personnel. Clearly, a 'Third Force' was required.

Security Agreement Civilian Police: The Third Force

The prospect of such a 'Third Force', however, was raised by a senior member of the Prime Minister's Department whilst the meeting took place in Bali. This took the form of the AFP.

> Prime Minister Howard asked whether Indonesia would accept a contingent of several hundred police officers. Habibie said this would be difficult given the small number of officers (250) in the Indonesian police force in East Timor. Habibie said that it was intended that the number of Indonesian police would be increased, but even without increased numbers the security situation in East Timor presented no problems: there was no international crisis occurring in East Timor…It was agreed that the UN would determine how many police would be adequate for the task. In a separate discussion with Defence Minister John Moore, Wiranto agreed that Indonesia would accept 200–300 international civilian police in East Timor.[42]

The dynamics of this meeting are instructive. Hugh White, a senior Australian Defence official present, later stated to the author that when the prospect of Australian troops was raised, the Chief of the Indonesian military, General Wiranto, emphatically opposed it. So much so that he physically waved his arm repeatedly in front of his own president and said loudly, 'No, no, no!'. This exchange speaks volumes about where real power resided in the embryonic Indonesian democracy.

Decision to send Australian Federal Police to UNAMET

The genesis of this decision-making process arose in early March when the UN Secretary General Kofi Annan had confirmed that a number of countries had been approached to contribute to a proposed UN mission in East Timor, although the exact scale and nature of the mission had not then been decided. Speaking on SBS Television on 13 March Mr Annan said that 'we would want [an] Australian contribution' to a UN mission to East Timor that he said at that time could be sent as early as late April'.[43]

Two weeks later, the Australian Foreign Minister Alexander Downer initially rejected the possibility of an Australian Defence Force component in any proposed UN mission in East Timor but later stated that the Australian Defence Force could have a role in assisting in a possible peacekeeping operation.[44]

Then of course, the meetings took place in Bali and in lieu of a military contribution to the UN mission, the AFP was to be deployed as acknowledged in the Parliament by Mr Downer on 11 May 1999: Australia expected to provide about fifty police officers to the UN mission.[45]

Australian Federal Police Expression of Interest 29 April-3 May 1999

The AFP response was agile and rapid, which is particularly impressive as very little pre-warning had been provided to the AFP prior to the Bali meetings on 27 April 1999.[46] The Australian delegation had raised the prospect of an armed international military peacekeeping force of between 12,000 and 16,000 and instead had emerged with a compromise of up to 300 UN police.

Upon return to Canberra, the AFP was contacted and at 1700 hrs on Thursday 29 April 1999 the AFP sent out calls for Expressions of Interest for what was an un-named mission in East Timor, referred to as the United Nations Peacekeeping Force in East Timor (UNCPIT).[47] The name UN-AMET was to emerge with the signing of the 5 May Agreements. The EOI closed five days later on Monday 3 May 1999 at 1600 hrs. This included a weekend.

Noteworthy is the selection criteria, roles, skills and background called upon in this EOI. These include:

Selection Criteria:
- Currently appointed as a police member under the AFP Act 1979 and have contemporary policing experience of not less than eight years
- Knowledge of the United Nations monitoring role in East Timor
- Demonstrated ability to exercise self-discipline, and a willingness to accept a military style working and living environment
- Knowledge of the ethnic culture relevant to East Timor/Indonesia and a sound knowledge of the history surrounding the United Nations commitment
- Demonstrated ability to be culturally aware, tolerant and sensitive in dealing with difference

- appointees should be aware that they will be required to adhere to, and implement UNCPIT directives and procedures

Roles:
- Implement and/or participate in the conduct of UN operations that relates to the monitoring of the East Timor Referendum
- Facilitate conflict resolution
- Facilitate liaison between all factions, Indonesian Officials and UN staff
- Facilitate liaison between UNCPIT forces and Indonesian authorities
- Provide advice to Indonesian National Police on law-and-order issues
- Provide high level advice to various parties as required, and as appropriate
- Special Role Requirements:
  1. Ability to operate in a harsh remote environment with minimal infrastructure, and volatile environment of unpredictable security
  2. An understanding of the political sensitivities that impact upon the East Timor situation, and an appreciation of the various ethnic culture relevant to East Timor and Indonesia
  3. Indonesian language skills would be advantageous

The following are mandatory:
- basic motor vehicle maintenance skills
- map reading skills
- current driver's licence
- 4-wheel drive skills
- firearms permit

First aid qualifications are desirable.

Demonstrated knowledge of OH&S policy and procedures and a demonstrated commitment to the principles of equity and diversity.

It should be noted that a warning in capital letters was also provided: APPLICANTS SHOULD NOTE THAT DEPLOYMENT WILL BE UNDER EXTREME HARDSHIP CONDITIONS, WITH THE POTENTIAL FOR MEMBERS TO BE EXPOSED TO PERSONAL RISK.[48]

These are not skills, background or experience readily at hand in any domestic Australian police force, let alone one with both ACT general policing and national investigative responsibilities. Yet despite this, the AFP received enough applications to field fifty members, and ten reserves of the First Contingent. Readers should be reminded that this sort of activity is not the core business of the AFP. Finding fifty members with Indonesian language skills, previous deployment experience, map reading, vehicle maintenance and 4-wheel driving skills and a working knowledge of the political and physical environment in East Timor, plus the willingness to live in 'extreme hardship conditions' and 'be exposed to personal risk...in a harsh remote environment with minimal infrastructure, and volatile environment of unpredictable security', among a workforce almost entirely devoted to domestic policing is a feat unto itself. Unlike the military, these, sorts of skills and attributes are not readily found. For them to be found over a five-day period including a weekend is extraordinary.

UNAMET AFP Pre deployment Training and Deployment

Selection and Training

Between the meeting in Bali on 27 April 1999 and the signing of the 5 May agreement the AFP quickly responded, to recruit and train the required number of members and several reserves. It should be noted that the AFP at this time did not have a standing deployable capacity, the contingent members were drawn from normal police duties throughout Australia. The AFP did, however, have a long and distinguished history of deploying relatively small civilian police to overseas missions such as Cyprus, Cambodia, Mozambique, Haiti and Bougainville.

Many of the members of the AFP UNAMET contingent had mission experience in these missions. Some were selected for language skills, some had previous military experience, and some had previous mission experience. They were all volunteers. UNAMET itself was raised at short notice and the AFP contingent which deployed to UNAMET was hastily selected, assembled, trained in basic language and culture and deployed within about six weeks of the commencement of the two-week training package, which took place in a caravan park on the outskirts of Canberra.

By necessity, training was rushed and ad hoc. It did include mention of the militia groups which had been active in East Timor since late 1998 and early 1999, but no specific mention was made of the relationship between the Indonesian military and these pro-integration militias nor of their organizational structure.

This period also included equipment issue and a use of force recertification, including the recertification on the police firearm. Significantly also, members were required to provide a blood sample for DNA purposes, and were also required to have a last will and testament,[49] presumably in the event of death; not an unreasonable precaution given the circumstances. They were also issued with military style identity discs, commonly known as 'dog tags', which was unusual for a UN police deployment.

UNAMET is Established: June 1999

Following the meetings on 27 April and 5 May, UNAMET was established on 11 June 1999. The 5 May Agreement allocated the sole role of security to the newly formed Indonesian police, which had only separated from the Indonesian military on 1 April 1999. UNCIVPOL were to act as advisors to the Indonesian police. The AFP provided the largest single national contingent of UNCIVPOL. This was also the largest contingent the AFP have deployed to that date.

As explained by Mules et al., the UN Resolution 1246[50] of 11 June 1999:

> Authorises until 31 August 1999 the deployment within UNAMET of up to 280 civilian police officers to act as advisers to the Indonesian Police in the discharge of their duties, and at the time of consultation, to supervise the escort of ballot papers and boxes to and from the polling sites.
>
> By virtue of UN Resolution 1246, 11 June 1999, UNAMET was mandated to include political, electoral, civilian police, information, military liaison officers and administrative components…The 5 May Agreements mandated the Indonesian police with the responsibility for the maintenance of law and order, with CivPol acting as advisors. CivPol were to be unarmed. CivPol were also mandated to supervise the escort of ballot materials to and from polling sites. To carry out these tasks the United Nations deployed 271 civilian police, with the first team deployed by mid-June.[51]

The Security Environment

Pursuant to the 5 May Agreement, all UNAMET staff had to rely solely on POLRI for protection. The daily role of UNCIVPOL was to liaise with and advise POLRI in their duties as they related to the ballot. POLRI had just separated from the military and was very much subservient to the TNI. As a result, they either would not or could not perform their normal policing duties, particularly when militia activities were involved. In many cases, unarmed UNCIVPOL essentially stood in the way of mass murder, as predatory pro-Indonesian militia groups, backed by the Indonesian military,[52] sought to harass, intimidate, coerce and eventually murder those they considered supporters of independence.

The initial strategy was to deny the entry of UNAMET. When this failed, the strategy changed to harassing and intimidating the East Timorese population into voting to remain with Indonesia. When this failed, the strategy became disrupting the ballot, especially in the western districts of East Timor. This was an attempt to discredit the ballot itself by having the ballot boxes from several polling places removed or destroyed to support a claim that the ballot was not universal. When that failed, and the results of the vote showed that nearly 80 per cent of the population rejected the Indonesian offer of autonomy or integration, the strategy became an overt, violent and destructive scorched earth campaign of terror. It was this violence and complete collapse that created the need for INTERFET.

It is also worth stating that due to the haste with which UNAMET was raised and deployed, there was no medevac capability and no medical facilities capable of dealing with lacerations or gunshot wounds. The nearest medical facility capable of dealing with injuries such as lacerations or gunshot wounds was the Royal Darwin Hospital, about a two-hour flight from Dili.[53] This was particularly important upon the announcement of the ballot result when the violence was overt and extreme.

There were several UN helicopters, but they were configured solely to convey personnel and ballot material and could not fly at night. They were not configured for medevac. In fact, as stated to the author, Indonesian BRIMOB (*Korps Brigade Mobil*, or the Mobile Brigade Corps) had orders to fire upon any aircraft flying at night, including UN helicopters.

Indonesian Perception of Australian Partisanship

Impartiality is a highly desirable requirement for UNCIVPOL service and is a trait of liberal-democratic policing. Impartiality and a well-developed ability to negotiate and de-escalate volatile situations played a significant part in maintaining a semblance of order during the UNAMET. This was sorely tested in East Timor during the UNAMET, and despite the challenging security circumstances and the volatile political situation, deploying unarmed was the correct decision.

The question put to the East Timorese electors related to an offer of 'autonomy' or 'integration' within the Republic of Indonesia advanced by the Indonesian Government or to reject this offer and pursue a path the eventual independence.

With little or no experience or understanding of police impartiality, some within the Indonesian military and their militia proxies erroneously believed that the UN and all its constituent parts, including Australian police working with the UN, had chosen a position and supported the pro-independence movement. This was a major challenge and ran contra to the principle of non-partisanship as mentioned by Shaw at the beginning of this chapter. In a highly charged environment such as that in East Timor during UNAMET, perception of partisanship is enough to create a high risk of death or serious injury. As discussed, if the AFP UNCIVPOL members supported their own government's position and assumed the stated policy of the Australian Government supporting autonomy, rather than the impartiality of the UN, they would have actually been justified in being actively pro-autonomy rather than pro-independence. The fact is, the AFP members were impartial, which is in line with their training and apolitical posture and impartial stance when dealing with crime in Australia. These are features of British-based liberal-democratic policing approaches and can be difficult concepts to grasp for people whose political experience and exposure have been entirely partisan, which was the case with the militia groups and politicised entities such as the military and police in East Timor. Nonetheless, their impartial posture and being unarmed provided international police with an environment where police traits of negotiation rather than the use of force, or the threat thereof, to resolve potential conflict in partnership with their Indonesian police colleagues, who themselves had recently split from their military. In fact, impartiality played a significant role in UNCIVPOL de-escalating some very volatile situations between armed militia groups and UN volunteers, as well as normal East Timorese community members. This approach saved countless lives in such a volatile situation, and there are numerous examples of extremely brave conduct by UNCIVPOL, including by many members of the AFP.

According to instruction from the UN Civilian Police Commissioner, the senior AFP member Alan Mills, the UN police were to apply the rule of strict neutrality, monitor the neutrality and observe the performance of the Indonesian police by creating a professional and sound working relationship with them, and to provide advice, assess threats and escort the ballot boxes to and from the polling sites. The objective was to encourage the preservation of law and order and inspire confidence among the community to allow them to register their vote in a 'free, fair and stress free environment'. The process of the ballot itself was well designed by the Australian Electoral Commission and very thorough and progressed through organised phases.

Armed Police?

The question as to whether the police should have been armed or not was raised at the time and continues to raise eyebrows in certain circles. East Timor in 1999 was a province of a sovereign nation recognised by Australia but not by the UN. As such, armed security was entrusted with the sovereign power of Indonesia. This was a controversial subject at the time and remains so. Most of those who were part of the first contingent, including the author, maintain that, had they been armed, they would have provoked a more hostile reaction from an already affronted Indonesian police and military structure. They were certainly outnumbered and outgunned, as they would only have been carrying police issue handguns, and they would have presented themselves as attractive targets by militia groups, who would see the police side-arms as desirable items and would have attempted to obtain them by any means available, including murder. Many militia members had access to military long arms from their Indonesian overseers. One of the initial tactics of the militia was to dissuade the implementation of UNAMET itself. One deliberate attack involving the murder of a member of UNAMET including UNCIVPOL would have been sufficient for a rethink in New York and Canberra as well as other capitals. AFP were attractive and identifiable targets as they wore the Australian National Flag on their UN Blue police shirts in accordance with UN requirements.

Paradoxically, in this case, being unarmed worked to the advantage of member safety. As Mules et al. explain:

> The question of whether CivPol would be armed was the subject of considerable discussion within the Australian Government. After extensive deliberation, the Government accepted advice from the AFP that Australian CivPol should be unarmed, in line with conventional UN practice.[54]

AFP Assistant Commissioner Alan Mills, who was the UNCIVPOL Commissioner in East Timor, in a later address to an International Policing Conference stated:

> The issuance of sidearms to CivPol should only be taken as a last and extreme measure. That issuance must be consistent with the mandate criteria and preferably in agreement with the parties to the conflict...the issuance of a sidearm for CivPol raises the bar in terms of visual acceptance as a peacekeeper, and increases the likelihood of the member becoming a target. In any case, when compared against the array of military type weapons usually carried by the parties to the conflict, the presence and capacity of a sidearm is totally disproportionate...The absence of weapons assists in clearly projecting a more positive image to the parties to the conflict and the community generally. In most cases it engenders respect that paves the way for a more positive communication process.[55]

Operation Global Clean Sweep: Ballot

The overt nature of Operation Global Clean Sweep went covert upon the arrival of UNAMET in June 1999; however:

> [i]n late June and early July, incidents of intimidation and violence directed at UNAMET served not only to highlight the larger problem with militia activities posed to a free consultation process, but also the question of whether UNAMET would be able to carry out the process at all. Throughout June, anonymous phone callers made repeated threats against UNAMET personnel, including, to lob grenades into UNAMET's Dili compound and

eateries favoured by international staff. Threats were also made to shoot down the helicopter transporting the Secretary-General's two representatives…A letter was received threatening 'rivers of blood' in East Timor, and the UNAMET VHF frequency was broken into with a message that all UNAMET personnel would be killed.[56]

This was the uncertain security environment that confronted AFP members who formed the largest contingent within the UNCIVPOL element of UNAMET. The helicopter report was made by AFP members in the Suai region after sightings of militia carrying long arms and what appeared to be shoulder-launched rocket launchers in the vicinity of the proposed landing zone.

These reports were dismissed by Commissioner Mills as 'alarmist and overstated', and the reporting AFP UNCIVPOL members were chastised. This did nothing to engender trust in Commissioner Mills among the Australian police. The helicopter situation was eventually resolved after the incident was brought to the attention of the Indonesian police, who then dealt with the suspects, not by arresting them but by ordering them to leave, albeit with their weapons un-confiscated.

AFP Role UNCIVPOL and the Relationship with the Indonesian Police

The role of the UNCIVPOL was outlined in UN Resolution 1246, in which UNCIVPOL was directed to monitor the neutrality and observe the performance of the Indonesian police. Specifically, UNCIVPOL was to (1) provide advice to the Indonesian police, (2) assess threats to the public order and advise the local authorities on it, (3) supervise the escort of ballot papers and boxes to and from polling sites and (4) assist the efforts of UN agencies and other civil components of the UN mission. All of this assumed a benign security environment: 'The agreement on security stated that an environment devoid of violence or other forms of intimidation was a prerequisite for holding a free and fair ballot.'[57]

Security was the sole responsibility of the Indonesian National Police (the state civilian Police of the Republic of Indonesia, or POLRI)[58]; however, they had only separated from the military in April 1999, and in many cases were intimidated by the Indonesian military and were clearly subservient to the Indonesian military and their militia proxies.

The Ballot

Upon arrival in East Timor, police were split into small groups and attached to electoral teams, as determined by the Chief Electoral Officer, which were then dispatched throughout the province to some very remote and inaccessible areas, often without supplies, communications or maps. It was in these areas, as well as in Dili, that much of the militia-inspired violence and intimidation took place. Increasingly, reports of these militia groups being supplied with alcohol and amphetamines by the TNI to increase aggression, and unpredictability, became apparent. This violence continued throughout the entire period UNAMET was active, and it escalated dramatically when the actual ballot result was announced.

Each electoral team consisted of two UN volunteers drawn from all parts of the globe, a local Timorese driver and a Timorese interpreter. The role of each team was to establish a registration and polling place, provide voter education, register voters and ultimately conduct the ballot. The role of UNCIVPOL was to liaise with POLRI to ensure that this process could proceed without disruption or interference. This was generally successful, however, in some areas, intimidation and coercion occurred to such an extent that voter registration and campaigning had to be suspended.

The most important role of UNCIVPOL was to secure the ballot boxes once the polling had ceased, the administration reconciled and the ballot boxes sealed. The ballot boxes were conveyed to secure locations overnight, collected the following morning and conveyed to the central tally office in Dili. At all times, these ballot boxes were to remain in the custody of UNCIVPOL. This included overnight security, where, in some cases, UNCIVPOL slept with the ballot boxes to ensure an unbroken chain of custody. This was a concept with which police were familiar, as it is the same chain of custody process used for the handling of evidentiary material in criminal matters.

Ballot Result

Despite extreme intimidation and coercion by militia groups and claims made by pro-Indonesian elements of bias and procedural irregularities by UNAMET, the people of East Timor registered to vote almost in their entirety, and in excess of 98 per cent of eligible voters actually voted on 30 August 1999. The ballot result was announced by UN Secretary-General Kofi Annan in the mid-morning of 4 September 1999:

> The result was an overwhelming rejection of Indonesia's autonomy proposal: 21.5 per cent (94,388) said yes to the offer; 78.5 per cent (344,580) rejected it and, in doing so, indicated a preference to separate from Indonesia.[59]

The effect on the ground was immediate, widespread and extreme. Most of the UN electoral volunteers had left East Timor immediately following the actual ballot and before the announcement of the result.

Most of the international media had departed also due to pro-Indonesian intimidation, although some brave media representatives remained to report on the rapidly deteriorating situation on the ground. The only remaining, and highly visible, UN presence was UNCIVPOL, with AFP members prominent among them. As result of the UN requirement that police members wear their national flag prominently on their shirts, Australians attracted the specific attention of militia violence. This was a very dangerous situation for UNCIVPOL, but specifically for AFP members, who were the most numerous and highly identifiable to militia groups. The Indonesian police stated to UNCIVPOL on several occasions that they could no longer guarantee their safety.

> One Australian Civilian Police (UNPOL) officer told us how his local POLRI (Kepolisian Negara Republik Indonesia: Indonesian National Police) commander tipped him off after the referendum result was announced in 1999: 'Tomorrow I've been ordered to remove your security at midday and not see what happens.' The Australian added that the local militia had a list of priority targets for assassination that he himself was on, but the POLRI commander was number one on that list.[60]

The shooting of American UNCIVPOL member Earl Candler from Chicago is a case in point. On the day of the announcement of the ballot result he was posted to Liquica, was mistaken for an Australian and was shot by an Indonesian soldier who discharged at least three rounds from a military semi-automatic weapon as Candler was in a clearly marked UN vehicle.

Australian UNCIVPOL had been directed to remove their UN police shirts that displayed an Australian National Flag as the Indonesians blamed Australia for the entire UNAMET process and the loss of face created by the ballot result. Australians were clearly identifiable by the flags on their shirts and were being specifically targeted. To avoid this, they reverted to wearing plain navy-blue T-shirts with the generic 'UNAMET' symbol visible. Although he came from the U.S., Earl took his police shirt off as well. He resembled an AFP colleague, working with him in Liquica, and it is strongly suspected this was the motive for the shooting. Earl only survived, because he had brought a ballistic vest with him from his previous mission in the Balkans, and he held this up against the window. The shots were aimed at his head, but when the high-velocity projectiles hit the ceramic plates in the ballistic vest, they were deflected into his abdomen. He was eventually evacuated to Dili and then the Royal Darwin Hospital, where he was treated and eventually recovered. It is also worth noting that, in addition to being deployed unarmed, the AFP was deployed without any sort of ballistic protection, such as ballistic vests or helmets. The reason for this appears to be a reluctance on the part of decision-makers in Canberra to avoid insulting the Indonesians by showing a lack of trust in the Indonesian security forces to fulfil their role.

Overreaction by TNI/Militias:
Operation Global Clean Sweep: Post-Ballot

As soon as the ballot result was announced, the overt phase of Operation Global Clean Sweep was implemented, and TNI and POLRI were dispatched throughout the province. Some members of POLRI donned their old military uniforms. In many remote and regional areas, smoke from burning villages and buildings was sighted and panic ensued. In Dili large groups of internally displaced persons were loaded aboard military transports and taken across the border to West Timor. The entire province generally descended into chaos and violence. The Indonesian police evaporated and the UNCIVPOL were left isolated in many remote and regional areas of the province. There was, thus, no control at all over the violence, and little restraint was being demonstrated by the perpetrators. This created a deliberate humanitarian crisis on the ground. Kingsbury explains:

> A further element of Operation Clean Sweep was to disrupt the UN process in East Timor. This problem escalated into August and had reached radical proportions by early September, with more than 350,000 forced into homelessness and hundreds, probably thousands, tortured and killed.[61]

Much of this was witnessed by UNCIVPOL, although there was a deliberate strategy by the Indonesians to corral UN staff, especially UNCIVPOL into controlled areas in Dili and Baucau, the two locations with airstrips large enough to accommodate C130 aircraft for the forced evacuation of international UNAMET personnel caused by the escalating violence. This corralling was the first stage of removing competent eyewitnesses to the slaughter that was to come. The Indonesian military action bore similar hallmarks to those of 1975, where military action was justified to suppress insurrection and to remove international witnesses, particularly UN police. Major Clinton Fernandes, an Australian Intelligence Officer with the Australian Army, wrote:

> The Indonesian military terror campaign was carefully calibrated in intent, timing and location. For all its visceral, punitive aspects, the aim was to reverse the result of the ballot. It would have to be discredited as rigged, by suggesting that a majority of Timorese were voting with their feet. The Indonesian military needed to remove all foreigners in order to execute its plan without the impediment of outside attention. Therefore, for all its

sensationalism and violent imagery, the execution of the terror campaign was carefully controlled.

The military campaign would work sequentially as follows: (1) Use the militia proxies to confine and remove foreign observers. (2) With foreigners gone, attack the local population and use logistics assets to move them across the border. (3) Provoke a desperate retaliation from Falintil...thereby drawing it into a conventional war. (4) Announce that the TNI was forced to intervene between the 'factions' and then, freed from restraints, attack and destroy Falintil in conventional warfare. (5) Create new demographic facts on the ground, ensuring that the results of the ballot were irreversibly overturned.[62]

The UN Compound Dili 4–14 September 1999

Most non-uniformed international UNAMET staff such as the District Electoral Officers (DEOs) had left their remote locations and had departed to their home locations, leaving only UNCIVPOL and locally engaged staff (LES) in situ. After a great deal of negotiation with POLRI and indirectly with the various militia groups. UNCIVPOL and many LES, eventually made their way to Dili and Baucau, as they were corralled into places they could be managed and eventually evacuated from the province altogether. It is no accident than both Dili and Baucau had airfields large enough to accommodate Hercules C130 aircraft. There is little doubt that this was a deliberate strategy by the pro-Indonesian elements to concentrate the remaining international staff in locations for evacuation, leaving the LES exposed. Once evacuated there would be no international staff to witness what was to come. Whilst in both locations the harassment continued as the following extract from a 2001 DFAT publication explains:

> Despite a visit to Dili on 5 September by General Wiranto and Foreign Affairs Minister Alatas, that afternoon the security situation in Dili deteriorated further. Harassment of the international presence increased significantly. UNAMET staff were increasingly confined to headquarters as UN vehicles were shot at in the streets, as was the Australian Consulate vehicle...That evening, machine gun fire in the close vicinity of UNAMET headquarters drove several hundred more terrified East Timorese to seek refuge in the UNAMET compound. Gunfire and grenade blasts continued throughout the night.[63]

The harassing fire, punctuated by grenade blasts, continued through the afternoon and evening and into the night. Indiscriminate machine-gun bursts, defined by the tracer bullets, were fired at fleeing East Timorese Internally Displaced Persons (IDP) and LES, seeking safety in the hills behind Dili. One member of the Indonesian forces entered the schoolyard next to the UN compound in Dili and discharged his weapon. Many frightened IDPs had gathered there as they sought sanctuary and safety close to the UN compound. This gunfire panicked them and they fled to the actual compound and attempted to scale the wall separating the school and the compound. This was topped with razor-wire and some of the terrified East Timorese threw their babies over the wall to what they thought was safety. A number were caught up on the razor-wire and were helped down by UNCIVPOL where they were given first aid for their lacerations. A small gate was eventually opened and a more orderly stream entered the UN compound. This ran the risk of overwhelming the existing space and provisions such as food and water as well as latrines. Attempts by UNCIVPOL to travel through the chaotic streets of Dili to obtain resupply from the UN warehouse at the waterfront were futile as they encountered roadblocks and on several occasions were fired upon.

Hygiene was likely to become a major problem quite quickly. Latrines were dug behind the auditorium as the harassing gunfire and grenade blasts persisted. A ballot was drawn up and the remaining UNCIVPOL was evacuated in small numbers to Darwin by two C130 aircraft, one UN (South African Air Force) and one Royal Australian Air Force. A small number of East Timorese LES and IDP accompanied them. When the security situation had deteriorated to a particularly dangerous level, UNAMET was given no option but to evacuate completely. Many remaining UNCIVPOL refused to leave until safe passage for the IDPs and LES in the compound could be arranged. This succeeded and the remaining East Timorese in the Dili compound were transported covertly from the compound to the airport and were evacuated to Darwin. Similar results occurred in Baucau.

Images of the destruction and violence were being transmitted by remaining media to an increasingly enraged public in Australia and elsewhere.

A fortnight of chaos, violence and destruction took place between the start of the withdrawal of UNAMET from regional areas to Dili and Baucau on 6 September and the eventual arrival of an international military force known as INTERFET on 20 September, negotiated by Australian Prime Minister Howard and the UN Secretary General, supported by U.S. President Clinton.

This fortnight was punctuated by the final withdrawal of UNAMET on 14 September and was characterised by multiple casualties and atrocities. Investigations by a follow-on UN mission (UNTAET) Serious Crimes Unit, revealed a confirmed murder of over 1200 East Timorese, the forced deportation of 250,000 East Timorese across the land border with West Timor and the destruction of an estimated 70 per cent of infrastructure by arson in a pre-planned scorched earth campaign. Acts of murder, kidnapping, torture and rape were commonplace.[64]

U.S. academic Geoffrey Robinson, in a 2003 report to the UN Commissioner for Human Rights detailed some of the atrocities in detail. He stated: The principal crimes committed in East Timor in 1999 included extra-judicial killing, torture and ill-treatment, sexual violence, forcible transfer of population, and destruction of property. These acts infringed a wide range of fundamental human rights recognized in international law, including the right to life, the right to personal security, the right to physical integrity, freedom of thought, freedom of association, and the right to own or hold property.[65]

The Casualty List and Indictments

Supplementing the findings by Robinson, the following table is compiled from the UNTAET Special Crimes Units Report.[66]

District	Mil Dist/ Kodim	Militia	Killed	A	B	C	Off Indict Actual
Lautem	1629	Team Alfa	53	53			26
Baucau	1628	Saka, Sera, Forum Komunikasi Partisan (FKP)	43	43			19
Manatuto	1631	Morok and Mahadomi (Manatuto Hatomi Otonomi – Manatuto Loves Autonomy)	32	32			5
Viqueque	1630	Makikit, 59/75 Junior	8–30	8–30			7
Dili	1627	Aitarak (Thorn)	192		192		68
Liquica	1638	Besi Merah Putih (BMP), Pana	183		183		23
Ermera	1637	Darah Integrasi, Darah Merah, Naga Merah, Team Pancasila, Aitarak	82		82		14
Ailieu	1632	Ahi	28		28		6
Cova Lima	1635	Laksaur, Mahidi	190			190	51
Oecussi	1639	Sakunar	170			170	47
Ainaro	1633	Mahidi, Laksaur	34			34	22
Manufahi	1634	Ablai	27			27	12

Bobonaro	1636	Halilintar, Dadurus Merah Putih, Firmi Merah Putih, Saka Loromonu, Armui Merah Putih, Guntur Merah Putih, Hametin Merah Putih, Harimau Merah Putih, Kaer Metin Merah Putih	229			229	131
Total			1293	158	485	650	431

Summary

Sector
A   158 killed   57 indicted
B   485 killed   111 indicted
C   650 killed   263 indicted
District militia leaders: all indicted
Sector A- (Leader of Team Saka militia Los Palos)
Sector B- (Leader of Aitarak militia Dili)
Sector C- (Leader of Mahidi militia Ainaro)

It is quite clear that the worst of the violence was experienced in Sector C, the westernmost districts bordering West Timor, followed closely by Sector B, especially Liquica and Dili. All three militia leaders from these districts were indicted, but none faced trial. In fact, one of the most violent militia leaders, Eurico Guterres was awarded the prestigious Bintang Jasa Utama Prize in August 2021 by Indonesian President Jokowi Widodo on the recommendation of the then Indonesian Defence Minister Prabowo Subianto, whose involvement in the initial raising of the East Timorese militia groups has been raised above but is yet to be fully explored. Prabowo Subianto was elected President of the Republic of Indonesia in 2023.

There were also eight National Indictments: These people were all indicted as individuals and superiors for the murder of hundreds of East Timorese and deportation or forcible transfer of the population and persecution of tens of thousands of East Timorese during 1999. The indictees all returned to Indonesia. None of these people have faced trial or have been called upon to answer these allegations. Some have attained high office within the Indonesian security and political arena.

Despite protestations by the Indonesian authorities that these militia groups were ostensibly spontaneous groups established by concerned civilians...it was clear that they were deliberately organised, trained, and supplied by military authorities, with assistance from civilian authorities.[67]

This is borne out by a later Truth and Reconciliation Commission[68] comprised of international lawyers and human rights experts in 2005.

The Commission found the following:

- Senior members of the Indonesian military, police and civil administration were involved in the planning and implementation of a programme of mass human rights violations intended to influence the outcome of the United Nations-organised Popular Consultation conducted in Timor-Leste in 1999.
- The militia groups were formed, armed, funded, directed and controlled by the Indonesian security forces.
- The programme conducted by members of the Indonesian security forces used violence and terror, including killing, torture, beatings, rape and property destruction in an attempt to force East Timorese voters to opt formally to 'integrate' with Indonesia. When this strategy failed to produce the intended result, the security forces and their auxiliaries went on a rampage of violence directed against people and property, and forcibly deported several hundred thousand East Timorese to West Timor.
- The massive human rights violations committed during 1999...were committed in execution of a systematic plan approved, conducted and controlled by Indonesian military commanders up to the highest level.
- The violations committed by the members of the Indonesian security forces during 1999 included thousands of separate incidents which constituted crimes against humanity. The Commission holds the leadership of the Indonesian security forces at the highest levels responsible and accountable for their role in planning and executing a strategy of which violations of human rights were an integral part, for failing to prevent or punish perpetrators under their command, and for creating a climate of impunity in which military personnel were encouraged to commit abhorrent acts against civilians known or perceived to be supporters of East Timorese independence.[69]

Indonesian military: Dwi Fungsi (Dual Function) Meets Resistance

It should be remembered that the Indonesian military is regarded, and regards itself as a revolutionary force, having secured Indonesian independence from the colonial Dutch in the 1940s. Part of the Indonesian approach to civil-military relations under President Suharto is a dual function (dwi fungsi). The primary role is to act as a traditional military and defend against external aggression and internal insurrection, and a secondary role is to live and work within the community throughout the Indonesian archipelago. This includes running businesses to supplement their military income. As a result, broadly speaking, because they are close to the community, the Indonesian military is generally very well respected by the community across the archipelago.

The Military-Militia Connection

As discussed above, the special forces elements Venus and Tribuana units were sent to East Timor to conduct covert operations, including the support to the militia groups raised and re-invigorated in East Timor in 1998 as a form of plausible deniability for activities which eventually amounted to gross violations of human rights and war crimes, for which any organised military would rightly be held to account.

In July 2001 the UN Serious Crimes Unit stated:

> Throughout 1998–1999 politically motivated violence carried out by the TNI and the militia correlated with the political negotiations and timetable leading to the signing of the 5 May Agreements, the 7 June Indonesian national elections and subsequently with UNAMETs Consultation timetable and beyond.[70]

Noted American academic Geoffrey Robinson, who worked as apolitical affairs adviser to UNAMET wrote a number of detailed and highly informative works on the militia in East Timor. One of these was a Report to the UN Office of the High Commissioner for Human Rights (OCHHR) in 2003.[71]

Robinson provides a comprehensive account of the formation of the militia groups:

> By October 1998 at least eleven militia groups were operational throughout East Timor. Like Halilintar, two other notorious groups were established early and at strategic locations in the western districts. Mahidi ('Dead or Alive for Integration') was centred around Cassa in southern Ainaro district, at the crossroads between Manufahi, Ainaro and Cova Lima districts. Besi Merah Putih (Red and White Iron) was based out of Maubara, on the border between Liquica, Ermera and Bobonaro districts. These three 'senior' groups were ideally placed to control the movement of the population in and out of the western districts and also to secede those districts if the need arose. Thus, it seems that these militia groups were established on a strategic basis most likely with input from the senior echelons of the TNI with previous experience in East Timor, perhaps as far back as 1975.

> Starting in late 1998, and with increasing frequency in early 1999, TNI, Police, and civilian officials took part in numerous ceremonies marking the formation of militia groups, or spurring those already formed to take action against pro-independence forces. Those documented included inaugural ceremonies in Cassa, (December 12, 1998), Same (March 11, 1999), Viqueque (March 11, 1999), Dili (April 17, 1999), Maliana (April 1999), Suai (mid-April, 1999), Oecussi (May 1, 1999), Manatuto (May 8, 1999), Lolotoe (May 10, 1999), Laclubar (May 18, 1999) and Gleno (April or May 1999). Without exception, the respective Dandim, Kapolres and Bupati were present at all of these ceremonies. In some cases, the ceremonies were attended by higher ranking authorities, including the East Timor military commander, Col. Tono Suratman.
>
> …by June 1999, the militias had been formally organized into a single military-type structure, with the explicitly military name of the 'Integration Fighters Force' (Pasukan Pejuang Integrasi – PPI), and were subject to commands and instructions from the leaders of that organization.
>
> Reflecting their close ties to the TNI, the militia groups adopted military rhetoric and modes of organization. They were organized into 'companies' and 'platoons' and their members were described as soldiers, or freedom fighters.
>
> The militia were allocated to three sectors named alphabetically from the Eastern (Sector A), Central (Sector B) and Western (Sector C).[72]

This is clear evidence of an organised group of armed and violent militias under some form of control, rather than random 'rogue elements', which remains the popularly held and publicly stated view of political, intelligence and policy elites in both Jakarta and Canberra.

Language is Important

How these militia groups have been characterised is important. The official Indonesian Government view was that they were 'rogue elements', not acting in accordance with official Indonesian Government policy. This was also the official position adopted by the Australian Government. This is a view which remains extant.

Formally known as Integration Fighters Force (Pasukan Pejuang Integrasi – PPI), generally, the Militias were referred to variously as 'pro-Indonesian', 'pro-autonomy' or 'pro-integration', rather than as 'anti-independence'. These terms are important, because they all disguise the fact that, although the Governments in Jakarta and Canberra may claim to not have been aware at the political level of what was occurring on the ground, the Militias were actually acting as proxy forces for elements of the Indonesian military, specifically Kopassus. Before and, during the actual UNAMET mission which ran between mid-June and mid-September, the primary targets of these militia groups were the pro-independence elements within the province.

These included the Timorese National Resistance Council (CNRT) and the armed pro-independence guerrilla force known as FALINTIL (Portuguese acronym for Forças Armadas de Libertação de Timor-Leste or Armed Forces for the Liberation of East Timor), which had been garrisoned, in accordance with UN requirements, to allow UNAMET to conduct the ballot.

Militia Targets

Initially there was little evidence that the Militias were directly and deliberately targeting international UNAMET staff, but they were certainly targeting locally engaged East Timorese staff working for UNAMET, and on many occasions unarmed UNCIVPOL were the only people who stood between armed Militia members and their intended targets, the pro-independence supporters. There were several incidents where international staff were subject to violence, intimidation and injury, including several incidents where they were shot at and in one case, actually shot.[73] To the participants on the ground with UNAMET, the precise intentions of the Militia was not known to them, and the perceived threat to their lives and to those of their colleagues was very real. This is made even more stark when the deliberate involvement of amphetamines use among the Militia was evident.

Under the influence of a drug colloquially referred to as Anjing Gila (Mad Dog), Militia members were in many cases, given military grade weapons and directed to use them indiscriminately. It is unclear how widespread this practice was, but clearly the influence of intoxicants such as amphetamines, known to increase aggression, raised the level of risk to international UNAMET staff. It certainly resulted in a degree of psychopathic violence unleashed on the pro-independence supporters in East Timor, as Robinson (2003) states:

> torture and ill-treatment in 1999 were...part of a strategy aimed at intimidating and terrorizing the population. The purpose of that intimidation varied over time. In the pre-ballot period, it was intended primarily to silence pro-independence voices in the context of the registration and campaigning, and to force recruitment into the pro-Indonesian militia groups. In the post-ballot period, it was used to force or 'convince' the population to flee.[74]

Plausible Deniability Meets Ground Truth

One of the problems with an attempt of plausible deniability is that comes in two parts: firstly, it must not only be deniable, but also that such denials be plausible.

Despite claims that the Militia were rogue elements and their activities were not official Indonesian Government policy, which was accepted and believed in diplomatic, intelligence and political circles in both Jakarta and Canberra, those who were on the ground in East Timor during UNAMET were witness to a very different version of events. They have attested that the pro-Indonesian Militias in East Timor, far from being rogue elements, were actually raised, trained, supported, armed and directed by the Indonesian military, in accordance with the above analysis. This was clear to those UNCIVPOL on the ground during UNAMET and was being reported formally through the chain of command, and eventually in desperation, informally through friends and contacts in Australia, and through the media when it was accessible. Yet the formal relationship between the Indonesian military and the militias, the activities of the militias, and the high level of risk exposure to death and serious injury by UNAMET staff, including AFP members, remains opaque in defence, intelligence and foreign policy circles in Canberra. They remain rogue elements in the minds of many in those circles. The question is why?

As stated by Hess (2020):

> There are significant reasons for the downplaying of the relationship between the Indonesian security forces and the militia groups, which created so much tension and fear throughout the entire UNAMET period, and whose post-ballot violence is the reason for the creation and deployment of INTERFET.
>
> The reasons behind this reluctance to acknowledge this link can only be guessed at, but must include the overriding interests in the health of the Australian-Indonesian strategic relationship.[75]

What is beyond dispute, but what has been deliberately suppressed, is the fact that elements of the Indonesian military, particularly the Kopassus special forces, in all probability acting under Ministerial direction, were actively involved in supporting and directing the militia groups in East Timor during UNAMET, and in some cases were actively involved in the commission of the violence. This relationship and militia intent and activities were known to intelligence, defence and foreign policy elements in Canberra but were not shared with those who faced the greatest risk of death or serious injury should things go wrong. This is both reprehensible and unforgivable.

Kopassus and the Secret Warfare Manual

In 2001 six East Timorese plaintiffs, known by their legal pseudonyms of Jane Doe and John Doe et al, brought the civil suit against Lieutenant-General Johnny Lumintang, the Deputy Chief of Staff of the Indonesian Army throughout most of 1999,'for designing, ordering, and directing a campaign of violence and intimidation against the people of East Timor which resulted in the wrongs suffered by the plaintiffs'. The U.S. District

Court had jurisdiction over the case under the provisions of at least two U.S. laws, namely the Alien Tort Claims Act 1789 (ATCA) and the Torture Victim Protection Act 1991.[76]

The core of the case against Lumintang was that he was derelict in his execution of his responsibilities as a legally appointed officer within the Indonesian Armed Forces. Under the doctrine of command responsibility, commanders may be held responsible for certain actions even though the commander did not participate in the criminal actions.[77]

Discovered in Dili after the Indonesian withdrawal, the manual, signed by Lumintang, the Deputy Chief of Staff of the Indonesian Army, is intended to systematise Army preparations for secret warfare, and the goals of training in particular. As the manual points out, the principal part of the Army using such secret warfare skills is the Special Forces Command [Kopassus]. The manual specified exactly what techniques were to be taught to Kopassus personnel, and how they were to be examined on paper and in the field:

- Tactics and Techniques of War of Nerves ['Strategy of Tension']
- Tactics and Techniques of Propaganda
- Tactics and Techniques of Abduction
- Tactics and Techniques of Terror
- Tactics and Techniques of Agitation
- Tactics and Techniques of Sabotage
- Tactics and Techniques of Infiltration
- Tactics and Techniques of Surveillance
- Tactics and Techniques of Wiretapping/Bugging
- Tactics and Techniques of Photo Intelligence
- Tactics and Techniques of Psychological Operations

The signed manual demonstrates not only Lumintang's knowledge and approval of conduct treated as criminal throughout the world…Nothing more clearly indicates the depth of the normalisation of universally condemned standards of morality in the culture of impunity.[78]

On 10 September 2001, Lumintang was found liable for torture, wrongful death, summary execution, assault, battery, and intentional infliction of emotional distress, however this judgement was later overturned in 2004 on the basis '..that the service of the summons and complaint on Lumintang at Washington Dulles International Airport in Fairfax County, Virginia, did not give the District Court in the District of Columbia personal jurisdiction over the defendant.'[79]

UNAMET: The Consequences

For a variety of reasons, much what actually occurred during UNAMET has been downplayed and in some cases deliberately suppressed by Defence and DFAT, and has been deliberately ignored at the political level by successive Australian Governments. These reasons include a desire to avoid a perception of offending Indonesian sensitivities, the protection of some professional reputations, both political and administrative in Australia and a focus on the ADF-led INTERFET mission which has completely over shadowed UNAMET.

Although the entire AFP UNCIVPOL contingent to UNAMET was awarded a Group Bravery Citation, which was very well received, this does not appropriately recognise the many individual acts of extreme bravery performed by UNCIVPOL. When the Group Bravery Citation was awarded in 2001, the links between the Indonesian Government, the Indonesian military, especially Kopassus, and their support of the militia were not widely known and certainly not publicly acknowledged. This relationship has never been officially acknowledged by Australian authorities.

Unbeknown to the AFP contingent of the UNAMET UNCIVPOL, the entire mission was awarded the Elie Wiesel Ethics Award in 2000. This was accepted by the UN Deputy Secretary-General Louise Fréchette.

Upon receipt of the award, she stated:

> UNAMET was entrusted with a unique mission, and overcame extraordinarily difficult conditions to conduct the popular consultations within the limited period of time, and with limited resources. The success of UNAMET was made possible, above all, by the courage and dedication of its staff. Several local staff of UNAMET lost their lives during its operation, and I would like to again pay tribute to them and their family members. This Elie Wiesel Ethics Award belongs to them.
>
> Helping East Timor stand on its own as a free and independent country is one of the greatest responsibilities ever given to the United Nations.
>
> UNAMET staff were the face of our Organization to the people for whom we exist: the poor, the vulnerable, those threatened by violence, and those seeking to build stable, democratic and prosperous societies out of the ashes of war.[80]

For twenty years the existence of the Elie Wiesal Ethics Award and its award to UNAMET was never made known to AFP UNCIVPOL members. It was only brought to the attention of the author by one of the British UNCIVPOL members of UNAMET when they met in Dili in 2019 for a 20-year reunion. In Dili in September 2024, at the 25th anniversary of UNAMET, the award was presented by Mr Ian Martin, the former UN SRSG to UNAMET, in an informal ceremony to those Australian and British UNAMET UNCIVPOL members present. A few days later a more formal presentation of the Timor Leste Solidarity Medal was made at the Presidential Palace by His Excellency Jose Ramos Horta, the President of the Democratic Republic of Timor Leste, who stated: that the medal

> symbolizes our nation's profound gratitude towards those who, from various parts of the world, played an active and crucial role in the development of our democracy. These brave officers stood with us during one of the most challenging periods in our history. Their dedication and work in the period before and after the historic referendum deserves to be highlighted and recognized for its contribution to peace and security.' [Press release: President Jose Ramos-Horta Awards United Nations Police with Timor Leste Solidarity Medal, Dili, September 3, 2024.]

The Senate

In December 2000 the East Timor Final Report of the Senate Foreign Affairs, Defence and Trade References Committee stated:

> 1.7 This premeditated action by the militias and the TNI was in breach of the undertaking, given by the Indonesian Government in the agreement of 5 May 1999 with Portugal and the United Nations, to preserve peace and security in East Timor in the interim phase between the conclusion of the popular consultation and the start of the implementation of its result, regardless of the outcome, and to guarantee the security of the personnel and premises of UNAMET (United Nations Assistance Mission to East Timor).

The Report acknowledged at para 3.45: '...the vital role played by civilian police in securing the popular ballot in East Timor and in subsequent efforts to restore order to the territory...'

In a Supplementary Submission to this Senate Report the Australian Electoral Commission commented on the conduct of UNAMET:

> UNAMET and its staff did an excellent job in conducting the ballot in a way that met the highest professional standards, and in the most difficult of circumstances. Many of those staff displayed conspicuous fortitude and bravery throughout the process.[81]

On 8 August 2000, Justice and Customs Minister Senator Amanda Vanstone, Minister responsible for the AFP said:

> AFP officers were amongst the first international contingents into East Timor, having served there since July 1999 when they played a significant role

in the successful conduct of the self-determination ballot. Let's remember they were there first, they were there unarmed, they protected the Timorese while the ballot was being undertaken and they protected the ballot boxes to make sure that the will of the people was properly recorded…

The men and women who went through the most dangerous time in Timor, who were there first, who were there unarmed before the army…[82]

3.48 The Committee believes that the police who served in East Timor as part of UNAMET had a more difficult and dangerous job than did the military as part of INTERFET. They were unarmed and served there during the height of militia harassment and violence in the lead up to the 30 August poll and afterwards in the systemic destruction of the territory. Indonesia, which demanded and got responsibility for maintaining security in East Timor during the UNAMET period, abjectly failed in fulfilling that responsibility.[83]

Also in August 2000, the then relatively junior Senator and official observer during UNAMET, Senator Marise Payne stated:

…for the three months preceding the ballot, all over the country members of the AFP in CIVPOL, unarmed, supported and protected their fellow members of UNAMET and local East Timorese from the excesses of militia activities. They, as part of CIVPOL, protected polling stations and ballot boxes on 30 August 1999 to ensure the integrity of the ballot and the safety of UN workers, East Timorese and international observers, like me.

I for one believe that without CIVPOL, and without the efforts and commitment of the AFP component of CIVPOL before, during and after the ballot, the fate of the East Timorese and their move to independence would have been very different. Long before September last year when the unfolding drama in East Timor filled our TV screens and radio waves every day and every night, these men and women were doing an extraordinary job for the East Timorese and our nation.[84]

Courage for Peace

Nearly a decade later, on 17 October 2019, in the Keynote Address at the opening of 'The Courage for Peace' exhibition at the Australian War Memorial, Senator Marise Payne, who had risen over the intervening two decades to Minister for Foreign Affairs and Minister for Women, via the Defence Minister portfolio, stated:

Australia has contributed to…many…peacekeeping operations and most of those unarmed…we don't shrink from the task of bringing peace and saving lives even…at the risk of our own. Indeed, generations of Australian governments have decided the building of peace is at least as important as the making of war.

It is both a necessity and a choice for principled nations like Australia to contribute to peace missions.

> ...if we are to live in a rules-based international order where we do not accept that coercion and force dictate the outcomes of disputes; if we choose a world where values and principles are worth defending, and the rights of nations to enjoy prosperity and harmony under international law are paramount; we genuinely believe that inhumanity, genocide, unchecked state-sponsored violence, perpetual instability have no place in the modern world; then we have no choice but to have the courage to stand up, step forward, share the burden of collective security, regional stability, and breaking the cycle of violence, so that peace has the room to re-establish itself...we are standing on the shoulders of giants...who served in Cambodia, in Timor Leste, in Somalia, in Cyprus, in Rwanda, in Afghanistan and elsewhere, some twice or more times.

Former AFP Commissioner Mick Palmer

In 2021 former AFP Commissioner Mick Palmer shared an excerpt from his unpublished memoir with the author in which he stated:

> During my time as Commissioner of the AFP...there were many occurrences and incidents which gave me reason for pride in the people of the AFP and their achievements. None, however, gave me more pride than the performance, courage, commitment, determination and compassion demonstrated by the AFP members who participated in the United Nations Mission in East Timor known as UNAMET between June and September 1999.

UNAMET in Summary

UNAMET was a seminal mission in many ways. UNAMET succeeded against severe odds created by a highly flawed security agreement and violent and active partisan behaviour by erstwhile protectors under that agreement. Nonetheless 98 per cent of registered voters actually cast a vote, of which 78.5 per cent rejected the Indonesian offer of autonomy. UNAMET paved the way for the eventual independence of Timor-Leste in 2002. UNAMET also raised the profile of the AFP in the eyes of Australian Prime Minister Howard. This in turn created an impetus for future AFP-led missions in the South West Pacific and the establishment of the International Deployment Group IDG to support those missions.

Follow-on UN Missions

The UNAMET mission was the first of many UN missions to follow in East Timor, later Timor-Leste. The AFP was involved in every one of these missions, until the UN withdrew in 2012. The AFP continues to be engaged in the new nation of Timor-Leste, established in 2002, through a police development program, the Timor Leste Police development Program (TLPDP).

After UNAMET in late 1999, and in tandem with INTERFET, the UN established the 'transition' mission of UNTAET, which had overall responsibility for the administration of Timor-Leste for a temporary period, including the power to make laws, govern and administer justice. The purpose of UNTAET was to establish the conditions and institutions needed for Timor-Leste to transition to governing itself as an independent and democratic nation.

UNTAET Serious Crimes Unit: Crimes Against Humanity

On 20 May 2002, full independence was achieved. The Democratic Republic of Timor-Leste became the first new nation-state of the 21st century.

UNTAET was followed by another UN mission, the UN Mission in Support of East Timor (UNMISET). UNMISET was established to assist the core administrative structures critical to the viability and political stability, to provide interim law enforcement and public security, to assist in the development of a new law enforcement agency (the East Timor Police Service [ETPS]) and to contribute to the maintenance of the external and internal security of East Timor.

The UN Mandate was extended twice, and UNMISET eventually ended in 2005, and responsibility was handed over to another small follow-on UN political mission – the United Nations Office in Timor-Leste (UNOTIL) – which was established by the Security Council to ensure that the underpinnings of a viable state were firmly in place in Timor-Leste. UNOTIL supported the capacity development of critical state institutions, including the East Timor National Police (PNTL), to strengthen democratic governance and to help build peace in Timor-Leste.

Unfortunately, democratic governance and peace in Timor-Leste were shattered by an outbreak of politically motivated violence in April–May 2006. The UN responded by establishing the UN Integrated Mission in Timor (UNMIT) in August 2006. This was a multidimensional, integrated UN peacekeeping operation that was mandated to support the Timor-Leste Government in 'consolidating stability, enhancing a culture of democratic governance, and facilitating political dialogue among Timorese stakeholders, in their efforts to bring about a process of national reconciliation and to foster social cohesion'. UNMIT concluded on 31 December 2012, and the UN withdrew completely from the region after more than twelve years.

Throughout this time, the AFP engaged in Timor-Leste in the police capacity development mission: the TLPDP. This mission is still in existence at the time of writing in 2024.

There are some commentators who regard UNAMET as a failure that required military intervention. While there is some merit to this if viewed through an exclusively military security lens, there are other more tangible and longer-term results for the ballot, as I observed in 2015:

> The cost for the East Timorese people was very high, in terms of post-ballot casualties, and it is they who should be the ultimate arbiters of whether the sacrifice involved in conducting the ballot was worth it or not.[85]

Xanana Gusmão, the current and former Prime Minister of East Timor who was an instrumental influence on the political destiny of East Timor, wrote:

> Our independence referendum was an uplifting event for our people that brought the promise of self-determination after many years of struggle. While we knew the wishes in the hearts of our people, we also knew best the situation on the ground in our country and the risks of a vote for independence. On 30 August the Timorese people came out to vote in a collective act of courage and determination. The referendum had a turnout rate of 98.6 per cent and 78.5 per cent voted for independence. The Timorese people had achieved what so many had told us was no more than a dream.
>
> Today, the referendum stands and testament to the bravery and dignity of our people. We knew that a vote for independence would provoke vengeance and retaliation. After the result was announced on 4 September, widespread violence broke out, spreading across our country. People were killed as a scorched-earth campaign of destruction was carried out, leaving most of our country in ruins. This was a bittersweet moment for our people as out joy turned to despair. Just as our dreams of freedom were becoming a reality we faced further brutality and fear. Our people were desperate. We were not certain if the international community would intervene with peacekeeping force, so desperately needed.[86]

Priority of Australian–Indonesian Relationship

It is worthwhile recalling that one of the over-riding influences over the way the UNAMET mission was created, implemented and under-acknowledged was, and remains the strategic relationship between the governments, foreign ministries and militaries of both Australia and Indonesia.

Hugh White stated this quite clearly in 2008 in his piece on the strategic decision-making where he outlines that this was related to the transition of Indonesia from autocracy under President Suharto and democracy under President Habibie:

> ...Australia's top priorities in the post-Suharto era was to support Indonesia's democratic transformation, and to sustain a good relationship with TNI.

This influenced a number of strategic priorities once the prospect of a UN-sponsored ballot became inevitable. White outlines them as follows:

> ....some principles were established and practical measures taken to adjust to the new circumstances. First, it was agreed broadly that Australia had...key policy objectives in relation to East Timor;
> - East Timor should remain part of Indonesia;
> - The relationship with Indonesia was more important to Australia than the future of East Timor, so that we should avoid outcomes which damaged or jeopardised that relationship;
> - The relationship with TNI was especially important, because of its expected role in Indonesia's political future, so special care should be taken to protect that relationship.[87]

Clinton Fernandes[88] in his 2008 response to Hugh White outlines that Habibie had his supporters in Jakarta but also his detractors concerning Habibie's East Timor policy. One of Habibie's supporters, Dewi Fortuna Anwar specifically highlighted that the Indonesian military could not be trusted with security for such a ballot and they were not impartial. Her public statements in this regard alarmed U.S. Government leaders so much that the Australian Secretary of Foreign Affairs, Ashton Calvert was asked by U.S. Assistant Secretary of State Stanley Roth about the prospect of an international peacekeeping force as the following excerpt makes clear:

> Dewi Fortuna Anwar sounded a public warning about the Indonesian military's forthcoming campaign of militia-backed terror. Writing in the International Herald Tribune, she said that "Indonesia's 500,000 strong military cannot be relied on to do the job [of providing security for the ballot] because it is not regarded as neutral". Alarmed, the U.S. Assistant Secretary of State Stanley Roth met the Secretary of Australia's DFAT, Ashton Calvert five days later in Washington DC. According to the highly sensitive transcript of the conversation, Roth was of the view that a full-scale peacekeeping operation would be an unavoidable aspect of the transition... Australia's position of keeping peace keeping at arms-length was essentially defeatist, and that it was necessary to go forth and persuade Congress and UN member states that it simply had to be done...Stating the Australian government's position, however, Calvert made it clear that Australia wouldn't support peacekeepers.

Adept or Inept Australian Diplomacy?

Desmond Ball (2002) expands on the reluctance by Ashton Calvert, Secretary of the Australian department of Foreign Affairs and Trade, for armed military peacekeepers as proposed by Stanley Roth the U.S. State Department's Assistant Secretary for East Asian Affairs at a meeting in Washington in February 1999. Calvert argued that such a peacekeeping force was unnecessary.

He said, according to the DFAT transcript of the meeting, that Australia had not sensed any broad international appetite for a large-scale UN intervention, though Canberra would be prepared, if necessary, to send military personnel; but not into a bloodbath. He said: to avert the need for recourse to peacekeeping, what we were proposing was to be active in the first instance.... Australia's preferred approach was designed to avoid a military option by the use of adept diplomacy.[89]

This line of thinking was no doubt influenced by over-riding considerations concerning the Canberra-Jakarta strategic relationship. Calvert's adept diplomacy was a serious miscalculation, based in part in a misplaced trust in the Indonesian authorities' capacity, ability and willingness to play by the rules, which were yet to be formulated and agreed to. As a result of the prioritisation of the Australia-Indonesia strategic and military relationship, and in furtherance of the discussion between Hugh White and Clinton Fernandes, Iain Henry[90] argues in 2013 that when the potential implications of the East Timor ballot were being deliberated the Government of Australia was forced into a balancing act between the relationship and the desire for a ballot to be conducted fairly, but clearly the relationship took priority:

> ...Australia was forced into a reactive policymaking posture...Australia's need to prioritise its relationship with Indonesia constrained its ability to pursue other strategic goals...Australia's primary challenge throughout 1999 was ensuring that strategic policy appropriately prioritised the two most important objectives—encouraging Indonesia's developing democracy and maintaining the Australia-Indonesia bilateral relationship.
>
> ...the top priority for Canberra—Australian Governments of both political persuasions have consistently prioritised the Australia-Indonesia relationship above almost all other concerns...

Perhaps an explanation as to why this relationship is such a priority is worthwhile and this is succinctly provided by Clinton Fernandes in two parts. Firstly, in his 2005 book Reluctant Saviour,[91] Mr Fernandes states:

> For Australia, the long-term construction of a 'good relationship' is designed to deliver a specific outcome: an Indonesia that is non-communist and

integrated into the western sphere of influence. This outcome has been a long-standing Australian foreign-policy objective.

Secondly the rationale, as stated by Mr Fernandes in 2021, is quite simple – pragmatism:

> Indonesia…was a founding member of the Non-Aligned Movement. It had the largest Muslim population in the world, and was therefore very influential in the Organization of Islamic Conference. It was also a member of the Association of Southeast Asian Nations, which had a policy of non-interference in one another's internal affairs.[92]

Transition – Past to Present: UNAMET and The Global War on Terror

One of the primary drivers of international policing and diplomacy is political prioritisation which in turn is dependent on political will. There are occasions where policy rather than law determines police actions despite the strict adherence to the separation of powers between government policy and police best practice. This was the case with East Timor, both with the initial AFP involvement as part of UNAMET and the resultant Australian-led INTERFET.

Combined, these created some serious foreign policy difficulties for Australian–Indonesian relations, among them the raising of Australia as a 'legitimate' target as a Crusader Nation in the eyes of al Qaeda. To justify bringing his version of global jihadism to the South East Asian region, Osama bin Laden stated that East Timor had been excised from the Islamic nation of Indonesia by the combined crusader forces of the United Nation and Australia. It was thus interpreted as an attack on Islam, making Australians legitimate targets. He was factually incorrect because, as a legacy of its Portuguese colonial antecedents, East Timor was, and remains, an overwhelmingly Catholic country. This was one of the factors underlining the problems between the Indonesian administration and the local people. There was truly a clash of cultures and of religion.

Indonesia: Counter-terrorism and the AFP Liaison Network

As the war against the Soviets in Afghanistan drew to a close in the late 1980s, many former international Mujahadeen fighters returned to their home countries. In South East Asia, this included Malaysia, the Philippines and Indonesia. Once in their home countries, many regrouped and began to pose a security threat both domestically and externally.

AFP Liaison Officers based in Indonesia developed sound and effective working relationships with their POLRI counterparts in the period following the East Timor deployments, specifically UNAMET, INTERFET and UNTAET. High on the list of priorities was the rise in militant political Islamic jihadism, which became particularly important with the Bali bombings in October 2002 as well as other bombings in Indonesia and attempted attacks in other parts of South East Asia. The AFP-POLRI relationship endures and has survived the political ebb and flow over numerous contentious issues. One senior former AFP intelligence representative opined that following the breakdown of relations between the Governments of Indonesia and Australia following the East Timor interventions, the AFP-POLRI relationship acted as a 'police-led recovery' of the government-to-government relationship. This illustrates the important diplomatic impact a professionally respectful, co-operative and collaborative police to police relationship can have regardless of what is occurring at the official government to government level. This reflects the truism that police perform best when they cooperate rather than compete with their foreign counterparts, and that the more they are separated from their respective polities they are, the more effective this cooperation can be as they deal with common problems related to crime and criminality.

The 9/11 Attacks, Prime Minister Howard and the AFP Close Protection Team

Probably the most significant manifestation of the rise of militant political Islam was the attacks in New York City and Washington D.C. on 11 September 2001. It was incidental but important that the Australian Prime Minister John Howard was on an official visit to the U.S. at the time.

As is standard practice, Prime Minister Howard was accompanied by an AFP Close Personal Protection (CPP) team. This CPP Team did not have any ability or authority to perform security itself, but was in close liaison with the U.S. Secret Service, which had primary jurisdiction for the protection of visiting dignitaries, including heads of government. Both AFP and Secret Service protection teams reacted as they had been trained and in accordance with planning, and secured Mr Howard and his family who were accompanying him.

On 12 September, Mr Howard had been scheduled to deliver an address to a Joint Sitting of Congress, which was no longer possible given the security circumstances. Nonetheless, he attended Congress, and his attendance was acknowledged by the Speaker of the United States House of Representatives, and he received a five-minute standing ovation. He then departed for Australia.

The previous day, the Australian Government had been offered the use of the Vice President's Boeing 747 (Air Force Two), to evacuate Mr Howard. Mr Howard, however, declined the offer, preferring to focus on the Western coalition and any role Australia could play in supporting this coalition.

Eventually, late on 12 September, Prime Minister Howard decided it was time to depart for Australia. The offer of Air Force Two still stood and was accepted. Significantly, beside U.S. Air Force military aircraft patrolling the skies over continental United States, this flight, direct from Washington D.C. to Hickham Air Force Base in Hawaii, was the only other aircraft flying across U.S. air space.

During this flight, the Team Leader of the AFP CPP Team had an opportunity to speak directly to the Australian Prime Minister. This is a unique situation where a relatively junior, but highly experienced operational member of the AFP had direct and unfiltered access to the leader of the Australian Government, without the input and interference of political and administrative obstacles and political gatekeepers. During this conversation Prime Minister Howard foreshadowed some of the challenges faced by Australia within the Western alliance and sought advice about what role the AFP could play in this and what resources it would require. This conversation was reported to the Commissioner of the AFP by the Team Leader upon return to Australia.

This experience gave Prime Minister Howard an early and graphic first-hand perspective of the new security threats that faced social cohesion and prosperity in the Western world. This included the value of a well-resourced and supported intelligence and policing framework and the role it can play as a major part of countering and mitigating these threats. The following year, on 12 June 2002, Prime Minister Howard returned to the U.S. and addressed a Joint Sitting of Congress.

In this address, he stated:

> The ANZUS Treaty of 1951 pledged each country to come to the aid of the other if it were under attack. And so it was that in a U.S. Airforce plane made available for my return to Australia on 12 September and high above the Pacific that I informed the U.S. Ambassador Tom Schieffer travelling with me our intention was that, for the first time in its fifty-year history, Australia would invoke the ANZUS Treaty. America was under attack. Australia was immediately there to help.[93]

Hence, Australia became involved in Iraq and Afghanistan. The latter will be discussed in Part V of this book. He also spoke of Australian involvement in East Timor by stating: 'Australia is proud of its leadership role in East Timor in gaining for a people so long oppressed the freedom and democracy available to our own citizens', which, as explained, caused a significant degree of political difficulty between Canberra and Jakarta.[94]

The 9/11 attacks changed the world and, in particular, the demeanour of the U.S. and the West generally. This resulted in military interventions in other parts of the world, including Afghanistan, which also resulted in ADF and later AFP members being deployed to that country between 2007 and 2013. Closer to home, in October 2002, eighty-eight Australians were among the 202 killed in Bali by bombs detonated by Jemaah Islamiyah. There were several other bombings in Indonesia and other attempts in regional South East Asia and domestically in Australia. This was the environment in which Australia and the AFP entered the third millennium.

There are some global priorities that are self-evident and require genuine international cooperation between police and intelligence agencies, including those from countries which do not practice a liberal-democratic policing posture. This includes the prevention of and response to global violent extremism.

Indonesia

On 20 September 2001, nine days after the attacks on New York and Washington on 11 September 2001, U.S. President Bush delivered an address to a Joint Session of Congress and the American people at the U.S. Capitol in Washington. He stated that the U.S. was:

> a country awakened to danger and called to defend freedom. Our grief has turned to anger, and anger to resolution. Whether we bring our enemies to justice, or bring justice to our enemies, justice will be done.
>
> Our war on terror begins with al Qaeda, but it does not end there. It will not end until every terrorist group of global reach has been found, stopped and defeated…We will direct every resource at our command – every means of diplomacy, every tool of intelligence, every instrument of law enforcement, every financial influence, and every necessary weapon of war – to the disruption and to the defeat of the global terror network.
>
> Every nation, in every region, now has a decision to make. Either you are with us, or you are with the terrorists. From this day forward, any nation that continues to harbor or support terrorism will be regarded by the United States as a hostile regime.[95]

Following so briefly after U.S. President Clinton threatened to melt down the Indonesian economy if the Indonesian Government failed to allow an international peacekeeping force into East Timor in late September 1999, the intent behind President Bush's words and the ability to deliver on them would not have been lost on the Indonesian Government. This softened the ground for improved AFP–POLRI relationships following the animosity and division created by the East Timor situation.

As discussed earlier, Australian governance evolved from an entirely different historical and cultural base from the majority of its neighbours in the region, including the stark contrast between the Commonwealth of Australia and the Republic of Indonesia. Historically there has been a fractious diplomatic relationship between these two states and a degree of mutual distrust and misunderstanding. A series of events in which police-to-police relationships, based on mutual respect and a shared responsibility to cooperate in the face of a growing Islamist threat in the region, played a significant role in improving the government-to-government relationship through the police.

Indonesia is the world's largest Muslim-majority country with an island chain extending from Aceh in the west, which has a sea border with the Indian Nicobar Islands and the Andaman Islands, to PNG in the east, with which it shares a land border, and Australia with the Torres Strait and the Arafura Sea to the south. Indonesia also has a land border with the Malaysian states of Sabah and Sarawak on the island of Borneo and has common archipelagic concerns with the southern Philippines. It is the most populous country in Southeast Asia and controls the sea lanes through which the bulk of Australian trade and commerce transits to markets deeper into Asia, and much of Australia's imports, including oil. Indonesia, like a number of maritime ASEAN states, has extant jurisdictional disputes with the PRC in the South China Sea. Indonesia is a founding member of ASEAN, which formed in 1967 as a bulwark to the southern expansion of communism at the height of the Cold War. It is a highly influential and strategically placed nation that links Asia to the Pacific and Australia to Asia.

The health of the Australian–Indonesian relationship is of very high significance to Australian strategic interests. As discussed in the section relating to East Timor, there has been strong bipartisan political support for this relationship, as well as support from those in the 'Jakarta Lobby'. Despite some political differences, both in the short term and permanently, the AFP has established, nurtured and maintained a close and effective working relationship with POLRI. The result has been the betterment of each other's respective communities and the broader government-to-government relations generally. This relationship is a good example of international police cooperation in the face of common threats.

The Relationship Between the AFP and POLRI

The AFP and POLRI have a formal relationship that predates the events in East Timor in 1999. On 5 August 1997, the AFP and POLRI signed a Memorandum of Understanding concerning law enforcement issues of mutual concern. At this signing, an address by POLRI National Police Chief General Dibyo Widodo stated, prophetically, '...we have to be prepared to anticipate the type of crime that is likely to happen or else we'll be left behind to do too little too late.'[96]

At that time, Indonesian President Suharto was still in power, and the police were still part of the Indonesian military. Although the police had operated as an autonomous agency in the immediate post-independence period in 1945, they were integrated into the military during the 1960s. As a result, the capacity of the national police suffered due to its militarisation, where its responsibilities were limited to lower-level crime and providing support to military-led internal security operations.[97]

The Suharto years featured an authoritarian approach, and when he stepped down in 1998, there were calls for democratisation and security sector reform, including reform of the police, by separating it from its military structure. POLRI was formally separated from the military in April 1999, just before UNAMET was deployed, which explains some of the security issues experienced in that mission. POLRI lacked capacity and experience, and were simply outgunned and intimidated by the Indonesian military and their militia proxies. The 2002 bombings in Bali created an environment in which close cooperation between police from all over the world (including Australia), despite their different cultural backgrounds, worked effectively in the pursuit of justice. This was a glimpse into the potential for international police cooperation in which there is more that unites police than divides them.

UNAMET, INTERFET and the Connection with Global Jihad: 1999–2002

The previous discussion outlined the relationship difficulties created by the involvement of the UN in East Timor in 1999 in which significant numbers of the AFP were engaged. One of the resulting global aspects of this intervention, particularly the Australian-led military intervention INTERFET, was the listing of Australia as a legitimate target by Osama bin Laden, the leader of the emerging Islamic jihadist organisation al Qaeda. On 3 November 2001, the Qatar-based media network Al-Jazeera broadcast a statement by bin Laden that specifically identified Australians as 'crusaders'. The British Broadcasting Corporation (BBC) quoted him as follows:

Let us examine the stand of the West and the United Nations in the developments in Indonesia when they moved to divide the largest country in the Islamic world in terms of population. This criminal, Kofi Annan, was speaking publicly and putting pressure on the Indonesian government, telling it: You have 24 hours to divide and separate East Timor from Indonesia.

Otherwise, we will be forced to send in military forces to separate it by force. The crusader Australian forces were on Indonesian shores, and in fact they landed to separate East Timor, which is part of the Islamic world. Therefore, we should view events not as separate links, but as links in a long series of conspiracies, a war of annihilation in the true sense of the word.[98]

The fact that he was factually incorrect mattered little to some in Indonesia, who were eager to hear his message. He was incorrect in stating that East Timor was Islamic; it was a predominantly Catholic province, which was one of the primary drivers behind its desire for independence from Muslim-dominated Indonesia. He was also incorrect in stating that it was the UN Secretary-General who directed Indonesia to separate itself from East Timor. The dynamics were far more complex than this simple statement, but this was the simple message received by those in Indonesia, who were already radicalising and were not interested in the polemics of nuanced arguments. In October 2002, a network of these radicalised individuals set off large bombs on the largely Hindu island of Bali, where Western tourists, including Australians, holiday in large numbers.

Three explosions were detonated on 12 October 2002 by Islamic extremists known as Jemaah Islamiyah (JI). The bombs killed 202 people, including eighty-eight Australians. The response from Australia was immediate and included the deployment of significant numbers of AFP members. This was aided by the relationship that had already developed between AFP Commissioner Mick Keelty and General Dai Bachtiar, the Chief of POLRI. This relationship had been developed by effective liaison work by the AFP Liaison Officer in Jakarta immediately following the East Timor intervention. In this capacity, the Liaison Officer overcame some of the political static and natural reluctance to engage, and he arranged a meeting between the two police chiefs, which developed into an enduring friendship.

The personal relationship between Commissioner Keelty and POLRI representatives was long-standing, in particular, the relationship with the POLRI commander in charge of the Bali bombing investigation, who had attended an AFP Management of Serious Crime (MOSC) course in Canberra in 1993. As McFarlane stated:

> The benefit of solid professional and personal friendships formed during the MOSC programs was clearly demonstrated in the aftermath of the first Bali

bombing in 2002. The Indonesian police commander in charge of that investigation, Inspector General Drs I Madi Pastika, was a graduate of MOSC-5 in 1993, at which time one of his closest colleagues was Mick Keelty.[99]

This is an example of effective police diplomacy at the senior level, which originated at the middle management level. In a reflection of the true nature of the combined efforts of AFP, POLRI and many others, the response to the Bali bombing in 2002 was named Operation Alliance. The AFP deployed specialist teams of investigators, intelligence analysts, bomb experts, post-blast analysts, search and rescue, forensic specialists, disaster victim identification specialists, crime scene analysts and many others within a very short timeframe. They developed their own relationships, both professional and personal.

Islamic Extremism in Indonesia

Due to its enormous diversity, both geographic and cultural, the Republic of Indonesia has experienced a number of separatist insurgencies seeking greater autonomy or even complete separation from the Jakarta-centred government. Timor-Leste is arguably the most prominent example, but others include Aceh and Irian Jaya at opposite ends of the Indonesian archipelago with entirely different dynamics. These have been predominantly geographic in nature, as remote and discrete areas sought to move away from central control from Jakarta. Although not unknown in the post-1945 period, internal terrorism based on ideology or religion was not widely experienced. The post-Suharto era, where the authoritarian approach to internal security was effectively used to suppress such activity, was relaxed, so there was an increase in internal, ideologically based, primarily Islamic, violence, as attacks and bombings against shopping centres and churches were perpetrated as expressions of anti-Christian and later anti-Western sentiment.[100]

The Australian Government National Security website states that the most notorious Islamic jihadist group in Indonesia is JI, which is inspired by the same ideology as al Qaeda.[101] JI was formed in Malaysia on 1 January 1993 by radical Islamist clerics Abdullah Sungkar and Abu Bakar Bashir and regards regional governments as illegitimate, including the Indonesian Government. It sought to revive and install a 'pure' form of Islam in an Islamic Caliphate governed by the tenets of Sharia (Islamic law) across the region by force. This region includes Indonesia, Malaysia, Singapore, Brunei, southern Thailand and the southern Philippines, namely, the original members of ASEAN.

It was members of JI who were the perpetrators of the bombings in Bali in 2002 and 2005, as well as a campaign in Jakarta, with two bombings of the JW Marriott Hotel in 2003 and 2009, the Australian Embassy in 2004 and the Ritz-Carlton Hotel in 2009. JI appropriated and maintained a network of about fifty religious boarding schools (or *pesantren*) that continually worked to inculcate future generations of Indonesian youths in their extreme form of Islam. The membership was estimated to range between 900 and several thousand active members. Incarceration of JI members does not disincentive them; rather, prisons 'provide a further avenue for recruitment, as some JI members proselytise to fellow prisoners and visitors in efforts to recruit members'.[102]

JI had connections to other radical Islamist organisations in the region, including Abu Sayef and the Moro Islamic Liberation Front in the southern Philippines, as well as radical organisations in the Middle East, including al Qaeda. A number of JI members travelled to Syria and Iraq under the auspices of Hilal Ahmar Society Indonesia, where they formed affiliations with other extremist networks in the region. The seizure and siege in Marawi on Mindanao in the southern Philippines in 2017 and the resultant violence inspired by Islamic extremism is an example of how potent this regional threat can be.

The Australian Government first proscribed JI as a terrorist organisation on 27 October 2002 and relisted it on 1 September 2004, 26 August 2006, 9 August 2008, 22 July 2010 and 12 July 2013. It remains a proscribed organisation by the Governments of Australia, New Zealand, Canada, Britain and the US. JI co-founder Abu Bakar Bashir, the Indonesian Islamic cleric who was charged and imprisoned for orchestrating the Bali bombings, as well as other bombings in Indonesia directed against the Indonesian Government of Megawati Sukarnoputri. Six days after the bombings in Bali, he preached anti-Western sentiments to the assembled media for the benefit of his followers in the mosque at Solo in Central Java:

> We reject all of your beliefs, we reject all of your ideologies, we reject all of your teachings on social issues, economics or beliefs. Between you and us there will forever be a ravine of hate and we will be enemies until you follow God's law.[103]

The Bali Bombing 2002

This vitriolic hatred manifested itself with three explosions on 12 October 2002 that deliberately targeted Western holiday-makers. The first bomb exploded at a bar called Paddy's Bar and was estimated to have involved between 500 g and 1 kg of TNT and was placed in the bar by a suspected suicide bomber. Later crime scene examination revealed pieces of metal intended as shrapnel. Shortly after the explosion at Paddy's Bar, a much larger device was detonated in a van parked outside another bar, the Sari

Club. It was estimated that there were more than 350 people in that location when the bomb exploded:

> The force of the blast was strong enough to register on Indonesian seismic instruments. It is estimated that this was a lower velocity, high explosive bomb with an effective weight of between 50 and 150kg. It consisted of potassium chlorate, sulphur and aluminium, was placed in a van outside the club, and was possibly remote detonated by mobile phone.[104]

A third bomb, estimated to involve between 500 g and 1 kg of TNT, was detonated approximately forty-five minutes later close to the U.S. Consulate, about ten km from the Sari Club and Paddy's Bar. It was believed to have been detonated remotely by mobile phone.

The bombings were reported by Federal Agent Paul McEwan,[105] who was holidaying in Bali at the time, and he immediately contacted the AFP in Canberra:

> He described seeing burning buildings, burning motor vehicles with occupants still inside and a relatively large crater in the street outside the Sari Club. He reported chaos, with people running from the scene and emergency services attempting to extinguish fires. He also advised that Paddy's Bar and the Sari Club were known to be frequented by Australian and other foreign tourists and that, because of the extent of the damage he could see, Australian casualties were likely to be significant.[106]

The AFP had renewed its focus on terrorism in the post-9/11 period and was, therefore, in a position to provide specialist and technical assistance very rapidly upon request from Indonesia. This included investigative, administrative and forensic staff to assist POLRI. The AFP's contribution was part of a DFAT-led response that also involved members from other agencies and departments, such as the Australian Security Intelligence Organisation (ASIO) and the APS.

Eventually, the range of Commonwealth Government agencies and departments was to involve: Prime Minister and Cabinet, Defence, the ADF, DFAT, the AFP, APS, Immigration, Customs, ASIO, Health, Family and Community Services, Centrelink, Parliament House, Transport and Regional Services, Emergency Management Australia, the Treasury, Finance and AusAID. The speed of the Australian response is an example of what can be achieved if consideration has been given to contingency planning and preparation:

> Within 24 hours: 20 government officials, nine DFAT and 14 AFP staff from Canberra and Jakarta on the ground in Bali. Operation headed by the Australian Embassy's Deputy Head of Mission from Jakarta. Staff placed

at Denpasar International Airport to facilitate departure of Australians and arrival of victim's relatives.[107]

By the fourth day, 80 staff comprising pathologists, odontologists, radiologists, forensic experts and police were working on the case.[108]

These members meshed with POLRI and other international police and pursued a joint investigation to identify the perpetrators and bring them to justice. This was made much easier by the fact that for many years, the AFP and POLRI had been conducting joint investigations and had shared intelligence in relation to criminal activities, such as drug trafficking, money laundering, fraud, child sex tourism and people smuggling. It is through this sort of collaboration that personal and professional relationships based on trust and mutual respect developed, and this formed the basis for Operation Alliance.

This cooperation and collaboration was not confined to the AFP and POLRI, as each Australian state and territory provided personnel and resources. International investigators and specialists from the U.S. Federal Bureau of Investigation (FBI), the German Federal Police, the London Met Anti-Terrorist Branch, the New Zealand Police, and police from Japan, France, South Korea, Hong Kong, Taiwan and Sweden also provided part of this international response. All of this took place in the sovereign nation of Indonesia, where international police, including the AFP, had no legal sovereignty. This was short-circuited by the Indonesian Government and a joint operations agreement was formalised between both governments on 18 October 2002 that outlined the command arrangements and formalised the basis upon which Australian and later other international participation was based under Operation Alliance. This streamlined much of the administrative and bureaucratic requirements to enable a whole-of-government and interagency approach to this incident.

While the Indonesian police, led by Brigadier General (Police) I Made Mangku Pastika, took the lead in the investigation, POLRI gave the AFP unprecedented access to the crime scene and witnesses from the very beginning and shared the task of analysing evidence in an open way. General Pastika worked closely with the lead AFP officer, Assistant Commissioner Graham Ashton, who said at the time:

> The dimension of the incident was such that a lot of the normal red tape-visa, quarantine clearances-were waived for us and that was an immediate sign from the Indonesian Government of their view of the importance of this issue. Since then, things have been fast-tracked-and continue to be fast-tracked. There is a whole-of-government approach to this and officials are co-operating elsewhere at a very high level.[109]

Arrest of Amrozi

Examination of the chassis of the van used to bomb the Sari Club revealed a chassis number. The original had been filed off, but in Bali, a second number was required. It was this number that revealed the van had been purchased by an individual named Amrozi, who was identified and arrested by POLRI. Upon questioning, Amrozi admitted that he had purchased the van and chemicals used to make the explosives and had attended meetings where the bombings were discussed and planned. He also identified his accomplices as Samudra, Idris and Dulmatin.

Disaster Victim Identification (DVI)

While the identification, arrest and interview of Amrozi was taking place, an extensive and painstaking DVI process was also occurring. DVI processes must comply with internationally recognised protocols, and a high degree of certainty is required before the remains of victims can be released to their relatives. The DVI process aims to accurately identify each victim by comparing and matching data available prior to death with post-mortem remains. This is done via a three-phase approach:

> The first phase involves collecting ante-mortem information such as physical descriptions, photographs of possible clothing and jewellery, fingerprints and DNA samples. The second, or post-mortem information collection phase, involves detailed examination by pathologists, odontologists, radiologists, forensic experts and police of the victim's remains. The third and final phase is the reconciliation of the collected information.
>
> It is only through this process that certainty of identification can be guaranteed. This certainty is needed not only for the victim's families' peace of mind but also for other legal processes and procedures that follow death.[110]

Domestic Response: Immediate

The AFP has had a presence at designated Australian international airports and in each mainland capital city since 1979. At each state and territory headquarters (Darwin, Brisbane, Sydney, Melbourne, Adelaide and Perth), the AFP established Major Incident Rooms (MIRs) with direct connectivity to the National Incident Co-ordination Centre in Canberra. The MIRs and the existence of AFP members at Australian international airports were a vital link between an international mass casualty event and its domestic implications and sped up the flow of information and evidence.

Thus, arrangements were already in place for the reception and evidence collection from returning victims. As the then General Manager Counter Terrorism, Assistant Commissioner Ben McDevitt, stated: 'We needed to be able to capture whatever information those people had. We also needed to gather any forensic evidence they might actually be wearing, including residue from the explosives.'[111] The efficacy of a national policing body, with representation in all mainland capitals and all international airports, was a major factor in securing information and evidence, as by 0230 on 13 October 2002, the first commercial flights, chartered by the Australian Government, evacuating survivors began arriving at Australian airports, where passengers were interviewed, statements were taken, and physical evidence was collected, by members of the AFP awaiting their arrival. This resulted in statements being taken from passengers from nineteen flights over a two-week period and the collation of information from 7340 passenger questionnaires, which led to 450 relevant leads.[112]

Why Police?

This response involved a great deal of contemporaneous activity, including the immediate response, forensic analysis, DVI and follow-up investigation. The incident involved a large number of victims from a wide range of countries:

> Of the 202 people who died there were 88 Australians; two Brazilians; 22 British; two Canadians; three Danes; four Dutch; one Ecuadorian; four French; six Germans; one Greek; 38 Indonesians; four French; two Japanese; three New Zealanders; one Pole; one Portuguese; two South Africans; two South Koreans; five Swedes; three Swiss; one Taiwanese; seven Americans and…three unidentified bodies.[113]

The investigations were conducted in accordance with internationally accepted standards at the actual crime scene, and the follow-up coordination at Australian international airports was greatly enhanced by the fact that the AFP was positioned nationally and was, thus, prepared for such a contingency.

The existing relationship with POLRI and the coordination with a range of other police agencies – both on the ground at the crime scenes in Bali and in Australia – with all state and territory police, in addition to other stakeholders, provides an example of professional operational policing as an effective form of international diplomacy with a direct link to the lives of ordinary citizens. It is this aspect of linking the community at the individual level that is prominent among the features that distinguish professional policing in terms of effective diplomacy. This is not an aspect of normal duties shared by other traditional international actors.

Police worldwide share certain features that make them uniquely placed to link many aspects of contemporary affairs. They include well-established relationships with the communities they serve; the authority to question, search, arrest suspects and seize material; well-established accountability measures and the legal authority to use force if required to enforce the extant law. Thus, there is an implicit understanding shared by all police officers worldwide and an ability to cooperate, communicate and collaborate, particularly in times of crisis.

International Policing

The bombings in Bali in October 2002 and the resultant Operation Alliance were significant milestones in the evolution of the AFP as an international police agency. The credibility gained from such a rapid and comprehensive response and the enhanced relationship with POLRI provided a foundation upon which a solid relationship continues to prosper. The respect for the eighty-eight Australians killed in Bali on that night is reflected in the fact that POLRI named their special operations police unit responsible for counter-terrorism activities 'Detachment 88'. The AFP responded along three primary lines of effort. The first was the immediate response to the incident. The first priority was to deal with the incident, which, as discussed, was made much easier by the existence of personal relationships and mutual respect based on professionalism. The heightened sense of security resulting from the 9/11 attacks in the US, then the Bali bombing in 2002 and others that were to follow uncovered a number of home-grown plots in Australia. The second was to further nurture the important relationship between POLRI and the AFP, which, despite the sometimes-acrimonious political relationship, steers a steady course between mutually respected professional organisations. As the AFP Commissioner Colvin stated in an address to the National Press Club in Canberra on 31 May 2017:

> Our relationship with the Indonesian National Police has for many years delivered outcomes that benefit both Australia and Indonesia's interests. This has been a resilient and continuous relationship despite the sometimes rocky diplomatic tensions between the Governments. Even more importantly, it has often been the catalyst for the broader bi-lateral relationship to come back on track.[114]

The third was to acknowledge that Australia indeed existed in a highly volatile region, and that the AFP is an asset that is multifaceted and highly professional. As a direct result, in 2004, two significant developments occurred. The first was the creation of the Jakarta Centre for Law Enforcement Cooperation (JCLEC), discussed immediately below, and the second was the IDG. (see Appendix 4). This approach emphasises the significance of the combined effect of cooperative police-to-police relationships and all that can derive from them, as well as a recognition that police interventions can restore trust in societies where there is a breakdown in trust and, therefore, address one of the precursors to violence.

Jakarta Centre for Law Enforcement Cooperation (JCLEC) 2004

The AFP maintains an International Liaison Officer Network in many locations of interest to Australian law enforcement. The largest of these posts is in Indonesia, with approximately thirty AFP personnel located in the Australian Embassy in Jakarta, in Bali and at the JCLEC, which is located within the Indonesian National Police Academy (AKPOL) in Semarang. It was established in November 2004 as an initiative of both the Australian and Indonesian governments arising as a direct result of the Bali bombings.

The trusting relationship between the AFP and POLRI has also provided entry into regional police forums such as the ASEANAPOL conferences. This has provided direct access to a highly diverse group of policing agencies in a region that is vital to Australia's interests. This is one aspect of police diplomacy, and it involves close cooperation at the strategic and operational levels based on issues of mutual interest.

Government and Academic Partners

The long-term development goal of the JCLEC is to contribute to the enhancement of the regional law-enforcement capacity to manage multi-jurisdictional investigations. It is primarily an education and training institution focusing on a cooperative relationship between Australian and Indonesian police, as well as other regional police representatives, and aims to disrupt transnational crime and violent extremism in the Asia-Pacific region. This includes (1) professional law enforcement education, (2) exchange of information and intelligence, (3) international law enforcement education standards and (4) emphasising the supremacy of the law.

JCLEC maintains relationships with the governments of Indonesia, Australia, Canada, New Zealand, Denmark, the U.S. Department State Diplomatic Security Service, the United Nations Office on Drugs and Crime, INTERPOL, and the Centre for International Legal Cooperation. Over 30,000 students from more than seventy countries have participated in several hundred training courses since it was established. The bulk of these students are from POLRI, but around 20 per cent of places are reserved for participants from other countries. JCLEC also engages with non-police law enforcement agencies, including those with border security, anti-corruption and judicial responsibilities.[115]

The establishment of JCLEC also maintains close affiliations with universities and other training centres in Australia and Indonesia, including the Australian Institute of Police Management (AIPM), Charles Sturt University and Griffith University in Australia, and Indonesia's own police colleges, the University of Indonesia, Gajah Mada University and University of Diponegero in Indonesia.

Another region in which Australia has had a long-term interest is the South West Pacific. However, the approach made by the AFP in this region is very different to that of Indonesia and Southeast Asia. The historical approach in the South West Pacific was along the lines of police capacity development, which commenced with a regional engagement in the troubled country to Australia's north-east, the Solomon Islands. This is another aspect of police diplomacy based on 'boots on the ground' involvement.

UNAMET and Consequential UN Security Council Resolutions

The failure of security by POLRI and the chaos and destruction which took place in East Timor after the ballot was announced on 4 September 1999 resulted in an immediate response by the UN in New York which had longer term implications for the AFP, and resulted in the establishment of the International Deployment Group in 2004.

On 8 September *A Report Of The UN Secretary General* was submitted to the UN Security Council.[116] This report does not identify East Timor or Indonesian specifically, but the timing and following commentary from the Secretary General make quite clear that the situation in East Timor was front of mind.

On 10 September 1999 UN Secretary-General Kofi Annan attempted to explain the failure of UNAMET to secure the province:

> 'We knew it was going to be difficult, we knew about the security problems, but not the carnage and the chaos we have seen. I can assure you that if those who were putting together the deal-and we must remember the agreement was signed by Portugal and Indonesia with the support of their leaders, unanimously endorsed by the [Security] Council-if any of us had an inkling that it was going to be this chaotic I don't think anyone would have gone forward...We are no fools.'[117]

Within a week the UN had passed a resolution condemning...the deliberate targeting of civilians in situations of armed conflict as well as attacks on objects protected under international law, and calls on all parties to put an end to such practices...and emphasised...the responsibility of States to end impunity and to prosecute those responsible for genocide, crimes against humanity and serious violations of international humanitarian law. This resolution recognised...the role of police in assuring the safety and well-being of civilians and, in this regard, acknowledges the need to enhance the capacity of the United Nations for the rapid deployment of qualified and well-trained civilian police...[118]

This in turn developed into two UN doctrines: The Responsibility to Protect and The Protection of Civilians.

The Responsibility to Protect (R2P) is a global political commitment which was endorsed by all member states of the United Nations at the 2005 World Summit in order to address its four key concerns to prevent genocide, war crimes, ethnic cleansing and crimes against humanity.

On 16 September 2005, Member States committed to the principle of the Responsibility to Protect by including it into the outcome document of that meeting (A/RES/60/1).

Within twelve months the UN published a Report of the Panel on United Nations Peace Operations on 21 August 2000, commonly referred to as The Brahimi Report, after its author.[119]

Between paras 118 and 126, this report makes specific mention of the importance of civilian police in Un operations and missions.

> Civilian police are second only to military forces in numbers of international personnel involved in United Nations peacekeeping operations. Demand for civilian police operations dealing with intra-State conflict is likely to remain high on any list of requirements for helping a war-torn society restore conditions for social, economic and political stability. The fairness and impartiality of the local police force, which civilian police monitor and train, is crucial to maintaining a safe and secure environment, and its effectiveness is vital where intimidation and criminal networks continue to obstruct progress on the political and economic fronts.
>
> ...a doctrinal shift in the use of civilian police in United Nations peace operations, to focus primarily on the reform and restructuring of local police forces in addition to traditional advisory, training and monitoring tasks. This shift will require Member States to provide the United Nations with even more well-trained and specialized police experts, at a time when they face difficulties meeting current requirements.
>
> ...the police component of a mission may comprise officers drawn from up to 40 countries who have never met one another before, have little or no United Nations experience, and have received little relevant training or mission-specific briefings, and whose policing practices and doctrines may vary widely.

Critically for the AFP and what was to become the International Deployment Group, between paras: 122 and 124, the reports states:

122. The Panel therefore calls upon Member States to establish national pools of serving police officers (augmented, if necessary, by recently retired police officers who meet the professional and physical requirements) who are administratively and medically ready for deployment to United Nations peace operations, within the context of the United Nations Standby Arrangements System. The size of the pool will naturally vary with each country's size and capacity. The Civilian Police Unit of DPKO should assist Member States in determining the selection criteria and training requirements for police officers within these pools, by identifying the specialities and expertise required and issuing common guidelines on the professional standards to be met. Once deployed in a United Nations mission, civilian police officers should serve for at least one year to ensure a minimum level of continuity.

The report recommended that police contributing nations...develop joint training exercises...regional training partnerships...offer assistance (e.g., training and equipment) to smaller police-contributing States to maintain the requisite level of preparedness...

124. The Panel also recommends that Member States designate a single point of contact within their governmental structures to be responsible for coordinating and managing the provision of police personnel to United Nations peace operations.

At para 126, a summary of key recommendations on civilian police personnel was provided recommending that police contributing countries:

- establish a national pool of civilian police officers that would be ready for deployment to United Nations peace operations on short notice
- enter into regional training partnerships for civilian police in the respective national pools in order to promote a common level of preparedness
- designate a single point of contact within their governmental structures for the provision of civilian police to United Nations peace operations

This was the basis upon which the International Deployment Group was founded in 2004, which followed Australian engagement in the Regional Assistance Mission to the Solomon Islands in 2003 in which the AFP played a leading part. This will be discussed in Part III.

The next major involvement Australia had in relation to the United Nations was a non-permanent member of the UN Security Council between 2013 and 2014. The roles the AFP played in both East Timor/Timor Leste and the Solomon Islands was used to underpin the legitimacy and credibility of Australia as a nation in the pursuit of the ideals of the UN, such as peace, justice, security and democracy, occasionally at great risk to deployed members involved.

During this term on the UN Security Council Australia was instrumental in passing two UN Security Council Resolutions relevant to Un Peacekeeping and police. These were 2014 UN Security Council Resolution 2151: Security Sector Reform[120] and Resolution 2185 United Nations peacekeeping operations S/RES/2185 (2014).[121]

These will be discussed in more detail in Part V of this book.

To formalize the adoption of the doctrines of the Responsibility to Protect and the Protection of Civilians, the AFP and ADF co-signed the Australian Guidelines on the Protection of Civilians[122] in December 2015. This was brokered by the Australian Civil Military Centre (ACMC). The author played a role in this as the AFP Adviser to the ACMC at that time.

While these guidelines focused on the AFP and ADF they were intended to provide a shared understanding across the whole-of-government arena, when engaged in offshore missions and operations.

The Guidelines state that:

> Australia plays a significant role in enhancing POC globally. During our 2013–14 UN Security Council term, Australia advocated for strengthening POC in Security Council mandates and sponsored Resolution 2185 on the role of police in peacekeeping, which emphasised the central role of the protection of civilians.
>
> The Guidelines confirm Australia's commitment to POC in accordance with international law and UN General Assembly and Security Council Resolutions. They are consistent with existing legal and policy frameworks and draw on best practice from the field.

The legacy of UNAMET is manifold. Not only did it secure a path of eventual independence of Timor Leste, it created the precursor for violent jihadist activities in Indonesia, and provided the basis for the genesis and formalisation of important humanitarian doctrines of the Responsibility to Protect and the Protection of Civilians. Sadly, these are being ignored in contemporary conflicts, including by Permanent Five (P5) of the UN Security Council, bringing the credibility of the UN into question. This is discussed in part V of this book.

The next major AFP regional engagement was the Regional Assistance Mission to the Solomon Islands (RAMSI), and further into the South West Pacific, which will be discussed in the next Part.

Part III

Capacity-building and the New Security Paradigm 2003–2014

The Solomon Islands, the South West Pacific and Papua New Guinea

Regional Assistance Mission to the Solomon Islands (RAMSI) 129
United Nations was Not Involved 130
Australian Government Change of Mind 131
Whole of Government and Region 132
Diplomats, Police and Soldiers 134
Independence 135
Request for Help 136
Road to Peace 137
Operation 'Helpem Fren': Engaging Armed Offenders 139
Harold's Day in Court 140
The Participating Police Force and Disarmament 141
Justice Being Done, & Being Seen Done 141
Path to Sovereignty: Re-arming Police 142
People's Survey 143
The Success of RAMSI 144
Implications of RAMSI for Pacific Region 145
Legacy for Solomon Islands 146
The Pacific and Establishment of International Deployment Group 147
The Pacific, Arc of Instability and Howard Doctrine 149
The Pacific: Early Claims 150
Colonisation and Principle of Effective Occupation 151
Pacific Governance 151
Pacific Regional Policing Initiative/Pacific Police Development Program 152
Years 2004–2008: Pacific Regional Policing Initiative 152
Year 2006: Howard Doctrine Faces Challenges in Pacific 153
Melanesian Spearhead Group 153
Enhanced Cooperation Project-PNG 2005 153
Solomon Islands: Prime Minister Sogavare and Julian Moti 2006 153
Prime Minister Sogavare Replaced by Prime Minister Sikua 2007 155
Timor-Leste: Dili Riots July 2006 156
Withdrawal of Fiji Police Commissioner Andrew Hughes 2006 157
Fiji-military Coup 2006 158
Year 2008: IDG Establishes Pacific Police Development Program 159
Samoa-Australian Police Partnership: SAPP-2009 160
Vanuatu Australia Police Project (VAPP) 2011 161
Pacific Islands Chiefs of Police 161
Pacific Transnational Crime Network 2004 162
Pacific Police Training Advisory Group 2011 162
Papua New Guinea, Early Colonialism 163
Independence 164
Urbanisation 164
Crime 165
Cape York Peninsula and Torres Strait 167
Enhanced Cooperation Program 2004–2005 167
Enhanced Cooperation Treaty 2004 168
Papua New Guinea Policing Partnership 2008– 'Wok Wantaim' 169
Regional Resettlement Program with Papua New Guinea 170
Future Trends 172
Melanesian Spearhead Group (MSG) and PNG 173
Australia–PNG Relationships 173

The concept of an 'Arc of Instability' to Australia's north has its roots in the perspective that Australia's main strategic priorities lie in its immediate neighbourhood. In this part, the way in which disrupted, unstable or fragile Pacific states pose a risk to Australia, particularly if they fall under influences inimical to Australia's interests or those of the broader Western alliance, is discussed. Such threats need not necessarily be foreign powers using military force; they can take the form of malign non-state actors such as organised crime groups or violent extremists unduly or unlawfully imposing their will to the detriment and peace of the communities concerned. They also involve the potential to exert influence on political elites' posture on things like access to sea lines of communication (SLOCs), which are vital for Australia as a trading nation and a vulnerability in times of conflict.

The underlying security and stability challenges need not be external or visible; they can often be internal and largely unseen, for example, in the form of political corruption and eventual social breakdown, or the other extreme, oppressive regime-protection styles of policing. This can create an erosion of host-nation institutional trust to the extent that international intervention is required. A number of these nations in Australia's neighbourhood are recipients of Australian foreign aid funding. History shows that the expectation in this region is that Australia will shoulder the burden of such interventions, although the PRC has now entered the field of strategic aid delivery in this region, including police assistance and advisory roles, which sets the scene for a bidding war between donors. The economic cost associated with such interventions is publicly funded, and the Australian taxpayer should quite justifiably expect that Australian taxes, so allocated, are being spent wisely and appropriately. The reality is that the limit to the funds available for foreign aid must be balanced with domestic political priorities. In a liberal democracy, for any government to remain in power, this expenditure should be as transparent as possible to enable electors to make their own judgements at the ballot box. Not so in an autocracy such as the PRC, which is already engaging in its own version of 'police diplomacy' which is perceived by some, as a foot in the door for further political influence and a possible change in the political systems concerned. This has the potential to entrench political elites and for the police to be used in a regime protection capacity rather than as an institution which respects and protects the rights of the community.

The Regional Assistance Mission to the Solomon Islands (RAMSI)

The 1999 intervention in East Timor, to Australia's north-west, has been discussed in the context of mixed success due to circumstances in its very inception in late 1998 and early 1999, and a highly flawed security agreement, which were largely out of the hands of the Australian Government. The next major 'boots on the ground' policing intervention involving the AFP was in the Solomon Islands, to Australia's north-east, commencing in 2003. It incorporated many of the lessons learned from the East Timor intervention in the preceding years. This was especially true in relation to a strong security posture and maximum Australian Government control over the planning and implementation of the intervention.

It was recognised by the Australian Government that a preventative strategy in the greater Pacific was an approach that would benefit both the local communities through higher quality policing and Australia as a donor through better relationships with more capable local police. According to Byrnes, 'Law and justice assistance became a foreign policy and development priority during the first decade of the 2000s, against a strategic backdrop of state fragility in our region.'[1]

The result was a better police-to-police relationship between the AFP and the host nation police in the Pacific, which is in line with the AFP's mandate of fighting, or at least deterring, crime offshore or at its source. From an operational policing perspective, the ultimate aim of such police interventions should be a strong, reliable, trust-based police-to-police relationship. This is different to the relationship police have with their own communities, which is their own form of social contract. From a community and host-government perspective, the relationships between the host government and the community should ideally be trust-based and culturally appropriate. Hence, the Australian Government made some considered decisions when deploying police in the troubled South West Pacific nation of the Solomon Islands.

The first and largest police mission in the Pacific was RAMSI, which was established in 2003, despite some reticence by senior politicians and their departmental advisors. It was Prime Minister John Howard who was the driving force behind the establishment of the RAMSI intervention. This was based on a renewed assertiveness and well-founded confidence in the two primary arms of international intervention, the diplomats and the military, as well as the 'third force', the AFP, whose members had acquitted themselves well in East Timor from 1999 and in response to the Bali bombings in 2002.

The United Nations was Not Involved

RAMSI had unique features that contributed to its success. Perhaps most importantly, it was Australian-led and deployed at the specific request of the Solomon Islands Government of Prime Minister Kemakeza. As Braithwaite et al. identified, Kemakeza had only approached the UN twice, both times in 2002, but it did not have the capacity to respond because the effect 'of Solomon's diplomatic recognition of Taiwan would be that China would veto any Security Council resolution to step up assistance...the United Nations played a more marginal role than is normally the case with an international peace operation'.[2] According to Breen, it was the opinion of the Australian Government that a United Nations force would not be able to solve the problems facing the Solomon Islands and that any such intervention by the UN would risk displacing the Solomon Islands Police and risk initiating a prolonged occupation by international military and police forces.[3]

Australian Government Change of Mind

The problems faced by the Kemakeza government in Honiara were significant, including extortion and political corruption to the extent that the Solomon Islands was on the verge of state failure; it was running out of funds to pay for essential services. In February 2003, Elsina Wainwright of the ASPI drafted a paper on the Solomon Islands, *Our Failing Neighbour*,[4] that was distributed by Hugh White, then the head of ASPI. The paper proposed an Australian-led multinational mission to assist in restoring law and order in the Solomon Islands.

The paper prompted Prime Minister Kemakeza to write to Prime Minister Howard requesting intervention by Australia. The request was not welcomed by the Australian High Commissioner to the Solomon Islands, who advised Canberra that:

> it was most unfortunate that ASPI had stimulated unrealistic expectations. Kemakeza was now tenaciously committed to an armed regional peacekeeping force. In Kemakeza's opinion, the Solomon Islands people would welcome such a force, provided that it could improve the law and order situation.[5]

Officials from the Prime Minister and Cabinet, Defence and DFAT prepared a paper in response to Kemakeza's letter that emphasised the intractability of Solomon Island's problems and stressed the risks and high costs of intervention. According to Breen, the report indicated that:

> [n]o intervention force could reshape the political culture of Solomon Islands. At best, it would give the Solomon Islands Government breathing space by securing Honiara and allowing the government to operate without the threat of violence, and to begin to purge the Solomon Islands Police and regain control of public finances.
>
> This outcome was precisely what Howard and, eventually, Downer had in mind-a circuit breaker to create a secure environment for recovery, not a panacea for all the problems facing Solomon Islands.[6]

The major Australian departments, Prime Minister and Cabinet, Foreign Affairs and Trade and Defence, were of a like mind that the Solomon Islands 'had not hit rock bottom' and that the endemic lawlessness and corruption was 'not sufficiently threatening to Australia's interests to warrant the cost of intervention on the scale required'. The decision rested on whether the Australian Government was willing to 'pay the price and take the risk of deploying Australian police and soldiers to deter, disarm and bring to justice those in Solomon Islands who were destroying its polity'.[7]

As a result, the ASPI paper caused reconsideration at many levels. Prime Minister Kemakeza read it and was supportive. He was in a perilous situation and had been rebuffed by the UN. Australian officials from both DFAT and Defence were against any intervention, as was Foreign Minister Downer initially, as Stephanie Koorey states:

> In January 2003, then Australian Foreign Minister Alexander Downer emphatically stated that Australia would not be sending troops to Solomon Islands. Downer contended that not only would such an intervention 'fail to solve the problem' but he was particularly acute to potential allegations of 'recolonisation', and decried the idea as 'folly in the extreme'.[8]

The Foreign Minister and the Defence Minister, however, changed their minds after consulting Prime Minister Howard, who had read the departmental report himself and had been reminded of Australia's responsibilities in its own region by U.S. President Bush upon his last visit to the U.S., as Breen explains:

> Howard disagreed with the departmental paper arguing against intervention in Solomon Islands, which he read on the plane after speaking with Bush. He decided then and there to confer with Downer and Hill on his return to Australia and to have them direct their departments to examine options for intervention.[9]

Whole-of-Government and Whole-of-Region

At the insistence of Prime Minister Howard and Foreign Minister Downer, there were several criteria that underpinned any possible deployment to the Solomon Islands. First, it had to be at the express invitation of the Government of the Solomon Islands; second, it had to be endorsed by the Pacific Islands Forum; and third, it had to involve police and military contributions from the Pacific Islands Forum member states. This was a watershed decision: 'Howard and Downer moved Australia from a "whole-of-government" approach to Solomon Islands to a "whole-of-region" approach.'[10]

The ASPI paper overturned the prevailing attitude in Canberra policy circles, which was based on a reluctance to intervene for fear of being perceived as 'neo-colonial'. This failed to recognise that the international community, via the UN and other organisations, was intervening in failing and failed states around the globe. This included the new nations of Timor-Leste in Australia's own region, whose extant status was due in large part to Australian intervention.[11] Both Breen and Braithwaite further argued that the attacks in September 2001 and the bombing in Bali in October 2002 influenced Prime Minister Howard's perspective on the region towards a more robust posture.

The 2003 ASPI paper also mentioned Australia's reluctance to intervene based on a lack of contemporary relevance. This appeared to be the opinion of the strategic advisors from the traditional diplomatic and military fields and arguably not from the AFP, whose concerns about transnational crime and other malign actors did not appear to register with the traditional policy advisors; the latter's emphasis remained steeped in traditional and somewhat anachronistic diplomatic, inter-state and defence-oriented relations. However, Breen identifies that the possibility of transnational organised crime or other malign activity was acknowledged and that an occupation:

> of Solomon Islands by a military power was unlikely, if Solomon Islands became a so-called failed state, there was potential for it to become a source or transit point for criminal and terrorist activities, that might affect Australia, as well as other countries in the region.[12]

Part of this thinking incorporated the non-military threats mentioned above, although, as Braithwaite identifies, the prospect of transnational criminals or terrorists gaining a foothold in the Solomon Islands was not a high risk:

> When Prime Minister Howard announced the intervention, he referred to the risk of the Solomons becoming a safe haven for 'transnational criminals and even terrorists'. It seemed implausible to people who knew the Solomons well that it could be a hospitable safe haven for transnational criminals or terrorists.[13]

Nonetheless, the Howard government pursued this policy of an Australian-led multilateral intervention of state-building until the job was done. This was based on Prime Minister Howard and Foreign Minister Downer concluding that failing states in Australia's region were a threat to Australian national security and regional stability. In this thinking, they were encouraged by the success of the Australian-led intervention in East Timor in 1999. As a result, they advocated for 'an armed Australian-led regional peace support force to act as a circuit breaker on violence in Solomon Islands, to coerce weapons disposal and to facilitate the rebuilding of its polity'.[14] The AFP led the security aspect of this mission with military support.

Diplomats, Police and Soldiers, In That Order

The AFP then began planning in earnest. Two AFP members drafted a basic four-phased plan in May 2003, which was called at that stage the Solomon Island Law Enforcement Mission (SILEM). This involved four contemporaneous phases: (1) 'separation' – arrest and detain 16 major militia commanders and criminals, (2) 'top down' – retrench senior Royal Solomon Islands Police (RSIP) and Field Force Special Constables, search homes with a view to arrest and prosecution, (3) 'recovery' – locate and impound all high-powered weapons and (4) 'enclaved lockdown' – cordon and search of Honiara-establish quarantine perimeter-checkpoints.[15]

The casual observer may ask: why the police and not the military? The answer is that the Solomon Islands situation was unique in many ways, which meant that police, as part of a broader law and justice mission, were a more appropriate instrument than the military. There are many reasons for this. The first is that the Solomon Islands does not have its own military. Security and public safety were the exclusive responsibility of the Royal Solomon Islands Police, and they had failed in this duty. The second is that the deterioration of the security situation was essentially a law-and-order problem and, thus, best addressed by a law-and-order agency: the police.

This was recognised by the first by the Australian Special Coordinator from Australia's Department of Foreign Affairs, which had overall authority over RAMSI, Nick Warner, who stated:

> Because of the purely criminal nature of most of their activities, it was decided that we would approach the former militants as a policing issue. After we arrived, teams of RAMSI police investigators were formed to investigate the many crimes that had been committed in recent years, mostly by former militants. These investigations were conducted quickly, but without fanfare.[16]

Contrastingly, Braithwaite (2010) stated:

> [t]he size of the intervention was much more than was needed. RAMSI Special Coordinator Nick Warner has said this was an explicit policy of 'shock and awe'…helicopters dropping troops in visible locations, landing barges crashing onto the beach loaded with troops…It worked in immediately transforming the climate of security…RAMSI replaced the rule of the gun with the rule of law very quickly.[17]

In this very visible sense, the military was extremely important.[18] Learning a lesson from the precarious and highly flawed security arrangement in UNAMET, where unarmed UNCIVPOL and electoral volunteers were exposed to a high level of risk at the hands of extremely violent Indonesian-backed militia groups, a large Australian military show of force was deployed in support of RAMSI to persuade anyone who may have been considering an armed challenge to RAMSI to reconsider. As stated by Warner upon his arrival in Honiara in 2003, 'Our immediate purpose is to restore law and order...should criminals seek to sabotage our assistance efforts, endanger public safety, or prevent the police from doing their duty, the military will not hesitate to act.'[19]

This was reflective of the proverbial posture to 'speak softly and carry a big stick'.[20] A full-scale military intervention into an island nation of approximately 500,000 people by a first world nation such as Australia could have had disastrous consequences for Australia's international standing, and allegations of neo-colonialism may well have been justified. The police, on the other hand, although uniformed, armed and responsive, provided a much lower profile more appropriate to the circumstances. This was 'firm' power which was as much about governance as it was about conflict. Some background on this 'road to crisis' in 2003 is required to explain why Australia, specifically the AFP, intervened. The troubles in the Solomon Islands date back to independence from Britain in 1978, the power vacuum that was filled by corrupt and criminal actors and the downward spiral towards state failure.

Independence

The decade of the 1970s saw a well-intentioned global move towards self-determination and the independence of former colonial possessions, which was encouraged by the UN but exploited by Cold War power blocs. This brought with it several challenges in relation to peace and stability as colonial administrations withdrew. Australia's immediate region has had its fair share of this experience, and Australia responded accordingly, but not always immediately. Following the independence of PNG from Australia in 1975, the Solomon Islands, a former British Protectorate, gained self-government in 1976 and full independence from Britain in 1978. It was not of strategic significance in the Cold War context, so it was essentially abandoned by Britain and left to its own devices.

The first Solomon Islands Constitution was created in 1970, but it was challenged, and a new Constitution was created in 1974. The withdrawal of colonial forces left a leadership vacuum filled by poor governance and foreign exploitation, which led to rampant corruption. With no effective political leadership, several militias emerged, and the situation descended into violence, the fronts of which were drawn on ethnic and geographic lines. Many of the issues faced by the Solomon Islands were the same as those faced by many other nations emerging from a colonial past: corruption, foreign-based resource exploitation, urban drift, high youth unemployment and the resultant crimes against person and property. A factionalised overlay complicated matters further.

Decades of deterioration in social cohesion culminated in a period known as the 'tensions' in the late 1990s, where resentment based on which ethnic group one belonged to, which originated from different islands in the archipelago, developed into violent clashes. The two main ethnic groups were the Malaitans and the Guadalcanal people (Guales), each of which formed their own armed elements: the Guales formed the Guadalcanal Revolutionary Army (GRA), otherwise known as the Isatabu Freedom Movement (IFM), and the Malaitans formed the Malaitan Eagle Force (MEF). Violent clashes between these groups further destabilised an already fragile environment.[21] AFP RAMSI Commander Ben McDevitt explains that the first aggressors appeared to be Guadalcanal people who resented the concentration of Malaitans in Honiara:

> At the height of this conflict some 20000 Malaitans were forced, through fear and intimidation, to flee their homes in Guadalcanal and return to Malaita. Young, dispossessed and aggrieved youth took up arms and clashes between rival groups became commonplace.[22]

Societal cohesion had broken down to such an extent that its primary features were '…guns, ethnic tensions, rogue police, corrupt politicians and business people, and armed criminals'. The Government of the Solomon Islands recognised that it was facing a set of problems that were beyond its own capabilities to resolve and sought assistance from its larger neighbour, Australia, but these approaches were initially rebuffed, so the situation deteriorated further.

Request for Help

The AFP for many years placed its representation in the South West Pacific region in the South Pacific International Liaison Officer (SPILO), one of whom was John Murray. His book, *The Minnows of Triton* (2005), provides a comprehensive background to the circumstances in the region in the 1980s and 1990s. Murray wrote:

> A number of requests made by the Solomon Islands Government to the governments of Australia and New Zealand for stability assistance were

rejected. Anecdotal information suggests that an overriding fear of criticism based on 'neo colonialism' prevailed in many influential circles.

Actual reasons cited for this rejection included that any intervention would not be supported by the Pacific region; that Australian taxpayers would not support any intervention; that intervention would require a long-term strategy with an ill-defined exit point, and it was believed that foreigners would lack a solution to what was perceived as a local cultural problem. Also among the reasons was an apparent reluctance for an Australian police Commissioner to use armed force.[23]

There were some compelling reasons that Australia might become involved linked to Australia's national interests by virtue of malign non-state actors gaining a foothold in such a fragile nation due to anaemic or corrupted policing so close to Australia because:

> a dysfunctional Solomon Islands held long term dangers for Australia and the region. A country beholden to armed thugs is a recipe for chronic instability…[s]uch instability is an open invitation to transnational crime. Experience elsewhere shows that weak states are also attractive as havens for money laundering, people smuggling, drug smuggling and terrorism. And while there was no evidence that transnational criminals were targeting Solomon Islands, there was no point waiting for this to happen.[24]

There was a recognition by some that action was required, but a breakthrough did not happen until the signing of the Townsville Peace Agreement (TPA) in the year 2000.

The Road to Peace

Murray provides a snapshot of the situation in the Solomon Islands. As many as 1100 armed Malaitan 'special' members of the RSIP:

> remained on the police payroll while engaging in torture, rape and the burning of 'enemy' villages. Murder and banditry went unabated elsewhere with former police employee Harold Keke and his gang held responsible for multiple abductions and massacres in the Weathercoast region of Guadalcanal including the killing of cabinet minister/Catholic priest Father Augustine Geve…many ranking officers became complicit in supplying MEF militants with weapons from the police armoury.[25]

In June 2000, MEF militants with rogue RSIP members formed a paramilitary unit known as the Joint Operations Force, which seized control of key installations and took Prime Minister Ulufa'alu hostage. He resigned in exchange for his release. He was replaced as Prime Minister in late June 2000 by Manassah Sogovare, who had previously been Finance Minister.

He was then replaced in December 2001 by Allen Kemakeza. According to Murray, during this six-month period, Sogovare had 'entered into arrangements with what was effectively a mercenary group to counter any opposition to the outcomes of the MEF cadres'.[26] This was the Solomon Islands Peace Monitoring Organisation (SIPMO).

SIPMO was formed in Melbourne and was codenamed Operation Unity. Its stratagem was to overcome by force 'those recalcitrant elements identified as a threat to the MEF's total assumption of control'. This plan was kept well out of the public domain and was later abandoned. Its initial planning used terminology such as 'neutralise the opposition', 'robust arrangements', 'rapid deployment', and 'enforce compliance'. It was intended that SIPMO operatives would possess sophisticated weaponry, explosives, marine resources and a BK 117 twin-engine multi-mission helicopter – a 'force multiplier' with the ability to fly 'hot and high' – with the purpose of deploying armed personnel throughout the islands.[27] This was partisan politics writ large with the real risk of ethnic cleansing.

Clearly, this was a situation Canberra could ill-afford to allow to continue in a Commonwealth country so close to its shores. This reinvigorated the impetus for Australian and New Zealand diplomatic assistance to bring militants to the negotiating table, which took place aboard HMAS *Tobruk* in July 2000. This concluded with a ceasefire agreement on 3 August 2000, and it created the momentum for further peace talks that became known as the Townsville Peace Agreement (TPA), which took place in Townsville, North Queensland in October 2000.

The TPA was signed by MEF, elements of IFM and the Solomon Islands Government and was followed by the Marau Peace Agreement in February 2001, signed by the MEF, IFM, Guadalcanal Provincial Government and the Solomon Islands Government. However, it was not signed by Harold Keke, the Guadalcanal militant leader, who was to become instrumental in the eventual restoration of order in the region. The indigenous SIPMO was charged with the responsibility of implementing the peace agreement with the assistance of the International Peace Monitoring Team (IPMT), which had been established under the TPA. The IPMT was largely ineffective and withdrew in June 2002.

Lawlessness continued, although Australia continued to assist – with help from a Law and Justice Sector Program aimed at strengthening the police, prison and legal services – the work of the National Peace Council, the United Nations Development Program project for the Demobilisation of Special Constables by providing financial support, and the police with communications and logistics support. In February 2003, shortly after the

British police Commissioner William Morrell arrived to replace former police Commissioner Morton Sirheti, Fred Soaki, was shot dead while dining at a hotel. Soaki was a member of the National Peace Council and was due to chair a Commission of Inquiry into the causes of civil unrest, which created misgivings among many people in positions of influence. A police sergeant, Edmund Sae, was arrested for the crime but escaped custody with relative ease.

Civil unrest continued. The Department of Finance, for instance, was surrounded by armed men when cash was due to arrive. There was a prevailing atmosphere of lawlessness, violence and extortion with an inadequate police response, which is what prompted Prime Minister Kemakeza to seek formal assistance from Australian Prime Minister Howard in April 2003, but only, as discussed earlier, after a request for United Nations intervention was deemed impossible due to the Chinese veto in the UN Security Council over diplomatic recognition of Taiwan by the Solomon Islands Government.

Following consultations between the governments of the Solomon Islands, Australia and New Zealand, a package of strengthened assistance was proposed and endorsed unanimously at a meeting of the Foreign Ministers of the Pacific Islands Forum (PIF). It was debated and endorsed by the Solomon Islands Parliament through the Facilitation of International Assistance Act 2003, commended by the UN Secretary-General Kofi Annan and supported by the Commonwealth's Ministerial Action Group and Secretary-General. This level of regional and international endorsement underwrote RAMSI's legitimacy.

Operation 'Helpem Fren': Engaging Armed Offenders by Negotiation, Not Enemies by Armed Force

The AFP Commander of the RAMSI Participating Police Force (PPF), Ben McDevitt, adopted a strategy of targeting Keke because he was seen by Solomon Islanders as 'almost like a demon'. The significance of this approach was that Keke was treated not as an enemy in a military sense but as an armed offender in a police sense. There is a major difference, and this approach proved to be successful. Braithwaite records that McDevitt wrote to Keke on 25 July 2003 offering to guarantee his safety in custody in return for surrendering weapons and submitting to justice. Keke replied in writing that he wanted peace and was willing to surrender 'as long as the first priority is to disarm the militants in Honiara and get rid of corrupt politicians'.[28]

Keke's Guadalcanal Liberation Front had declared a unilateral ceasefire on 5 July 2003, three weeks before McDevitt's letter.[29] A direct message was sent in a letter to all militants from Warner and McDevitt:

> In our talks with militia leaders, we have made it very clear that we are not here to negotiate or make deals…It is in your interest to hand in all guns. Anyone found with a gun after midnight 21 August will be breaking the law and will face up to 10 years in prison and a S$25,000 fine…We are able to deal with any situation and track down illegal weapons. We will not be stopped by threats or intimidation.[30]

This approach eventually allowed McDevitt to negotiate the peaceful surrender and arrest of Keke on 13 August to face criminal charges. Two weeks after the arrival of RAMSI, Warner and McDevitt met with Keke in his own village. They told him it was time to end the conflict, and it was best to pursue matters through legal processes, where he would have an opportunity to tell his side of the story. He was informed that he had an outstanding arrest warrant and that he would have to give himself up at some stage.

Negotiations took place over three meetings, after which Keke and some of his key commanders surrendered. Breen states that Keke was originally arrested for aggravated burglary and the theft of an outboard motor to persuade him to agree to accompany police to the RAMSI Headquarters in Honiara for further questioning. He was accompanied by his family in special accommodation at the Guadalcanal Beach resort, which was the RAMSI Headquarters. He was also accompanied by his Chief of Operations, Ronnie Cawa, who had ordered most of the murders, executions and other atrocities on the Weather Coast. He apparently boarded the helicopter because he had never been in one before.

Harold's Day in Court

Upon the departure of Keke and Cawa, it is reported that around fifty members of Keke's Guadalcanal Liberation Front militia held a formal parade after Keke and his entourage had left and handed in their weapons. One man raised his arm and loudly declared, 'The war is over!' and others joined the chant: 'The war is over! The war is over!' As indicated by McDevitt, Keke ultimately surrendered to have his day in court: 'He wanted to tell his side of the story about what had happened to him and I think that was a pretty powerful incentive for him-one of several. He wanted to say how he had been wronged.'[31]

On 18 March 2005, Keke and Cawa were sentenced to life in prison for the murder of former Cabinet Minister and clergyman Father Augustine Geve at Mbiti in 2002.[32] According to Braithwaite, Keke 'was a mentally unstable man who had convinced others of his mystical indestructibility'.[33] This was confirmed by Special Coordinator Warner:

Keke's behaviour was erratic and unpredictable. Just before our arrival seven Anglican brothers from the order of Melanesian Brothers who had been taken hostage by Keke's followers in May, were killed. Keke's surrender was a key milestone in RAMSI's operations. Other militants and police had used his belligerency as a justification for holding onto weapons. After his arrest, there were no more excuses. Keke's arrest was another major confidence boost for the whole country, especially on Guadalcanal where many had lived in fear of his raids.[34]

This was the catalyst for the seizure and public destruction of weapons, which in itself had a positive, profound and visible influence. A 21-day amnesty, between 31 July and 21 August 2003, was announced by Prime Minister Kemakeza. Anyone found in possession of a firearm after that date would be subject to a 10-year term of imprisonment. This had an immediate effect, and firearms were handed over in large numbers.[35]

The Participating Police Force (PPF) and Disarmament

As the RSIP had been disarmed, the management of crime was left to the PPF, which was under the command of RAMSI. The PPF consisted of police representatives from fourteen Pacific Island nations, which gave a 'Pacific face' to this intervention. These PPF members were recruited locally in their own countries and trained in Australia by the AFP at the IDG facility at Majura. In a similar fashion to the UN police in East Timor during the UNTAET mission, the international police in RAMSI performed an executive policing function and actually enforced the criminal laws of the Solomon Islands.

The PPF set about disarming the militants, and 'more than 3730 weapons and more than 30000 rounds of ammunition were removed from the militia. About 700 of those were high-powered military style weapons'.[36] These were destroyed publicly before large crowds of onlookers 'in a potent display of our commitment to ridding the nation of firearms'.[37]

Justice Being Done and Being Seen to be Done

In addition to the arrest of Keke and the disarming of the police and the militants, the PPF, led by the AFP, commenced investigating and prosecuting the offenders, who had been the cause of so much of the political instability:

> Dozens of senior police…along with politicians and bureaucrats were put before the courts and imprisoned for rapes, murders, abductions, thefts and falsification of accounts. Andrew Nori was charged with corruptly receiving SI$5 million and Alexander Bartlett for illegally importing firearms, demanding money with menaces, arson, lodging false compensation claims and inciting to commit offences. Justice Minister Michael Maina had to

explain a theft of SI$15000, while former ministers Kemakeza, Benjamin Una and Francis Zama faced a spectrum of corruption and office-based abuse claims. Ex backbencher John Maetia was arrested on 10 charges for obtaining over SI$198000 and attempting to solicit a further SI$14000 for supplying naturalisation certificates for Chinese nationals.[38]

By July 2004, 3316 people had been arrested on 4788 charges. This success was made possible through evidence collected and secreted by Royal Solomon Islands Police (RSIP) who remained loyal during the tensions. Similarly, the security situation in the Solomon Islands had stabilised to such a degree that military personnel were drawn down in the second half of 2004…Eventually 25 percent of the RSIP was either arrested and charged with corruption offences or discharged from the force. More widely, an ombudsman, a magistrate, numerous lawyers, multiple public servants, corrections officers and four government ministers were arrested in a very public and transparent cleansing of corruption.[39]

This was not only justice being done but was justice being seen to be done, which had a positive effect on restoring public confidence and societal trust. The PPF, in which the AFP was significantly represented, was instrumental in this effort. In this way, RAMSI continued for the next decade, during which time the PPF gradually stepped back from front line policing roles and allowed the newly reconstituted and renamed, but still unarmed, Royal Solomon Islands Police Force (RSIPF) to assume more general policing duties.

On the Path to Sovereignty: Re-arming the Police

This set in motion a gradual rearmament of the RSIPF beginning with PPF-trained CPP members responsible for the armed protection of high office holders and visiting foreign dignitaries, and Airport Police, which is in accordance with international requirements. Both sections were trained by AFP trainers and mentors. The re-arming of the police created some disquiet in some sections of the Solomon Islands community, whose trust in the police remained low. In 2013, RSIPF Commissioner Matthew Varley, himself on secondment from the AFP, acknowledged these concerns but identified that:

> More than two thirds of the RSIPF has been recruited since the tension period. We've had heavy investment in training by RAMSI and development over that time. The officers that are involved in this limited rearmament program have been trained to the highest standards and I'm pretty confident that those officers are well disciplined and ready to take on that extra responsibility.[40]

RAMSI finally withdrew after fourteen years on 30 June 2017, leaving behind forty-five AFP members with the Solomon Islands Police Development Program (SIPDP) to continue to advise the RSIPF. This then became the

RAPPP, the Royal Solomon Islands-Australia Police Partnership Program. The RAMSI mission is broadly lauded as a success. One commentator in 2009 remarked:

> From the beginning, the AFP/IDG contribution to RAMSI has been marked by a number of achievements. The first of these was the ability of the Mission to rapidly deploy to the Solomon Islands and diffuse the turmoil that was spreading across the country. By achieving this tasking through regional consensus and collaboration rather than using direct assistance from the United Nations, a model has been established for Pacific intervention that is both more responsive and less cumbersome than traditional peace-keeping models. This success is what prompted the establishment of the IDG in 2004 and has led the Australian Government to adopt a policy preference toward law and order as the lynchpin of stability in the Oceanic region. Furthermore, the emphasis on achieving law and order as a means toward nation-building has put the AFP at the forefront of Australia's regional security program.[41]

The People's Survey

One feature of RAMSI that helped maintain direction and connection with the Solomon Islands community was the People's Survey. A selection of statistics and comments is provided below, from which some conclusions can be drawn about the popularity of RAMSI, the issues that have been addressed and the issues that remain.

In 2006, 92 per cent of respondents considered youth unemployment as a threat to security. In 2008, many respondents considered gang-based violence among unemployed youth to be a response to disempowerment in an unforgiving urban environment. Nepotism and 'wantokism' (see Appendix 6 The Melanesian Wantok system) were consistently seen as problems, particularly within the political and police circles. Some understood that this was a 'cultural expectation'.

In 2009:

> Weak policing and a poorly disciplined police force were frequently mentioned as contributing to law and order problems, especially by the Men and Young Men groups. There were many negative comments and examples of bad police behaviour and police providing poor role models.[42]

In relation to conflict resolution, in 2006, 41 per cent of respondents indicated a preference for customary law rather than modern law to resolve disputes. In 2007, 93 per cent of respondents indicated that they would resolve their disputes entirely within their own community, either through customary law, the church or 'working it out themselves'. Only 4.2 per cent of conflict resolution involved RSIPF or RAMSI. The following year, in 2008,

84 per cent of respondents expressed a preference for customary law, and 5 per cent and 7 per cent of disputes involved RSIPF or RAMSI, respectively. By 2011, 60 per cent of respondents indicated they would seek help from a chief to resolve a dispute, and 15 per cent indicated they would seek help from RSIPF.[43]

In 2010, the main suggestions from respondents for improving the dispute resolution processes were: 'more respect for chiefs' (46 per cent), 'kastom' (26 per cent), 'elders' (19 per cent) and 'church' (19 per cent). 'More community policing' was suggested by 15 per cent and 'more access to RSIPF' by 10 per cent. Less than 10 per cent mentioned courts and other modern sources of justice and dispute resolution. Support for RAMSI in 2008 was 89 per cent of respondents, which dropped to 86 per cent in 2013. In that same year, 48 per cent said RAMSI's biggest achievement in Solomon Islands was bringing peace to the country, and 40 per cent said it was restoring law and order.[44] Recalling the portmanteau maxim that peace is not merely the absence of conflict but the presence of justice and government, in terms of policing, the bringing of peace and the restoration of law and order are one and the same.

The Success of RAMSI

There is little doubt that, despite early misgivings about the prospect for success of such an intervention, RAMSI has been one of the most successful international interventions ever, regionally or globally. This is due to a range of factors, including the following:

- It was a regional agreement by the PIF.
- It was led by Australia but had a 'whole-of-region' approach.
- It had a 'whole-of-government' approach.
- The political support from Australia was not influenced by the political cycle but by intervening for as long as it took to get the job done.
- The security aspect was police-led.
- The police were not confined to 'Western' interventionists from Australia, but the police instead adopted a regional 'Pacific face' via the PPF.
- The PPF was prepared to perform all executive powers of a police force, not just general duties and public order, and was able to address some of the underlying issues of corruption and poor governance through justice mechanisms.

This was not achieved by the police acting alone; it also required a viable and legitimate court system.

Many lessons came from the Australian experience in RAMSI. Among them are:

- The invitation of the host government is essential for cooperation. This is not always straightforward, as simple pride often prevents sovereign governments from asking for help.
- Nefarious activities by government actors, including corruption, exacerbate the problem.
- Regional consultation and a genuine long-term partnership with the host government are essential.
- The inclusion of all agency perspectives, including those of the police, during the planning process tends to minimise coordination problems on the ground.

The adoption of a 'Pacific' style under the PPF allowed for a much more credible voice on behalf of the intervening force. This Pacific voice was, on occasion, able to deliver harder messages in a softer way than more unfamiliar or unwelcome 'Western' voices. The leadership provided by a senior diplomat who was capable of seeing the 'big picture' and coordinating efforts accordingly was no doubt part of the success of RAMSI. The 'optics' of a police-led security posture rather than a military one was a much softer yet effective form of 'firm' intervention. The fact that the militants were regarded by the police as criminal actors rather than armed 'enemies' provided for a more nuanced and flexible approach to what was essentially a problem of lawlessness. An interesting observation is that the UN changed to 'integrated missions' around this time, and perhaps there were some lessons from RAMSI that were translated to the UN.

Implications of RAMSI for the Pacific Region

RAMSI helped consolidate Australia as a trusted partner in the Pacific, even in places where Australia traditionally had little or no interest, such as Micronesia, which had a traditional partnership with the U.S., and Polynesia, whose traditional partner was, and remains, New Zealand. This was by virtue of the diverse Pacific membership of the PPF, which reflected the PIF membership more broadly. The appropriate levels of political support and resourcing were also extremely important.

Many positives arose from RAMSI, including a safer and more stable region, the provision of a successful formula upon which similar interventions could be based, an enhanced understanding of regional dynamics, increased understanding and appreciation of individual agencies' methods of operation, including constraints, restraints and requirements; and the development of strong police-to-police peer networks. Discussed in another section, such relationships have become increasingly important. It is instructive to mention that short-term versus long-term time perspectives, and different timeframes adopted by various Australian agencies in relation to such interventions are as follows:

> McDevitt explains that the military representative said in securing the strategic military points would take 32 days, and then the military would be ready to withdraw. Mr McDevitt then explained that the community had lost trust in the RSIP and the police component of the mission could take up to 10 years. He says a representative from another agency then talked at length about endemic corruption in the country. Further there was a need for significant programs in infrastructure, finance and all other departments. The assessment was it would take a generation to make the necessary changes.[45]

RAMSI adopted and applied a comprehensive approach that combined peacemaking, peacekeeping and peace building. Seen through Australian eyes, particularly those of the police, RAMSI was, in short, the beneficiary of a rare combination of political will and a regional imperative, and in that sense, it was a diplomatic success. In terms of the legacies left behind, however, there may be less grounds for optimism.

It is worthwhile to re-state that the RAMSI intervention was intended as a circuit breaker to create a secure environment for recovery, not a panacea for all the problems facing Solomon Islands. These underlying problems remain and can only be addressed by the Solomon Islanders themselves as they negotiate the terms of their own social contract.

Legacy for the Solomon Islands

Urban drift, youth unemployment, 'wantokism', nepotism, political corruption, foreign-based resource exploitation and a fragile path to economic self-sufficiency remain concerns for the future peace, order and good governance of the Solomon Islands. RAMSI has provided some basis for development along these lines but has not addressed the underlying causes; it was never designed or intended to. RAMSI was intended to provide breathing space to allow the Government of the Solomon Islands to re-establish itself. In that, RAMSI succeeded. It is now up to the Solomon Islanders themselves. As RAMSI Special Coordinator Nick Coppel stated:

> RAMSI [was] a unique initiative, never before attempted by the countries of our region or elsewhere for that matter. The mission's commitment to assist Solomon Islands [went] well beyond simply creating a stable environment and strengthening the capacity of the security sector, to a much broader commitment to assist Solomon Islanders in their efforts to strengthen the

functions of the state in areas such as economic management and good governance. This was an ambitious but very deliberate decision, reflecting the unanimous views of the Pacific Island Forum Leaders that the mission should assist Solomon Islanders to address the fundamental causes of their nation's near collapse and not just be a 'quick-fix' focused on security.[46]

The AFP within RAMSI was very much at the forefront of this pioneering effort and, as such, has consolidated a growing and impressive list of achievements, both in terms of operational outcomes and effective diplomacy. In the case of RAMSI, both Australia's national interest and regional good citizenship were consistently demonstrated.

The rapid withdrawal of extant governance control, and the resultant power vacuums in the post-colonial period, have been partially to blame for some of the problems in Australia's region. To avoid repeating this problem, it is important to note that the closure of RAMSI has not meant the end of AFP involvement in the Solomon Islands. When the UN withdrew from Timor-Leste in 2012, the AFP maintained a police capacity development mission there: the TLTDP. In a similar fashion, the AFP continued its police capacity development in the Solomon Islands with the SIPDP with forty-five members. This has now been renamed the Royal Solomon Islands – Australia Police Partnership Program (RAPPP). This kind of phased withdrawal is one of the salient lessons learned from the AFP's experience in both Timor-Leste and the Solomon Islands. Proactive engagement was another.

The Pacific and the Establishment of the International Deployment Group (IDG)

The year 2004 was a highly significant one for the way in which the AFP engaged at an international level. As discussed, the JCLEC was established as a joint AFP–POLRI initiative in response to the Bali bombing in October 2002. Another initiative in 2004 was in response to the demands placed on police administration, logistics and training by contemporaneous police activities in Timor-Leste and the Solomon Islands, where RAMSI had been established the previous year. The extant arrangements were somewhat ad hoc and not designed to sustain large missions long-term, so the IDG was formed at Majura on the north-eastern outskirts of Canberra in the ACT.

Following the East Timor deployments, particularly the UNAMET and UNTAET deployments between 1999 and 2002, and noting the effect they had upon deployed members, the AFP reviewed its pre-deployment training. The original model closely resembled the pre-deployment training conducted by the ADF for AFP members deploying to Bougainville. This period also coincided with the Report of the Panel on United Nations Peace Operations sometimes referred to as the Brahimi Report, discussed above, which was a direct descendant of the UNAMET mission in East Timor in 1999.[47]

This report made a number of observations and recommendations based on the changing nature of UN interventions, in which police were playing an increasingly significant role. This included civilian police involvement in East Timor, in which the AFP was playing a continuing role in tandem with, and following on from, INTERFET. An important observation in the report, in a domestic donor-nation sense, was that there can often be less opposition to deploying civilian police in lieu of military forces, but that the availability of such police is often impractical, as they are structured to meet domestic needs alone, and there is, therefore, little or no excess capacity to provide police for international missions. The report further acknowledged that police from a range of backgrounds and cultures could experience difficulties working in a cohesive manner if forced to work together in the field for the first time.

The report noted that in its global operations, deployed civilian police personnel were only second in numerical terms to deployed military personnel, and that the demand for police in UN missions was high and likely to remain high. The report highlighted the fact that unique features of policing in such environments included fairness and impartiality and noted the disruption to political and economic progress in fragile states caused by crime. This is compounded by associated intimidation, violence and other criminal activity, and police reform in such states was recognised to be as important as training, advising and monitoring.

The report made a number of recommendations that included the establishment of (1) a national pool of civilian police that is 'administratively and medically ready for deployment to United Nations peace operations, within the context of the United Nations Standby Arrangements System'. (UNSAS), (2) regional training partnerships for civilian police and (3) a single point of contact for the provision of civilian police to United Nations peace operations.'

As a result, the AFP established the IDG to service the existing and evolving UN mission in East Timor and the growing multi-lateral RAMSI deployment to the Solomon Islands. The IDG was an appropriate mechanism to provide a national pool of deployable police, develop a regional training regime that trained all PPF members from the Pacific nations deploying to RAMSI, and act as a single point of contact for international police deployments for Australia.

Finally, the panel report recommended that 'parallel arrangements to these recommendations be established for judicial, penal, human rights and other relevant specialists, who with specialist civilian police will make up collegial "rule of law" teams.' This was in part addressed by the Australian Civilian Corps (ACC) established by Prime Minister Rudd in 2011 under DFAT.

The Pacific, the Arc of Instability and the Howard Doctrine

The formation of the IDG also accorded with the prevailing Australian Government foreign policy doctrine, which became known as the Howard Doctrine. This featured a more robust regional posture involving police support as an alternative, or as a supplement to, other means of intervention. Australian Prime Minister John Howard stated in early 2004:

> the purpose of this group [the IDG] will be for deployment in the region. Nobody should construe from the formation of this group that we have in mind deployment further afield. The whole purpose is to consolidate and put on a proper dedicated basis the evident need for this country in the years ahead to provide police, professional police support, to many of our neighbours in the Pacific. Many of these countries need trained police, as much if not more than they need military personnel[,] and one of the best things that Australia can do, on an ongoing dedicated professional basis[,] is to provide an effective police presence and police advice in these countries.[48]

The regional focus was to become somewhat stretched with UN deployments to Sudan (UNMIS) and South Sudan (UNMISS), and also bilateral deployments to Jordan and Afghanistan. Due to Prime Minister Howard deciding to deploy the AFP to East Timor in 1999 and to deploy AFP to the Solomon Islands, 'the Howard Doctrine' was coined by journalists as an expression to reflect that Australia became known colloquially in the media as the 'Deputy Sheriff' in the region, which created some raised regional eyebrows.

As Breen recorded, the new 'peace-building approach', in which police played a vital role in securing stability and justice-based outcomes, was built upon the successes of East Timor in 1999, where a national police force was established following independence, and by the early successes of the RAMSI mission in the Solomon Islands.[49] Despite the fondness of journalists and cartoonists to use the 'Deputy Sheriff' title, the Howard government's contrary intentions were made clear on 27 September 1999 after the deployment of INTERFET, when he addressed the House of Representatives:

> We do not seek ever to impose our views on other countries; we do not seek any kind of regional police role. We seek rather to act in concert with friendly nations within our region to achieve mutually shared objectives.[50]

This was reinforced the following day when Mr Nugent, the Liberal Member for Aston, addressed the House of Representatives in response to a question by the Leader of the Opposition concerning the Bulletin article on the Howard Doctrine:

> Let me reiterate what the Prime Minister has already said very specifically: the government does not see Australia as playing the role of deputy for the United States or, indeed, any other country in the region. Neither does the government see the United States playing a role as regional policeman.[51]

The Howard Doctrine focused on the 'Arc of Instability' as it applied to the island nations in the South West Pacific. The Pacific is the largest ocean in the world. It stretches from the Arctic to the Antarctic circles and is surrounded by the archipelagic region of Southeast Asia, the continents of East Asia, North and South America and Australia, and its vast interior contains several island groups inhabited by racial and ethnic groups broadly categorised as Melanesian, Polynesian and Micronesian. At 165 million square kilometres, it is larger than all the earth's land areas combined. It has been a contested area for the past century, as littoral states have waged actual and strategic conflict for control or influence. Australia's recent history saw Imperial Japanese military forces come very close to Australian territory, and since 1942, Australian policy has been one of strategic denial to powers whose aspirations and intentions were inimical to Australia's.[52]

The Pacific: Early Claims

There have been some ambitious claims of ownership of this vast and sparsely populated expanse of water. This first European claim came from the eastern side of the Pacific by early Spanish explorers:

> Columbus reached Central America in the Santa Maria in 1492; he never saw the Pacific, but by 1513 the Spaniards reached the Pacific coast and learned that Columbus had not been crazy after all. There lay the mightiest ocean of all! Keats has told us of that breathless moment when the Spaniards 'stared at the Pacific, silent upon a peak in Darien.' Balboa, the leader of this expedition, waded into the ocean, clad in full armour and sword in hand, and took possession of the Pacific in the name of the sovereign of Spain.[53]

Like many who have tried to deal with the Pacific as a single entity, Balboa was perhaps more than a little ambitious. Of the nations on the Pacific Rim, three are global behemoths: China, Russia and the U.S. Other major industrial powers such as Japan and South Korea also have significant interests in the Pacific, as does one of the most populous nations in ASEAN, the Philippines. The Pacific is divided broadly into ethno-centric groupings:

Melanesia, consisting of PNG, the Solomon Islands, Vanuatu, Fiji and New Caledonia; Micronesia, made up of Pohnpei, Kosrae, Chuuk and Yap; and Polynesia: Hawaii, a state of the U.S., Samoa, Tonga, Tuvalu, Cook Islands, New Zealand, Tahiti (French Polynesia) and Easter Island/Rapa Nui, which is administered by Chile. The vast and widely-spread Polynesian Triangle extends from Hawaii in the north to Stuart Island at the bottom of the South Island of New Zealand in the south-west to Easter Island/Rapa Nui in the south-east.

The Pacific, simply put, is immense and diverse, and there is, therefore, no unique or universal Pacific culture, religion, ideology, political system or approach, nor is there a shared history, colonial or otherwise. The closest thing the Pacific has in terms of commonality is probably the Christian religion, which was introduced by missionaries over the centuries, particularly in the second half of the 19th century, although earlier attempts were made by Spanish missionaries from South America.

Colonisation and the Principle of Effective Occupation

There are many nations, particularly among the islands, that are former colonies of European powers, primarily Britain and France but also Germany, which had a brief foray into global colonialism in the late 19th century. Of note is a principle related to colonial possession developed in relation to the 'scramble for Africa'. The Principle of Effectivity, or Effective Occupation, was developed at the Berlin Conference in 1884–85. Also known as the 'Congo Conference' (*Kongokonferenz*) or the Berlin West Africa Conference (*Westafrika-Konferenz*), the principle was developed to prevent European powers from setting up colonies in Africa in name only:

> The Principle of Effective Occupation stated that powers could acquire rights over colonial lands only if they actually possessed them: in other words if they had treaties with local leaders, if they flew their flag there, and if they established an administration in the territory to govern it with a police force to keep order.[54]

This principle was recognised in the 19th-century German colonies in the Pacific, which were based primarily in Samoa but included north-eastern New Guinea, the Bismarck Archipelago, the northern Solomon Islands, including Bougainville, the Marshall Islands, as well as Carolines, Palau and the Marianas. Samoa was a German colony for twenty years from 1900 until 1920.

Pacific Governance

Although it was written with colonial administration in mind, from a governance perspective, the Principle of Effectivity or Effective Occupation is a good benchmark from which to measure the basic provision of administration by all governments. Rather than 'treaties with local leaders', the 'social contract' with the community is a more relevant term for contemporary observation related to police and policing. Noteworthy is the ability to administer the territory and the requirement for police to keep order.

This has not always been a strong feature of governance and policing in a number of nations in the South West Pacific. The Solomon Islands and PNG, in particular, are each discussed in their own section. From aspirational possession by Balboa and effective administration by European colonisers to contemporary dialogue and aspirational partnerships in the post-colonial environment, the nations of the South West Pacific have traditionally sought assistance for governance from liberal democracies such as Australia and New Zealand. Building on their experience in East Timor and the Solomon Islands, police capacity development was seen as a way forward in other parts of the Pacific. The combination of the Australian national interest and international good citizenship as it applies to the region have been highly prominent features of the AFP approach to the Pacific.

Until the Howard Doctrine, the AFP had a loosely coherent approach to the Pacific, starting with the SPILO, who was part of the International Liaison Officer Network. Following significant AFP involvement in East Timor and the Solomon Islands, there was an increasing recognition that the AFP was in a position to play an important role in stability and rule-of-law interventions in the South West Pacific.

From the Pacific Regional Policing Initiative to the Pacific Police Development Program

The Years 2004–2008: The Pacific Regional Policing Initiative (PRPI)

The year 2004 saw the effective implementation of the Howard Doctrine with the establishment of the JCLEC to respond to Islamic violent extremism in Southeast Asia, and the IDG to support ongoing operations in Timor-Leste and the newly formed RAMSI. The year 2006 was one in which the dynamics of the Pacific created the catalyst for a renewed focus on peace, order and good governance in the Pacific, as the Arc of Instability lived up to its name. The reaction by the Australian Government under Prime Minister John Howard involved the AFP in multifaceted and ongoing engagements.

At the Pacific Islands Forum in August 2003, the Prime Ministers of Australia, New Zealand and Fiji announced the creation of the Australian-led PRPI. This was to be based in Fiji and was intended to enhance capacities to address crime and corruption, coordinate and deliver standardised training for regional police and foster police networking across the Pacific. Significantly, this initiative included Fiji; however, events in late 2006 had a follow-on effect on the PRPI and regional policing for the Pacific was transferred from Fiji to Australia, specifically the IDG. This manifested itself in a renewed sense of Melanesian identity in the form of the Melanesian Spearhead Group (MSG) based in Fiji.

The Year 2006: The Howard Doctrine Faces Challenges in the Pacific

Melanesian Spearhead Group (MSG)

The MSG has its genesis in a renewed sense of unity among the members of Melanesian nations Fiji, Vanuatu, the Solomon Islands, PNG and the French territories in the form of the *Front de Liberation Nationale Kanak et Socialiste* (FLNKS), a group of pro-independence parties in the French Territory of New Caledonia. The first MSG member to flex its muscles against Australian-led intervention aimed at better governance, including an attempt to tackle political corruption, was PNG.

Enhanced Cooperation Project (ECP)-PNG 2005

In 2005, the AFP deployed 115 AFP members to PNG under the ECP. This saw AFP members working alongside their Royal Papua New Guinea Constabulary (RPNGC) counterparts in an armed executive policing role. This involved legal indemnity from prosecution under PNG law and provided legal immunity from civil prosecution in what is a highly litigious population. This aspect of the program was successfully appealed by Luther Wenge, Governor of Morobe Province, to the PNG Supreme Court on the basis that it was unconstitutional. The ECP was disbanded, and AFP members returned to Australia in May 2005.

Solomon Islands: Prime Minister Sogavare and Julian Moti 2006

The next MSG member to flex its political muscle was the Government of the Solomon Islands under Prime Minister Manasseh Sogavare. The appointment of Snyder Rini as Solomon Islands Prime Minister after the 2006 general election sparked rioting in Honiara amid allegations that the election and subsequent appointment of Rini were 'fixed'. As tensions escalated, parts of Honiara were razed and looted, and Chinese-owned property was targeted. He was replaced by Manasseh Sogavare, who had previously served a term as Prime Minister in 2000–01.

Sogavare was known to be opposed to the presence of RAMSI, perhaps because RAMSI had commenced addressing the corruption, fraud and theft that had caused the 'tensions'. He sought to install a Fijian-born Julian

Moti QC, who was a dual Solomon Islands and Australian citizen, as his Attorney-General. The appointment was opposed by the Australian Prime Minister and Foreign Minister based on advice from the Australian High Commissioner to the Solomon Islands, who had indicated that Moti was unfit to take this office due to outstanding criminal charges from a court in Vanuatu under the Child Sex Tourism Act. The allegations involved multiple charges of rape of a teenage girl in Vanuatu and New Caledonia in 1997.

Attempts to have Moti extradited from the Solomon Islands had failed. On 29 September 2006, Moti was returning to Honiara from India via Singapore and Port Moresby. He was returning to support Prime Minister Sogavare, who was facing a no-confidence motion. He was arrested in October 2006 in Port Moresby while in transit to the capital, Honiara, where he was to be sworn in as Attorney-General.

Moti was held in PNG unwillingly and illegally by virtue of the express authority of the PNG Deputy Prime Minister Don Poyle, who was acting for Prime Minister Sir Michael Somare, who was away in the provinces at the time. An attempt to have him extradited to Australia from PNG to face criminal charges saw him take refuge, under diplomatic protection, in the Solomon Islands High Commission in Port Moresby. While there, he was contacted by Joseph Assaigo, the Chief of the PNG Intelligence Branch, who informed him that the PNG Government could no longer guarantee his safety, and that a secret operation had been planned. PNG PM Somare denied any involvement in this affair. [55]

On 10 October 2006, Moti was conveyed on a clandestine PNG Defence Force flight from Port Moresby to Munda in the western provinces of the Solomon Islands. According to Dr Susan Merrell in the PNG Echo, 'He had been dumped in the middle of Papua New Guinea police armed with machine guns who were confronted by a RAMSI Land cruiser obstructing the runway. The Australians were waving revolvers and shouting threats.'[56] He was conveyed to Honiara.

In the meantime, the Australian High Commissioner Patrick Cole was declared persona non grata in September 2006 by the Sogavare government. This was to be followed in December 2006 by RSIP Commissioner Shane Castles, who had been seconded from the AFP to take up this position in 2005. The existing tensions between the Governments of the Solomon Islands and Australia were aggravated by actions taken by the RSIP under Commissioner Castles with assistance from the RAMSI PPF, including some Australians. They had obtained search warrants and searched the office of the Solomon Islands Prime Minister, seeking to obtain evidence for the prosecution of Moti.

Commissioner Castles Declared an 'Undesirable Immigrant' December 2006

Mr Castles was declared an undesirable immigrant in late December 2006 when he was on leave in Australia. He never returned to the Solomon Islands. The Foreign Affairs Minister for the Solomon Islands, Mr Patterson Oti, indicated that the return of Mr Castles 'would be prejudicial to peace, defence, public safety, public order, public morality, security and good governance in the Solomon Islands'.[57]

This created some consternation in Canberra. National Manager of IDG Assistant Commissioner Paul Jevtovic stated in a Media Release on 12 January 2007:

> In relation to the search warrant on offices associated with the Prime Minister, a search warrant was sought through the Director of Public Prosecutions and issued by an independent Magistrate, who authorised the police action. The process to issue the search warrant and the subsequent search of the Prime Minister's Office complied with the laws of the Solomon Islands in all respects.[58]

Prime Minister Sogavare Replaced by Prime Minister Sikua December 2007

In December 2007, Prime Minister Sogavare was replaced in a parliamentary no-confidence motion by Prime Minister Derek Sikua, who was well disposed to the presence of RAMSI and the Australian Government generally. The incoming Australian Government of Prime Minister Kevin Rudd, elected in November 2007, supported the extradition of Moti to Australia to face criminal charges in the Supreme Court of Queensland. In a media interview on 13 December 2007, Prime Minister Rudd stated:

> on the question of the Moti matter, the position of the Australian Government is absolutely clear cut. This individual is the subject of criminal charges and because of the application of Australian domestic law; we have activated our extradition arrangements with the Government of the Solomon Islands. Nothing has changed on that score. We therefore intend to prosecute that to the full. The reason being is that the normal operation of the criminal law of the Commonwealth of Australia, and through its properly constituted agencies, including the Australian Federal Police, international extradition arrangements should proceed unimpeded and that will remain our position.[59]

Extradition of Julian Moti

In December 2007, Mr Moti was extradited to Australia, and was bailed, to face criminal charges in the Supreme Court of Queensland, where his case was heard by Supreme Court Judge Debra Mullins in December 2009. Justice Mullins ruled against Mr Moti's claims that the investigation and prosecution, under the Child Sex Tourism Act, was politically motivated by the then Howard government's fears of the lawyer's growing backroom influence in the region. Justice Mullins acknowledged that the investigation had commenced after concerns raised by Australian High Commissioner to the Solomon Islands, Mr Patrick Cole. She stated: 'There is no evidence of any impropriety associated with the AFP's approach to the investigation of the conduct of (Mr Moti) that is the subject of the charges'.[60]

However, she also raised some concerns about the way in which the AFP provided funding to support the family of the victim of the original crimes and the prime witness. She stated:

> It raises questions about the integrity of the administration of the Australian justice system, when witnesses who live in a foreign country, where it is alleged an Australian citizen committed acts of child sex abuse, expect to be fully supported by the Australian government, until they give evidence at the trial in Australia of the Australian citizen…The conduct of the AFP in taking over the financial support of these witnesses who live in Vanuatu is an affront to the public conscience.[61]

This led to a series of legal cases that culminated in a permanent stay of prosecution by the High Court of Australia in 2011.[62] The PNG Echo stated that it was an 'abuse of process' that the High Court of Australia found when it granted a permanent stay of prosecution to Moti at the end of 2011 on the regurgitated Australian charges of sex with a minor that the Vanuatu courts had thrown out over a decade previously. During his tenure, Sogavare reversed the Solomon Islands' diplomatic recognition of Taiwan to the diplomatic recognition of the PRC in 2019 and signed a security pact with the PRC in 2022. This has had major implications for the liberal-democratic legacy of the policing efforts of the PPF under the RAMSI mission and following deployments. The full implications of this are yet to be seen, but they are likely to herald increased PRC police 'assistance' to the Solomon Islands and perhaps elsewhere in the Pacific, particularly in Melanesia. This influence is unlikely to enhance liberal-democratic practices and has the real potential to pave the way to a longer-term strategic threat to Australian sovereignty.

Timor-Leste: Dili Riots July 2006

As all these events were taking place in the Solomon Islands, another incident to test the resource base of the IDG was not in the Pacific but in Timor-Leste in July 2006. This saw approximately fifty AFP IDG members deploy in a Public Order Management (POM) capacity to assist the ADF, who had deployed under Operation Serene. Rioting broke out following the dismissal of 600 soldiers from the Timor-Leste Defence Force.[63]

Operation Tokoni: Tonga November 2006

This outbreak was followed by riots in the Tongan capital, Nuku'alofa. On 16 November 2006, approximately 750 to 1000 people rioted in the Tongan capital of Nuku'alofa following a period of pro-democracy protests. As a result, a large area of the capital's central business district was destroyed by fire, scores of buildings were looted, and seven people died as a result of a deliberately lit fire. Properties owned by the King of Tonga, the Prime Minister and Chinese businessmen were specifically targeted. A state of emergency was declared and the Tongan Government sought assistance from the Australian and New Zealand governments during the evening of 16 November 2006.

Early on 18 November 2006, an initial AFP commitment of thirty-four personnel deployed to Tonga to re-establish law and order and to support the Tonga Police Force's investigation into the criminal activity of 16 November 2006. The deployment was named Operation Tokoni, after the Tongan word for 'friendship'. A total of sixty-five AFP personnel deployed to Tonga between 18 November 2006 and 19 December 2006. The contingent consisted of personnel from IDG, the Operations Response Team (ORT), AFP Forensics, The Victorian Institute of Forensic Medicine, AFP Information and Communications Technology, and AFP Protection portfolios. This deployment formed the basis of what was to become the Tonga Police Development Program (TPDP).

The three public order events in Timor-Leste, the Solomon Islands and Tonga were the catalyst for the formation of the Operational Response Group (ORG), which performed a specialist response capability within the IDG. This was to later amalgamate with the ACT Policing Special Operations Team (SOT) to become the Specialist Response Group (SRG), which became an AFP-wide asset in 2015 as the IDG was dissolved and its duties absorbed by the AFP International Operations portfolio. As the public order issues throughout 2006 attracted the attention of the AFP IDG, the situation in relation to Mr Castles as Commissioner of the Royal Solomon Islands Police was replicated by the situation of another AFP nominated Commissioner, Mr Andrew Hughes, in Fiji.

Withdrawal of Fiji Police Commissioner Andrew Hughes: November 2006

The final incident in 2006 involving the AFP, which had implications for the IDG, occurred in Fiji in November and December 2006. Hughes was another seconded senior AFP officer who assumed his position in 2003. As Commissioner of the Fiji Police Force, Mr Hughes made sincere attempts to reconcile some of the ethnically-based differences between the indigenous

Fijian population and the Indian population. He also sought to address corruption and had been a major instigator of the PRPI.

Mr Hughes had been nominated by the AFP following a request by the Fijian Constitutional Officers Committee. Fiji had experienced political instability and a coup in 2000 in which the Fijian military had deposed the elected government of Prime Minister Mahendra Chaudhry. This had resulted in a number of pending prosecutions, and it was felt that a non-Fijian citizen would better project an image of fairness and impartiality with coup-related cases.

Mr Hughes vigorously pursued investigations impartially against high-profile citizens in relation to the coup events of 2000. His targets included chiefs and politicians, including some government ministers. This occasionally strained his relationship with the Government of Fiji. His main area of disagreement with the government concerned the Reconciliation, Tolerance, and Unity Bill, which proposed to establish a commission empowered to compensate victims and pardon perpetrators of the coup. Mr Hughes expressed serious reservations about the amnesty provisions and opposed government attempts to cap expenditure by the police and the military. Relations between Mr Hughes and the military commander, Commodore Frank Bainimarama, deteriorated during 2006, to the point where Commodore Bainimarama demanded Hughes's resignation in November of that year.

Mr Hughes was critical of the Fijian military throughout the later part of 2006. The military consequently demanded that he be fired by the government. 'Mr Hughes had endured intense political pressure while maintaining the rule of law in Fiji, in the lead-up to an eventual military coup in December. Apart from personal threats, threats were also made against the well-being of his family'.[64] His family left in November 2006, and he followed shortly afterwards.

Fiji-military Coup December 2006

A military coup deposed the government on 5 December 2006, and on 6 December, according to the Fiji Live news service, the military junta announced that it had dismissed Mr Hughes from office, citing 'dereliction of duty.' However, as AFP Commissioner Keelty stated in 2007:

> For a long time now the AFP has been committed to assisting the development of police forces not only in the Solomons and Fiji but also Vanuatu, Tonga, Timor-Leste, Cambodia and Asian countries. It is important to stand up for the apolitical nature of policing-it has to serve the community as well as the Government.[65]

Unfortunately, there are some political influencers in the region, in both Southeast Asia and the South West Pacific, to which this degree of impartiality, based on the application of an apolitical posture, remains inimical. The regional isolation of Fiji intensified in 2009 after Bainimarama failed to hold the elections he had promised or, indeed, to open any discussion about the return to democracy. In response, the PIF and the Commonwealth suspended Fiji. Fiji expelled Australia's High Commissioner in November 2009 and New Zealand's High Commissioner in 2010 and cut diplomatic communications down to the bare minimum. This effectively spelt the end of the PRPI. The Final Report of the PRPI in October 2006 stated:

> There are very mixed messages being delivered across the Pacific about policing priorities. Most Forum Island Countries (FICs) will never be in a position to have the sophistication of policing to address regional and global transnational crime problems. The primary focus of support for capacity development is at the basic functions of community policing: Pacific government budgets are unlikely to afford anything more. Other arrangements are necessary to ensure FIC access to other specialist police services when they are required.[66]

The Key Stakeholders' Group, comprising representatives of AusAID, NZAID, Fiji Government, PIFS, PICP, AFP, New Zealand Police (NZP) and PRPI. Five years after its inception, as the PRPI at the PIF in 2003, the AFP IDG established the Pacific Police Development Program (PPDP) in 2008, which adopted many of the same objectives as the PRPI and much of the same membership, with the notable exception of Fiji.

The Year 2008: The IDG Establishes the Pacific Police Development Program (PPDP)

The PPDP was a joint initiative between the AFP and the Attorney-General's Department in close cooperation with Australia's development agency, AusAID. It was designed to provide a more coherent Australian response to police development needs in the Pacific to improve the rule of law in the region.

The PPDP had two broad components that incorporated country-specific programs in Nauru, PNG, Samoa, Tonga and Vanuatu, as well as a regional component, the PPDP-R. The latter provided country-specific support on a fly-in-fly-out basis to the remaining members of the PIF countries: Kiribati, Niue, Tuvalu, The Republic of the Islands (RMI), Palau, Cook Islands and the Federated States of Micronesia (FSM).

The PPDP-R was designed to meet the specific needs of the seven host nations and incorporated joint planning and resource sharing. It had two primary outcomes: (1) the encouragement of legitimacy and accountability within the host country police and (2) increased capacity for law and justice agencies to operate within legal frameworks that are just, effective and support the rule of law.

The PPDP-R has provided funding and technical advisory support to PICP-established working groups, including the Forensic Working Group, Cyber Safety Pasifika, the Pacific Policing Training Advisory Group (PPTAG), the PICP, the Women's Advisory Network and the Pacific Prevention of Domestic Violence Program, which were managed by the NZP and start-up funding for the Pacific Police Information Technology Program Working Group.

Training supported by PPDP-R included police leadership courses specifically delivered to future and current female police leaders, management of investigations, basic intelligence, sexual offences first response and community engagement. The PPDP-R also provided assistance in the reform and development of corporate policy, planning and legislation and worked collaboratively with Australian Department of the Attorney-General (AGD) International Legal Assistance Branch in relation to the review, reform and implementation of police-enabling legislation.[67]

Samoa-Australian Police Partnership: SAPP-2009

The AFP took responsibility for the management of the Samoa-Australia Police Partnership (SAPP) from AusAID on 1 January 2009. On 1 August that year, the AFP deployed the first Project Manager to Samoa, who, in consultation with the Commissioner of the Samoa Police and Prison Service (SPS) and other key stakeholders, initiated the development and implementation of the SAPP Strategic Framework 1st January 2010 to June 2012. The SAPP is staffed by three members of the AFP.

This framework focused on three key objectives: (1) improve public safety by strengthening general policing and investigative capacity, (2) improve police responsiveness to community perceptions and (3) improve corporate and administrative support capacity to underpin Samoan Police Service operations. Much of this administrative support was captured by the introduction of a crime reporting system and case management system within the Criminal Investigations Department and the Professional Standards Unit. Police responsiveness was enhanced by encouraging members of the SPS to attend training courses such as the Emergency Management and Executive Development Program with the support of the AIPM to strengthen police management, encourage change and improve police performance. Media Skills Workshops were conducted to positively shape community perceptions of the police through improved media management and response.

Qualifying courses at the Constable and Sergeant levels were also introduced. Name plates were introduced for police to enhance accountability, and a law reference book was compiled and distributed to members so they could be better informed of their powers and important legislation. An enhanced Police Code of Conduct in both English and Samoan was also promoted throughout the SPS. In September 2011, the PPDP funded a forensic laboratory and a Pacific Automated Fingerprint Identification System.

The SAPP continued to focus on more advanced police capability development in areas such as investigative capacity, brief preparation and case management, police responsiveness, police visibility, customer service, training, information management, intelligence, inter-agency communication and coordination (including disaster management), performance management, executive development, media management, traffic management and radio communications. It is noteworthy that the Pacific Transnational Crime Network (PTCN), formed in 2004, has its headquarters in Samoa.

Vanuatu Australia Police Project (VAPP) 2011

The Vanuatu Australia Police Project (VAPP) was a 'whole-of-government' project aimed at providing support to the Vanuatu Police Force (VPF). The project commenced in February 2011 following the conclusion of the Vanuatu Police Force Capacity Building Project. This was a partnership between the AFP, AusAID (DFAT), the Government of Vanuatu and the VPF.

The aim of the project was to provide support to the VPF and build and develop the capacity of the VPF to assist and provide members with the tools and resources to effectively carry out their duties. This included the provision of training and development courses, including Middle Management Courses at the AIPM in Sydney, the modernisation of the VPF communications system, the construction of police buildings, the provision of a twelve-metre police vessel as well as several police vehicles. The support has also included improved governance procedures and processes relating to finance, budgeting, workforce planning, police accountability and improved firearms control.

Pacific Islands Chiefs of Police (PICP)

The Pacific Islands Chiefs of Police, of which the AFP Commissioner is a member, is responsible for various police programs in the Pacific, with certain nations assuming lead responsibilities. These include the Pacific Forensic Working Group (FSM), the PTCN (Samoa), the Pacific Police Training Advisory Network (Palau), Cyber Safety Pasifika (Australia), Women's Advisory Network (French Polynesia), Pacific Police Domestic Violence

Program (Niue), Pacific Police Crime Prevention Program (Cook Islands), Pacific Police Information and Technology Program (Solomon Islands).

Pacific Transnational Crime Network (PTCN) 2004

In addition to the formation of JCLEC and the IDG, the year 2004 also saw the establishment of the PTCN, in which the AFP plays a significant role. Based in Samoa, the PCTN and its coordination centre, the Pacific Transnational Crime Coordination Centre (PTCCC), links Transnational Crime Units (TCU) in each member country and collects, analyses, and disseminates criminal intelligence. It thus provides a proactive intelligence network for Pacific police agencies, including the AFP. This sort of operational cooperation in the South West Pacific region is important in a constantly changing global criminal environment, which poses an increased threat to Pacific Island nations as well as Australia. The sort of criminal activity targeted by the PCTN includes narcotics trafficking through the region, including cocaine from South America destined for Australia, fraud, money laundering, illegal resource exploitation and irregular people movements.

The membership of the PCTN consists of Vanuatu, PNG, Fiji, Samoa, Tonga, FSM, Palau, Marshall Islands, Commonwealth of Northern Mariana Islands, Solomon Islands, Kiribati, Cook Islands, Niue, Australia, New Zealand and the US. It links TCUs in each country with the broader global law enforcement network via its links with the AFP, NZP and, significantly, with the U.S. Joint Inter Agency Task Force West (JIATF-W) based in Hawaii. The JIATF-W links directly to the extensive U.S. global law enforcement network. It has links to the Pacific Islands Forum Secretariat, Oceania Customs Organisation, Pacific Immigration Directors Conference and the ADF-funded Pacific Patrol Boat Program. The AFP also provides PTCN advisors to the PTCCC in Samoa, PNG, Fiji and the PICP Secretariat. This provides a vital regional Pacific linkage into the AFP's criminal intelligence network. This is an example of the type of new diplomatic networks required to meet the emerging challenges in the region.

Pacific Police Training Advisory Group (PPTAG) 2011

In 2011, the AFP formed the PPTAG, which seeks to address holistic training needs for the region and works in conjunction with the PPDP-R. One of the major programs involves 'Cybersafety Pasifika', which is:

> a youth project aimed at developing knowledge around cyber-crime and safety matters with an emphasis on internet and technological devices. The mission of CSP is to ensure that the children of the Pacific will be safe and

secure by providing them with the skills and knowledge to navigate the digital landscape safely and responsibly.[68]

Papua New Guinea – Early Colonialism
Bismarck's Principle of Effective Government

The Berlin Conference of 1884, which resulted in the Scramble for Africa, was called for by Portugal and organised by Otto von Bismarck, the German Chancellor. One of the principles to emerge from this conference was the Principle of Effective Occupation for European powers, which could acquire rights over colonial lands only if they actually possessed them, that is, if they had treaties with local leaders, if they flew their flag there, and if they established an administration in the territory to govern it with a police force to keep order.

Although it applied to the European colonisation of Africa, the metaphorical and practical application of this principle in relation to law, justice and policing, and their relationships with peace, order, good government and prosperity, should not be overlooked in the post-colonial setting in the South West Pacific. This is of particular relevance to Papua New Guinea, as the north-eastern quadrant of the island of New Guinea was colonised by Germany in the1880s, and the Principle of Effective Occupation would have been directly relevant to that territory. The German-administered territory was policed by the New Guinea Police Force. The south-eastern quadrant, known as Papua, was administered by the British until 1905, when it changed from British to Australian administration. It was policed by the Royal Papuan Constabulary.

The German territory, then known as New Guinea, was ceded to Australia following the Treaty of Versailles in 1919 under a League of Nations mandate in 1920 and joined the south-eastern quadrant, Papua, which had been reluctantly colonised under the British Crown. This followed precipitous action by the colonial Government of Queensland in the 1880s due to alarm over German activities in the region. Once amalgamated, they became the Australian Territory of Papua and New Guinea (TPNG) and eventually the new nation of Papua New Guinea upon gaining independence in 1975.

The Australian Territory of Papua and New Guinea (TPNG) and the 'Kiaps'

Policing between 1945 and 1975 was done via Australian Patrol Officers, known as 'kiaps', a pidgin term derived from the German word for captain (*kapitän*). In all, about 2000 young Australian men performed duties as Patrol

Officers in the TPNG. Prior to taking up their posts, they were trained at the Australian School of Pacific Administration in Sydney:

> In the field, kiaps juggled the multiple roles of ambassador, policeman, judge, administrator, explorer, farmer, engineer and anthropologist. Away for weeks at a time, kiaps patrolled vast areas on foot with the help of an indigenous police force.[69]

A recruitment advertisement from 1959 provides a snapshot of an era offering positions for 'Cadet Patrol Officer; Cadet Agricultural Officer; Cadet Veterinary Officer; Cadet Education Officer; Cadet Forest Officer; Cadet Valuer; Co-operative Officer-in-Training, and Clerk' to male British subjects aged between 18 and 24. '[T]hey were administrators, census takers, policemen, magistrates and gaolers. Some were required to go on arduous patrols into unexplored territory. At times it was dangerous work'.[70] The kiaps were assisted by the amalgamated native police forces, the New Guinea Police Force in the north and the Royal Papuan Constabulary in the south. These were later amalgamated to form the Royal Papua New Guinea Constabulary (RPNGC) upon independence in 1975.

Independence 1975

The kiaps ceased duties in 1975 with independence, and the RPNGC assumed primacy. It could be argued that since independence in 1975, PNG has not demonstrated 'effective occupation' and, in terms of governance, has seen a gradual but consistent decline in internal security and stability, an eroded standard of living and chronic neglect of basic services such as health, education, and law and order. This has occurred despite sincere and costly efforts on the part of international aid donors (including the Australian Government and its taxpayer base) to assist the human development of the people of PNG, the economic and social development of PNG as a nation, and its placement in the global community of nations.

Urbanisation

In concert with other parts of the Pacific, particularly in Melanesia, rapid urbanisation and increased crime rates have exacerbated an already extant disparity situation between rich and poor. This urban drift started in the immediate post-independence era when large groups of men from rural areas moved to urban centres seeking employment. In a familiar pattern, a lack of work and pressure on general facilities unable to handle this influx resulted in the development of squatter camps. As the squatter camps continued to grow, due to the high rate of unemployment, low education levels and boredom, they provided a steady stream of recruits to criminal gangs, which became known as 'raskol' gangs.

These groups provided disenfranchised youth with a sense of worth and belonging within the existing and culturally accepted 'wantok' hierarchy. This extended into various government organisations, including the police and military, as well as into mainstream politics, which provided a pool of 'mercenaries' for use in extortion, robbery, bribery and other violent and predatory crimes. These include vandalism, theft, physical violence, racial attacks targeting foreigners, violent sexual attacks and mutilation, drug taking, murder, extortion and armed robbery.

Crime

Law and order in PNG remains a serious issue, and PNG is seemingly at a constant risk of breaking down completely into a state of anarchy. Corruption is endemic, often masked by the 'wantok' culture, which is widely accepted as a part of the PNG culture. This affects not just the long-suffering, law-abiding members of the community but also the risk-based decisions relating to foreign investment. A Special Report by ASPI in 2014 lists five broad areas of crime: (1) violence against women, (2) corruption, (3) public order, (4) crimes against the person and property and (5) transnational crime and money laundering.[71]

Many of the drivers underpinning this combination of criminal activity include culturally accepted or ingrained behaviours, particularly in relation to violence against women, corruption and public order. PNG is a male-dominated culture; therefore, the RPNGC has a male-dominated culture. This is highly problematic and difficult to address by cultural outsiders without risking exposure to accusations of cultural imperialism. This is not to say that international police should not or cannot attempt to address these issues, quite the contrary, but strategies designed to do so need to factor in the cultural aspects of a male-dominated 'warrior' culture and work towards changing male behaviours, as well as championing the cause of inclusiveness of women's participation in community activities, including policing. Such changes are unlikely to take place in the short term and are likely to be resisted by an entrenched patriarchy.

Corruption is endemic and pervasive and can often be masked by the 'wantok' culture. Inaction by the authorities, such as the police, to seriously address such issues has led to a culture of impunity and the inevitable culture of violence. This has a negative effect on investor confidence and, therefore, upon the prospects of enhanced peace and prosperity. Transparency

International rates PNG as 'highly corrupt' and ranks it among the bottom third of nations surveyed.[72]

Similarly, the Asia-Pacific Group on Money Laundering used a standard comparative assessment to report in 2011 that PNG faces very serious risks from money laundering. The World Bank rated Port Moresby and Lae as two of the least safe cities in the world in 2010 based on their thirty-three and sixty-six homicides per 100,000 inhabitants, respectively. Regular surveys of community, business and investor confidence, as well as academic studies, support widespread perceptions that the country is badly affected by violence and crime.[73]

Violence along tribal and ethnic lines is a serious issue but appears to be in a different category to the urban violence perpetrated by the raskol gangs in Port Moresby and Lae. Additionally, the lines between tribal and urban violence appear to be blurred, particularly in the urban fringes. Connery and Claxton identify that:

> large fights, mainly over land issues that may go back decades, involve hundreds of warriors using military, high-powered and homemade guns. Intergroup clashes on the outskirts of cities and towns stem from friction as newer settlers from 'outside' groups are blamed for taking work and causing crime.[74]

One result of this combination of widespread corruption and semi-officially sanctioned crime is that there is widespread cannabis cultivation, particularly in the Highlands. The AFP, with the RPNGC, has intercepted, investigated and prosecuted numerous attempts at importation of narcotics and other contraband from PNG to Far North Queensland by light aircraft and vessels. This area is remote, and as such, police resourcing is very thin on the ground. The AFP has offices in Cairns, and two officers are posted on Thursday Island in the Torres Strait, which is the narrow waterway between the tip of Cape York Peninsula in Far North Queensland and the Southern Province of PNG, which is only about 100 kilometres wide and is populated by a number of islands known as the Torres Strait Islands. The ability of Australian authorities to detect and respond to criminal activity in this remote region is extremely challenging. In part, effective Australian border control relies on timely and accurate reporting between the AFP and RPNGC, which is fostered through peer-to-peer relationships. The covert smuggling at this stage has only involved illicit drugs, primarily cannabis, but the remoteness of the region and the relative absence of effective mechanisms to intercept light aircraft in particular leave it open to other malign actors with more dangerous illicit cargo, including biological agents or terrorists.

Cape York Peninsula and the Torres Strait

The Department of Immigration and Border Protection is also active in the area. The Queensland Police Service also has members posted to police stations on Thursday Island in the Torres Strait and throughout the Cape York Peninsula. Their primary role is community-based policing rather than border protection. Therefore, a deterioration of circumstances in PNG has direct implications for Australia due to its proximity and the regional vulnerability to covert border penetration. A state of lawlessness, or a state where malign non-state actors, such as organised crime groups, hold influence over affairs in PNG, increases the risk of such activities affecting Australia.

This is compounded by the possibility that a state power whose interests are inimical to Australia's and has influence in PNG poses a direct threat to Australian sovereignty. This nearly came to pass in the 1940s with the expansion of Imperial Japanese forces in the region. As ASPI strategist Joanne Wallis recalled:

> renowned strategic thinker T.B. Millar once reflected, Papua New Guinea is an 'an exposed and vulnerable front door', as if it was in 'hostile hands' it would 'make attacks on our east coast much easier—Port Moresby, after all, is closer to Sydney than Darwin is.[75]

Therefore, an unstable PNG means Australia is vulnerable; clearly, this is a situation that Australia cannot ignore. There are global, regional and domestic considerations in the relationship between PNG and Australia, and very real incentives for Australia to invest heavily in social stability and economic progress in PNG. However, if one were to apply a PESTEL (political, economic, social, technological, environmental, legal) analysis to the relationship, it is the political and the legal that have been the most influential in the development of the policing aspect of the broader PNG-Australian relationship, and this has been detrimental to actual progress, and as a by-product, harmful to the reputation of the AFP. The recent involvement of the AFP in PNG can be seen in two stages: (1) the PNG ECP in 2005 and (2) the PNG-Australia Police Partnership (PNG-APP), which ran in phases from 2008 to the present.

Enhanced Cooperation Program (ECP): 2004–2005

For many years, the forerunner to AusAID, the Australian International Development Aid Bureau (AIDAB), provided police advisors to the RPNGC under contract. However, in the mid-2000s, under the Howard Doctrine, which had enjoyed relative successes in East Timor and the Solomon Islands, the AFP deployed serving members to work alongside their RPNGC counterparts in an executive policing role. This had mixed success due to a range of factors, not because of the successful constitutional challenge to the immunities under which Australian police deployed to PNG in 2005.

The governance underpinning this deployment commenced with the 'Enhanced Cooperation Program: RPNGC-AFP ECP Policing Assistance Component: Implementing Agreement', signed in August 2004, also referred to as the 'Madang Agreement' or the 'ECP Treaty', which was enacted into PNG law in the *Enhanced Cooperation between Australia and Papua New Guinea Act 2004 (ECP Act)*. This included the deployment of both Assisting Australian Police Personnel (AAPP) as well as other Australian government personnel deployed to work with their counterparts in PNG government departments and agencies. The objective of the ECP was to work in partnership with the Government of PNG to address core issues in law and order and justice, as well as capacity in the RPNGC.

Enhanced Cooperation Treaty 2004

A number of administrative and legal arrangements were included in the ECP Act of 2004. These included the granting of 'functions, powers, authorities and privileges exercised by members of the RPNGC' under Article 3 (7). Crucially, AAPP members were not 'members' of the RPNGC for the purposes of carrying out their duties. Further, they were subject to command and control by the head of the AAPP, a deployed AFP senior officer who was required to report administratively to the Commissioner of the RPNGC but was also operationally responsible to the Commissioner of the AFP. There was, thus, a conflict of sovereignty. To which Commissioner did these police owe their loyalty?

In acknowledgement of the highly litigious nature of PNG society, and due to the exposure AAPP members would have to vexatious and malicious prosecutions, AAPP members were granted immunity from the civil jurisdiction of the PNG courts with respect to acts or omissions done in the course of, or incidental to, their official duties. It was these aspects of 'privilege' and 'immunity'[76] and the dual nature of reporting to two Commissioners that formed the basis of the successful constitutional challenge by the Governor of Morobe Province, Mr Luther Wenge. In its judgement, the PNG Supreme Court made a number of determinations, including:

1. The command structure, whereby AAPP were subject to the direction of the head of the AAPP, was held to be invalid because it undermined the constitutional requirement that the Commissioner of the RPNGC

have superintendence and control of the PNG Police Force (s.198 of the PNG Constitution).
2. The arrangements for dealing with criminal jurisdiction were held to be invalid because they were inconsistent with the unfettered prosecutorial discretion given to the PNG Public Prosecutor and members of the RPNGC under the PNG Constitution (ss.176 and 197(2) respectively).
3. The immunity from civil jurisdiction with respect to acts or omissions done in the course of or incidental to their official duties was held to be invalid to the extent that it affected the rights of persons to enforce rights and freedoms guaranteed by the PNG Constitution.[77]

This was deemed to be an unacceptable risk by the AFP, and the Australian Government withdrew the police component of the ECP in May 2005. This marked the end of the first serious attempt at addressing some of PNG's law and order issues by a large Australian 'boots on the ground' police intervention. There is no way of accurately assessing whether this approach would have been successful, but one lesson learned was that not everyone welcomes such interventions. Despite strong political support at the national level, the existence of such missions can be successfully challenged through an active judicial system, which embodies the rule of law and proves the existence of the separation of powers in PNG. It also raised the risk profile associated with such deployments by including exposure to legal risks as legitimate considerations for incorporation into mission planning alongside the security, physical and health risks.

Papua New Guinea Policing Partnership (PNG-APP) 2008–Present: Operation 'Wok Wantaim'

The period between the end of the ECP in 2005 and the commencement of the PNG-APP in 2008 featured two significant events relevant to the AFP IDG and its reputation. The first was the election of the Rudd government in 2007 and its changed posture in relation to the region, and the second was the deployment of AFP members to Afghanistan, which will be discussed in detail in a later section. The PNG-APP will be discussed below.

Following the withdrawal of the ECP in 2005 due to its conflict with the PNG Constitution, the AFP under the Rudd government negotiated an agreement with the PNG Government of Prime Minister Peter O'Neill for the deployment of a relatively small number of AFP advisors to the RPNGC. This was known as Phase I. These seventeen members were deployed to the Bomana Police College and the Internal Affairs Directorate and carried out a range of support roles. In October 2011, the then Australian Parliamentary Secretary for Pacific Island Affairs, Richard Marles, stated:

> The sense of the need to have more police on the ground, more federal police, is certainly an issue that was raised on the PNG side, and it's certainly one we take very seriously and we're keen to assist.[78]

In 2012, Phases II and III of the PNG-APP were implemented, increasing the number of members deployed by eleven sworn and five unsworn, who focused on training, logistics, professional standards, governance and accountability management frameworks, fraud and anti-corruption. All AFP international deployments, including those to PNG, were affected by changing political circumstances in Canberra. The ECP under the Howard Doctrine had failed due to circumstances beyond the control of the AFP, both at the strategic level and the operational level. The Howard government was replaced in 2007 by the Rudd government in a landslide victory for the ALP. This started a cycle of political instability in Australia that distracted from issues such as police development in places such as PNG. This was exacerbated by a singular issue involving border control, which diverted attention away from most other government programs.

Regional Resettlement Program with Papua New Guinea

After eleven years in office, the conservative Howard government was voted out in 2007; Prime Minister Howard lost his own seat of Bennelong in Sydney. The Howard Government was replaced by the energetic government of Kevin Rudd, a progressive multi-lateralist with a strong belief in the UN and Australia's role in the Asia-Pacific region. Rudd himself was replaced by Julia Gillard after a leadership contest in June 2010. Rudd again took the prime ministership after another internal leadership contest in June 2013, shortly before the government was to face the electorate.

Between 2007 and 2013, the Rudd-Gillard-Rudd governments saw a significant influx of irregular maritime arrivals, including people from as far afield as Africa, the Middle East and Pakistan seeking asylum in Australia after transiting through Malaysia and Indonesia. This was electorally unpopular and was considered, at the political level, that a loss of control of borders would result in a loss of government. Shortly after Prime Minister Rudd replaced Prime Minister Gillard in 2013, he announced a Regional Resettlement Program with PNG, whereby those seeking asylum by arriving by boat from Indonesia would not be settled in Australia. In the lead-up to the 2013 federal election, *The Guardian* reported on 19 July 2013:

All asylum seekers who arrive in Australia by boat will be sent to Papua New Guinea for processing and resettlement and none will be allowed to stay in the country, the prime minister has announced, as he sent out a draconian pre-election message that Australia's borders are closed to refugees.

In what he said was 'a clear and undiluted message to every people smuggler in the world that your business model is basically undermined', Kevin Rudd said the new rules would apply initially for one year and there was no limit on the numbers of asylum seekers PNG would take.

In return, the government announced new aid to PNG for hospitals and universities and said it would pay unspecified 'resettlement costs' for the refugees as well as bearing the costs of the expansion and upgrade of the Manus Island processing centre. Rudd said only that the package would 'not be inexpensive' but no cost details were immediately available.[79] [80]

The Relationship Between Perceived National Interests and International Good Citizenship Exemplified

Although not overtly stated, the connection with an expanded police program in PNG was assumed, and in 2013, the AFP expanded the PNG-APP mission by fifty frontline police officers, known as Phase IV, following the agreement between Prime Ministers Rudd and O'Neill. That agreement included a small group of AFP officers deployed to Lae.

In September 2013, the Rudd ALP Government was replaced by a Liberal Government led by Prime Minister Tony Abbott, who continued both the Regional Resettlement Plan and the PNG-APP. Prime Minister Abbott was replaced as Prime Minister by Malcolm Turnbull in September 2015 due to a leadership vote in the Liberal Party. Prime Minister Turnbull continued both programs, although the Regional Resettlement Program was in its final stages, as the PNG Supreme Court deemed the detention centre illegal in May 2017 and ordered its closure by the end of 2017.

Despite the political and legal challenges, the PNG-APP mission now stands at forty-two members primarily in Port Moresby and Lae. These members are ostensibly involved in 'publicly visible policing activities', but lack executive police powers and have no authority. They are involved in training, prosecutions, station management, custody management, specialised crime squads and corporate management. Members also undertake joint foot patrols in community areas, including markets and shopping centres.

Throughout 2017, a significant number of these members were involved in duties related to the APEC meeting hosted by PNG in 2018. Much of this involved training and advising RPNGC members in duties specifically related to APEC. They included: traffic control, including motorcycle escorts, police intelligence, airport policing including counter terrorist first response, bomb search, canine operations, water police, CPP, hostage negotiations, investigations, custody management, gender issues, family and sexual violence, internal investigations, and POM. It should be noted that the RPNGC remains the sovereign authority in PNG and that the AFP activity is confined to advising and training. These are all areas in which the AFP has a particularly comprehensive skills and experience base. These tasks are important for the RPNGC to deliver the secure conduct of the APEC meetings and have had follow-on value for post-APEC policing in PNG.

Future Trends

One of the most serious challenges facing international police participating in an intervention involving police capacity development is the issue of community trust. As discussed, the nature and the level of crime in PNG are difficult to address via a liberal-democratic policing approach, particularly when the international police, in this case, the AFP, lacks authority and adequate capacity to make a meaningful contribution to addressing the underlying causes of crime. In the case of PNG, this appears to be a combination of cultural factors, such as tribal disputes, and social factors created by trends such as rapid urbanisation, high youth unemployment and an environment in which organised crime and corruption seem to thrive with impunity. Addressing these issues in any meaningful way in PNG through enhanced policing involves acting on two assumptions identified by ASPI in a Special Report by Connery and Claxton in October 2014[81]: first, that the PNG Government wants an effective police force and second, that Australia will continue to support an ongoing commitment to PNG's police force. A third assumption, not stated in the ASPI report, but raised in this book, is that PNG will prefer international assistance to come from Australia in the south rather than from Asia in the north. The latter remains an active issue.

The first assumption, that the PNG Government wants an effective police force, involves effective policing in all of its aspects, including an objective and impartial anti-corruption capability with authority and the capacity for it to deliver. It also involves developing a stronger relationship with the community. One significant lesson to come from the RAMSI mission in the Solomon Islands is that re-establishing community trust in the police once it has been lost can take many years. The situation in PNG is manifestly more complex than the Solomon Islands, and as the ASPI report identifies 'creating an effective RPNGC that can promote the rule of law, prevent crime, use resources to their maximum effect and contribute to a positive human rights situation in PNG is a generational undertaking'.[82]

The second assumption is that Australia will support an ongoing commitment to PNG's police. There are other Australian-led programs in PNG aimed at enhanced justice. They include: the PNG–Australia Law and Justice Program (PALJP), the Strongim Gavam Program and the Combating Corruption Project (CCP), all of which are funded by DFAT. The PNG-APP is the only program in this sector that is not funded by DFAT and, as such, is exposed to occasional unfavourable commentary from DFAT.

The impetus behind the decision to boost the PNG-APP in 2013, combined with the Regional Resettlement Program, no longer exists, as facilities on Manus Island have closed down and the pre-APEC incentive for enhanced training dissipated post-APEC. The underlying causes of crime will, in all likelihood, remain unaddressed, which will create a favourable environment for more organised criminal activity on Australia's vulnerable northern approaches and the potential risks attached. The influence in PNG of other regional actors such as the PRC in the policing sphere in PNG remains an open question.

The Melanesian Spearhead Group (MSG) and PNG

The third assumption, not stated by the ASPI paper, is that PNG will prefer international assistance to come from Australia in the south rather than from Asia in the north. The MSG has a 'Look North' policy, whereby it seeks greater connectivity with Asia, particularly China, in terms of investment and cultural exchange. The dynamics with the MSG are interesting in this regard, as they also have an impact on the PIF, which has been the pre-eminent supra-national body in the South West Pacific and was the authority that underwrote the RAMSI intervention in the Solomon Islands. Notably, the PIF membership includes Australia and New Zealand. An alternative group with connections with the MSG is the Pacific Islands Development Forum, which excludes Australia and New Zealand. Wallis states that this is 'an alternative caucus grouping at the United Nations, the "Pacific Small Island Developing States" (PSIDS) group, which has effectively replaced the PIF in this role'.[83]

Australia–PNG Relationships

The MSG 'Look North' posturing has obvious implications for regional dynamics, particularly as they relate to the Australia–PNG relationship. There are already other interested parties engaging with PNG and more broadly in the region. Carter and Firth (2015) identified some of these parties:

> China is a rising power in the region, the United States is responding to that rise, and Indonesia is claiming a Melanesian identity for its easternmost provinces as part of a concerted effort to forge closer links with the island

countries of the western Pacific. Japan, China, the United States, Korea, India, Indonesia, Israel and the European Union are all counted among the external states that have deepened their long-term connection with Melanesia in recent years, while the United Arab Emirates, Russia and Georgia are recent minor players on the scene. France is a Pacific Islands power with three Pacific territories.[84]

The implications of this sort of regional engagement for Australia are unknown. In relation to crime and criminal activity which may impact upon Australia or Australians, the AFP maintains a strong liaison presence in Port Moresby, independent of the PNG-APP mission. The duties of this post include participation in the PNG intelligence group responsible for monitoring activities in the Torres Strait, assisting the RPNGC with its conduit with INTERPOL, and the provision of support to the RPNGC TCU within the PTCN.

Australia has a unique relationship with PNG, particularly since it is a former Australian-administered territory. Since independence in 1975, the relationship has been seen primarily through the prism of PNG acting as a sentinel state for potential hostilities in the region or as a recipient of considerable amounts of foreign aid funding, and very little attention has been paid to its internal governance or its implications for Australia, which has the potential to affect Australian sovereignty and its peace and prosperity. The way in which Australia responds to the challenges posed by internal governance issues in PNG remains unclear. It is reasonable to assume that the AFP will have some sort of involvement, both in terms of protecting the safety and security of the Australian community and the promotion of humanitarian values within a culturally appropriate social contract in PNG.

Part IV

Applying The Rule of Law in Challenging Environments Further Afield 2007–2014

Afghanistan and Ukraine

AFP in Afghanistan from 2007 to 2014   177
Soviet Invasion and Occupation   178
UN and al Qaeda   179
9/11 Attacks – Connection with bin Laden   180
Northern Alliance   181
Bonn Agreement and International Security Assistance Force   182
NATO-ISAF   183
AFP Deployment to Afghanistan 2007   184
From Howard to Rudd: Political Optics   185
Police Operational Mentoring and Liaison Teams   186
No Peace to Keep, Corruption and Lucrative Cash Crop   187
Prime Minister Rudd December 2008   188
Counter-narcotics Intelligence 2008   189
Regional Command (South) 2008   190
Transfer and Transition 2009   191
Counter-terrorism to Counter-insurgency   192
Provincial Training Centre (PTC) Tarin Kot   194
A Reality Check   195
A Deteriorating Situation   196
President Obama's Exit Strategy   197
NATO Withdrawal 2020–2021   199
AFP and Afghanistan: Police Diplomacy?   201
MH17 Operation: Malaysia Airlines Flight MH17, 14 July 2014   202
International Diplomacy   204
International Justice   206
Russian Obstruction   207
Prosecution in The Netherlands   209
AFP and INTERPOL   210
MH17 AFP Operation 2024 Tried and Sentenced in Absentia   211

The AFP in Afghanistan from 2007 to 2014

As previously discussed, it needs to be borne in mind that when the Howard Government established the International Deployment Group in 2004, it was expressly stated that the intention was for the IDG to be a regional capability. It is worth repeating that Prime Minister John Howard stated in early 2004:

> the purpose of this group [the IDG] will be for deployment in the region. Nobody should construe from the formation of this group that we have in mind deployment further afield.[1]

Nonetheless, due to the relatively good reputation of the AFP IDG in Timor-Leste and the South West Pacific, and the AFP's good international reputation as an effective counter-narcotics agency, in 2006, a request was made by the British Foreign Secretary Jack Straw to Australian Foreign Minister Alexander Downer for assistance with the British Government's efforts in Afghanistan regarding the opium trade and its connections with the Taliban insurgency.[2]

This was the beginning of a seven-year series of deployments during which the focus continued to change along with the strategic and political environment. Afghanistan has a very complex history, and this made for an extremely complex operating environment.

A Complex History

Prior to a discussion of Australian involvement generally and AFP involvement specifically in Afghanistan, a brief discussion of the complex history of Afghanistan is necessary to provide background and context to its more contemporary troubles.

Afghanistan itself is an area of land that has never been centrally controlled and has been occupied by warlords for centuries. Its boundaries were created by the desire for a 'buffer' state between the Russian Empire in the north, Iran or Persia in the west and the frontier with the British Empire, usually referred to as the North West Frontier in what is now Pakistan. To prevent any part of the British Empire from directly bordering the Russian Empire, at the end of the Second Anglo-Afghan War in 1893, a line called the Durand Line was drawn through areas in what is now North West Pakistan. This created the present border between Pakistan and Afghanistan. Pakistan was part of British India during the Raj in the 19th century before the violent and bloody partition of India and Pakistan in 1949. The entire region is Islamic, predominantly Sunni, with the exception of Iran, which is Shi'a, and an ethnic group in central Afghanistan, the Hazaras, who are also

Shi'a. These are the descendants of the invading Mongol armies of Genghis Khan in the 13th century. The invasion and occupation by the Mongols were brutal and violent, and this has shaped present-day attitudes toward the surviving Hazaras, who are frequently victims of cultural violence and are largely confined to the remote highland provinces in the Hindu Kush mountain range that runs through Afghanistan from east to west.

When the Soviet revolution occurred in 1917, many Islamic people fled to Afghanistan, fearing the spread of communism into the old Russian Empire regions of Tajikistan, Turkmenistan and Uzbekistan, which are all directly north of and bordering Afghanistan. This displaced many of those who were already there, including the Pashtuns, who are ethnically and culturally related to their counterparts on the other side of the Durand Line in what is now present-day Pakistan. This naturally led to a great deal of resentment on the part of the Pashtuns.

The Soviet Invasion and Occupation

In 1979, the Soviet Union invaded Afghanistan from the north to support its puppet government in Kabul. The Afghan tribes put aside their differences and banded together to fight the Soviets in a war that lasted a decade and played a large part in the eventual fall of the Soviet Union and European communism. The Afghan fighters, known as Mujahideen, were joined by Islamic fighters from around the region, including Osama bin Laden from Saudi Arabia, and further afield, and they were supported by advanced weaponry from the U.S. Central Intelligence Agency (CIA), including Stinger anti-aircraft missiles, which were very effective against Soviet military helicopters. This was all part of strategic efforts at the height of the Cold War. The Soviets eventually withdrew in 1989, as did the U.S., which left a significant power vacuum filled largely by warlords who returned to their traditional ways.

The Taliban

With the end of hostilities, many Pashtun Mujahideen went to Madrassas in Pakistan to study the Holy Koran. These religious scholars were known as Talibs. They united as the Taliban to return to Afghanistan 'to restore peace, disarm the population, enforce Sharia, or Islamic law, and defend Islam in Afghanistan'.[3] They re-entered Afghanistan from the south and took Kandahar, Afghanistan's second-largest city, in 1994, followed by Herat in the west and the capital Kabul in 1996, and finally Mazar-e-Shariff in the north in 1998, massacring more than four thousand Hazaras, Tajiks and Uzbeks. They were financed by Saudi Arabia and the United Arab

Emirates through Pakistan's Inter-Services Intelligence (ISI), which had direct connections to the Taliban through its tribal affiliations. The Taliban then formed a government called the Islamic Emirate of Afghanistan (IEA). During this period, an Islamic scholar in the Kandahar region called Mullah Omar formed a relationship with the Saudi Arabian former Mujahideen Osama bin Laden, and they lived together in Kandahar in 1996:

> The CIA already considered bin Laden a threat, but he was left alone to ingratiate himself with Mullah Omar by providing money, fighters and ideological advice to the Taliban. Bin Laden gathered the Arabs left behind in Afghanistan and Pakistan from the war with the Soviets, enlisted more militants from Arab countries, and established a new global terrorist infrastructure called al Qaeda.[4]

The significance of the relationship with Mullah Omar was that bin Laden now had an entire country at his disposal to train global Islamic jihadists. There had been training camps operating in Afghanistan, which were financed by the ISI, to train insurgents for use in the disputed province of Kashmir on the Indian–Pakistan border. Bin Laden used these camps to train thousands of extremists to extend al Qaeda operations globally. It was during this period that bin Laden planned the bombings of the U.S. embassies in Kenya and Tanzania on 7 August 1998, which killed 224 people and wounded nearly 5000 and made bin Laden a man wanted by the U.S. authorities.

The UN and al Qaeda

As a result of these attacks, the UN Security Council passed Resolution 1267 in October 1999, which demanded that the Taliban in Afghanistan surrender bin Laden and cease providing sanctuaries to terrorists. This was followed by UN Security Council Resolution 1333 in December 2000, which imposed an arms ban on the Taliban government, the seizure of the Taliban's assets outside Afghanistan and demanded the closure of the training camps. These UN Security Council Resolutions were ignored by the Taliban government and its ISI backers. Finally, on 30 July 2001, the UN Security Council passed Resolution 1363, which authorised monitors on Afghanistan's borders to ensure that the UN arms embargo was enforced. This angered the Taliban government in Afghanistan and their Pakistani supporters, who threatened to kill UN monitors.

While the U.S. authorities were closely monitoring the situation, they appear to have underestimated the immediacy and the magnitude of the threat. Rashid states that between January and September 2001, 216 internal threat warnings were issued by the FBI, and thirty-three National Security

Agency intercepts relating to the possibility of an al Qaeda attack were reported. In July, a briefing paper by the CIA to President Bush stated:

> We believe that [bin Laden] will launch a significant terrorist attack against U.S. and/or Israeli interests in the coming weeks…attack preparations have been made…and will occur with little or no warning'.[5]

9/11 Attacks – Connection with bin Laden

On 11 September 2001, nineteen militants associated with al Qaeda hijacked four airliners in the north-east of the U.S. and carried out suicide attacks against iconic targets in the U.S. Two planes were flown into the towers of the World Trade Centre in New York City, a third plane hit the Pentagon just outside Washington, DC, and the fourth crashed in a field in Pennsylvania. The attacks resulted in extensive death and destruction with over 3000 fatalities, including over 400 police officers and firefighters as first responders. The reaction by the U.S. was calculated and deliberate. In addition to the warning given to nations who may be harbouring terrorists or their associates, there was specific mention of Afghanistan. The rationale for this was the connection between bin Laden, Mullah Omar and the IEA: the Taliban. Further to the plan to attack the World Trade Centre, the Pentagon and other targets in the U.S., bin Laden provided two potential Saudi suicide pilots and two Yemeni volunteers who ultimately were unable to obtain U.S. visas. The Saudis had no problem obtaining visas to enter the US. They practised with flight simulators on personal computers and were supplemented by four volunteers from the German city of Hamburg, who travelled separately to and from Kandahar on a regular basis to meet with bin Laden.

According to Woodward, al Qaeda was deliberately recruiting from thirty-five countries whose citizens did not require visas to enter the U.S. and was bringing them into the ungoverned regions in Afghanistan in large numbers to train them in all aspects of asymmetric warfare, including the use of explosives and chemical agents, and was trying to acquire biological weapons.

The CIA was aware of Islamic extremists generally in Germany and sought assistance from the German police, but were largely unsuccessful, as German courts placed strict limitations on police intrusion, and some German politicians and intellectuals dismissed American concerns over global Islamic terrorism as overblown and even naïve; a legacy of the reaction to Germany's Nazi past in which policing was both highly intrusive and extremely violent. The plot by these specific individuals was missed by the Americans, which is not surprising, as once they had entered the US, they lived as normal members of the community for a period of time, during which they amassed 364 false names between them to avoid detection as they planned and eventually carried out the attacks on 11 September 2001.[6]

The United States Reaction: Operation Enduring Freedom

On 20 September that year, President Bush addressed a Joint Session of Congress, which was broadcast worldwide. In this address, President Bush made specific reference to Afghanistan. He stated:

> Al Qaeda is to terror what the mafia is to crime. But its goal is not making money; its goal is remaking the world…and imposing its radical beliefs on people everywhere.
>
> This group and its leader…a person named Osama bin Laden…are linked to many other organizations in different countries…The leadership of al Qaeda has great influence in Afghanistan and supports the Taliban regime in controlling most of that country.
>
> And tonight, the United States of America makes the following demands on the Taliban: Deliver to United States authorities all the leaders of al Qaeda who hide in your land…Close immediately and permanently every terrorist training camp in Afghanistan, and hand over every terrorist, and every person in their support structure, to appropriate authorities. Give the United States full access to terrorist training camps, so we can make sure they are no longer operating.
>
> These demands are not open to negotiation or discussion. The Taliban must act, and act immediately. They will hand over the terrorists, or they will share in their fate.[7]

Northern Alliance

The 9/11 attacks engendered significant international support for the U.S., and international pressure mounted against the Taliban Government in Afghanistan. A number of exiled Afghan leaders joined forces to take up an armed offensive against the Taliban administration. Their coalition was known as the Northern Alliance, but it was officially known as The United Islamic Front for the Salvation of Afghanistan. Iran, Russia and India, which had funded and armed the Northern Alliance, stepped up their military support. The Northern Alliance fought a two-month campaign against the Taliban-led IEA and took Kabul in December 2001.[8] The resultant Afghan administration was known as the Government of the Islamic Republic of Afghanistan (GIRoA).

The involvement of Iran and India broadened the dimensions of the strategic environment, as Shi'a Iran was fighting a proxy war against its Sunni Islamic rival, Saudi Arabia, which was, in part, funding the Taliban-led IEA through Pakistan. India was similarly fighting a proxy war with its regional rival Pakistan, whose connections with the Pashtun Taliban have been discussed. The involvement of India and Pakistan raised the stakes considerably, as both countries are nuclear powers. The involvement of Russia naturally attracted the attention of the U.S. The potential involvement of nuclear weaponry was not confined to the nuclear powers mentioned but extended to al Qaeda itself.

According to Rashid:

> In the first months after 9/11, the CIA was deeply fearful of a follow-up nuclear or bio-logical weapons attack on the American mainland by al Qaeda. In 1998, bin Laden had said that obtaining nuclear weapons was a 'religious duty' and he spoke frequently about creating an American Hiroshima. The discovery at al Qaeda safe houses in Afghanistan of computer disks, laboratories, and even a crude diagram of a nuclear bomb, showing that al Qaeda was experimenting with biological and nuclear warfare, only confirmed the worst about al Qaeda's intentions.[9]

It was clear that the primary way to prevent al Qaeda from obtaining nuclear material was through a relationship with Pakistan. Bin Laden had fled to the remote *Federally Administered Tribal Areas (FATA)* in Pakistan in December 2001 following the U.S. reprisals for the 9/11 attacks in the form of Operation Enduring Freedom (OEF), which complemented the military offensive by the Northern Alliance. The FATA became the new base for al Qaeda.[10]

Bonn Agreement and The International Security Assistance Force (ISAF)

While OEF and the Northern Alliance were having an impact on the ground in Afghanistan, the international community was seeking a long-term, sustainable solution to stability in Afghanistan once the 'peace' was 'made' by military force. This was arranged by Germany, which had acted as a broker during the Afghan civil war in the 1990s by hosting an unofficial dialogue between the UN, the Taliban and the Northern Alliance. Germany was regarded as an honest broker by these parties, and the German Government hosted discussions in the former capital, Bonn, in December 2001. An agreement, known as the *Agreement on Provisional Arrangements in Afghanistan Pending the Reestablishment of Permanent Government Institutions*, was promulgated from the Bonn discussions. The declaration specifically included a new Afghan security force, but no specific mention was made of a new Afghan police force.

The Bonn agreement also created a second international intervention force, the ISAF, under UN Security Council Resolution 1386 of 20 December 2001. ISAF was given an enforcement mandate under Chapter VII of the Charter of the United Nations. ISAF was not initially under the command of NATO but under British, Turkish, German and Dutch command before coming under the command of NATO in August 2003.

ISAF was initially tasked with providing security in the capital, Kabul, but in August 2003, once NATO assumed command, a UN Security Council Resolution authorised ISAF to expand beyond Kabul. This took the form of Provincial Reconstruction Teams in each province to be led by a NATO member. Simultaneously, four cross-cutting nation-wide lines of effort were devised, and Britain assumed leadership for counter-narcotics, Germany assumed leadership for policing, Italy assumed leadership for justice, and the U.S. assumed leadership for training the Afghan military.

As a result, there were now two separate command structures for foreign forces in Afghanistan: the NATO-ISAF command responsible for 'peacekeeping' and 'nation-building' based in Kabul and the provinces, and the U.S.-led Coalition hunting for terrorists under OEF. The UN also had a presence in Afghanistan in the form of the United Nations Assistance Mission to Afghanistan (UNAMA); however, due to the non-permissive security environment throughout the country, particularly in the south, its influence was negligible.

NATO-ISAF

It needs to be acknowledged that Afghanistan was an active conflict zone and that NATO was one of the belligerents. It also needs to be stated clearly that Australia is not a member of NATO and, thus, required a host member nation of NATO to participate. This was done via an arrangement between the British Ministry of Defence and the Australian Department of Defence. There were several iterations of ADF engagement in Afghanistan[11] prior to the initial AFP deployment in 2007. The AFP is not part of the Australian Defence apparatus and, as such, had to be hosted by the ADF and also be formally invited by the Government of the Islamic Republic of Afghanistan (GIRoA) to deploy there. There was a growing suspicion as time went on that the ADF was seeking an exit strategy and that it saw a handover to the AFP as part of that strategy.[12] This line of thought has its genesis in the heavily military-oriented concept of Security Sector Reform (SSR).[13] Further complicating this thinking, funding for such engagement came largely from ODA, which had severe restrictions on the type of activities international police deployments could engage in (See Appendix 7). This created the absurd situation whereby the Australian Government of the day requested the AFP to deploy to an active war zone with poorly defined objectives and desired outcomes and was expected to submit funding proposals for it to do so.

It was in this highly complex geopolitical strategic environment that the AFP commenced its seven-year engagement in Afghanistan.

AFP Deployment to Afghanistan 2007

Australia's role in Afghanistan spanned four phases: 2001 to 2005, 2005 to 2008, 2008 to 2013 and 2014 onwards. The AFP was primarily involved from 2008 to 2013, with an extra year on either side of this period. The legal basis for Australian involvement in operations in Afghanistan was twofold: authorisation under United Nations Security Council Resolution (UNSCR) 1883 and at the invitation of the GIRoA. Australia's military commitment to Afghanistan operated as part of the NATO-led ISAF as a peace-enforcement mission under Chapter VII of the UN Charter. British Foreign Secretary Jack Straw made his request for an Australian police contribution to assist with mentoring the newly created Counter Narcotics Police of Afghanistan (CNPA) in early 2006. Due to administrative difficulties relating to visas to enter Afghanistan and some negotiations between Canberra and Kabul concerning duties and immunities, the deployment was delayed until the second half of 2007.

In addition, ISAF had established a US-led Combined Security Transition Command-Afghanistan (CSTC-A), which had assumed the role of reforming the Afghan National Police (ANP) from the Germans to collectively deliver a professional police force to enhance the security of the Afghan people. One AFP member was seconded to CSTC-A to advise an exclusively military and a predominantly U.S. command structure on elements of police reform. Among the contributions made by this member was the adoption of an amended police recruit training package from the AFP College in Barton, Canberra. There was also a need for advice on criminal investigations to the Ministry of the Interior within the GIRoA, so one member, the Mission Commander, was tasked with these duties.

In the meantime, in February 2007, the Afghan Ambassador to Australia, Mr Mohammed Anwar Anwarzai, highlighted the narcotics problem in Afghanistan, its connection with the Taliban insurgency and the risk this posed of creating a 'narco-state.'

As Mark Dodd of *The Australian* wrote:

> Afghanistan has warned it could unravel into a terrorist-backed narco-state unless Australia and the rest of the international community send specialist

police to combat the heroin trafficking which is funding the Taliban insurgency.

The war-battered nation's ambassador to Canberra, Mohammed Anwar Anwarzai, said yesterday Australia's military deployment had helped build local trust, but a dangerous vacuum existed in the wake of their withdrawal last year. 'Unfortunately, we are now on the verge of becoming a narco-state. I can confess to that.' Mr Anwarzai told The Australian.

In its first acknowledgement of the extent of the problem, Canberra is planning to send four AFP agents to Afghanistan to help with police training and monitoring of illicit opium exports. Two armed AFP agents will be based in the opium heartland of Jalalabad to gather intelligence on opium smuggling.[14]

On 16 October 2007, four AFP officers were deployed to Afghanistan. Two members were deployed to Kabul, working under the auspices of the CSTC-A and the Afghan Ministry of the Interior, respectively, and two members were located in Jalalabad and worked under the auspices of the British Embassy Drug Team with the CNPA. Significantly, their life support was provided by a private British security firm known as ArmorGroup, which was later acquired by G4S. The expense this incurred was to influence the way the AFP was postured in Afghanistan with the incoming Rudd government in 2007.

From Howard to Rudd: Political Optics

When the Howard government was voted out of office and replaced by the Rudd government in 2007, there was an immediate change of posture in relation to the AFP in Afghanistan. When in opposition, Prime Minister Rudd had been highly critical of the Howard government for its involvement of the Australian military in the U.S. invasion and occupation of Iraq. He had been less vocal in relation to Afghanistan and, in fact, had supported Australia's military involvement there primarily because it was a reaction to the 9/11 attacks and because the international involvement in Afghanistan, both OEF and ISAF, had the authority of the UN. Significantly, the four original AFP members had only been in Afghanistan for a short time when the Rudd government was elected, and he was taking advice from many quarters in relation to Afghanistan, but crucially, it seems, not the AFP.

In May 2008, Raspal Khosa from the ASPI wrote a paper that highlighted the importance of SSR in Afghanistan and urged the use of the AFP IDG based on its record for capacity-building, mentoring and peacekeeping operations. Khosa specifically referred to the use of the AFP to mentor the ANP via a police Operations Mentoring Liaison Team (OMLT) to be based in Uruzgan Province, whereby 'the Australian Government would realise the synergies with any proposed ADF training activity, particularly the instruction of police in small arms and other tactical activity'.[15]

Police Operational Mentoring and Liaison Teams (POMLT)

The OMLT concept was used by the ISAF military whereby military trainers, mentors and liaison officers accompanied their Afghan National Army (ANA) counterparts in the field. From a policing perspective, this concept, dubbed 'POMLT' (Police Operations Mentoring and Liaison Team), was highly problematic due to the profound differences in field operations and daily duties between the respective roles, composition and structure of the military and the police in such endeavours. These differences were exacerbated by the non-permissive environment of southern Afghanistan in 2008.

The military is generally well armed, moves in groups and is well supported by force protection. Its duties in conflict, including in insurgencies such as Afghanistan, are dirty, dangerous and difficult but relatively straightforward: to train in the use of weapons and tactics, oversee leadership decisions and ensure effective communications are maintained, and when in direct contact with their adversaries, employ as much force as required, with the expectation of immediate fire support and medical evacuation if needed. The military is well suited and equipped for this role; after all, this is its raison d'être.

Policing, on the other hand, is generally done on an individual basis or in small groups and, if it is done correctly, involves maximum community engagement and interaction and often unseen investigations to detect, deter, disrupt and prevent crime, including violent crime, and other criminal activity, such as corruption and narcotics dealing. While there is an active insurgency, policing can be equally dirty, difficult and arguably more complex and dangerous due to exposure and vulnerability to those hostile to police activities, including violent extremists, those involved in the narcotics trade and those whose actions are corrupt. The latter may include some of the host police themselves, particularly at a leadership level, where the incentives for corruption are the highest, which exposes international police mentors to danger from the very people they are tasked to assist and with whom they would be intimately dealing with a view to their arrest prosecution. A dangerous endeavour in Australia; a death warrant in southern Afghanistan. This sort of proposal for the deployment of AFP members to an active war zone in Afghanistan was a long stretch from Howard's clear statement that the IDG was only for limited regional deployment in Australia's immediate, and relatively benign, region.

No Peace to Keep, A Low Base, Corruption and a Lucrative Cash Crop

The role of the police is to engage with the local population to prevent crime, identify offences, bring offenders to justice, and generally keep the peace. The existence of the latter underpins all three other functions; to administer justice and 'keep the peace', there must be a 'peace to keep'. There is no prospect of justice, very little chance of detection of offences and almost zero chance of benign crime prevention, in a liberal-democratic sense, until there is such a peace. In the case of Afghanistan, particularly in Regional Command (South), including Uruzgan Province, such a peace was highly elusive.

An additional complication for policing, as opposed to military mentoring, in southern Afghanistan was that the ANA was predominantly composed of soldiers from the ethnic groups from the north of Afghanistan, the Tajiks, Uzbeks and Turkmen, whose predecessors had formed the Northern Alliance and ousted the Pashtun dominated Taliban IEA Government, with U.S. support, in the immediate aftermath of 9/11. The ANP, however, were locally recruited from the predominantly Pashtun population in the south of the country. The prospect of a 'blue on blue' incident was a very real prospect based on this aspect alone, to say nothing of the vulnerabilities created by exposure to the criminal activities detailed above.

Among the shortcomings of the ANP, in addition to illiteracy and inadequate training, was the fact that corruption was widespread, and there was an ambiguous relationship between the police and the public as a result. This cannot be addressed by training or mentoring in the field without intimate supervision and highly intrusive protocols. A further complication involved the connection between police corruption and the burgeoning trade in opiates. Opium poppies are a cash crop in many parts of Afghanistan. The UN had a 'line of control' below which they recommended that enforcement action not take place. This was to protect the livelihoods of local poppy farmers and their employees; thus, the only part of the supply chain that could be addressed by policing at a local level was the actual heroin production and its distribution by road to its worldwide market. The execution of search warrants and the interception of such road transport was a highly dangerous activity, particularly because any authority to pursue these activities under the rule of law, such as local warrants, was made almost impossible because police and courts in particular came into favour as specific Taliban targets.[16] Either that, or they were active participants in the drug trade themselves.

The AFP members deployed to Afghanistan were armed with Glock 9 mm Self Loading Pistols for self-protection, not law enforcement and in any circumstance in Afghanistan, such lightly armed police were outgunned. Any involvement in the POMLT concept, which included mentoring the ANP in enforcing dubious laws 'outside the wire'[17] dealing with well-armed and well-connected criminals in a highly lucrative trade in illicit narcotics, where English was rarely spoken, was a risk the AFP was not prepared to take. Such activities in Australia, where the AFP legitimately enforces criminal law, would be subject to detailed risk assessments and judicial oversight with every precaution taken to ensure member safety. For the AFP to engage in such POMLT activities 'outside the wire' in an environment such as Uruzgan Province was suicidal and ultimately futile, a fact recognised by those on the ground but apparently not by their political masters in Canberra. The depth of analysis appeared to be in part based on the similarity of the abbreviations of the AFP and the ANP nomenclature: 'Australian Federal Police similar to Afghan National Police. Good enough. Deploy and do "police stuff".'

Prime Minister Rudd December 2008

When Prime Minister Rudd and his security advisor Duncan Lewis travelled to Tarin Kot (TK) in Uruzgan Province just before Christmas 2008, the latter made a direct approach to the senior AFP member present who had just assumed the role of AFP narcotics intelligence coordinator in TK. The exchange, as related to the author in a personal communication, went as follows: "'If money and security weren't a problem, could you do POMLTs?" The response was, "If money and security aren't the problem then we can basically do anything asked of us."' This exchange was reported to the AFP in Canberra via the Team Leader of the Afghanistan Mission Desk at the IDG who reported it up the chain to the National Manager IDG (NMIDG), and alarm bells rang immediately at the IDG at Majura.

There is no evidence of prior consultation by Government with the AFP in Canberra, so the first time this concept was made known to the AFP was when a high-ranking official in the Prime Minister's party, a former senior military officer, approached a relatively junior officer in the field directly. This 'outside the wire' approach to police mentoring was repeated during another visit by Mr Rudd, this time as Foreign Minister, in TK in March 2011. This is indicative of the ad hoc approach to policy involving police deployments under this particular government, which appeared to have been based on concepts advanced by the Canberra 'Good Ideas Club' without consultation with the people who would actually have to perform these duties, namely, the police themselves or their agency heads, who had a duty of care and were ultimately responsible for their safety and welfare.[18]

Refocus AFP Efforts to Regional Command (South) and 'Leverage as Much as Possible from the ADF'

The reason this member was in TK was due to a direction from the government, pending the rotation of the first four members deployed, for the AFP to increase its numbers to eight, go to Regional Command (South) (RC[S]) and leverage the ADF as much as possible. The rationale for this was based on the cost of life support by G4S for the Kabul-based members. The two Jalalabad-based members had spent six months in that location working with the CNPA. Their means of transport between Kabul and Jalalabad was via a UN aircraft, which was withdrawn for passage by the AFP members for unspecified reasons.

The AFP members involved were in Kabul when this decision was made and returned to Jalalabad via a local bus service, which took them approximately six hours due to delays created by roadworks. This exposed them to an unacceptable risk of death, serious injury or kidnap, and, as a result, the Jalalabad post was closed forthwith by the AFP in Canberra, and these members were relocated to Kabul. When the direction came from the government in Canberra to refocus AFP efforts on RC(S), it was these members who conducted the initial scoping in Kandahar Airfield (KAF), the Headquarters of RC(S).

The broad directions to AFP for the second deployment were interpreted by AFP members, at the operational level, as being more related to the political optics of comparison between the new, fresh and progressive Rudd Government with the old, tired and conservative Howard Government. Such a perspective is given added credence when the instructions from the government also contained a direction to increase the number of AFP deployed to Afghanistan to twelve the following year.

The most confusing part of this direction was the fact that no further guidance was provided as to what the AFP members deployed to an active conflict zone were expected to actually do, other than a broad reference to 'counter-narcotics intelligence' and 'criminal intelligence'. In an effort to maximise the value of this increased commitment, an AFP delegation engaged interlocutors from the major law enforcement contributors to Afghanistan – the U.S., Britain, Canada and the Netherlands – to identify strategic opportunities to complement existing efforts.

Counter-narcotics Intelligence 2008

The general government intention behind the deployment of AFP to southern Afghanistan was to enhance support for international stabilisation operations in Afghanistan through the deployment of civil policing expertise to Australian whole-of-government activities in southern Afghanistan and other international efforts based in Kabul. The focus was on counter-narcotics and criminal intelligence by providing strategic, analytical and intelligence advice on counter-narcotics activities as part of the international stabilisation activities in cooperation with GIRoA to shape counter-narcotics activities. Kilcullen (2009) states that:

> [a]ccording to officers of the National Directorate of Security (NDS)-the Afghan intelligence service…the Taliban adopted a five-line information strategy, in the form of series of slogans, in early 2006. These were 'Our party, the Taliban'; 'Our people and nation, the Pashtun'; 'Our economy, the poppy'; 'Our constitution, the Shari'a'; and 'Our form of government, the emirate.'[19]

The configuration of the mission was, therefore, in three separate locations engaged in entirely different duties. Two members were located in Kabul, where the Mission Commander continued duties with CSTC-A and the Ministry of the Interior, and an embedded member with the Interagency Operations Coordination Centre (IOCC) dealing with the U.S. Drug Enforcement Agency (DEA) and the British Serious Organised Crime Agency (SOCA). Three members were located at KAF, where the intention was to locate two members as liaison officers and analysts in secure compartmentalised intelligence cells: the Kandahar Intelligence Fusion Centre (KIFC) and the Kandahar Fusion Centre (KFC), and a third member and supervisor of all members in RC(S) to act in the capacity of a law enforcement liaison officer with the British SOCA at KAF dealing primarily with the counter-narcotics effort.

The third location was in TK, Uruzgan Province. Three members were located at TK, with one member working as a SSR Adviser to the Dutch Commander responsible for police and SSR in the province. One acted as an intelligence officer within the TK Secure Compartmentalised Intelligence Fusion Team with a focus on force protection. The third member worked within the Tarin Kot Fused Intelligence Team, which acted as a clearing house for raw intelligence.

Regional Command (South) 2008

A significant challenge from an AFP perspective was that, aside from the Kabul-based positions, despite assurances in Canberra and assurances by ADF members on the ground in Regional Command (South) when the positions were first arranged, things and people had moved on, and the incoming AFP members arrived 'cold' to establish their own roles within this heavily militarised environment dominated by the U.S. military in an active conflict zone. Two of the positions in KAF required an extremely high-level security clearance, a fact not relayed to AFP Canberra, which resulted in two members not being able to enter the secure intelligence cells for a number of weeks until arrangements could be made for them to enter the Kandahar Intelligence Fusion Centre (KIFC). The KIFC was a military targeting cell, so AFP presence in this area was ill-advised, and would have been a breach of the funding guidelines under Official Development Assistance (ODA). On the ground in KAF, the senior AFP members there negotiated placement within a newly formed outpost of the Interagency Operations Coordination Centre (IOCC) in Kabul known as the Combined Joint Inter Agency Task Force-Nexus (CJIATF-N), which was a U.S.-led targeting cell.

The role of the AFP members in this cell was to look for connections between the insurgency and the narcotics trade and attempt to engender an opportunity for the Afghan authorities to deal with this connection via judicial and police action rather than kinetic military responses. There was, however, a disconnect between the AFP and the ANP in KAF, as the AFP were not permitted to leave the base and the ANP were not permitted on the base. The counter-narcotics mission was known as Operation Contego. This mission, however, was relatively short-lived, as the strategic direction changed again in 2009.

Transfer and Transition 2009

When the Obama administration took office from the Bush administration in January 2009, there was a changed strategy towards the situation in Afghanistan. Bob Woodward, in his 2011 book *Obama's Wars*, makes it clear that President Obama was seeking an exit strategy. In 2009, for the first time, the words 'transfer' and 'transition' appeared. 'The model had be-come clear, hold, hold, hold, hold and hold. Hold for years. There was no build, no transfer.'[20] The question was transfer or transition from what to what?

The answer was to transfer from an international guarantee of safety and security to a host government guarantee of safety and security, preferably with host-state police primacy. The solution, after a number of reports, was a full counter-insurgency (COIN) strategy, which involved one member of the security forces (international or domestic) for every forty or fifty members of the Afghan community nation-wide. This was later amended to consider the north relatively benign, as the main insurgency was in the south among the Pashtun Taliban, who considered themselves to be the legitimate government, the IEA, in exile.

Australian Whole-of-Government Strategic Objectives 2009

In April 2009, Prime Minister Rudd identified the whole-of-government strategic objectives and focuses for Australia's contribution to Afghanistan. These included stabilisation of the Afghan state through a combination of military, police and civilian efforts to consolidate the gains made by Afghan and international military forces, support for counter-narcotics efforts in Afghanistan, the re-establishment of security and rule of law in Afghanistan as an essential requirement for broader development aspirations, and the promotion of the capabilities of the ANP and policing agencies.

The AFP's expertise in building the capacity of community police overseas was considered well suited to the training and mentoring of the ANP at the Provincial Training Centre (PTC) in TK.[21] The AFP delivered tailored programs on values, ethics, general police duties and human rights. This was an attempt to apply internationally accepted processes and policies regarding the role of a police force within a democratic society to generate public confidence. This appeared to mesh with the transition from a Counter-Terrorism (CT) focus to a Counter-Insurgency (COIN) focus. CT is 'enemy' focussed and COIN is 'population-centric', however, as explained below, from a police and justice perspective, they are largely one and the same thing. As Kilcullen identifies:

> Counterinsurgency policing is substantially different from policing in a peacetime environment. The three key components required for effective police work in a counterinsurgency environment are community police officers, who act to secure and protect population centres and delivers basic public order and rule of law; field police (paramilitary organisations sometimes called constabulary or gendarmerie units), who conduct normal police duties but in a higher threat environment and typically are better armed and more mobile than community police; and a police intelligence or police special operations capability (sometimes called a 'special branch') that specifically targets and arrests insurgent underground cells.[22]

Counter-terrorism to Counter-insurgency

With the election of the Obama administration, the strategic approach changed from a predominantly counter-terrorism (CT) posture to a predominantly COIN approach. The confusing and grossly misunderstood aspect of this from a policing perspective is that both terrorists and insurgents do the same things: they use violence to attempt to achieve political ends. The NATO definitions do not leave much room for distinction between the two as far as their actual activities are concerned. The NATO definitions are as follows:

Terrorism
[t]he unlawful use or threatened use of force or violence against individuals or property in an attempt to coerce or intimidate governments or societies to achieve political, religious or ideological objectives.

Insurgency
[a]ctions of an organized, often ideologically motivated, group or movement that seeks to effect or prevent political change or to overthrow a governing authority within a country or a region, focused on persuading or coercing the population through the use of violence and subversion.

Counter Terrorism
offensive measures taken to neutralize terrorism before and after hostile acts are carried out. Note: Such measures include those counterforce activities justified for the defence of individuals as well as containment measures implemented by military forces or civilian organizations.

Counter Insurgency
Comprehensive civilian and military efforts made to defeat an insurgency and to address any core grievances.[23]

Both terrorism and insurgency involve the threat or actual use of force or violence to influence political outcomes based on a political, religious or ideological basis. From a policing perspective, these activities are considered crimes, and they are addressed in the same way; namely, all efforts are made to detect, deter, prevent and disrupt them, or if offences are actually committed, all efforts are made to identify the offenders and have them brought to justice. Herein lies the difference between the way police perceive and address such things and the way the military counters them. In the case of the U.S. military under the Presidency of George W. Bush, offensive CT measures meant using military force. In Afghanistan, this was OEF, which included aerial bombardment and missile attacks launched from U.S. Navy ships combined with aggressive action by special forces and CIA operatives on the ground. The OEF 'enemy-centric' CT operations continued while the NATO-ISAF focused on 'population-centric' COIN. This confused everybody: the Afghans, the military strategists, the military and, in particular, the police. To try to build a consent-based policing model within a non-existent justice sector while an active and offensive CT operation was in progress was an impossibility. Yet, those were the directions from Canberra emanating from the very top, acting on extremely poor advice and in the full knowledge that the risk-to-return equation was heavily weighted in the direction of extremely high risk with virtually zero return.

This had longer-term implications for the reputation of the AFP in the eyes of many of its whole-of-government partners, as the following illustrates. The AFP was ill-fitted for all the roles, as a 2016 Lessons Learned Report on Afghanistan commissioned by the Australian Civil Military Centre (ACMC) stated:

> For all their professionalism and experience...the AFP is not set up, trained or equipped as the sort of paramilitary force that would have been required to undertake joint counter-insurgency training patrols with the ANP and some of what was expected of the AFP went beyond what it is trained, prepared and equipped for, which led to some frustration.[24]

These are all well-intentioned aspirations and theoretically achievable from the safety and certainty of a policy office in Canberra. However, concepts such as stabilisation, security and the rule of law, and the application of internationally accepted processes and policies regarding the role of a police force within a democratic society to generate public confidence were not easily achieved in a place such as southern Afghanistan in 2009. Nonetheless, increased pressure was placed on the AFP to deploy 'outside the wire' along the lines of the highly risky POMLTs. It was patently clear to the AFP members on the ground and to a number of support staff in Canberra that this was highly risky, both physically in Afghanistan and politically in Canberra. There was also a growing suspicion that the ADF was looking for an exit strategy and saw the AFP as part of that strategy. This also begs the uncomfortable question as to whether the AFP was set up to fail in deploying to Afghanistan to attempt to achieve the unachievable. This remains an open question.

The Provincial Training Centre (PTC) Tarin Kot

As good fortune would have it, the Dutch were destined to leave Uruzgan Province as their involvement in Afghanistan became very unpopular, and the Dutch Government had collapsed in February 2010 as a result of the Labour Party withdrawing from the coalition over the extension of troop deployments after 2010. As a legacy project, the Dutch financed and constructed a Provincial Training Centre (PTC) for police in Uruzgan. The reason was that police recruited locally from Uruzgan Province feared for the safety of their families in their absence if they had to travel to the adjoining province of Kandahar. Negotiations occurred on the ground with the Dutch authorities for AFP trainers to take up positions at the PTC, which was quickly endorsed by AFP Canberra. On 29 April 2009, the Australian Prime Minister announced an additional AFP commitment of up to ten personnel to act as advisors to ANP training staff at the PTC at Camp Holland in TK in the Uruzgan Province. These personnel and roles were known as Operation Synergy.

The curriculum for the ANP basic patrolman's course was a basic eight-week training program developed under the Focused District Development (FDD) initiative. A member of the initial AFP deployment had significant input into the development of this program in his role as advisor to the CSTC-A. The FDD basic police curriculum was continuously reviewed and enhanced to best meet the needs of the ANP. This is fortunate because the U.S. Commander ISAF Gen. David Petraeus reviewed the FDD police training course in 2009, and as Woodward states:

> Petraeus had immersed himself in the details. He studied the police training schedule for an eight-week course. He kept looking at it. Something was missing. He soon realised there was no time on the shooting range.[25]

A Reality Check

An event described by Australian diplomat Ian (Fred) Smith, involving ANP members in TK township, provides an explanation as to the efficacy of this basis para-military policing approach in a non-permissive security environment such as southern Afghanistan during this period. Mr Smith, a DFAT representative in Uruzgan Province, was due to meet some Afghan representatives from the Provincial Governor's office, who were held up by an incident involving a suicide bomber waiting in ambush for them. The bomber was shot in the face by the ANP members present; this is a good example of why a liberal-democratic policing approach to generate public confidence was a flawed approach.

Smith recorded how:

> The governor said the bomber had been waiting outside the compound for him but when he did not emerge had moved towards the adjacent bank building, where Afghan National Police officers were drawing their salaries as they usually did on Sunday mornings. An ANP officer spotted the bomber and quietly alerted two colleagues; one grabbed the bomber's left arm, the other grabbed his right arm (thereby preventing him from touching together the two detonation wires hidden up his sleeves). The third shot the bomber in the face. Not a bad effort; the governor was pleased.[26]

In Australia, this would be regarded as police murder, and the police concerned would be prosecuted to the full extent of the law. In Afghanistan, it was applauded by the governor. The difference lies, in large part, in the permissiveness of the environment and the commensurate tolerance for such forceful policing.

A Deteriorating Situation

There are indications that Mr Rudd was aware of the deteriorating situation on the ground in southern Afghanistan, both as Prime Minister and as Foreign Minister, and that the increasing casualties of Australian soldiers was taking its toll politically. In March 2009, SBS News reported that a recent poll indicated that 65 per cent of those polled were against increased troop deployments to Afghanistan. In the same article, it was reported that 'the situation in Afghanistan was becoming even more challenging and would require a continued commitment and that progress in Afghanistan would require a better integrated strategy, involving military, police and development assistance'.[27]

On 29 April 2009, just a month later, on the ABC 7.30 Report, Michael Brissenden interviewed Prime Minister Rudd, who stated:

> Australia concurs with the United States that the current civilian and military strategy is not working. If anything, security in Afghanistan is deteriorating…I think this is going to become progressively an unpopular war. I accept that for the reality that it is. I am also seized of the fact that we have a responsibility to prevent Afghanistan from becoming a training base again for terrorists to go out and kill more Australians, and that we have a responsibility to our American ally consistent with our treaty obligations.[28]

The deterioration of the security in Afghanistan was known to Mr Rudd as early as 2008, as a Sydney Morning Herald report from 2010 indicates, with reference to the mass leaking of diplomatic cables by Wikileaks. The article, titled 'Rudd: "Scared as Hell"' by Philip Dorling and Nick McKenzie on 10 December, stated that the government was deeply pessimistic about Australia's engagement in Afghanistan, and that some officials had described the task of training police in Afghanistan as hopeless.

The article further stated:

> Referring to Australia's plan to increase funds for training Afghan police - a task undertaken by more than two dozen federal police officers - Mr Smith warned it might involve 'putting good money into a bad situation'.
>
> Another cable, from December last year, says that:
>
> Smith [Australian Foreign Minister] questioned what the AFP would be able to accomplish given the 'train wreck' that they had to be given to work with in the Afghan National Police.
>
> A cable from October 2008, which records what Mr Rudd told a group of visiting U.S. congressmen, says he 'concluded by noting that the national

security establishment in Australia was very pessimistic about the long-term prognosis for Afghanistan'.

The U.S. cables also reveal that the head of the AFP's IDG, Assistant Commissioner Frank Prendergast, had also raised concerns about what federal police officers could achieve in Afghanistan.[29]

Nonetheless, Mr Rudd was prepared to place increased numbers of AFP members in harm's way in the full knowledge that the security situation was badly deteriorating and that AFP members were unlikely to achieve anything significant in Afghanistan.

President Obama's Exit Strategy 2009-2011

Although the COIN strategy was implemented in April 2009, the situation was further complicated in December 2009 when President Obama promulgated his Final Orders for the Afghanistan-Pakistan Strategy, which included the intention to deny safe haven to al Qaeda and deny the Taliban the ability to overthrow the Afghan Government. This was based on a strategic concept of degrading the Taliban insurgency while rebuilding sufficient Afghan capacity to secure and govern Afghanistan, thereby creating conditions for the U.S. to commence a reduction of forces by July 2011.[30]

Once a timeframe had been made known, the Taliban government in exile was able to increase its intimidation of the population and regularly used direct threats against them via 'night letters', which threatened retribution on those who cooperated with the international forces. This announcement allowed the Taliban to adopt a posture where the internationals had 'all the watches', but the Taliban had 'all the time'. In terms of justice and governance, as David Kilcullen has stated, 'a government that is losing to an insurgency is not being outfought, it is being out-governed.'[31]

The Taliban, as an alternative government, was administering its own form of 'justice' and dispute resolution. Those who advocated for the application of internationally accepted processes and policies regarding the role of a police force within a democratic society to generate public confidence in Afghanistan were oblivious to the fact that the internationals might have 'all the law', but the Taliban had 'all the justice'.

Operations Synergy and Contego were combined in 2010 to form Operation Illuminate, which continued in all three locations: Kabul, Kandahar and TK. The AFP eventually closed its mission in Afghanistan in 2014.

2012-2014

The AFP deployed personnel to several Kabul-based roles between 2007 and 2014, including an SES-level representative from June 2011 until September

2013. The initial role of this member was as Senior Advisor to the NATO Training Mission-Afghanistan (NTM-A), Deputy Commander-Police and Executive Police Advisor to the Afghan Government's Deputy Minister for Security. In 2012, this member occupied a lead role on the International Police Coordination Board, the main coordination body for police reform in Afghanistan.

Other experienced AFP officers undertook advisory roles with either NATO or Afghan authorities or assisted the European Union Police training mission in Kabul. Others performed duties with the Major Crime Task Force in conjunction with the U.S. FBI.

The most salient lesson learned from an AFP perspective was the inappropriateness of attempting to apply liberal-democratic policing approaches in a non-permissive environment. As stated by the ACMC report:

> The international military intervention, which began as a counter-terrorism campaign increasingly, took on the characteristics of a counter-insurgency campaign and, in significant parts of the country, stabilisation operations of the kind usually seen in post-conflict situations were not possible. Perhaps the best that can be said is that stabilisation-type activities were undertaken in parallel with continuing conflict.[32]

If this was a challenge for the ADF, whose role is to engage in both CT and COIN, these challenges were amplified for the AFP IDG, which was established for capacity development in relatively benign environments[33] such as the South West Pacific rather than active combat zones such as southern Afghanistan, as per the Howard Governments intent when establishing the IDG in 2004.

Opium

Another context, and the primary reason the AFP was initially deployed to Afghanistan in 2007, was narcotics. According to Rashid, the opium problem in the region began in Pakistan in the 1980s, where the Mujahideen were encouraged to grow and sell opium and heroin to fund their anti-Soviet activities while the Pakistani ISI and the CIA turned a blind eye. In addition, as the Taliban expanded through Afghanistan, they assumed control of the opium trade and its export through Pakistan, Iran, Central Asia and the Arabian Gulf through al Qaeda contacts.[34]

Crop eradication was seen as problematic because so many low-level farmers and micro-economies were dependent upon the cash crop of poppy harvests. Drug money and its associated corruption permeated all levels of society so that nothing could be done without the permission of the drug lords. Nothing could compete with the profits, including substitute crops.

No ordinary jobs paid as much as the lucrative drug industry. Drug money funded the Taliban and compensated the families of suicide bombers. According to Rashid:

> one of the major reasons for the failure of nation building in Afghanistan and Pakistan was the failure to deal with the issue of drugs. In 2006 the State Department belatedly conceded that 'Afghanistan's huge drug trade severely impacts efforts to rebuild the economy, develop a strong democratic government based on the rule of law, and threatens regional stability'.[35]

Here also were very strong links between the drug trade and senior members of the GIRoA and their families. The corruption and political and economic distortion this created will never be fully assessed, but the detrimental effect, as observed by Rashid, is profound.

NATO Withdrawal 2020–2021

In February 2014, a roundtable was hosted by the Asia Pacific College of Diplomacy at the Australian National University. At this conference, one of the academics present outlined the practical logistics challenges faced by the U.S. withdrawing equipment from a land-locked country such as Afghanistan:

> It is estimated that 60 percent of U.S. military equipment must pass through Pakistan by road en route to a sea port for repatriation. This equates to one truck every seven minutes over a three-year period.[36]

Events since the withdrawal of AFP from Afghanistan in 2014 provide a salutary warning.

In January 2015, NATO launched the Resolute Support Mission (RSM) to train, advise and assist Afghan security forces and institutions to fight terrorism and secure their country.

The U.S. and the Taliban signed an agreement in February 2020 on the withdrawal of international forces from Afghanistan by May 2021. Pursuant to this, NATO Foreign and Defence Ministers, in April 2021, decided to withdraw all Allied troops from Afghanistan within a few months.

Following the completion of the withdrawal of all RSM forces in August 2021, the mission was terminated in early September 2021. The withdrawal of U.S. troops was completed at night on 30 August. Following the withdrawal of all American forces from Afghanistan, the security situation deteriorated rapidly. The withdrawal was chaotic and involved numerous casualties. There was a great deal of military equipment left behind by NATO-ISAF and the U.S. military in particular.

Remnants of War

Below is a list of the equipment left behind by the US' rapid and poorly coordinated withdrawal from Afghanistan:

- 2,000 armoured vehicles, including Humvees and MRAPs
- 75,989 total vehicles: FMTV, M35, Ford Rangers, Ford F350, Ford Vans, Toyota Pickups, Armoured Security Vehicles, etc.
- 45 UH-60 Blackhawk helicopters
- 50 MD530G Scout Attack choppers
- ScanEagle military drones
- 30 Military Version Cessnas
- 4 C-130s
- 29 Brazilian-made A-29 Super Tucano Ground Attack Aircraft
- 208+ total aircraft
- at least 600,000+ small arms M16, M249 SAWs, M24 Sniper Systems, 50 Calibre, 1,394 M203 grenade launchers, M134 Mini Gun, 20 mm Gatling Guns and ammunition
- 61,000 M203 rounds
- 20,040 grenades
- Howitzers
- mortars +1,000s of Rounds
- 162,000 pieces of encrypted military communications gear
- 16,000+ night vision goggles
- newest technology night vision scopes
- thermal scopes and thermal mono goggles
- 10,000 2.75-inch Air to Ground rockets
- reconnaissance equipment (ISR)
- laser aiming units
- explosives ordnance C-4, Semtex, Detonators, Shaped Charges, Thermite, Incendiaries, AP/API/APIT
- 2,520 bombs
- administration encrypted cell phones and laptops, all operational
- pallets with millions of dollars in U.S. currency
- millions of rounds of ammunition, including, but not limited to, 20,150,600 rounds of 7.62 mm, 9,000,000 rounds of 50. calibre
- large stockpile of plate carriers and body armour
- US Military HIIDE, for Handheld Interagency Identity Detection Equipment Biometrics
- lots of heavy equipment, including bulldozers, backhoes, dump trucks and excavators.[37]

The outcome of this is that the world now has a well-armed, failing, potential narco-terrorist state that seamlessly links China with Iran and the Middle East and the 'Russias' with the Persian Gulf. The strategic implications of this cannot be overestimated.

AFP and Afghanistan: Police Diplomacy?

Establishing a functioning rule of law or even a basic post-conflict policing capability within Afghanistan was always going to present a significant challenge to the international community. Given the history of the region, its diverse ethnic makeup and its difficult terrain, which, combined with governance issues and a fragile economic base, it was unrealistic to expect anything approximating a Western-style democratic rule of law within any reasonable timeframe. The AFP recognised that Afghanistan's narcotics industry posed a major threat to stabilisation efforts in the region and that it helped fuel the Taliban insurgency, whose goal was undermining government legitimacy. It was this aspect that the AFP could have made a more meaningful contribution to the NATO-ISAF effort. Yet, it was this line of effort that was completely disregarded by the Australian Rudd government of the day, arguably in an attempt to politically differentiate itself from its predecessor. The best that can be said of the Australian Government's desire to deploy an ever-increasing number of Australian police to Afghanistan is that they were arguably well-intentioned but poorly informed.

The AFP was asked to deploy into a complex active conflict zone for the initial task of assisting our British friend and ally with a chronic narcotics challenge in Afghanistan. Changes of government in both Canberra and Washington and a rapidly changing strategic environment on the ground caused demands to be made of the AFP that it was not trained for nor equipped to fulfil. These were high-risk endeavours for virtually zero return other than a possible political dividend by allowing politicians to claim they were actively seeking to transition from an aggressive CT, enemy-centric approach to a more 'progressive' population-centric, COIN approach. This was poorly thought out and reflected the relative ignorance of the political decision-makers and their advisors, particularly in Canberra, who seemed to lack an appreciation of the roles and limitations of liberal-democratic policing in an active conflict zone.

The whole notion of POMLT illustrates the fact that police were solely considered security sector actors, and their primary role as justice sector actors was completely ignored. Had this aspect of policing been more carefully considered, it would have been quickly realised that if 'peace is not just the absence of conflict but the presence of justice', and if the decision-makers had addressed the simple question of 'when does the blue take over?' they would have found the answer from the AFP that 'when the military wins the war, the police can keep the peace'. Throughout the entire seven years of AFP engagement in Afghanistan, there was 'no peace to keep'. Furthermore, if peace is not just the absence of conflict but the presence of justice, then there is arguably still no peace with the Taliban back in control.

As for diplomacy: the AFP IDG was specifically designed for the types of activity for furthering international good citizenship in the South West Pacific. When the AFP was deployed to Afghanistan, and their roles continued to change in relation to political direction and expediency, they were almost exclusively performing a national interest function in a highly contested part of the world, a long way from the South West Pacific, in which Australia had virtually no interests of its own.

The national interest, in this case, was the maintenance of the alliance with the U.S. The ADF tragically lost forty-one members during its engagement in Afghanistan. The Chief of Army, General Peter Leahy, once rhetorically asked how he could look the mother of a deceased Australian military member in the eye if they had died in Afghanistan only to maintain an alliance with the U.S.; a very difficult question to answer and hard to justify. Arguably more so for the mother, father, husband or wife of a lightly armed police officer in an active conflict zone on the other side of the world. Yet, to the political class, like earlier missions such as UNAMET in East Timor, it seems that police are more expendable than soldiers.

MH17 Operation: Malaysia Airlines Flight MH17, 14 July 2014

In July 2014, many of the operational capabilities of the AFP were called upon for a mass casualty event involving almost 300 people, including several Australians. This was an incident of which the victims had no knowledge and no warning in an area of the globe involved in an active conflict in which Australia had no direct interest. The response by the AFP was immediate and effective, as members with the required skills worked alongside their international counterparts in a hostile environment over a crime scene covering a large area and were tasked with the massive undertaking of retrieving the remains of the victims for identification and repatriation, in accordance with the wishes of their surviving kin. The AFP response to this incident was known as Operation Arew. This was not a deployment from the IDG, but skillsets were drawn from the wider AFP and also a number of State police agencies. This operation culminated in the prosecution of several citizens of Russia and a Ukrainian in absentia in the Netherlands and the conviction of three of those charged. This remains one of the greatest crimes of the century.[38]

The Incident: 17 July 2014

Shortly after midnight (AEST) on 17 July 2014, Malaysia Airlines flight MH17, a Boeing 777 en route from Amsterdam, the Netherlands to Kuala Lumpur, Malaysia failed to respond to calls from Rostov-on-Don air traffic control and vanished from its intended flight path. The morning media in Australia reported almost three hundred bodies lying in burnt fields near the city of Donetsk in eastern Ukraine. This area was contested between the Ukrainian government and pro-Russia and Russian-backed rebels, who sought unification with Russia. This was not a small-scale fight involving small arms; it was a heavily contested war zone in full-scale conflict involving weaponry such as:

> tanks, very heavy calibre artillery, mortars, air defence weapons and people wandering around with high power long arms, Kalashnikovs…The aircraft was shot down…likely by a separatist-fired, Russian-supplied SA11 (BUK) surface-to-air missile, in what was probably a case of rebels-who are fighting to break from the Ukraine-mistaking it for a Ukrainian military plane near Hrabove village, Donetsk Oblast. Neither side claimed responsibility. The culprits were either the Ukrainian or the Russian-backed separatists-or one of them trying to make it look like the other.[39]

Why the Police?

The decision to deploy the AFP into this heavily contested zone was made by Prime Minister Abbott following a meeting of the National Security Committee (NSC) of Cabinet. According to some accounts, the Prime Minister was convinced of the efficacy of this strategy by the ability of the AFP to deploy rapidly. Some accounts indicate that when asked how long it would take the ADF to assemble and respond to this crime scene, the Chief of the Defence Force responded that it would take approximately two weeks. Apparently, when asked the same question, the AFP Commissioner responded that he could deploy a full team immediately.

One senior AFP member involved in Operation Arew indicated that prior to this NSC meeting, the ADF had made an offer of a C17 heavy lift aircraft to transport AFP to Europe in response. This offer was apparently withdrawn following the NSC meeting for unexplained reasons, but it was suspected by this AFP member to be churlishness on the part of the ADF at not being allocated as the lead agency. Regardless of the politics behind this, the fact was that there were several hundred bodies lying in a large field of debris, which was difficult enough on its own. As a crime scene, natural decomposition and animal scavenging called for a timely response, and the AFP was able to fulfil the requirements by using civilian air carriers.

James Brown, then Research Director and an Adjunct Associate Professor at the U.S. Studies Centre, University of Sydney, stated:

> After considering the sensitivities of operating in a war zone and within the shadow of the border of a faded superpower with one of the world's largest conventional militaries, I concluded that the presence of the military would be counter-productive. This mission would be best left to federal police and diplomats, preferably unarmed to emphasise the non-military forensic nature of their work. If the situation was unstable enough to require means of immediate self-defence, the AFP should carry side-arms. As an afterthought, I forwarded my blog post to a friend working in the national security field. He replied almost straightaway to let me know he was thinking along the same lines.[40]

International Diplomacy

Diplomatic negotiations were complex and were conducted by DFAT officers. These negotiations involved the carriage of firearms by foreign police (AFP) in other jurisdictions and the governments of the Netherlands, Ukraine and the Organization for the Security and Co-operation in Europe (OSCE). The Ukrainian government agreed to cede sovereignty in this case and allow international police to conduct the investigations. The governments of Ukraine and Australia agreed to a Dutch-led response, and the search scene response was to be coordinated by Australia. This was to have two facets but a combined DVI and CT investigation response. The AFP's experience with the 2004 Boxing Day Tsunami and various bombings in Indonesia underpinned this decision.

Access was arranged by members of the Organisation for Security and Cooperation in Europe (OSCE), but it was quite restrictive, as Australian Special Envoy Sir Angus Houston stated:

> [t]he conditions of access were, you can't stay overnight and you can't carry arms. We never took arms out-they were never needed out there…and had we needed them, we would have been in a heap of trouble. This is high-end conventional type warfare. We didn't want to get anywhere near that and it worked for us.[41]

A Challenging Crime Scene

On 22 July 2015, a presentation on Operation Arew was given by AFP Commanders Buchhorn and Harrison and Dr Simon Walsh to the United

Services Institute in Canberra. The following is a precis of that presentation. A number of challenging issues were evident on the ground, including (1) access to the scene, (2) geographic isolation, (3) long supply lines, (4) substandard convoy transport, (5) security, (6) technological limitations, (7) coordination with partners-Ukraine/Netherlands/Malaysia and (8) few searchers had trained with previous experience in an active conflict zone.

Priority Taskings

The priorities for the police teams were in order: (1) recover remains: due to the altitude and the manner in which the aircraft was destroyed, there was severe 'disarticulation' of body parts strewn over a wide area. The debris field was approximately twenty-three kilometres in dispersal length and covered an area of approximately fifteen square kilometres; (2) recover personal effects – these had already been searched or interfered with by local Ukrainian authorities prior to arrival, and (3) recover the wreckage. While the international police teams had 'permission to do certain things, it should be noted that "permission" in this case was "permission at the end of an AK47"'[42], and as such, evidentiary material was the last of the three priorities, and on occasion was actively discouraged by the local people on the ground.

There were also issues with identification from the ground level due to the crops of sunflowers and wheat obscuring the view. Thus, an aerial perspective was required. This was provided via the 'Five-Eyes' intelligence community, of which Australia was the only member among the nations represented. This allowed a process known as geo-tagging to be used for the first time in such an operation. The potential search areas were 'sectorised', and 'clusters' were identified for 'highest yield of human remains'.

The search on the ground was a mixture of AFP, Dutch and Malaysian police and was led by an AFP Sergeant, Sergeant Rod Anderson from Gungahlin Police Station in the ACT, who doubled as the DVI Commander for ACT Policing. There were Cadaver K9 dogs, Explosive Ordinance Device, Chemical Biological Radiation and military medics in support. All were unarmed, with limited and optional ballistic protection available. Time on task was determined by the prevailing security environment, which was fluid. There were five search teams of five police, each using a pre-loaded GPS from the sectoring and clustering geo-tagging process.

Safety and Security at the End of an AK47

From a safety perspective, the following risks were identified: (1) landmines, (2) gun fire/cross-fire, (3) indirect fire (mortars), (4) risk of hostage-taking, (5) aircraft carbon filaments similar to asbestos, (6) poison oak, which can cause severe allergic reactions including rashes if direct contact is made with the skin, (7) tuberculosis, which was endemic in this region, (8) polluted drinking water, (9) dehydration, which was a particular problem for the Dutch police who were unused to working in hot conditions, and (10) chemical safety; this was an issue especially during the post mortem phase due to the use of formaldehyde by the Ukrainian authorities to preserve the bodies when they first responded to the incident.

Disaster Victim Identification (DVI)

DVI is conducted in four phases in accordance with INTERPOL Guidelines and the Australia and New Zealand Policing Advisory Agency (ANZPAA) DVI Committee (ADVIC). These are: Phase 1, recovery of remains at the scene; Phase 2, post-mortem to establish cause of death; Phase 3, ante-mortem, to obtain information from family to assist with identification; and Phase 4, reconciliation.

International Justice

At the formal diplomatic level, the Australian Government, through Foreign Minister Julie Bishop, was pursuing justice in conjunction with the governments of all other nations who lost citizens when flight MH17 was shot out of the sky. By sheer coincidence, Australia was a non-permanent member of the United Nations Security Council for a two-year term in 2013–14. Australia, through Foreign Minister Bishop, proposed a resolution condemning the downing of the flight and demanding immediate access to the site, the dignified repatriation of the remains of the victims and an independent international investigation. UN Security Council 2166 was passed unanimously by the Security Council. Minister Bishop had previously consulted the Australian Ambassador to the U.S. Kim Beazley, CIA Director John Brennan and the U.S. Director of National Intelligence James Clapper. The content of this meeting is not available; however, it can be safely assumed confidential information relating to suspected culpability was passed to Minister Bishop.

Australia urged the council to pass Resolution 2166, which:

> underlined the need for a full, thorough and independent investigation into the crash and demanded all military activities in the area cease to enable access to the site…[and was a]…vital point of pressure on those who controlled the crash site to allow access for investigators from Australia and other countries and enabled the victims of flight MH17 to be repatriated and returned to their loved ones.[43]

On the twelve-month anniversary of the passing of Resolution 2166, Foreign Minister Bishop published a media release in which she explained that Australia, Belgium, Malaysia, the Netherlands and Ukraine, the countries were undertaking an independent criminal investigation into the downing of MH17. She further explained that a separate independent air safety investigation had been conducted in full compliance with all International Civil Aviation Organisation (ICAO) guidelines and Appendix 13 of the Chicago Convention, and stated that this had the full confidence and support of the United Nations, indicating that the purpose of the aviation investigation was to determine the cause to the incident, rather than to conduct a criminal investigation into culpability.

Foreign Minister Bishop further stated that:

> Alongside the air safety investigation, the law enforcement authorities of Australia, Belgium, Malaysia, the Netherlands and Ukraine have been cooperating in a Joint Investigation Team to conduct a criminal investigation. This investigation has been equally comprehensive and independent, carried out in accordance with the highest international standards.
>
> The AFP is the Australian police representative in the Joint Investigation Team, and as such will contribute to the evidence presented in the Dutch prosecution of any offenders identified and charged. This is not only serving justice, but has potentially global diplomatic consequences.[44]

Russian Obstruction

On 21 July 2014, Resolution 2166 was passed unanimously by the Security Council, including Russia, which later created an obstacle to its implementation. One year later, the Government of Malaysia, supported by Australia, the Netherlands and Ukraine, proposed a resolution to the UN Security Council to establish a tribunal to investigate this event. This proposal was vetoed by the Russian Federation as a permanent member of the UN Security Council. The protection of civilians was highlighted by most speakers during the debate on Resolution 2166. Ironically, as the resolution was being debated, the Russian representative stressed that such protection was a national responsibility and that national sovereignty should be respected. On the subject of the protection of the civilians aboard the aircraft, Russia remained silent.

Of the fifteen-member council, eleven voted in favour of the proposal by Malaysia, Australia, the Netherlands and Ukraine, while three countries abstained: China, Angola and Venezuela. A number of excerpts from various statements provide some background to the positions adopted by some of these nations.[45]

Russian representative Vitaly Churkin said:

> the Russian Federation did not support the creation of an international tribunal under Chapter VII, as resolution 2166 (2014) had not considered the downing of the aircraft a threat to international peace and security.

This was vehemently disputed by most of the other nations, who made statements. The Angolan representative, Joao Iambeno Gimoleica, 'emphasized the need to hold the perpetrators accountable, bring justice to the victims and their families and ensure the safety of civil aviation' but further stated that 'the establishment of an international tribunal was premature, given that the investigations were ongoing'.

Venezuelan representative Rafael Dario Ramirez Carreno stated that 'Justice must prevail' and added, 'We must not prejudge or reach conclusions that are un-founded'. Tellingly, no suggestion was made as to how well-founded conclusions can be drawn without such a tribunal. The Chinese representative Liu Jieyi justified abstention on the basis that there was no consensus, which indicated that the 'focus should be on seeking justice and ending impunity…Consensus on the draft would have sent a positive message, whereas a divided Council would impede the cause espoused'.[46]

This, of course, is consistent with justifying China's own veto power when it is required over issues such as Taiwan and the South China Sea.

There was an overwhelming number of voices supporting the Malaysian proposal. Most objections related to the fact that attacking civilian passenger aircraft was a threat to international peace and security in direct contradiction with Russia's rationale for the veto. This extended to the actual and perceived impunity afforded to the perpetrators by the Russian veto and the message of impotence it sends to those malign actors, including ideologically based terrorists who would seek to target civilian passenger aircraft. This diverse group of voices included those of Malaysia, Indonesia, Vietnam, Chad, the U.S., Australia, New Zealand, France, Germany, Israel, Lithuania, Chad, Spain, Chile, Britain, Belgium, the Netherlands, Canada, Ireland, the Philippines and Ukraine. The Ukraine representative Pavlo Klimkin, the Ukraine Minister for Foreign Affairs, summed up the unspoken sentiments of many when he stated:

> There is no reason to oppose such a move unless you are one of the perpetrators…The Russian Federation's role in the conflict in Ukraine was clear and well known…and its veto needed to be seen in that context. The hope for justice remained alive. The Russian Federation's use of the veto may have killed the draft resolution today; it would not be able to kill the hopes of people around the world to see justice prevail.[47]

Evidence for Prosecution

The joint investigations team continued in its duties. One member, AFP Detective Superintendent Andrew Donoghoe, observed:

> An overwhelming amount of information has already been collected. This includes video files, photographs, interviews, witness statements, telephone intercepts, and lots of intelligence. A vast amount of forensic examination work has been completed. It's a very big repository of evidentiary information that takes time to meticulously scour-and access to the AFP's electronic resources for our members in the Ukraine can also be challenging. But we continue to look for the clues that are going to lead us to the right solution to the problem we have.[48]

Prosecution in The Netherlands

On 5 July 2017, the Government of The Netherlands announced that the members of the Joint Investigations Team (JIT), Australia, Belgium, Malaysia, The Netherlands and Ukraine, had decided that the suspects should be prosecuted in The Netherlands and that the Dutch Public Prosecution Service will make appropriate decisions regarding criminal prosecution at the appropriate time. All JIT countries expressed their full confidence in the Dutch legal system, and the criminal investigation continued to enjoy virtually unanimous support from the international community. This saw members of the AFP giving evidence in a Dutch court against those who eventually stood trial accused of this crime.

This involved the charging and conviction, in absentia, of senior members of the Russian military. The London-based freelance investigative body Bellingcat provided information to the JIT based in the Netherlands in which it identified Russian Major General Sergey Nikolaevich Dubinsky as 'a key—or perhaps even the key—figure in organizing the transport of Buk 332 from Donetsk to a field south of Snizhne on the day of the tragedy' and linked him to the incident via a series of photographs and telephone intercepts.[49]

It is noteworthy that not even a Russian veto in the UN Security Council could prevent these charges from occurring. This is testimony to the underlying principle of the separation of powers, even on a global scale, between the executive, in this case, the UN Security Council, and the justice system, in this case, the combination of the Dutch judicial system and INTERPOL.

The AFP and INTERPOL

The relationship the AFP has with the UN dates from 1964 when the Commonwealth Police deployed to Cyprus. Since then, a credible history has evolved, which has resulted in a platinum standard training capability for police from the South West Pacific for deployment to RAMSI and Australian police to other missions including UN missions. This contributed to Australia securing a non-permanent seat on the United Nations Security Council. During its term on the council, Australia influenced global affairs in relation to international policing, in part relying on the AFP's involvement. The AFP's experience was, therefore, able to provide a demonstrable link between the theoretical and the practical through two unanimously adopted resolutions relating to police. The involvement of the Australian Foreign Minister in the unanimous adoption and subsequent pursuit of the offenders in relation to the mass murder of passengers aboard MH17 and Australia's response on the ground, which involved the AFP deploying large numbers to an active war zone far away from the Indo-Asia-Pacific region, is a direct link between Australian foreign policy and its implementation at the highest global level, namely in the Security Council of the United Nations.[50] This was practical diplomacy in uncharted waters. It was operational and firmly in the national interest.

The fact that the UN was unable to follow through on Resolution 2166 due to a veto by the Russian Federation is an unfortunate result of the highly flawed and anachronistic construct of the UN generally, and the Security Council specifically, upon its inception in the mid-1940s. The fact that there is a separate international policing organisation independent of the UN (INTERPOL) is a testament to the utility of that independence. The UN focuses its international policing efforts on the provision of uniformed police responding to long-term crises and capacity development, and the AFP has played its part in this. For a more detailed discussion on INTERPOL, please see Appendix 8.

The AFP is also the Australian representative for INTERPOL, which is the organisation that assisted in bringing the MH17 offenders to justice via a prosecution by the Dutch Government and the subsequent issue of INTERPOL Red Notices for arrest of those involved.

Expect the Unexpected

The AFP's Operation Arew thrust the AFP into the global spotlight once again in the wake of a tragic event that involved the loss of a significant number of Australian lives and victims from other countries. The AFP response was rapid, and the way in which members meshed seamlessly with their international colleagues stands as testimony to their versatility and professionalism. They served their nation with pride, courage and skill. This event was unexpected, but like the other tragic mass casualty events discussed in this book, these tragedies are now on the threat horizon as a reality. It may not be a surface-to-air missile next time, but there are enough ideologically driven extremists with the intent and capability to target civilian airline traffic indiscriminately to state firmly that the next mass casualty event involving airlines somewhere in the world is only a matter of time. The AFP's performance in Operation Arew in 2014 is evidence of the preparedness to respond in a similar way if required.

As AFP Commissioner Colvin stated at a Lowy Institute address in March 2015:

> Had you asked me 12 months ago if could I see a situation where the AFP would deploy teams of unarmed men and women to the heart of an active conflict zone in eastern Ukraine – with no notice, no area familiarity, no established links or local partnerships – to identify and bring home the remains of Australian victims, and to investigate the shooting down of a passenger plane, I would probably have told you that even as a hypothetical exercise, it was a bridge too far. But we did it, and we did it very well.[51]

MH17 AFP Operation 2024
Tried and Sentenced in Absentia

As of 2024, three of the four people charged with the serious crime of shooting down a civilian airliner, killing almost 300 innocent people, were convicted in absentia in a Dutch court and sentenced to life imprisonment.

The Dutch-led JIT was established on 7 August 2014 for the criminal investigation into the MH17 disaster. On the basis of this investigation, it was decided on 19 June 2019 that four suspects would be prosecuted. On 9 March 2020, at the first court session of the MH17 trial, the public prosecutor announced the charges against the suspects. Prosecutors alleged they were jointly accountable for downing flight MH17.

The Dutch Public Prosecution Service prosecuted and on17 November 2022 the District Court of The Hague sentenced, the following persons:

Igor Vsevolodovich Girkin: also known as Strelkov or Perviy, is a former colonel of the FSB, the Russian Federal Security Service. On 17 July 2014, Girkin was Minister of Defence and commander of the army of the self-proclaimed Donetsk People's Republic which is the district from which Flight MH17 was shot down. As the highest military officer he maintained contact with the Russian Federation. Girkin was found guilty and sentenced to life imprisonment.

Sergey Nikolayevich Dubinskiy: nicknamed Khmuriy, is a former military officer of the GRU, the Russian military intelligence service. Dubinskiy was one of Girkin's deputies in 2014 and also head of the intelligence service of the Donetsk People's Republic. In this capacity he also maintained regular contact with officials in Russia. Dubinskiy was found guilty and sentenced to life imprisonment.

Leonid Volodymyrovych Kharchenko: also known as Krot, was the only Ukrainian suspect investigated by the JIT. He received his orders directly from Dubinskiy and in July 2014 he was commander of a combat unit in the Donetsk region which at the time, was in armed conflict between pro-Russian militia and the Ukrainian armed forces. Kharchenko was found guilty and sentenced to life imprisonment.

Oleg Yuldashevich Pulatov: also known as Giurza, was a former military officer of the Russian Spetznaz-GRU, the special unit of the Russian military intelligence service. In 2014, Pulatov was deputy head of the intelligence service of the Donetsk People's Republic and one of the Dubinky's deputies. Pulatov was acquitted on all charges.[52]

The AFP provided significant input into the initial response and follow-up JIT investigations into the downing of MH17 in 2014. All of those prosecuted and convicted were tried in absentia. It is unlikely they will ever serve the sentences imposed by the Dutch court. The fact remains that the Russian Federation, a member of the Permanent Five of the United Nations Security Council is protecting these convicted criminals, found guilty for one the greatest crimes of the century: a crime of mass murder. This is an indictment on those individuals, the Russian Federation and the UN. This entire event has been overshadowed by the invasion of Ukraine by Russia under the Putin regime. At the time of writing this open conflict in which civilians appear to be deliberate targets on the eastern edge of Europe continues.

Summary and Conclusion

It should be noted that the response under Op Arew was not deployed under the International Deployment Group, but was drawn from the broader AFP capability base. The response to the downing of flight MH17 demonstrated that, arguably, there is no other organisation in Australia, or in its region, that has the combined experience-based attributes of flexibility and versatility to respond as rapidly as it did to such an unexpected event. The versatility and experience-base within its own ranks also helped to ensure that a response such as this was as comprehensive as possible. This ranged from the DVI, Forensic, Search and Rescue, Investigation, Intelligence, Special Response Group, Family Investigative Liaison Officers and the Ceremonial and Protocol Officers. The fact that these elements exist under one command is evidence that the AFP, in such circumstances, is capable of effectively linking a professional response to a tragic event with the families of its victims.

The fact that the AFP played a significant part in the criminal trial of senior Russian military figures places them in as high a profile as any ordinary police officer can be placed. Their evidence formed part of a successful prosecution and restricted the ability of those convicted to travel. This is only partial closure for the victim's relatives, but it is also a significant advancement in global justice and the dismantling of impunity, which has served to undermine confidence in the international rules-based order.

The fact that the Russian authorities refused to cooperate and that those convicted remain at large in Russia stands as testimony to the callous nature and impunity with which this autocratic former superpower and permanent member of the United Nations Security Council operates. With such an eroded legitimacy, it is difficult to envisage how such a country can continue to hold such a prestigious and influential position in a global body such as the UN.

In Australia's immediate region, we are witnessing the slow but steady encroachment of authoritarianism in Indo-China, Southeast Asia and the South West Pacific, as the PRC, also a permanent member of the UN Security Council, extends its influence closer to Australian shores. This has direct implications for police and how policing is done in Australia's immediate region. This is discussed in Part V below.

Part V

Australian Security and Sovereignty in the Asian Century 2014–2024

China and Australia's Northern approaches

Liberal Democracy in Indo-Pacific Region: Police Perspective   217
Rise of China   217
Taiwan   217
South East Asia and South West Pacific   218
Australia's Future as Liberal Democracy   220
United Nations   223
2024: Assessment of 60 Years of AFP International Engagement   224
Cyprus 1964–2017   224
Timor-Leste 2024   225
China and the South West Pacific 2024   228
Melanesian Spearhead Group (MSG) 2024   228
Solomon Islands 2024   230
Papua New Guinea 2024   231
The AFP in the South West Pacific 2024   231
Pacific Police Development Program-Regional   235
Pacific Community for Law Enforcement Cooperation   236
Police Diplomacy: AFP 1964–2024   237
1964–1998 International Good Citizenship: AFP and UN   238
1999–2007 Australia's National Interest: East Timor, Bali and the Solomon Islands   239
2007–2014 Challenging Missions in Afghanistan, Papua New Guinea and Ukraine   242
2014–2024 National Interest and Rise of China: Australian Security and Sovereignty in Asian Century   243
Achievements of the AFP 1999–2024   245

The Rise of China and the Future of Liberal Democracy in the Indo-Pacific Region: A Police Perspective

The West, specifically Western liberal-democratic values, are under considerable challenge in this first part of the 21st century. The actual or perceived decline[1] of the U.S. and the Western alliance system has emboldened more autocratic powers to combine their efforts to attempt to replace Western dominance and the rules-based international order through which it operates with something else. Whatever that 'something else' is, it is unlikely to feature a benign and benevolent approach to policing and justice as the status quo. Central to this discussion is the rising influence of the People's Republic of China (PRC).

The Rise of China

Xi Jinping was the Vice President of the PRC from 2008 to 2013, the has been the General Secretary of the Chinese Communist Party since 2012 and assumed office as the President of the People's Republic of China in March 2013. Since coming to power as president, Xi Jinping has embarked on an unprecedented expansion of the PRC's military and territorial claims, especially in the South China Sea and East China Sea. This has not only threatened the sovereignty of its neighbours in Indo-China and maritime Southeast Asia but has also threatened maritime sea routes, sometimes referred to as Sea Lines of Communication (SLOCs), between the sources of energy, primarily oil in the Middle East, and some industrialised consumers in the Far East, notably Japan and South Korea, both of whom are pro-West.[2]

Taiwan

In the sense of trade, this is of concern to Australia, as China, South Korea and Japan are significant trading partners for Australian raw materials. Freedom of access through these SLOCs is of vital importance to the future peace and prosperity of a trading nation such as Australia. One of the most vulnerable SLOCs is the Strait of Taiwan between the Chinese mainland and the island nation of Taiwan, which Xi regards as a renegade province and has declared it will be subsumed into the PRC. Should the PRC be successful in this pursuit, it will create a potential choke point for both general trade and oil supplies to South Korea and Japan. This is a vitally strategic waterway for the Western alliance. The loss of Taiwan to the PRC would also do significant damage to U.S. prestige and trust in the region. This has direct consequences for Australia as a liberal democracy.

South East Asia and the South West Pacific

The PRC has also extended its influence into the nations of the Association of Southeast Asian Nations (ASEAN), with particular influence in newly admitted countries such as Cambodia and Myanmar. While the PRC expansion into maritime Southeast Asia risks conflict with countries such as Vietnam, Indonesia, Malaysia, the Philippines and Indonesia, Cambodia and Myanmar have become almost vassal states of the PRC. This has split ASEAN into two camps.

In the South West Pacific, the PRC has exerted its influence in a number of countries where Australia has a direct strategic interest. Chinese influence in the Solomon Islands has seen decades of post-conflict police development efforts by the AFP challenged by a growing Chinese policing influence due primarily to a political decision by the most recent Prime Minister, Manasseh Sogavare, who is known for his anti-Australian and anti-Western sentiment. He switched diplomatic recognition from Taiwan to China in 2019 and struck a security deal with China in 2022.

As former Australian national security official Mike Hughes told the ABC, China is intent on consolidating a security presence in the Solomon Islands.

> 'What that means is having states like Solomon Islands, and influential elites like Mr Sogavare, who will defer to China's interests in everything they do. We know from how China behaves across the world that they have no qualms bankrolling people with authoritarian ambitions. It raises all sorts of questions over how far Sogavare is willing to go, and what he'd be willing to do to stay in power.'[3]

A General Election was held on Wednesday 24 April 2024 Sogavare's Ownership, Unity and Responsibility (OUR) Party stood against the CARE Coalition consisting of the Democratic Party, the United Party and two other single MP parties Umi for Change and the Democratic Alliance Party.

The role attitudes of local people to Chinese influence cannot be accurately assessed but as Al Jazeera reported on 24 April 2024:

> Analysts previously told Al Jazeera that while the international community might be focused on China relations, Solomon Islanders were more concerned with "bread and butter" issues such as the cost of living, health and education.

Al Jazeera further reported that: United Party leader Peter Kenilorea Jr, had promised to switch ties back to Taiwan.[4]

As Terrance Wood observed of the Development Policy Centre observed:

...a small minority of voters in Solomon Islands did vote with China on their minds – and who can blame them, China's presence in their country isn't benign – but the evidence really doesn't fit with the hypothesis that the poor performance of the OUR party was driven by voters' dislike of China... local personalities and connections are crucial to competition in individual electorates. If you've got clan, community or church leaders on your side, sometimes it doesn't matter which party you're from.[5]

The election result did see Prime Minister Sogavare stand down before the result was announced. His successor, former Foreign Minister Jeremiah Manele, has indicated that his stance on diplomatic recognition of China would not change.

As reported in The Guardian on Monday 29 April 2024:

Sogavare, who narrowly held his onto seat in last Wednesday's election, announced he would not be a candidate for prime minister at a televised press conference on Monday evening.

Sogavare said his government had been 'under pressure from the United States and western allies' and he had been 'accused of many things'.

"Geopolitics is at play, after we made a very important decision in 2019," he said, referring to his government's decision to switch diplomatic recognition from Taiwan to Beijing.

Mr Manele said that if he was elected as prime minister he would have the 'same foreign policy basis – friends to all and enemies to none'.[6]

On 2 April 2024 Mr Jeremiah Manele was elected as Prime Minister of the Solomon Islands. He is a member of the OUR Party and was Foreign Minister under the Sogavare Government when the Solomon Islands switched recognition from Taiwan to China and when the security pact with China was signed in 2022. When asked if his Government would keep this pact, he said '[i]n terms of foreign policy, yes, that agreement is there. If there is a need to review that, it will be a matter for China and Solomon Islands to discuss'.

Mr Manele is a former diplomat and has represented Solomon Islands at international forums, including the United Nations General Assembly, Pacific Islands Forum and the Melanesian Spearhead Group.[7]

A similar outcome has emerged in Timor-Leste, where the AFP has served continuously since the deadly and destructive period of UNAMET and INTERFET in 1999. Both the Solomon Islands and Timor-Leste are adjacent to SLOCs that are of direct strategic importance to Australia, both in terms of trade and naval and maritime support in times of conflict. Timor-Leste also controls the Strait of Wetar and the Strait of Ombar directly on its northern coastline. These two straits are important SLOCs for the transit of U.S. submarines from the Pacific to the Indian Ocean and vice versa.

One question raised by these developments is whether this part of a longer-term strategic attempt at partial encirclement, which is possibly combined with a policy of domestic political infiltration through elites, with a potential for a more authoritarian future, regionally and domestically.

Australia's Future as a Liberal Democracy

> Today authoritarianism is on the march everywhere, becoming more aggressive, asserting the superiority of its political systems, taking a more belligerent military posture and even invading or threatening to invade neighbouring countries.[8]

Tactics and approaches employed by the PRC include 'muscularity', 'assertiveness', 'strongman tactics' and 'wolf-warrior diplomacy' and an increasing tendency to 'shirtfront' its way to achieving its interests.[9]

This can also include other less confrontational approaches, such as interference, including conduct that is 'covert, coercive or corrupt'.[10] The fine line between influence and interference needs to be made at this point. Influence is a legitimate element of traditional diplomatic statecraft, but interference is not.

In any case, it is difficult not to view the influence and potential interference of the PRC on both the Solomon Islands and Timor-Leste as long-term strategic positioning moves by the PRC and, as such, a threat to Australia's sovereignty, peace and prosperity.

After all, as James Curran identifies, 'the threat of the use of military force or coercion against Australia does not require invasion'.[11] Australia's vulnerability in this regard cannot be overstated.

As Molan, in his 2022 book *Danger on Our Doorstep*, states, 'Australia is extraordinarily dependent on sea trade even for basic commodities such as liquid fuels, pharmaceuticals, fertilisers and IT.'[12] Molan identified that in recent years, China has been building up its naval and military capacity and is unlikely to telegraph its intentions. It instead has a preference for the element of surprise and overwhelming force, starting with space and cyber-attacks, first knocking out communications satellites and then deploying missiles to defeat the U.S. military and strategic assets and bases in the region.

The implications for this eventuality for a liberal-democratic Australia should not be underestimated and cannot be overstated:

> If China were successful in a sudden attack…it would then be essentially in control of the region, with little or no threat from the US. This is when the real test for Australia would begin, as we could be on our own for quite

some time…A regionally dominant China represents an existential threat to Australia as a liberal democracy. It should be expected that, at the very least, China would demand access to Australia's resources at very favourable prices… or to obtain cheap materials for its industries…China might even establish a military presence in this country to guarantee access to resources and to stop the U.S. using Australia as a military base for launching a counter-offensive.[13]

There is an insidious aspect to this strategic manoeuvring. As Michael Green identifies, 'Xi's call for a "Community of Common Destiny" is eerily reminiscent of Japan's Greater East Asia Co-Prosperity Sphere. That contest for influence in South East Asia and the Pacific will continue'.[14] This 'common destiny' approach, was precisely the anti-colonial, propaganda-based strategy employed by the Imperial Japanese in the 1940s, which imposed the Greater East Asia Co-Prosperity Sphere over all the occupied territory in Southeast Asia. With its catch cry of 'Asia for the Asians', the anti-Western parallels in the 2020s are hauntingly familiar.

As Molan further states:

with the U.S. out of the region, Asia will once again be for Asians… Australia must now recognise that its region has changed and if Australia wants to maintain any shred of sovereignty, if it wants to open its sea routes to commercial shipping and import and export goods, then it has to reject any involvement with the U.S. military. In effect, Australia must become a tributary state of China.[15]

As Varral identifies quite succinctly, 'Australia matters because of our resources-coal, iron ore and lithium',[16] and, as Curran identifies, 'This is driven by…Beijing's ongoing need for growth-to ensure its internal stability and therefore the Chinese Communist Party's control-and its continuing hunger for Australia's natural resources'.[17]

In terms of the way policing could amend its approaches to force, intrusion and especially dissent, any thoughts that public disapproval and dissent via media, social media or public demonstrations under such an eventuality should be reconsidered. None of these would be tolerated in the form that exists at present. Western liberal democracy is seen by communist hardliners as weak and decadent, and the relatively benign Peelian policing approach is viewed as symptomatic of that weakness and decadence. It is also a direct descendant of Australia's imperial and colonial past. This model in its current apolitical form would not last long in a region under a dominant authoritarian power such as the PRC exerting its influence over a compliant political system in Australia. But what would replace it? Although conjecture, this would in all probability involve a more politicised policing approach with increased inconsistency in how public order, dissent, for and intrusion are used by police under this 'new normal'.

One only need consider what has occurred in Hong Kong to see what implications this would have for policing, particularly public order policing in the face of considerable community dissent.

As Davidson states:

> Hong Kong experienced a significant decline in autonomy following the PRC's imposition of the Hong Kong National Security Law in June 2020. At Beijing's behest, Hong Kong authorities used mass arrests to silence pro-democracy activists and curb further dissent by eroding the pro-democracy movement's political power, weakening Hong Kong's free press and promoting pro-Beijing education in Hong Kong's schools. Meanwhile, PRC security organizations have established an official presence in the city under the auspices of the Office for Safeguarding National Security, enabling Beijing to closely monitor Hong Kong residents and enforce the National Security Law. Through these heavy-handed efforts to impose authoritarian control over Hong Kong affairs, the PRC has demonstrated the hollowness of its 'one country, two systems' model.[18]

Sadly, this is a very real long-term outcome for policing in both the Solomon Islands and Timor-Leste should the present AFP programs be terminated and the liberal-democratic approach to policing and justice be replaced by a more autocratic model intolerant of political dissent and public demonstrations of dissatisfaction with the politics or government of the day. Because there is no element of public consent involved in such policing models, any such demonstrations are likely to be met with extreme state-sponsored violence and could well serve as a pretext for more foreign police intervention from the PRC, which could easily translate into a more permanent security and military presence. The longer-term implications for Australia's security and future as a liberal democracy of a PRC military presence in the region are profoundly pessimistic.

Any prudent Australian government should adhere to its first duty, namely, the protection of the nation and its citizens, and regard the potential threat to both from an increasingly emergent and proximate authoritarian presence in Australia's immediate region as serious. Among its highest priorities should be to ensure that the PRC never establishes military bases in the Pacific, which can threaten Australia's national interests and national sovereignty directly, territorially and also via Australia's vital sea lines of communication.

The global nature of this increasingly expansionist authoritarianism is accentuated by the coalescence and cooperation between the PRC and other malign influences ranging from the Democratic People's Republic of North

Korea to its east to the Islamic Republic of Iran to its west. The fall of Afghanistan in 2021 provides a direct and seamless territorial link between these entities. None of these countries feature tolerance in their political cultures. A direct strategic nexus to the former Soviet Union, now the Russian Federation, provides these autocratic powers a major landmass with attendant resources from which to grow their strength and exert their influence.

There are some who posit that recent hostilities in Ukraine and Gaza are linked, and that the PRC may use these Iranian proxies to stretch Western resources, test Western resolve and use the distraction to make its move on Taiwan and push the U.S. out of the western Pacific. These conflicts have already created significant division within the pluralist populations of western counties including Australia, with attendant allegations of inconsistent policing of public order. This has the potential to seriously erode trust in the police, as a precursor to more civil unrest and an eventual breakdown of social cohesion.

There are some commentators who believe that a serious challenge by the PRC to invade Taiwan is highly likely to lead to either conflict or surrender on the part of the U.S. With the U.S. presently socially, economically and politically divided and perceived as weak by these autocracies, it is quite possible that autocratic moves in Australia's near region are not far away. The implications for Australia generally, and as a liberal democracy specifically, are profound. Unfortunately, as an ally of the U.S., Australia, in such an eventuality, would be unable to appeal to the UN for support or assistance, as that body has been badly compromised, by autocratic actors such as the PRC and the Russian Federation.

United Nations

The UN was established in the aftermath of the 1939–45 wars in Europe and Asia, and consists primarily of a General Assembly and a Security Council. Its Security Council consisted of the victorious powers in 1945: China (Nationalist), the Soviet Union, the UK, the U.S. and France. These now form the Permanent Five (P5), all of which have veto power. Its entire rationale was based on the prevention of a return to the 'scourge of war'. One of the unfortunate ironies of the contemporary system of international affairs is its anachronistic nature. Both the PRC and the Russian Federation may veto any UN resolution advanced to attempt to solve the problems and challenges facing global peace and prosperity. Any resolution to sanction the PRC should it threaten Australia, directly or indirectly, is likely to be vetoed by both the PRC and Russia.

The UN is badly in need of reform. As a founding member of the UN General Assembly in 1945, Australia has a right to make a meaningful contribution to that reform. The AFP has made a significant contribution to UN and UN-sanctioned efforts to improve peace, prosperity, safety and security both in Australia's immediate region and further afield. What follows is a brief contemporary audit at the 60-year mark since Australian police first deployed to the troubled island of Cyprus in 1964.

2024: An Assessment of 60 Years of AFP International Engagement
Australian Police Diplomacy Update 2024 UNFICYP Cyprus 1964–2017

Australian police first deployed to the troubled Mediterranean island of Cyprus in 1964 due to intercommunal violence between Greek and Turkish Cypriot communities. They deployed under UNFICYP. The Australian police were called upon after an initial refusal by the Australian military to serve in Cyprus due to more pressing regional responsibilities in Southeast Asia.

These police were initially state police who deployed as Commonwealth Police officers. Deployment gradually transitioned to Commonwealth Police and then to the AFP when it was established in 1979. The AFP withdrew from UN service in Cyprus in 2017 after fifty-three years. UNFICYP remains a textbook peacekeeping mission that maintains a UN Buffer Zone between two belligerent parties who have done nothing since a ceasefire was established in 1974. The ceasefire lines remain in situ and intact.

The situation in Cyprus and with UNFICYP is one of a stalemate. No party is willing to give in to the other, and no international power has the influence or incentive to move things forward and resolve the situation by force. Diplomacy continues but has not yielded anything positive in the sixty years since the AFP first deployed there. It is a situation suspended in time as events over the past sixty years have passed it by.

Ironically, the nations backing the belligerent parties, Greece and Turkey, are members of NATO. Greece and Cyprus are both members of the European Union, but Cyprus is not a member of NATO. Turkey is a member of NATO but not a member of the European Union, despite its long-held ambitions to join.

In 2024, the military element of UNFICYP is 740, consisting of Britain (252), Argentina (252), Slovakia (236), Paraguay (12), Hungary (11), Serbia (8), Chile (6), Russia (4), Austria (3) and Pakistan (3).

The UNCIVPOL component of UNFICYP is sixty-eight, consisting of Ireland (11), Romania (7), Bosnia Herzegovina (6), Finland (5), Jordan (5), Montenegro (5), Russia (4), Slovakia (4), China (3) and Italy (3).

With conflict again in Eastern Europe and the Middle East, the situation in Cyprus is likely to experience heightened tensions, and UNFICYP is likely to face a similar heightened threat level. Community tensions are likely to increase, and the situation facing the Turkish government and the Turkish military, as a NATO member, could well be at odds with sentiments held by the Turkish community and Turkish Cypriot community in general over the escalating tensions and hostilities between Israel and Palestinians in Gaza and with Hezbollah in Lebanon.

With the involvement of the Islamic Republic of Iran, suspected to be backed by the PRC,[19] the potential for this conflict to escalate and spread throughout the region and even into Western nations via large and active diasporas is significant. The immediate future of the situation in Cyprus and UNFICYP is uncertain, but if tensions grow and expand into the island, UNFICYP will face challenges it has not faced in decades.

Timor-Leste 2024

In a succinct and informative November 2023 paper titled *Timor-Leste's uncertain future*,[20] Parker Novak discusses in frank terms the existing situation and prospects of Timor-Leste. He identifies the present elitist leadership consisting of five political figures from the resistance period of 1975 – the 'Generation of 75' – as hindering institution building. He identifies that the handover of power can take one of three possible courses: (1) a tidy handover, (2) a power vacuum or (3) muddling through.

He outlines some concerning economic and demographic factors:

> Timor-Leste's population is estimated to be 73% under 35 years of age, with a poverty rate of 42% and an official unemployment rate of 4.9%.
>
> Much of the country's wealth is concentrated in and around its growing capital Dili, and those who live in rural areas face starker poverty than their urban counterparts.
>
> More than 70% of Timor-Leste's population draws income from the agriculture sector. In 2021, the country exported US$16.3 million worth of coffee. According to the World Food Programme, Timor-Leste imports 60% of its food. In 2021, nearly 40% of Timor-Leste's imports came from Indonesia, and more than 73% of its exports went to Indonesia.

Novak further states that in December 2022, the World Bank report noted:

> Timor-Leste remains overly reliant on hydrocarbon production for sustaining its economy…without the oil revenues, the undiversified economy of the country will solely rely on the rapidly depleting Petroleum Fund to bridge the considerable fiscal gap in its annual budget.

When the state's Petroleum Fund—the sovereign wealth fund from which more than 90% of government revenue is derived—is projected to run dry. If nothing is done to change this trajectory, Timor-Leste will eventually see its state coffers completely depleted.

He then outlines that the development of the Greater Sunrise gas and oilfields is vital to the economic prosperity and political stability of Timor-Leste:

> Timor-Leste's economy is dependent on oil and gas revenues, and, under current projections, state finances are headed for a 'fiscal cliff' within the next decade if the Greater Sunrise gas field is not developed. The development of Greater Sunrise will be the single most important factor in determining Timor-Leste's course.
>
> Under a worst-case scenario, Greater Sunrise is not developed by the late 2020s. It fails to deliver anywhere near its promised economic potential, and diversification does not occur. This makes ASEAN accession less likely and pushes state finances off a fiscal cliff, necessitating international financial intervention to avoid insolvency and state failure. The political transition is thrown into chaos, with old divides resurfacing and violently destabilising the country. History repeats itself, and the Timorese unwillingly forfeit much of their economic sovereignty to external powers. Timor-Leste at risk of having Chinese financial backing as its only viable option. Chinese investment could give Beijing outsized influence over Timor-Leste's economic affairs.

Strategic Impact

Such a worst-case scenario has some significant strategic geopolitical implications. Timor-Leste lies near the middle of the Indonesian archipelago, which is a key determinant of stability in Southeast Asia. In addition, Timor-Leste is positioned along the Ombai-Wetar Strait, the deep waters of which provide undetected access for submarines between the Pacific Ocean and the Indian Ocean. This is of strategic interest to Beijing, Canberra, Jakarta and Washington. This also has significant implications for Australia's SLOCs and trade routes.

State of Play: 2024

At the 25th anniversary of the 1999 UNAMET ballot, the situation remains that 1293 murders have been confirmed by the UNTAET SCU, and the primary suspects still face 431 indictments. Most of these suspects are in Indonesia and have not been held to account for their actions. A number of these were or are high-level security and political elites in Indonesia.

The Australian Government has washed its hands of the entire affair for fear of exposing a matter that risks offending Indonesian sensitivities, embarrassing officials in Australia who sent unarmed international police, including members of the AFP, into a known hostile environment without adequate protection, such as ballistic vests, or acknowledging that unarmed UNCIVPOL performed heroically in securing a very difficult environment to enable a free and fair ballot to be conducted, which paved the way for the eventual independence of Timor-Leste. As discussed it was actually advantageous for UNCIVPOL to be unarmed during service with UNAMET as it allowed complete impartiality to be demonstrated. However, this has come at a cost.

Many AFP members of UNAMET suffer from both PTSD and moral injury as a result of their service with UNAMET but are denied any meaningful support by the Department of Veteran's Affairs, as they are not regarded as 'veterans' because they were not members of the ADF. These issues remain largely unaddressed due to Australian government inertia and an official unwillingness to acknowledge what actually happened during UNAMET.

Nonetheless, one of the outcomes of the UNAMET mission is the increased confidence of the Howard government in the AFP and international police engagement as an effective instrument of foreign policy. This was particularly important as, with the end of the Cold War, the security environment changed from traditional inter-state conflict to strategic challenges such as terrorism, intra-state conflict and asymmetric threats, including state and non-state criminal threats. The AFP was at the forefront of Australian Government efforts aimed at addressing these and other challenges.

Timor-Leste and China

As discussed above, the geostrategic situation has changed a great deal in the past decade with the rise of China.

Paraphrasing an article titled *Playing the China card of a serious regional threat? Timor-Leste's new deal with Beijing* from The Guardian on 28 September 2023, it is quite clear that an independent Timor-Leste is not living up to expectations and is seeking to strengthen ties with the PRC. This raises some serious strategic concerns for Australian policymakers as Timor is situated less than 700 km from the port of Darwin, which itself, is on a long-term (99-year) lease to the PRC. Timor-Leste is one of the world's poorest countries, with about 40 per cent of people living in poverty and high rates of malnutrition. This is the pretext upon which increased contact between the PRC and Timor-Leste is based:

> A joint statement released by China's Xi Jinping and the Timor-Leste prime minister, Xanana Gusmão, said the new partnership was a sign of increased

cooperation and 'mutual political solidarity'. It followed a recent speech to the UN general assembly by the Timorese president, José Ramos Horta, who said that talk of China as 'a menace' was 'unjustified and unfair' – and the world should not fear any of the global superpowers.

However:

> a…controversial security pact [was] signed between China and Solomon Islands in July, which would allow China to deploy soldiers or police to the country and make naval visits, according to a leaked draft.
>
> Beijing is by far the more powerful partner – it is 600 times Timor-Leste's size with 1,000 times more people and a GDP 5,000 times larger. But it gains regional influence from the agreement, and another global voice giving support to its stance in Taiwan. It could also gain some strategic advantages with the military ties.[21]

Although the specific intent is unclear, there appears to be a consistent course of action at play here. The Solomon Islands is very close to important SLOCs for Australian sea traffic and Timor-Leste is strategically situated on two significant SLOCs: The Timor Sea, through which significant amounts of Australian trade sails, and the Straits of Ombai and Wetar to Timor's north. Australia, particularly the AFP, has been engaged in 'international good citizenship' missions and programs in East Timor and Timor-Leste since 1999. It seems by doing so, Australia's national interests are being directly threatened.

Coupled with the PRC's efforts in the South West Pacific, it is not difficult to draw the conclusion that, aside from direct assistance to governments in places such as Timor-Leste, the PRC has a longer-term agenda at play in relation to Australia and, in particular, potential access to Australian resources, by direct threat, coercion or actual force. These are not the actions of friendly nations.

China and the South West Pacific 2024

Melanesian Spearhead Group (MSG) 2024

As stated in its own website the purpose of the MSG 'is to promote and strengthen inter-membership trade, exchange of Melanesian cultures, traditions and values, sovereign equality, economic and technical cooperation between states and the alignment of policies to further MSG members' shared goals of economic growth.'[22] Its membership consists of the four Melanesian states of Fiji, Papua New Guinea, Solomon Islands and Vanuatu, and the Kanak and Socialist National Liberation Front of New Caledonia. Noteworthy is the fact that these Melanesian countries are situated to

Australia's near north east and are the closest Pacific Island countries to the Australian mainland. They form an arc from due north to east-northeast at a distance averaging between 500 and 900 kilometres and straddle important shipping routes. The MSG shares a vision and a political desire to seek the complete decolonisation of the Melanesian countries and territories still under the colonial rule in the South Pacific based on the concept of Melanesian Socialism and Melanesian Solidarity in a continuous struggle for self-determination, independence and freedom.[23]

In March 2023 The Melanesian Spearhead Group (MSG) Secretariat moved toward closer engagement with China for cooperation on matters of security.

Following a meeting between the Chinese Special Envoy to the Pacific, Qian Bo and the Director General, Leonard Louma, the MSG also considered partnering with the PRC as its first official 'development partner'.

> 'The Secretariat will now be crafting an Agreement that would be signed later this year between the Chinese Government and the Secretariat with the purpose of making the Chinese Government the first officially designated 'Development Partner' of the MSG Secretariat'.
>
> Louma further noted, 'My members have affirmed in very strong terms that no one will choose their friends or enemies for them. They have made it clear that they do not see any reason why their countries cannot receive security assistance, be it in training or equipment, from different development partners.'
>
> 'Consistent with our Members approach, the Secretariat is not averse to cooperation with China in implementing certain aspects of the Strategy and will be carefully looking at the Strategy to determine areas where cooperation might be possible', DG Louma said.[24]

Noteworthy is the stance taken in early 2024 by the Government of Fiji, an influential member of the MSG.

Paraphrasing an online ABC article by Movono, Lice and Stephen Dziedzic: Fiji PM orders Chinese police out of country, saying no need for them in Pacific police force, the Fijian Prime Minister Sitiveni Rabuka has been walking a tightrope in its relationship with China. His government has been working to draw investment and development funding from the PRC but 'has also been a critic of China's attempts to embed itself more deeply in Pacific nations like Solomon Islands and Kiribati.' Mr Rabuka, elected in 2022, has expressed concerns that China's presence in the region could undermine democratic systems in the Pacific:

> "A lot of people do not think about the inner peace brought about by a democratic system with tested legal systems…we have different legal systems

and policing and investigating methods…The fundamental rights of people and the government's respect for those…Those are the things that could happen if we were to be taken over by a new set of ideologies and approaches to life and living."

Mr Rabuka suggested that many Pacific leaders might be wary that intensifying Chinese influence in their countries could eventually erode democratic norms and values…Mr Rabuka said the China police agreement would be kept under constant review by Fiji and he still wanted senior Fijian police officers to continue training in China.

Prime Minister Rabuka told the ABC that while the government had decided to keep the policing MoU with China, he had ordered Chinese officers who had been based with Fiji's police force to leave the country.

[H]e added that he still wanted senior Fijian police officers to continue training in China, "particularly on the administrative side of senior command", saying officers had "benefited" from it over the years.[25]

Solomon Islands 2024

Following the signing of a security pact between the Solomon Islands and the PRC in March 2022, the security situation in that nation has become a major concern for Australian policymakers.

> "While PM Sogavare has said that Australia remains his country's primary security partner, his most recent comments would seem to cast doubt on his commitment to that position. If a security issue arose in future, and China was called on at the same time as Australia, that could be very difficult to manage."

Mr Batley, former senior DFAT RAMSI representative, now with the Australian National University indicated that most Solomon Islanders would be perplexed, and dismayed, by Prime Minister Sogavare's hostile and aggressive language against Australia. This is particularly disappointing because historically, Australia led the 'regional' RAMSI from 2003 to 2017, and continues to provide training to the Royal Solomon Islands Police Force with the RSIPF-Australian Police Partnership (RAPP).

Head of the ANU National Security College (NSC) Professor Rory Medcalf said there is a very real prospect of Chinese security forces becoming the preferred provider of internal security in the Solomon Islands could lead to a vicious circle of repression and chaos. He stated:

> "A catalyst for rioting in Honiara has been anger at the government's new closeness to China, so using Chinese forces to suppress such discontent will ultimately aggravate it…the Solomon Islands will pose an immediate test for the true quality of our diplomacy and what it means to be a Pacific partner", he said.[26]

Papua New Guinea 2024

The fact that China is seeking to expand its influence into the SW Pacific region including into countries such as Papua New Guinea places it in direct strategic competition with the West. This is of particular significance for Australian security as the PNG southern coastline forms the northern border of the Torres Strait, through which much shipping, Australian and international passes.

PNG is part of the Belt-and-Road Initiative and in 2018, China's President upgraded the Sino-Pacific relations to a 'comprehensive strategic partnership'. For PNG, the approach of 'friend to all, enemy to none' has been successful to date, however this is not a situation conducive to Australia's security interests.[27]

The AFP in the South West Pacific 2024

The South West Pacific is an area of significant interest to Australia for many reasons, and Australia has a long history of cultural, diplomatic, military and police engagement. The AFP has had a long-standing commitment to promoting stability and development in the Pacific through peacekeeping missions and capacity development programs. The AFP's operational engagement with Pacific partners has also expanded over the last two decades to combat a rise in transnational crime in the region. This includes an increase in drug trafficking through the region to lucrative markets in Australia and New Zealand, much of which originates in South America, transiting the Pacific destined for lucrative markets in Australia.

The extent of the AFP's investments in the SW pacific region is reflective concerns about this trade and by Australia's proximity as well as long-standing ties with police in these Pacific Island Countries (PICTs) and the related wide-ranging security interests we share. The challenges of Pacific policing are significant and include large and fragmented jurisdictions, spread over wide areas of open ocean, limited resources and increasingly sophisticated transnational crime.

In a region with small populations spread across numerous islands, Pacific police are stretched by the need to serve many dispersed and diverse communities. Increasing crime rates driven by rapid social change, including urbanisation and weakening community ties, also pose significant for the effectiveness of Pacific policing. Contemporary evidence suggests that rates of violence against women and children across the region are persistently high, and that increasing substance abuse is a contributing factor to this violence as well as and other criminal behaviour. The strategic location, porous borders and weak governance of PICTs have made them a target of increasingly sophisticated transnational and organised criminals, including as transit points for drug and human trafficking. Official corruption, money laundering, environmental crime, cybercrime as well as broader security threats such as civil unrest and the prevalence of natural disasters in the region are concerns in the Pacific, and by extension are of concern to police in Australia.

In the post-colonial period, PICTs have sought to establish more professional and independent police organisations, but there are still some significant challenges. In many remote communities in the Pacific contact with government agencies is limited, and traditional cultural approaches to policing predominate. There is significant diversity in policing practices across PICTs, which reflects their individual histories, cultures and politics. In most PICTs, policing is a hybrid of traditional dispute resolution and Western models of law enforcement. Traditional approaches typically involve peacemaking by chiefs or other community leaders with reference to customary norms as well as Christian ethics.

All of these challenges are compounded by the resource management constraints of Pacific police organisations which reinforce the need for strong partnerships at both international and community levels to help fill gaps, build capacity and strive towards increased professionalism in policing and justice administration. These developments are very much in Australia's interests generally and in the AFP's interests specifically.

The AFP Commissioner is a member of the Pacific Islands Chiefs of Police (PICP), which is the umbrella organisation leading efforts to improve regional collaboration and interoperability. Regional mechanisms such as Pacific Community for Law Enforcement Cooperation (PCLEC) deliver police capability development under the direction of PICP, which assists in facilitating a more collaborative, locally-led approach.

The AFP received $317.4 million in the 2023–24 Federal Budget to enhance its policing engagement in the Pacific through the AFP Pacific Police Partnership Program (AP4).[28]

Australian whole-of-government policy is shaped, informed and influenced by the UN Sustainable Development Goals and international humanitarian law, and funding for development programs is provided by ODA from the OECD. The AFP acts within these parameters and that of its own Act, the *Australian Federal Police Act 1979*. From this comes the AFP International Engagement Strategy. This is renewed periodically and generally has the following as its objectives:

1. maximum impact on international criminal activity affecting Australia or Australians
2. international peace, stability and security
3. strong and mutually beneficial partnerships for international activities
4. protection of Australian High Office Holders, members of the foreign diplomatic corps, witnesses and international aviation users remain safe and relevant property.

The most relevant of these to the AFP Pacific engagement are its efforts towards international peace, stability and security, and strong and mutually beneficial partnerships for international activities.

The AFP's Pacific engagement is multifaceted and includes involvement in both the International Network and the Pacific Police Partnerships Program as well as other elements. The International Network is focused primarily on operational policing and police cooperation targeted at countering violent extremism and transnational crime. It deals with criminal operations and criminal intelligence.

The AP4 was formerly referred to as 'missions' and has evolved from a long history of Pacific police engagement, which started with RAMSI in 2003. The language has changed from 'missions' to 'partnerships' to reflect the mature nature of this engagement as it has evolved.

There are currently seven Pacific Police Partnerships. The brief details of these programs are:

Timor-Leste

TLPDP 2023–28: Ten AFP members. AFP assistance to Timor-Leste since 1999 UNAMET. Co-funded by DFAT. Current focus on community policing, PNTL institutional resilience, gender actions plans.

Papua New Guinea

PNG-APP 2022–26: Forty-two AFP members. One of the largest AFP Pacific Partnerships. Current focus on operations, training and corporate reform.

Samoa

SAPP 2021–25: Three AFP members. Since 2009, and AFP assistance from at least 2004. Current focus on investigations and general policing skills, community perceptions of SPS and SPS corporate support capacity.

Nauru

N-APP 2020–25: Two AFP members. Since 2020, and AFP assistance to Nauru from at least 2004. Administered from PNG. Current focus on operational command and strategic direction, community-based policing services and specialist policing capabilities, especially investigations.

Solomon Islands

RSIPF-Australia Police Partnership Program (2021), RAPPP 2021–25: Thirty-five AFP members. Built on earlier assistance of RAMSI since 2003. Current focus on frontline policing, corporate enabling services, transnational crime, regional policing partnerships and police leadership.

Vanuatu

VAP JP 2020–24: Five AFP members. Since 2017, and AFP assistance goes back to 2001. A justice and policing program co-funded and co-delivered by DFAT and AFP. Current focus on frontline policing, community engagement and sector coordination.

Tonga

TAPP 2022–26: Two AFP members. Since 2006, and there was previously a partnership between Australia, New Zealand and Tonga. Current focus on national security, illicit drugs and transnational crime. Frontline response to domestic violence. Ethical and responsive policing.

Tonga Families Free of Violence (FFOV) 2022–26: One AFP member. Since 2017. Partnership with Women's Affairs and Gender Equality Division of the Ministry of Internal Affairs and the Tonga Police Force. DFAT funded. Current focus on frontline response to family violence and implementation of the family Protection Act.

These AP4 all involve AFP members deploying to the seven Pacific Island nations concerned for periods up to twelve months.

The types and categories of engagement in these programs includes:

- advisory (short and long term)
- training and train the trainer
- policy and corporate advice and support
- on the shoulder mentoring
- direct provision
- infrastructure and asset provision, improvements and maintenance
- coordination with other donor programs

- professional development opportunities (e.g., twinning, shadowing, exchanges, secondments)
- police-to-police arrangements to support joint operations
- grants.

Pacific Police Development Program-Regional (PPDP-R)

In the broader Pacific, the AFP also engages in PPDP-R programs. This is serviced from Australia and generally involves AFP members travelling to the nations concerned to deliver specific programs. The ethos this program conducts itself by is 'By the Pacific For the Pacific'. These nations include Palau, the Federated States of Micronesia, the Republic of Marshall Islands, Kiribati, the Cook Islands, Niue and Tuvalu.

Pacific Islands Chiefs of Police (PICP)

The PPDP-R also covers Australia's engagement and involvement in the PICP forum, which covers a vast oceanic area spanning all of Melanesia and Micronesia and a large section of the Polynesian Triangle. This brings together the heads of police of twenty-one Pacific nations from as far east as French Polynesia (Tahiti) and as far north as the Northern Marianas Islands and the Marshall Islands. Australia is represented by the Commissioner of the AFP.

The twenty-one members of the PICP are:

- Australia
- New Zealand
- Palau
- France (New Caledonia)
- French Polynesia (Tahiti)
- Vanuatu
- Fiji
- Guam
- Marshall Islands
- Cook Islands
- Niue
- Kiribati
- Solomon Islands
- Northern Mariana Islands
- Federated States of Micronesia
- Tuvalu
- Nauru

- Samoa
- American Samoa
- Kingdom of Tonga.

Pacific Community for Law Enforcement Cooperation (PCLEC)

Falling under the PICP is the PCLEC. This is a regional delivery mechanism that supports capability development in priority areas as identified by the PICP. It aims to deliver quality, Pacific-led initiatives that align with the strategic priorities of the PICP. The mechanism is delivered by the AFP.

There are additional programs that fall under the PICP, including:

- The PICP Women's Advisory Network (WAN)
- The PICP Pacific Police Training Advisory Group (PPTAG)
- The PICP Pacific Forensics Working Group (PFWG).

Other AFP programs related to Pacific engagement include:

- Cyber Safety Pasifika (CSP), which is an AFP commitment under the DFAT International Cyber and Critical Technology Engagement Strategy. It is jointly funded by the AFP and DFAT and aims to deliver cyber capability programs in the Pacific.
- The Pacific Faculty of Policing (PFP) at the AIPM. This is a joint program between the AFP and AIPM and was established to provide opportunities for leadership and development for senior police from the Pacific region.
- The Pacific Transnational Crime Network (PTCN), which was established in 2002 to form a criminal intelligence network for Pacific law enforcement agencies to target transnational, serious and organised crime. The PTCN consists of twenty-eight locally staffed TCUs across twenty countries in the Pacific region. The PTCN is coordinated by the PTCCC, located in Samoa. The AFP has a member posted to Samoa with the PTCN and PTCCC as part of the International Network.

The AFP International Network also has members posted to New Zealand, Fiji, PNG and Vanuatu.

The AFP International Network 2024

The following is a list of countries the AFP International Network has posts:

Europe	London		Middle East	Ankara
	The Hague			Beirut
	Lyon			Amman
	Belgrade			Dubai
	Paris			Abu Dhabi
	Berlin			
The Americas	Los Angeles		Southeast Asia	Jakarta
	Mexico City			Bali
	New York			Singapore
	Pittsburgh			Kuala Lumpur
	Washington			Bangkok
	Huntsville			Manila
	Bogota			Ho Chi Minh City
				Hanoi
				Yangon
China	Hong Kong		South West Pacific	Samoa
	Guangzhou			Port Moresby
	Beijing			Vanuatu
				Suva
Sub-Continent	Islamabad		Africa	Pretoria
	New Delhi			
	Colombo			

Police Diplomacy: AFP 1964–2024, A Summary

The past sixty years of AFP international deployments includes the bulk of the Cold War from 1964 to the present. This period includes the 'post-colonial' transition in many countries, the fall of European communism in 1989–90 and the resurgence of expansionist East Asian communism from 2013 onwards. There are five broad chronological phases over these sixty years. The first comprises primarily UN missions with little or no effect on Australia domestically. They were all missions with international good citizenship as their primary focus. This changed in the second phase that began around the new millennium with the UN mission to East Timor in 1999, which had a major repercussion: this intervention precipitated the jihadist mass casualty event in Bali in 2002. Ironically, this crime was in part intended to drive a wedge between Australia, a Western nation, and Indonesia, the largest single Islamic population in the world. However, it did the exact opposite, mainly through effective and professional police-to-police relationships between the AFP and POLRI. This second phase also led directly to the third phase which included successful police interventions in the South West Pacific, with particular emphasis on the Solomon Islands. This period was a hybrid between international good citizenship and the national interest. The fourth phase involved missions and operations in Afghanistan, PNG and Ukraine, which wore the cloak of international good citizenship but had national interest at its core. The fifth and most contemporary phase encompasses the rise of a more assertive and authoritarian China rapidly exerting influence in Australia's immediate region and posing a long-term threat to Australia's national interests.

1964–1998 International Good Citizenship: The AFP and the UN

The role the AFP performed in most of the deployments between the commencement with UNFICYP in 1964 and Bougainville in 1998 was primarily monitoring and representation. There were aspects of communication, including negotiation and reporting, but these were generally at the local level. This was especially true with UN missions, as reporting to national capitals outside the UN chain was not required, and such communication was discouraged by the UN.

There was a genuine cultural affinity for the long-term presence of Australian police, who were identifiable by the prominent display of the Australian National Flag on their uniforms, with members of the Greek and Turkish communities on both sides of the UN Buffer Zone in Cyprus, many of whom have relatives in Australia.

The AFP is the international representative of Australian policing and has a long, proud and highly credible history of international police engagement, primarily with the UN. During 'The Great Peace' experienced by the Australian military in the post-Vietnam era, the AFP was active in international 'boots on the ground' missions in Cyprus, Cambodia, Mozambique,[29] Haiti and in other places, including Bougainville. This resulted in increased recognition by the government that, if used judiciously, police and policing, particularly through the AFP, could be an effective alternative to traditional means of projecting national values and protecting national interests via traditional diplomacy and military deployment.

As Whiddett said of a 1991 Senate report on UN peacekeeping:

> [i]n passing reference to the role of police...the report asserted that it was 'useful in the UN context to preserve the distinction between police serving in a non-military capacity and the more usual military police units...Depending on the tasks to be performed, the United Nations may have a 'need for civilian police personnel in the future, as operations become less exclusively military...

[I]t may also be that some of the tasks that have traditionally been carried out by military personnel would be performed by UN civilian police.[30]

This concept was to be fully tested by the UNAMET deployment in 1999, which protected the UN-sponsored ballot to ascertain the political destiny of the population of East Timor. The AFP played a lead role in this mission in lieu of the Australian military.

1999–2007 International Good Citizenship and Australia's National Interest: East Timor, Bali and the Solomon Islands

The UNAMET deployment was a major turning point in the way the AFP was perceived by the Australian government of the time, led by Prime Minister John Howard. The confidence held by Prime Minister Howard in the AFP underpinned many of the activities of the AFP in the following decade and a half. It was during this period that the credentials of the AFP as an international actor came to the fore.

The period after the East Timor deployments of UNAMET and INTERFET involving Australia, Indonesia and East Timor to the 9/11 attacks in 2001, which caused Prime Minister Howard to invoke the ANZUS Treaty, was a watershed period for the AFP, and it started a series of seismic shifts in the way it was perceived by the Australian government of the day. All the diplomatic qualities of 'a quick mind, a hard head, a strong stomach, a warm smile and a cold eye' were applied to various degrees by the AFP and its members throughout this period. With the best of intentions, the AFP's participation in the UNAMET regional engagement ignited regional and global dynamics that sparked the deployment of AFP members in response to a mass casualty event in Bali, killing over 200 people, including eighty-eight Australians. The primary mission objectives of this response, known as Operation Alliance, were to respond immediately and bring the offenders to justice. This was achieved through networking and collaboration between police professionals in Australia and Indonesia. Operation Alliance was operationally focussed and justice-based.

Coupled with the U.S.'s global war on terror, Australia and the AFP was thrust into the world of global violent extremism. A silver lining of the Bali bombing was the enhanced relationship between the AFP and the Indonesian POLRI, who worked together on endeavours such as narcotics trafficking, people smuggling and Counter-terrorism (CT) efforts. This provided the impetus for further expansion of AFP networks throughout the Southeast Asian region to address transnational criminal activity. This in itself supports the assertion that the AFP, as an international actor, is worthy of consideration as diplomats, even if by default, and that effective and accountable international policing should be considered to operate on its own diplomatic Track.

These events were preceded by significant AFP participation in the UNAMET mission in East Timor. The diplomatic impact of policing is further reinforced by the fact that it was the efforts of fifty-two unarmed AFP members alongside their international police counterparts during UNAMET that created a security presence of such sufficiency that the people of East Timor had the opportunity to register and vote in large numbers to pave the way for their ultimate independence from Indonesia.

When Prime Minister Howard sent his letter to Indonesian President Habibie in December 1998, it set in motion a series of decisions and events over which Australia had no control. The result was a hastily created UN-sponsored ballot process with a severely flawed security agreement. The AFP was called upon in lieu of the ADF, which was deemed unacceptable by the Indonesian Government. The UNAMET mission has been viewed as a security failure due to the post-ballot violence that erupted from the ballot result. This resulted in an emphatic statement by U.S. President Clinton, who, in no uncertain terms, informed the Indonesian Government that the consequences of a failure to halt the violence would be severe. This allowed a relatively permissive, non-contested environment for the Australian-led military intervention, known as INTERFET, to deploy and restore stability. The effect of both UNAMET and INTERFET emboldened Osama bin Laden and al Qaeda to regard Australia as a 'crusader' nation and its citizens and interests to, therefore, be legitimate targets for violent action. This was not to manifest itself regionally until 2002, when bombs exploded in Bali, killing over 200 people, including eighty-eight Australians.[31] Between the East Timor interventions in 1999 and the Bali bombings in 2002, al Qaeda attacked New York and Washington and killed 2977 people. This resulted in U.S. President Bush warning all nations that unless they were with the U.S., they were against it and with the terrorists. Coming so close to President Clinton's warning to Indonesia, the Indonesian Government had a decision to make. Fortunately for Australia, it decided to side with the U.S., which paved the way for an enhancement of the AFP–POLRI relationship. This relationship was to be given further impetus in the immediate aftermath of the Bali bombing in 2002 and the response to the 2004 Boxing Day Tsunami as well as jihadist bombings in Indonesia, in particular the bombing of the Australian Embassy in Jakarta in 2004. It is a relationship that endures to this day, and in fact, it was Indonesian sponsorship that allowed Australia to be a dialogue partner in ASEANAPOL in 2007.

In the Solomon Islands, Commander PPF Ben McDevitt's dealings by letter with GRA leader Harold Keke upon the arrival of RAMSI in 2003, although old fashioned, led to a peaceful end to the militancy and paved the way for an eventual return to sovereignty in the Solomon Islands from the brink of state collapse. The AFP was not only a participant in this mission, but it was also the lead security agency and approached the armed militants as 'criminals' rather than as 'enemies'. The resolution was achieved through a voluntary and peaceful submission to justice. The follow-on investigation saw 'justice being done and being seen to be done', which served to reinstate community trust in its institutions. The RAMSI intervention was given the operational name Operation Helpem Fren because that is exactly what the mission was intended to do – help a friend. The involvement of the PIF and the PPF nations in RAMSI, at the insistence of Prime Minister Howard, was an inspired piece of regional diplomacy. The creation of the IDG to service RAMSI and the East Timor missions provided the basis for greater police engagement in the Pacific.

The instrumental role played by the AFP and its members in UNAMET, Operation Alliance and Operation Helpem Fren are demonstrative of these individual diplomatic qualities. They all had regional implications which resulted in improved and enduring police-to-police relationships between trusted police partners.

The AFP has made a significant contribution to stabilising what was once referred to as Australia's 'Arc of Instability'. This success is based on myriad reasons, including implicit over-arching direction from successive U.S. administrations, an acknowledgement that some of the issues facing sovereign governments in the region were beyond the capacity of their resources and a willingness to seek assistance, and the confidence of Australian governments in the AFP to deliver. The AFP's success was due to adopting culturally appropriate approaches and strategies that, in the case of RAMSI, involved a 'Pacific face' with Australian training. This was a 'force multiplier', as Pacific police members gained training, experience and contacts that they returned with to their own nations. The IDG concept was a 'platinum standard' but was expensive and poorly understood by some AFP executives.

Australia has direct and indirect interests in the South West Pacific region related to a vested interest in ongoing stability, security, good governance and economic prosperity. In some countries in the region, cultural, social, economic, gender, security and governance issues continue to hamper sustainable development. If not addressed sensitively, these could undermine stability in the region and have the potential to create conditions that could be exploited by malicious state and non-state actors, including criminal elements, which require future interventions.

The 2013 Australian Defence White Paper stated:

> [The] region's big strategic challenges will last for decades and their mismanagement could have significant consequences. Regional forums and multilateralism have proven well worth nurturing, even if they remain a modest supplement to long-practised bilateral statecraft.[32]

Police capacity development programs run by the AFP and participation in a wide range of police-related forums have played a significant role in this form of multilateral and bilateral statecraft. With a change in government in Canberra from Prime Ministers Howard to Rudd came a change in foreign policy strategy and the deployment of AFP IDG members to missions where expectations were high and difficult to meet, which resulted in adverse effects on political support. Three examples are Afghanistan, PNG and Ukraine.

2007–2014 National Interest Cloaked in International Good Citizenship: Challenging Missions in Afghanistan, Papua New Guinea and Ukraine

Establishing a functioning rule of law or even a basic post-conflict policing capability within Afghanistan was always going to present a significant challenge to the international community. Given the history of the region, its diverse ethnic makeup, its difficult terrain, governance issues and fragile economic base, it was unrealistic to expect anything approximating a Western-style democratic rule of law within any reasonable timeframe. The AFP recognised that Afghanistan's narcotics industry posed a major threat to stabilisation efforts in the region, and that it helped fuel the Taliban insurgency aimed at undermining government legitimacy. It was this aspect that the AFP could have made a more meaningful contribution to the NATO-ISAF effort. Yet, it was this effort that was completely disregarded by the Australian Rudd government of the day, arguably in an attempt to politically differentiate itself from its predecessor. The best that can be said of the Australian government's desire to deploy ever-increasing numbers of police to Afghanistan is that they were arguably well-intentioned but poorly informed.

The AFP was asked to deploy into a complex active conflict zone with the initial task of assisting our British friend and ally with a chronic narcotics challenge in Afghanistan. Changes of government in both Canberra and Washington and a rapidly changing strategic environment on the ground caused demands to be made of the AFP for which it was not trained nor equipped to fulfil. These were high-risk endeavours for virtually zero return other than the possible political dividend of allowing politicians to claim they were actively seeking to transition from an aggressive CT, enemy-centric approach to a more 'progressive' population-centric, CI approach. This was poorly thought out and reflected the relative ignorance of the political decision-makers and their advisors, particularly in Canberra, who seemed to lack an appreciation of the roles and limitations of liberal-democratic policing in an active conflict zone.

Yet, to the political class, based on advice provided solely through a 'security lens', by which police missions and operations appear to be assessed, like earlier missions such as UNAMET, it seems to be the case in the eyes of some that police are more expendable than soldiers.

The period from 2007 to 2014 was one in which the versatility of the AFP was called upon by a new government where expectations were unrealistically high and tinged with the optics of politics. The challenging situations faced by the AFP in both PNG and Afghanistan had some similarities, including difficult geographic and human terrains and a politically driven attempt to fit a liberal-democratic policing template in culturally inappropriate contexts. The inability of the AFP to meet unrealistic, politically driven expectations resulted in frustration and the eventual financial stifling of the IDG concept. Nonetheless, the achievements of the AFP, particularly the IDG, formed part of the successful pitch by the Australian government for a non-permanent seat on the United Nations Security Council. Ironically, it was during Australia's term on this council that three resolutions in which the AFP had a direct stake were passed: two related to UN policing and security sector reform, and the third related to the downing of Malaysian Airlines flight MH17, an incident to which the AFP deployed rapidly and effectively.

The MH17 response was called Operation Arew, which is an archaic word meaning 'in a row'. The immediate, medium and long-term engagement of the AFP in relation to this atrocity resulted in offenders being tried and convicted in absentia in a court in the Netherlands and travel restrictions being placed upon military officials from a resurgent superpower. The response, the evidence, the prosecution and the eventual convictions in absentia in the Netherlands and international action through INTERPOL all served justice in an unprecedented circumstance, and the AFP was one of the major participants.

2014–2024 National Interest and the Rise of China: Australian Security and Sovereignty in the Asian Century

The decade between the rise of China following the assumption of power as President of China in 2013 by Xi Jinping and 2024, which marks the 60th anniversary of AFP international engagement commencing in Cyprus in 1964, has been marked by a discernible change in the global and regional environment.

Political developments in sovereign nations in Australia's immediate region, in particular Timor-Leste and the Solomon Islands, in which Australian police individuals and the AFP institutionally have invested enormous effort over decades, have seen a long-term potential threat arise directly to Australia's national interests, featuring closer security cooperation with China, a regional autocracy.

Despite the adverse implications that can be drawn from the discussion of the influence of the PRC globally, regionally and domestically, there is one area of direct cooperation between Australia and the PRC. This is known as Taskforce Blaze, which is a joint taskforce between the AFP and other Australian law enforcement agencies, and the Chinese Narcotic Control Bureau, focused on opiates and methamphetamine, and it commenced in November 2015. This has resulted in the seizure of several tonnes of illicit drugs and precursor chemicals and hundreds of arrests both in China and Australia. The cooperation has included sharing intelligence and evidence in joint investigations, including statements, forensic reports and photographs, and samples.[33] The rising trade in Fentanyl and its precursors is a litmus test of the efficacy and level of trust arising from this relationship.

Taskforce Blaze forms part of a series of bilateral and multilateral efforts aimed at addressing Transnational and Serious Organised Crime (TSOC). The cost of organised crime is estimated to be in excess of $60 billion. This includes illicit drugs and other illicit commodities, organised fraud, enablers, crimes against the person, cybercrime and more.[34] The AFP is one of Australia's primary agencies tasked with addressing TSOC. An emerging aspect of this fight against globalised criminality is the adoption of international cooperation between the Five-Eyes countries in five domains: police, border, military, intelligence, and science and technology. This is a formidable capability with a truly global reach.

The behaviour of the Russian Federation throughout the investigation of the flight MH17 crash site and the prosecution of offenders involved in the deliberate killing of nearly 300 innocent civilians demonstrates the disregard and indifference for the rule of law of this regime. The illegal and unprovoked attack and partial invasion of Ukraine is further evidence of this disregard for international rules and mores.

The fact that both China and Russia are Permanent Five members of the United Nations Security Council, and are colluding with other less than liberal states such as Iran and North Korea, gives rise to questions about the credibility and legitimacy of that supra-national body. Both of these nations, as well as other P5 members such as the United States, have used their veto powers to engage in questionable conduct, attempting to thwart justice in the case of Russia and the MH17, and given recent reports and observable events, undermining the entire ethos of the UN by verging on a return to the 'scourge of war'. This follows the UN failing to pursue the prosecution of the alleged Indonesian murderers in East Timor during the UNAMET period in 1999, some of which were witnessed by AFP UNCIVPOL members. The unfortunate aspect of this is the questionable legacy it leaves in the minds of those Australians, especially those members of the AFP who have served proudly, and in some cases risked their lives, under the UN flag in Cyprus, Mozambique, Cambodia, Sudan, South Sudan, East Timor, Timor-Leste and elsewhere, and those AFP members who have deployed to non-UN operations and missions, in the sixty years between 1964 and 2024.

Nonetheless, the legacy of the AFP's international deployments is one they can be proud of, particularly in the last twenty-five years.

Some of the Remarkable Achievements of the AFP 1999–2024

It needs to be borne in mind that the AFP is essentially a domestic crime agency with international responsibilities. Nonetheless, the AFP has had some significant input in enhancing the reputation of both itself and, by default, the Australian government. This type of recognition is also a part of diplomacy. In the past twenty-five years alone, the AFP has:

- played a major role in paving the way for a new nation in Timor-Leste (1999–present)
- resolved serious inter-communal violence in the Solomon Islands (2003–present)
- restored a largely broken relationship with Indonesia created by Australian involvement in East Timor in 1999, by the response to the Bali bombings in 2002 and the Boxing Day Tsunami in 2004; 230,000 people died, including twenty-six Australians, as well as several jihadist bombings in Indonesia. AFP pathologists and disaster victim identification officers deployed.
- AFP Assistant Commissioner Andy Hughes, APM, (deceased) appointed as Republic of Fiji Commissioner of Police (2007–9) and then Police Adviser to the United Nations and Head of Police Peacekeeping, involving 12,500 police from 100 contributing countries involved in eighteen missions around the world (2007–9). Also a member of the Executive Committee of INTERPOL (2000)

and Chairman of two separate UN Boards of Inquiry into fatal attacks on the UN in Afghanistan (twelve International staff killed).
- responded to a mass casualty event in an active conflict zone in Eastern Ukraine in 2014 and was part of an effort to prosecute representatives of a former superpower
- provided rapid response to an emergency situation in the caves in Thailand in 2018, where a soccer team was trapped by flood waters
- provided and continues to provide close personal protection to Australian High Office Holders, Diplomats and visiting dignitaries
- restrained criminal assets domestically and offshore worth $187 million (2020–21)
- served as Australia's INTERPOL representative, including 4422 new referrals actioned (2020–21)
- conducted Operation Ironside, including 993 arrests domestically and offshore (2020–21).

United Nations Security Council Resolutions (UNSCR)

The AFP's efforts in Timor and the Solomon Islands played a large part in helping Australia secure a non-permanent seat on the UN Security Council 2013–14. While on the council, three resolutions were passed with much input from Australia based in large part on the efforts of the AFP, including UNSCR 2151 SSR and UNSCR 2185 Police as an Integral Part of UN missions. The roles police played, especially in East Timor and the Solomon Islands, were influential in both resolutions. Additionally, Australia was instrumental in the adoption of UNSCR 2166 concerning the deliberate downing of Malaysian Airlines flight MH17. AFP responders, investigators, intelligence analysts and forensics were part of the Dutch-led joint investigations team. In 2023, three of those charged were convicted in absentia in the Netherlands.

These are all efforts worthy of consideration not only for their immediate operational effect but also for their longer-term diplomatic outcomes. This is police diplomacy, actual and potential, and is why effective international policing can be justifiably regarded as having its own diplomatic track based on the notion of 'firm' diplomacy.

How this newly defined diplomatic track can make a meaningful contribution in an era of strategic uncertainty and increased authoritarianism remains a question yet to be answered. It is likely that answering these questions will involve less of a focus on the benevolence of international good citizenship and more of a Realpolitick focus on Australia's national interest, with a specific focus on security and stability.

Conclusion

The Future: Police Diplomacy in the Age of Regional Strategic Competition

Australia and New Zealand, as long-standing liberal democracies, are outliers in a part of the world that has experienced high levels of political volatility and violence, both inter-state and intra-state. Thankfully, it appears this era of politically motivated violence ended with the end of the Cold War, but there are some who postulate that we are entering a new Cold War, and the possibility exists that this could be a precursor to a broader conflict, with some viewing the current era as the foothills of a third world war.

As the age of strategic uncertainty transitions to the era of strategic competition, the risk of conflict in Australia's immediate neighbourhood increases. This trend involves a direct competition between autocracy and liberal democracy. Policing and, more broadly, the administration of justice are at the very heart of this competition, and in Australia's case, the competition is taking place in three broad areas: domestically, regionally in the South West Pacific and in Southeast Asia. These three areas are different environments and have different characteristics, but the clearly observable trend is away from liberal democracy towards a more authoritarian approach to governance.

There is no scope in this book for a discussion of Australian domestic circumstances other than to state that this is a trend being seen in all Western nations, particularly those in the 'Anglosphere'.

The trend in Southeast Asia has been to split the ASEAN partnership by China co-opting a number of countries, notably Cambodia and Myanmar, towards a more Sino-focused outlook and more authoritarian approaches to police and policing. The trend in the South West Pacific is one of China's co-opting of national governments at the elite political level. Of the four levels of the criminal justice system, it is at the elite political level that the least effort is required to coerce and co-opt, and there is a trend away from a pro-Western stance towards a pro-China stance and, thus, a potentially more authoritarian, regime-protection, governance posture. How police are positioned, equipped and directed and how they interact with the community are all hallmarks of this.

This book has outlined the historical contribution the AFP has made in regional and global efforts aimed at peace and stability, encouraging the rule of law and promoting institutions to support these endeavours over the past sixty years.

It is quite clear that there is a requirement that the rationale surrounding AFP engagement in the South West Pacific needs to change from prioritising 'good international citizenship' to an emphasis on Australia's national interest. In this regard, police diplomacy, both at the individual and the institutional level, has more prominence than it has had in the past. The difference between an emphasis on the national interest and an emphasis on good international citizenship relates to primary motive. If Australia's goodwill surrounding regional engagements is likely to be repaid with co-option of regional political elites by an authoritarian power which poses a direct long-term threat to Australia's national security interests by threatening Australia's SLOCs, then perhaps the taxpayer's funds that finance these programs could be revised and could be better spent elsewhere.

Unfortunately, the AFP is constrained in its ability to operate offshore in the South West Pacific, as the AP4 are in large part determined by the United Nations Sustainable Development Goals, adherence to international humanitarian law and are largely funded via the OECD ODA, which has its own set of criteria. These are all focused on 'good international citizenship' approaches to the delivery of police programs and completely disregard the operational imperative to effectively address crime and criminality, which is one of the primary reasons police exist at all.

There is a clear disparity between the aims of the UN Sustainable Development Goals relating to peace, justice and strong institutions and the way police programs are funded to implement them. This is particularly so with specific challenges such as operational police efforts targeted at criminal activity such as the illicit flow of finance and arms, the recovery and return of stolen assets, organised crime, bribery and corruption and violent extremism such as terrorism. These are all operational police areas, and, as such, international efforts, including programs with police cooperation and coordination at their core, run the risk of not being funded by ODA. This is a sad reflection of the anachronistic manner in which many international bodies, including the OECD and UN, view the role and potential of such international police programs. Strategic competitors in the field of policing and justice, such as the PRC do not face such restrictions on their activities or the way they are funded.

Presently, there is strategic competition between authoritarianism and liberal democracy. The social contract between the government and the governed, particularly in the way policing is done, is at the epicentre of this competition. This has global and regional implications, and decisions need to be made now as to what the future of policing looks like. In all its international endeavours, AFP members have demonstrated the characteristics of diplomats. They have communicated and negotiated in very challenging circumstances, and they are representatives of the Australian Government and its humanitarian values. The AFP, as part of broader efforts with institutions such as the UN, have provided a supplement to international society through effective networking.

The AFP continues to be well positioned within government, law and intelligence and security circles in Australian and international contexts through an extensive network in Southeast Asia, the South West Pacific and more broadly. The AFP has shown itself as capable and ready to respond effectively to extant and emerging challenges and, as such, has earned a place in foreign policy discussions and considerations at the highest diplomatic levels.

At present, the AFP has an International Network with approximately 150 members posted to more than thirty posts in the countries listed above and has seven AP4s in Timor-Leste, PNG, Solomon Islands, Vanuatu, Nauru, Tonga and Samoa. Some of these programs have evolved from missions and have seen a continuous AFP presence for more than two decades.

The AFP provides a distinctive and direct link between the global, the regional and the domestic, which matches the globalised and networked Australian community it represents. International policing, as practised by the AFP, acts as a distinctive aspect of Australian 'firm' diplomacy and supplements the more traditional elements of international engagement between 'soft' traditional diplomacy and 'hard' military intervention. It does not seek to replace either, but it should be acknowledged that this aspect of police diplomacy is increasingly important in a period of strategic uncertainty in international affairs.

The primary observation of this book is that the structure, interconnectivity and actions of the AFP, as one of several 'thin blue lines' of policing, domestically, regionally and globally, serve as a guideline for the way in which values-based policing could be considered more broadly. (See Appendix 10). The proposition is that this extension of 'thin blue lines' into an effective network, a 'wide blue net', serves diplomatic ends by underwriting peace and prosperity while balancing individual rights and freedoms with broader community expectations of safety, security and freedom from interference by malign non-state actors such as organised criminals and violent extremists. It is preferable that Australia export its liberal-democratic values rather than import the illiberal values of autocratic governments, violent extremists and organised criminal groups.

The book concludes that although not officially acknowledged as a 'diplomatic' actor, the AFP is an 'international' actor whose activities, actions, responses, influences and effects are diplomatic in nature. The book further concludes that traditional theory that categorises diplomacy as official government Track I diplomacy and non-government engagement as Track II diplomacy should be reviewed to account for the new actors in the globalised environment, and that police diplomacy is rightfully deserving of being considered on its own track. In addition, this reconsideration of police activities as 'diplomatic' in influence should extend the funding model under existing OECD DACC ODA guidelines under which many police programs are funded.

In 2024, as its 60th anniversary of Australian police 'peacekeeping' approaches, the AFP continues to play a significant role as part of 'Team Australia' on the ground and with the strategic leadership within the police in the South West Pacific. This has been a long-standing and sincere engagement based on personal and professional relationships and encouraging institutional resilience. In some cases, these efforts have been undermined by political elites intent on pursuing their own self-interest and moving away from a liberal-democratic and accountable approach to law and justice towards a more autocratic, opaque and politicised form of law enforcement, with a trend towards a form of 'regime protection' policing. This is an unfortunate result of the geopolitical competition playing out between liberal democracy and autocracy worldwide. The implications for the people of the Pacific are yet to be determined, but it is quite clear that Australia's national interest is not well served by this trend.

The longer-term strategic effect of a compliant political elite in the Pacific and a politicised and authoritarian policing posture is the ability of malign actors such as the PRC to suppress dissent or unrest by force, possibly by foreign military force, with a tendency to remain in situ as a foothold to the establishment of 'warehouses' and other storage facilities that could quite easily be converted into military facilities with the potential to threaten Australia's SLOCs. The nations of the Solomon Islands and Timor-Leste are very well situated geographically for this to occur. It is also possible that, should conflict break out between China and the U.S., as an ally and as a rich and largely unprotected source of agricultural and mineral resources, such an outcome could be used to threaten the Australian mainland directly. It is in Australia's national interest, therefore, to pursue the 'international good citizenship' in the Pacific that the AFP continues to engage in. The stakes are high, and the AFP is playing a vital role in trying to deny a strategic foothold

Conclusion

to any regional actor with designs on Australia's peace and prosperity. This is the epitome of police diplomacy.

This relates to an under-recognised aspect of international good citizenship: a better social contract between the government and the governed in host nations. This encourages enhanced peace, order and good government, which are the precursors for stability and, thus, improved prospects for social security in these nations. Thus, there is less fertile ground for malign foreign actors, both nation-state and criminal. It also tends to reduce the potential for international military intervention from countries like Australia. This ultimately serves Australia's national interest.

We should bear in mind the notion that the reason we become involved in these interventions is to promote peace, which is the precursor to stability and underpins prosperity. It should be acknowledged that 'peace is not just the absence of conflict, but the presence of justice', which is the firmest pillar of good governance. The notions of peace and justice are inextricably intertwined. The role effective international policing can play in the promotion of peace through justice-based solutions under the rule of law is vital, as is the prevention of intra-state conflict, which is often the precursor to broader conflict.

A review and discussion of the major AFP engagements over the past sixty years, however, reveals some undesirable trends.

The situation in Cyprus is an anachronistic stalemate in a highly strategic but volatile region. With both belligerents as members of NATO, this situation is unlikely to change in the favour of liberal democracy and could become a flashpoint once more. This has no direct implications for Australia's national interest but could herald a possible split in NATO, which is a vital component of Western security.

The situation in Timor-Leste appears to be trending towards a more friendly disposition towards the PRC, as does the Solomon Islands and the MSG. It seems that all the efforts to encourage liberal-democratic policing practices and accountable justice mechanisms have been undone by decisions at the political level in these sovereign nations. These developments have direct implications for Australia's national interests, as they can form the basis for an increased influence and presence of security sector elements from the PRC, which brings them within striking distance of both the Australian landmass and Australia's SLOCs.

The democratisation of Indonesia in the post-Suharto era, and following the turmoil surrounding Timor-Leste and global jihadism, particularly the Bali bombings in 2002, has progressed well; however, it should be noted that 'a political oligopoly has emerged in Indonesia with nine national parties, which are either dynasties or oligarchies and which are deeply embedded in the country's richest families and conglomerates'.[1]

Indonesia is the single largest member of ASEAN, a body initially formed as a bulwark against the southern expansion of communism, which itself is at severe risk of being split by the PRC as Myanmar and Cambodia trend towards PRC's influence. The PRC has extant jurisdictional disputes with all the maritime states of ASEAN as it encroaches further and consolidates its position in the South China Sea.

Specifically related to the members of the AFP and other UNCIVPOL who deployed to East Timor with UNAMET in 1999, the murders of over 1200 East Timorese in 1999 at the hands of Indonesian military, police and militia proxies remain unanswered. The UN SCU laid over 430 indictments for murder and other human rights atrocities. Most of those indicted fled to Indonesia, and very few have ever been called to account for their actions. This speaks volumes about the integrity of all of those involved, particularly the governments of Australia and Indonesia, as well as the UN. What does this say about Australia's commitment to the rule of law? It is not beyond imagination that Australia's position in relation to these atrocities is based on prioritising strategic pragmatism above liberal-democratic principles. Indonesia has long been seen by strategists as a bulwark against communist aggression and southward expansion.

The most proximate nation to Australia, PNG, suffers from many problems and overtures have been made to it by the PRC. To date, these have met with limited success, but this is unlikely to stop further efforts on the part of the PRC. Should they be successful at the political level, as they have in Timor-Leste and the Solomon Islands, Australia's national interests would come under direct and immediate threat, as the Torres Strait is a vital SLOC lying between the tip of Cape York Peninsula and southern PNG.

A regionally dominant China represents an existential threat to Australia as a liberal democracy, and there is every sign that this regional dominance is drawing closer, with regional governments of sovereign nations complicit in its expansion. This has implications for the rule of law and how criminal matters such as mass casualty events are dealt with in the short term and potentially catastrophic implications in the longer term. This includes war.

As the late Senator for NSW, Jim Molan, stated in his final interview with Sky News in January 2023:

> Because we have been at peace for the last 80 years, many people find the prospect of serious war beyond their comprehension.
>
> We are well and truly within the strategic warning time for the next war.

I'd say to every Australian what we take for granted in the sovereignty, the freedom and prosperity in this country should never be taken for granted.[2]

What does war in the Indo-Pacific region mean for liberal-democratic policing? While we are possibly in the grey zone or foothills of the next major war, the rule of law remains the primary determinant for dispute resolution. Mass casualty events caused by hostile military action or by ideological or proxy actions such as terrorism, even in these foothills, are an increased likelihood as tensions build and as the capabilities of malign actors are enhanced. This will severely test the adherence to the rule of law internationally, regionally and domestically.

Reading the seminal work by Ross Babbage, *The Next Major War*, will enlighten the reader in relation to China's current status and indicators of future hostility and aggression. There is no doubt that China has the means and the motive for expansion by force if necessary. The burning question is whether it is awaiting its opportunity, and if so, when is that likely to be? There is no place in this book for such predictions except to state that should this eventuate, it is the stated intention of China to rewrite the international rule book in its own favour. Short of a major conflict, however, we are left with the rule of law under existing frameworks and structures in which the AFP has participated with credibility and will continue to do so.

The AFP responses to mass casualty events in Bali in 2002 and in eastern Ukraine in 2014 demonstrate the value of the sort of cooperative international police engagement highlighted in this book. Both involved endemic skills held by the AFP, and both resulted in successful prosecutions in Indonesia and the Netherlands, respectively. The fact that those tried for the MH17 atrocity were held in absentia due to obstruction by the Russian Federation speaks volumes about the credibility and integrity of this country, which incidentally holds a veto power as a Permanent Five member of the UN Security Council. The PRC, an autocratic country with an oppressive system of government and policing, is another Permanent Five member of the UN Security Council with a veto. It must be said that the U.S. backing of Israel in its activities in Gaza, involving allegations of indiscriminate bombing of civilians following the atrocities committed by Hamas in southern Israel on 7 October 2023 has brought into question the integrity and liberal-democratic credentials of the U.S. as a Permanent Five member of the UN Security Council as well. It seems the 'scourge of war', the very basis upon which the UN was established to prevent, is making a return and that the major members of the UN Security Council are either directly involved in hostilities, supporting belligerents and their proxies, or abstaining from taking preventative action. This is not a positive trend.

The chaotic and humiliating withdrawal of NATO from Afghanistan in 2021 not only damaged U.S. and Western credibility but also territorially linked North Korea, China, Iran and Russia. None of these societies has any aspect of liberal-democratic tendencies in their political cultures. Quite the opposite, in fact, and they are now increasingly emboldened, and their influences are moving physically closer to Australia and to Western Europe, liberal-democratic societies at either end of the Eurasian landmass. For a more detailed discussion of the autocratic outlook of both Xi Jinping and Vladimir Putin concerning state security and the role of the state, please see Appendix 9.

At the very start of this book, the question was posed to the military: what are we defending, and what are we defending it from? The reader was also asked to consider what is diplomacy and why it is done? This book has discussed the point that a large part of what we are defending and, in some cases, advancing are Australian values and principles; prime among those are liberal-democratic policing approaches and justice-based solutions to problem solving under the rule of law. How long Australia as a society can afford the luxury of clinging to these values and principles is an important question. In a volatile region that is rapidly adopting more authoritarian approaches to governance under increased influence from the PRC, and in potential future isolation from the U.S., which itself is being weakened and divided, these questions are of vital significance to Australia as a peaceful liberal democracy.

If we take Patrick Shaw's Minute to the External Affairs Minister in April 1964 re-deploying Australian police to Cyprus as a benchmark from which to review Australian international police engagements over the past sixty years, we have seen thirty-five years of adherence to the principle of UN Police Contributing Countries being selected because they have no strategic interests in the subject nation. This all changed with the UNAMET deployment to East Timor in 1999 where there were perceived and actual Australian strategic interests at stake which placed unarmed Australian police and their international UNCIVPOL colleagues in mortal danger. This mission led to other repercussions including a violent attack which included Australian holiday-makers in Bali as legitimate targets in the eyes of the offenders.

This was the catalyst for a strong and more respectful relationship between Australian and Indonesian police peers. It also enhanced the confidence in the eyes of the government of the day in the utility of the Australian Federal Police as an instrument of foreign policy. This in turn led to the creation of the International Deployment Group and a significant leadership role in another regional engagement in the Solomon Islands with RAMSI. In accordance with the Brahimi Report, a direct descendant of the UNAMET mission, further police to police partnerships in the South West Pacific evolved. The current situation has competing notions of policing and justice, one liberal-democratic and one authoritarian, under active consideration by the sovereign nations in this contested region close to Australia. Rather than being deployed because of an absence of Australian strategic interest, AFP members are now being deployed to these countries, in part, because there is a direct Australian strategic interest in the preservation of liberal-democratic, rather than autocratic, regime-protection approaches to policing and justice in Australia's near region. This is now based more on Australian national interests than international good citizenship, and is the inevitable result of a direct strategic challenge by the PRC, a Permanent Member of the UN Security Council, a powerful, autocratic regional power with its eyes on Australian land and resources.

UNAMET in 1999 and the inertia concerning the murders of over 1200 East Timorese, the obstruction of the Russian Federation, also a Permanent member of the UN Security Council, in relation to the pursuit of justice for the victims and families of the MH17 atrocity in 2014 brings into question the legitimacy of the United Nations itself. It seems that if the nation concerned has sufficient influence in elite political circles, contemporary realpolitik in the UN does nothing to encourage the pursuit of actual justice and does nothing to discourage such offenders from literally getting away with murder. Over the past sixty years, specifically the past twenty-five years, professional police members of the AFP have borne witness to these strategic changes with some concern.

The AFP International Network and the combined domains among the Five-Eyes countries is an encouraging development in preserving the rule of law and by extension, the essential role liberal-democratic policing can play in upholding the rule of law internationally. This remains an effective track of police diplomacy, but times are changing. There is little doubt that the 'international good citizenship' basis for AFP policing programs needs to be reconsidered, and that more focus on 'national interest' as a basis for such deployments should be re-prioritised in an era where serious conflict within the foreseeable future, is a real possibility. Perhaps the concept of liberal-democratic police, internationally and domestically, in times of war is a matter for further discussion and consideration in a follow-up book.

Appendix 1: Police Capacity Development

Police Development and the Rule of Law

The AFP IDG definition of Police development is:

> the support provided to police in post-conflict and developing nations, to build their capacity to provide sustainable and quality policing to their citizens. This support develops the operational capacity, enabling services and leadership that police services require to be accountable to their citizens, and to build and maintain the legitimacy required to support the delivery of the rule of law.

There is a direct relationship between police development, the observance of the rule of law and human rights. Police, however, are only one part of the institutional framework that underpins a well-functioning criminal justice system, as the following UN definition of the rule of law illustrates:

> For the United Nations, the rule of law refers to a principle of governance in which all persons, institutions and entities, public and private, including the state itself, are accountable to laws that are publicly promulgated, equally enforced and independently adjudicated, and which are consistent with international human rights norms and standards. It requires as well, measures to ensure adherence to the principles of the supremacy of law, equality before the law, accountability to the law, fairness in the application of the law, separation of powers, participation in decision-making, legal certainty, avoidance of arbitrariness and procedural and legal transparency.[1]

Military interventions are expensive and rarely result in a sustainable peace to keep. Early in this book, the distinction was made between the military as peacemakers and the police as peacekeepers. This is deliberately simplistic; however, in a preventative sense, to not consider these policing activities in tandem when making the peace runs the risk of increasing continued breakdowns of social contracts when the peace is actually made, to the extent that international military interventions may be prolonged. It does not take very long for a liberating military to be regarded as an occupier. By advocating transition to best practice, humanitarian approaches to policing, especially regionally, are not only the national interest served but also the prospect of a sustainable peace to keep by virtue of improved social contracts between the community and its government. Furthermore, this serves the Australian community's interests by enhancing connectivity between police agencies working to mitigate the influence of crime.

Appendix 2: Peel's Nine Principles

The philosophy of policing by consent

Sir Robert Peel served as Chief Secretary of Ireland from 1812 when that troubled land was still under British control. Law and order was breaking down in many rural areas and the local authorities were unable to maintain order amidst the factional fighting. Peel established a Peace Preservation Force in 1814 and later set up a system of county constabularies and then, in 1822 under the Constabulary Act. A single Irish police force, the Constabulary of Ireland, was established in 1836 after he returned to England. His experience in Ireland no doubt influenced his formation of the London Metropolitan Police when he was Home Secretary. London at the time was plagued by crime, but did not have the factional issues as Ireland. This provided an environment in which a more benign approach to law and order could be introduced.

Although there is some doubt concerning the actual probity of the of-quoted Nine Principles of Effective Policing, also referred to as the Peelian Principles, there is little doubt about their benign and benevolent intent. There is no firm evidence that Peel compiled an actual list, now known as the Nine Principles, and it is more likely that the first and joint Commissioners of the Metropolitan Police, Sir Richard Mayne, a barrister and Sir Charles Rowan, a soldier, discussed the sentiments which are reflected in the Nine Principles.

Sir Robert Peel's *Bill for Improving the Police in and near the Metropolis* of 19 June 1829, received Royal Assent on 29 September 1829. This was based on some basic guidelines for ethical policing which emphasised the paramount importance of trust and accountability as essential for the concept of consent-based policing. Sir Richard Mayne, is quoted as stating:

> The primary object of an efficient police is the prevention of crime: the next that of the detection and punishment of offenders if crime is committed. To these ends all the efforts of police must be directed. The protection of life and property, the preservation of public tranquility, and the absence of crime, will alone prove whether those efforts have been successful, and whether the objects for which the police were appointed have been attained. (Sir Richard Mayne 1829).

According to Hilton, this quotation first appears in the Frontispiece of the *Metropolitan Police General Order* and in *Instruction Books* from 1873 onwards. Hilton further states that Mayne's name and the date 1829 was only added during the 1948 revision of the *Instruction Book*.

There is little doubt that the establishment of the London Metropolitan Police was based on the principle of consent-based policing. Czerny highlights the influence the reformer Jeremy Bentham had on the concept of consent-based policing. Czerny states that Bentham 'who called for a strong and centralised, but politically neutral police force for the maintenance of social order, for the protection of people from crime and to act as a visible deterrent to urban crime and disorder.' To further distance the new police from the military Peel structured and organized the Metropolitan Police along civilian, rather than paramilitary lines. A good indicator of this is the deliberate choice of the colour blue for police uniforms, to distinguish them from the scarlet tunics of the British Army of the day.

Reith, quoted in Civitas, notes that Rowan and Mayne's conception of a police force was 'unique in history and throughout the world because it derived not from fear but almost exclusively from public co-operation with the police, induced by them designedly by behaviour which secures and maintains for them the approval, respect and affection of the public' (p. 140).

Regardless of whether the Nine Principles were written by Peel, Mayne or Rowan, or whether they were written in 1829 or later in the 19th century, there is no doubt that they were based on a unique and enlightened view of the consent-based social contract which was revolutionary in its time. Although sometimes observed in principle rather than practice, they eventually spread throughout the world via the British Empire, to places as far flung as Oceania, the Caribbean, the Sub-Continent, Africa and North America. As such, they are worth quoting in full, and deserve serious consideration as a set of guiding principles for policing generally, including contemporary police development missions and partnerships.

It is also worth noting that the colour blue continues to be strongly associated with police and policing worldwide and that the date 29 September is acknowledged in Anglophone countries including Australia, as National Police Remembrance Day.

1. To prevent crime and disorder, as an alternative to their repression by military force and severity of legal punishment.
2. To recognise always that the power of the police to fulfil their functions and duties is dependent on public approval of their existence, actions and behaviour, and on their ability to secure and maintain public respect.
3. To recognise always that to secure and maintain the respect and approval of the public means also the securing of the willing co-operation of the public in the task of securing observance of laws.

4. To recognise always that the extent to which the co-operation of the public can be secured diminishes proportionately the necessity of the use of physical force and compulsion for achieving police objectives.
5. To seek and preserve public favour, not by pandering to public opinion, but by constantly demonstrating absolutely impartial service to law, in complete independence of policy, and without regard to the justice or injustice of the substance of individual laws, by ready offering of individual service and friendship to all members of the public without regard to their wealth or social standing, by ready exercise of courtesy and friendly good humour, and by ready offering of individual sacrifice in protecting and preserving life.
6. To use physical force only when the exercise of persuasion, advice and warning is found to be insufficient to obtain public co-operation to an extent necessary to secure observance of law or to restore order, and to use only the minimum degree of physical force which is necessary on any particular occasion for achieving a police objective.
7. To maintain at all times a relationship with the public that gives reality to the historic tradition that the police are the public and that the public are the police, the police being only members of the public who are paid to give full-time attention to duties which are incumbent on every citizen in the interests of community welfare and existence.
8. To recognise always the need for strict adherence to police-executive functions, and to refrain from even seeming to usurp the powers of the judiciary, of avenging individuals or the State, and of authoritatively judging guilt and punishing the guilty.
9. To recognise always that the test of police efficiency is the absence of crime and disorder, and not the visible evidence of police action in dealing with them.

Ref: An Act for improving the Police in and near the Metropolis. 10 Geo. 4. c. 44. Commonly known as the London Metropolitan Police Act 1829

Appendix 3: Roles of the Military and the Civilian Police[1]

There are many aspects of various policing models that are largely reflective of the type of society they police. Much relates to the type of social contract, specifically the level of public consent, or the degree of coercion, between the 'government' and the 'governed'. Much relates to historical evolution, which in Australia's case is directly related to the British inheritance in the pre-federation colonial period. The British-based liberal-democratic policing approach, like the criminal law, is evolutionary rather than the more autocratic policing approach, which is generally more associated with revolutionary societies and systems of government.

It is also worth remembering that five countries in the South West Pacific region – Australia, New Zealand, PNG, the Solomon Islands and Tuvalu – retain the Crown, specifically King Charles III, as their Sovereign. In the case of Australia and New Zealand, the police and the judiciary swear their allegiance on Oath of Affirmation to the Crown to conduct themselves and perform their duties 'without fear, favour, affection or ill-will'. It is worth exploring the situation in these other nations as to the existence of similar oaths of affirmation and the degree of adherence to the sentiments of conduct 'without fear favour, affection or ill-will'.

The tables below illustrate the primary differences between liberal-democratic police and normal military entities. They are categorised as: Societal Role (Activities), Accountability (Individual v Collective) and Structure (Organisation).

Societal Role

Activities	Police	Military
Principal Purpose	Law Enforcement/Crime Prevention	Combat Deterrence
Objective	Justice	Victory/Political aim
Focus	Law and Order-Internal	Security-External
Activity	Constant	Preparatory and Periodic
Relevant Law	Domestic Law	Law of Armed Conflict
Constitution	Instrument of Law / No Political Influence	Instrument of Policy/Political Control
Accountability	Domestic Courts / Rule of Law	Chain of Command / Executive Government

Appendix 3

Procedures	Gather Evidence / Need for Proof	Limited Information/ Decisions Under Uncertainty
Use of Force	Minimum	Graduated

Accountability

Individual	Police	Military
Responsibility	Individual 'Office of Constable'	Primarily a Member of a Unit
Duty	To the Law/Judiciary	To the State/Monarch
Knowledge	Law	Lethal Force
Unlawful Orders	Uphold the Law	Refuse Lawful Order
Status	Citizen with Special Powers	Citizen with No Special Powers
Service	Voluntary	Voluntary or Conscripted
Career	Starts 'On The Beat'	Soldier or Office Entry

Structure

Organisation	Police	Military
Control	Local/Central	Central
Structure	Hierarchical	Strongly Hierarchical
Personnel	Uniformed/Non-uniformed	Uniformed
Origins	Emerged in 19th Century	17th Century and Earlier
Public	Direct Relationship, Practical Cooperation	Desire for General Support, Public Esteem
Mobility	Limited	Part of Core Function

Appendix 4: John Martinkus on Prabowo Subianto

Prabowo Subianto's human rights abuses in Timor-Leste
John Martinkus

The Saturday Paper 2–8 March 2024

[https://www.thesaturdaypaper.com.au/news/law-crime/2024/03/01/chasing-prabowo-timor-leste#hrd]

Prabowo was finally thrown out of the army in 1998 following the detention and disappearances that year of pro-democracy Indonesian activists in Jakarta, who were protesting against Suharto and calling for his overthrow. Thirteen of the activists disappeared and were never seen again, presumed killed by Kopassus troops who were under his command. Prabowo was given a travel ban to the United States, where he had previously trained in counter-insurgency with U.S. special forces at Fort Benning and Fort Bragg, and to Australia. He has always denied his involvement in kidnapping, torture and killings, and has never been charged in relation to any of the allegations against him and his men.

Prabowo orchestrated the strategy of separating those fighting for independence and the population. In Timor-Leste, Aceh and West Papua, troops under his command carried out countless casual human rights abuses. Coopting former resistance fighters into his own control was one of the lessons he learnt in America and he put it into effect firstly in Timor-Leste. He created auxiliaries called Hansips and later two notorious Indonesian-led but Timorese-staffed battalions, 744 and 745. Both were among the most brutal towards their own people. They killed civilians, students, nuns, priests and journalists, right up until the final Indonesian withdrawal in 1999.

I remember talking to Munir, an Indonesian human rights leader who had come to Timor-Leste after the fall of Suharto in May 1998 to document the abuses of the Indonesian military there. In August 1998, he told me about Prabowo's role in recruiting and organising the Indonesian-led and funded militias that were starting to form back then in Timor-Leste. Munir was later killed by a poisoned cup of orange juice on a Garuda flight to Singapore as he tried to flee Indonesia after reporting on Indonesian military abuses in Aceh. Kopassus was blamed.

Appendix 5: International Deployment Group

The IDG was formed in 2004 as a result of demands placed on the AFP by large police missions in Timor-Leste and the Solomon Islands. The IDG was a separate portfolio within the AFP and was headed by an SES Band 2 (2-Star) National Manager (National Manager IDG-NMIDG). The IDG was based in Majura just north of Canberra Airport and had three broad components: the mission component, the A-Based component and the Operational Response Group (ORG). It was given extra emphasis in 2006 following several outbreaks of violence in the Pacific in Dili, Timor-Leste; Honiara, Solomon Islands and Tonga.

The mission component involved members actually deployed to missions from a general pool of suitable members trained through the IDG-designed-and-run Pre-Deployment Training, which was conducted in classrooms and a specific training village also in Majura. These mission pool members were utilised in accordance with a 'hubbing' concept when not actually deployed or on leave. This involved working in areas in the AFP that did not involve operational work likely to result in a court appearance. This became slightly problematic, as police members 'hubbing' could not be fully employed to their full capacity. It was a compromise solution with many such members working on the Mission Support Desks within the A-Based component.

The A-Based component was the support mechanism for the training and administration of the mission component and included the IDG Executive, led by the National Manager IDG (NMIDG), the Mission Support Desks, a training component and a small logistics element. In addition to Timor-Leste and the Solomon Islands, the IDG supported a number of other missions, including UN missions in Cyprus, Sudan and South Sudan, capacity development missions in Tonga, Samoa and Vanuatu, the Enhanced Cooperation Mission in PNG, operations Contego, Synergy and Illuminate in Afghanistan and the Pacific Police Development Program-Regional, a fly-in, fly-out capability development mission in Micronesia. The IDG also managed the police response to the Northern Territory intervention and the responses to the Victorian bushfires and the Wellington earthquake.

The ORG was the specialist component that included tactical operators, negotiators, marine and aviation specialists as well as a number of other capabilities such as POM.

The IDG was amalgamated with the broader International Liaison Officer Network in a newly named International Operations (IO) portfolio in 2015 and later changed to International Command. International Command is headed by an SES Band 3 level National Manager International Commands. The International Command portfolio manages all of the international operations and missions conducted by the AFP. International Command is based in the AFP HQ building in Canberra, known as the Edmund Barton Building. The logistics and ORG elements of the old IDG remain in Majura and have become AFP-wide assets, as the ORG was amalgamated with its ACT Policing counterpart, the Special Operations Team (SOT), to become the Specialist Response Group (SRG). The SRG is available for response throughout Australia, including Norfolk Island in the Pacific and Christmas and Cocos (Keeling) Islands in the Indian Ocean, as well as internationally to the region as required upon request and assessment by the Australian Government.

Appendix 6: Melanesian Wantok system

In tribal-based societies everything revolves around the relative welfare of the tribe and clan members as a whole. Therefore face-to-face relationships, inter-marriage, kinship and reciprocal exchange are paramount in creating strong ties to keep the tribe together.

The wantok system[1] in Melanesian countries generally, links group identity, community belonging and reciprocity as well as expectations related to family, clan and tribal wellbeing. The term relates to relationships that link people in families, tribes, islands, provinces, nationality and even more superficially at greater Melanesian sub-regional aggregates. Various aspects of the wantok system are called different names by distinct language groups in Papua New Guinea, Solomon Islands and Vanuatu. The word wantok originates from the English words 'one talk', which literally means in Melanesian pidgin (Tok Pisin, Pijin and Bislama), speakers of the same language.

It is especially strong in remote and rural communities based on expectations of reciprocal support and a shared attachment to locality. It is a strong and enduring form of group identity which distinguishes one group from another.

The Wantok system can be thought of as a kind of traditional social safety net that made sure nobody went hungry and everybody had somewhere to live. Wantoks who gain positions of power, influence and responsibility are expected to look after their wantoks. This includes business, politics and government service, including police service.

Adherence to the wantok system is also related to respect so saying no is not an option to maintain respect and social status in their community. On occasion this has led to cases of fraud, embezzlement and other fraudulent activity as well as perceptions of corruption at the political level.

The wantok system is an enduring form for protection of community identity and cohesion in a tribal-based society, however, in terms of western notions underpinning modern approaches to policing, namely political independence, objectivity and impartiality, it creates a challenge for police development.

Appendix 7: Legal and Funding Parameters UN SDG International Human Rights Law (IHL) and ODA

Official Development Assistance (ODA)

Not all money spent on overseas policing efforts to assist police forces in developing countries is eligible for ODA.

ODA is defined by the OECD Development Assistance Committee's (DAC) Converged Statistical Reporting Directives for the Creditor Reporting System and the Annual DAC questionnaire (DAC Directives) as follows:

> Official development assistance (ODA) is defined as government aid designed to promote the economic development and welfare of developing countries. Loans and credits for military purposes are excluded.

The DAC's list of countries eligible to receive ODA is updated every three years and is based on per capita income.

Peace and Security Efforts

In 2016, the DAC agreed on updated rules for the eligibility of peace and security expenditures. This was to better recognise the marginal but actual developmental role that military actors sometimes play, notably in conflict situations, while clearly delineating it from their main peace and security function.

Broadly, the activity must be focused on assisting the economic and social development of the country. Activities that are purely related to security are excluded.

The following are generally ODA eligible:

- training and education of local police forces (classroom and non-classroom)
- community policing
- equipment (i.e., computers) and some capital works
- capacity building (sharing knowledge and mentoring).

The following are generally not ODA eligible:

- the supply of the donor's police services to control civil disobedience
- intelligence gathering and CT activities
- the supply of weapons and other lethal force equipment.

While this reflects the good international citizenship and benevolence of international policing programs, such restrictive funding criteria disregard the actuality of policing in any environment, namely, that civil disobedience is an unfortunate fact of life, and it is police agencies that are the primary responders to such events. This, on occasion, involves the use 'weapons and other lethal force equipment'. Similarly, addressing criminal activities by the use of intelligence gathering and addressing CT, prevention, response and investigation are core police functions. These restrictive funding criteria fail to reflect the reality of policing in a globalised criminal world and often politically fragile environments.

United Nations Sustainable Development Goals

Following many decades of effort pursuing sustainable global peace, prosperity and security, in 2015, the UN adopted a shared blueprint for global peace and prosperity. This is known as the 2030 Agenda for Sustainable Development. This began 17 Sustainable Development Goals (SDGs). The most relevant of these to the AFP and its international effort is SDG 16 relating to peace, justice and strong institutions.

SDG 16 Peace, Justice and Strong Institutions

16.1	Significantly reduce all forms of violence and related death rates everywhere
16.2	End abuse, exploitation, trafficking and all forms of violence against and torture of children
16.3	Promote the rule of law at the national and international levels and ensure equal access to justice for all
16.4	By 2030, significantly reduce illicit financial and arms flows, strengthen the recovery and return of stolen assets and combat all forms of organized crime
16.5	Substantially reduce corruption and bribery in all their forms
16.6	Develop effective, accountable and transparent institutions at all levels
16.7	Ensure responsive, inclusive, participatory and representative decision-making at all levels
16.8	Broaden and strengthen the participation of developing countries in the institutions of global governance
16.9	By 2030, provide legal identity for all, including birth registration

16.10		Ensure public access to information and protect fundamental freedoms, in accordance with national legislation and international agreements
16.a		Strengthen relevant national institutions, including through international cooperation, for building capacity at all levels, in particular in developing countries, to prevent violence and combat terrorism and crime
16.b		Promote and enforce non-discriminatory laws and policies for sustainable development

International Human Rights Law

With its origins in international treaties and conventions, customs, generally agreed principles of law and jurisprudence, IHL seeks to advance and protect human rights by providing legal guarantees with the goal of protecting individuals and groups against actions by governments that seek to interfere with fundamentally accepted freedoms, rights and dignity.

These include the right to life, liberty and the security of the person; the prohibition of slavery, torture, cruel or degrading treatment; the prohibition of arbitrary arrest, detention or exile; the prohibition of any form of discrimination based on race, ethnicity, religion, gender or disability; the right to be recognised by the law and the right to a fair and public hearing by an independent and impartial tribunal and the right to freedom of thought, expression, movement, association and assembly.

These all have clear implications for the police and the way police conduct themselves when carrying out their duties. This is not only directly applicable to Australian police in their domestic duties but also when deployed internationally, both in their own conduct and in relation to the training, advice or mentoring of other police they may work within their international duties. This includes the South West Pacific.

Appendix 8: INTERPOL

The badge of the International Criminal Police Organisation (ICPO or OIPC: *Organisation Internationale de Police Criminelle*) depicts a globe with Europe and Africa in its centre surrounded by a wreath of olive leaves symbolising peace, a vertical sword representing police action, and scales, the universal symbol of justice. It contains the acronym 'INTERPOL' and the initialisms ICPO/OIPC. Australia is depicted in the bottom right.

The vision of INTERPOL is 'Connecting Police for a Safer World'.

The four official languages of INTERPOL are Arabic, English, French and Spanish.

INTERPOL is the world's oldest and largest international criminal intelligence organisation dating from 1914, when the concept was first raised at the International Criminal Police Congress held in Monaco. It was officially established as the International Criminal Police Commission (ICPC) in 1923. In 1926, the General Assembly, held in Berlin, proposed that each country establish a central point of contact within its police structure: the forerunner of the National Central Bureau (NCB); a structure adopted in 1927. The ICPC dealt primarily with currency counterfeiting, criminal records and passport forgery. In 1935, the ICPC launched an international radio network that provided an independent telecommunications system solely for the use of the criminal police authorities at national levels.

In the following year, the German National Socialist (Nazi) Government took control of the ICPC after deposing its president and moved the headquarters to Berlin in 1942. During this period, the ICPC effectively ceased to function as most countries withdrew their participation. In 1946, Belgium led the rebuilding of the ICPC and the headquarters was moved to Paris. Democratic processes were established for the election of the President and the Executive Committee, and 'INTERPOL' was chosen as the organisation's telegraphic address. The organisation itself became known as INTERPOL in 1956. There are currently 190 member nations. In 1949, the UN granted consultative status as a non-government organisation and was granted recognition as an intergovernmental organisation in 1971. The General Secretariat of INTERPOL moved to Lyon, France in 1989 and in 2003, established a Command and Control Centre at Lyon, which enabled INTERPOL to operate twenty-four hours a day, seven days a week. INTERPOL maintains a Criminal Information System database, which was established in 1998. It allows instant, direct access to a number of criminal databases and contains millions of records contributed to by countries across the world. The latest innovation for INTERPOL is the establishment of the INTERPOL Global Complex for Innovation in Singapore in 2015 that combats cybercrime and assists police around the world to address emerging threats through innovation and training. INTERPOL currently has 190 members that provide global coverage for international criminal activities, including international INTERPOL Red Notice arrest warrants under the INTERPOL colour-coded notice system.

The INTERPOL Colour-Coded Notice System

INTERPOL's system of notices is used to issue international alerts for fugitives, suspected criminals, persons linked to or of interest in an ongoing criminal investigation, persons and entities subject to UN Security Council Sanctions, potential threats, missing persons and dead bodies. Details are stored in a database known as the INTERPOL Criminal Information System, which also contains personal data and the criminal history of people subject to request for international police cooperation.

The INTERPOL colour-coded notice system was established in 1946 as follows: (1) Red Notice – to seek the location of and arrest wanted persons with a view to extradition or similar lawful action, (2) Blue Notice – to collect additional information about a person's identity, location or activities in relation to a crime, (3) Green Notice – to provide warnings and intelligence about persons who have committed criminal offences and are likely to repeat these crimes in other countries, (4) Yellow Notice – to help locate missing persons, often minors, or to help identify persons who are unable to identify themselves, (5) Black Notice – to seek information on unidentified bodies, (6) Orange Notice – to warn of an event, a person, an object or a process representing a serious and imminent threat to public safety, and (7) Purple Notice – to seek or provide information on modus operandi, objects, devices and concealment methods used by criminals.

INTERPOL Areas of Interest

INTERPOL's activities are not confined to terrorism. INTERPOL maintains a number of databases that are useful for criminal investigations. They include the following:

(1) Fingerprints and DNA

The International Child Sexual Exploitation Image Database, the Automatic Fingerprint Identification System and DNA profiles contain the DNA information of offenders, crime scenes, missing persons and unidentified bodies but do not store any nominal data linking a DNA profile to any individual.

(2) Stolen and Lost Documents

Stolen documents can be used by criminals to facilitate criminal activity, so INTERPOL maintains Stolen and Lost Travel Documents and Stolen Administrative Documents. INTERPOL also provides the Electronic Documentation and Information System on Investigation Networks, which provides examples of genuine travel documents to help identify fakes, which is extremely useful for border control agencies.

(3) Stolen Property

Stolen property, particularly motor vehicles, vessels and works of art are trafficked internationally, and INTERPOL maintains a database for each. It is noteworthy that the Works of Art database contains descriptions and pictures of cultural objects reported as stolen by INTERPOL member countries and international partners such as the International Council of Museums and UNESCO. It includes items looted during crisis periods in Afghanistan, Iraq and Syria. Items such as works of art are regularly trafficked by organised crime groups.

(4) Firearms and Ballistics

The INTERPOL Firearms Reference Table provides a standardised methodology to identify and describe firearms, which enables an investigator to obtain or verify the details of a firearm. The INTERPOL Ballistic Information Network provides a global platform for the centralised collection, storage and cross-comparison of ballistics imaging. The INTERPOL Illicit Arms Records and tracing Management System (iARMS) facilitates information exchange and cooperation between law enforcement agencies on firearm-related crime and allows them to trace a firearm from the point of manufacture or of legal importation into a country through the lines of supply to the last known point of possession.

(5) Radiological and Nuclear Materials

The Project Geiger database is used to collate and analyse information on illicit trafficking and other unauthorised activities involving radiological and nuclear materials. It combines data from the International Atomic Energy Agency, open-source reports and law enforcement channels.

(6) Maritime Piracy

The maritime piracy database stores intelligence related to cases of piracy and armed robbery at sea, including data on individuals, telephone numbers, email addresses, piracy incidents, locations, businesses and financial information.

Appendix 9: Xi Jinping and Vladimir Putin as Autocratic Leaders

Xi Jinping

Over the past decade, Chinese President Xi Jinping has initiated a series of hardline moves that hark back to PRC founder Mao Zedong.

Mao's doctrine of the 'People's War,' has had his 'thoughts' written into the Chinese Constitution, and Xi has emphasized the absolute leadership of the Chinese Communist Party (CCP) in all aspects of the society. Xi himself imitates Mao on many occasions, including his gestures, dress, and rhetoric.

Xi is following three key Maoist ideals in governing China:

(1) the CCP at the centre; (2) control of history and avoiding the Soviet path; (3) rejuvenation of China.

Mao followed Lenin's ideas about one-party communist rule and the CCP maintains leadership in agriculture, commerce, education, military, and politics, which has been reiterated by Xi Jinping and written into the CCP Constitution in 2017. Noteworthy is that the People's Liberation Army does not report into the government, but the Party. The Maoist slogan that Xi repeats frequently 'East, West, North South and the Center. The CCP controls everything.'

What is officially ignored or conveniently forgotten are Mao's gross human rights atrocities the Great Leap Forward and Cultural Revolution, in which millions were killed.

For more information in Xi Jinping please see Marquis, C. (2022) *What Xi Jinping Draws From Mao's Legacy*. [https://time.com/6222018/xi-jinping-maos-legacy-china/ 13 October 2022]

Vladimir Putin

Putin, who has thrived in closed worlds, first as a KGB intelligence agent, defends the Soviet-era intelligence service to this day. He witnessed firsthand the momentous finale of the Cold War, from the front line in Dredsen in the former communist East Germany. Putin has expressed enthusiasm for reasserting the role of a strong state.

The biggest intelligence operation was the East German secret police, the Stasi, who monitored hundreds of thousands of citizens and kept millions of documents on file. The broad Stasi network was used often by the KGB, and the raw intelligence sent directly to Moscow. The Stasi poked into every aspect of life; in Dresden alone, the documents they preserved on citizens now stretch nearly seven miles in the archives.

The KGB was known to the Stasi as 'the friends,' and it relied on the Stasi for support. Putin's work with the Stasi won him a bronze medal in November 1987 from the East German security service.

For more on Vladimir Putin, please see Hoffman, D. (2000) Putin's Career Rooted in Russia's KGB. Washington Post Foreign Service. 30 January 2000. [https://www.washingtonpost.com/wp-srv/inatl/longterm/russiagov/putin.htm]

Appendix 10: Thin Lines

Although recently adopted by politically-motivated groups, particularly in the United States, the Thin Blue Line terminology has its genesis in events in the mid-19th century.

During the Crimean War, at the Battle Balaclava in October 1854 an understrength force of the 93rd Sutherland Highlanders, under the command of Gen Sir Colin Campbell. 1st Baron Clyde, successfully formed a defensive line against superior numbers of charging Russian cavalry.

Campbell reportedly said to his men: 'There is no retreat from here, men. You must die where you stand.' Sir Colin's aide John Scott is said to have replied, 'Aye, Sir Colin. If needs be, we'll do that.'

There were insufficient numbers to for a conventional defensive square four-men deep so one was formed two-men deep. This was the 'Thin Red Line', where the 'red' is derived from the scarlet tunics worn by the British military of that era, an effort to maintain morale in battles by camouflaging the blood from wounds, hence the common name of the British Army of the period: Red Coats.

Ironically, several decades earlier, the British deliberately chose the colour blue for the Metropolitan Police when it was established in 1829. This was a deliberate decision to differentiate the newly formed police from the military. It should be borne in mind that the Metropolitan Police was established under principles known as the Peelian policing principles, after ten years of parliamentary debate, following significant loss of life at St Peter's Field near Manchester in 1819, at the hands of the British Army, which in the absence of an organised presentative or responsive police force, reacted as it was trained and equipped to do to maintain public order during a civil rights gathering. This became known as the 'Peterloo Massacre', a corruption of Waterloo.

The colour blue has been adopted for many police agencies throughout the world, particularly in the Anglosphere. The Thin Blue Line typically refers to police and policing as the line between law and order and chaos and anarchy. In many British-based policing cultures the adoption of a Sillitoe Tartan has also been adopted. Taken from the Glengarry pattern of many Scottish Regiments, this is the chequered band seen on police headdress in all Australian jurisdictions, New Zealand and Britain. Canada has not adopted the Sillitoe Tartan, but some police forces in the United States have, including the Chicago Police Department. This was first adopted in Glasgow under the Chief Constable of that force, Sir Percy Sillitoe in 1932.

The Thin Red and Thin Blue Lines and variations of the Sillitoe Tartan have been adopted in similar fashion by Emergency services, many of them volunteer-based: (Orange), first aid (Green), Paramedics (White), Emergency Dispatchers (Gold) and Corrections Officers (Silver/Grey). Many of these organisations and agencies in Australia conspicuously display an appropriately coloured variation of the diced or chequered ribbon on their headdress, both formal and operational.

In relation to police and policing, the Thin Blue Line is often displayed as a thin blue coloured line across a nation's national flag.is is not an exclusive 'club', but it appears to be largely confined to the Anglosphere. There is no global prohibition on the police in less than liberal countries from displaying their political impartiality and autonomy by also placing a Thin Blue Line across their own national flag. The probability of censure by the government in those countries for doing so rather proves the point that police and policing in the Anglosphere is far more politically impartial and therefore objective than can be said of more autocratic systems. This is patently obvious but is worth emphasising to illustrate the point that the Thin Blue Line actually symbolises liberty rather than the opposite as some would advance.

Rather than representing a small group of disaffected and disgruntled group of politically-motivated individuals in the United States, the legitimacy of the Thin Blue Line and other Thin Lines in Australia therefore can trace their antecedents directly to the brave actions of British soldiers nearly two hundred years ago and is regarded by police a symbol of honour and service above self, often against very challenging odds, a sentiment shared by other emergency service workers. Any concerns about the Thin Blue Line being misrepresented needs to be put to rest as its legitimacy should be reclaimed by those who have actually served as police officers and restored to its rightful dignified position in police and justice symbolism.

Notes

Introduction

1 https://www.snopes.com/fact-check/einstein-world-war-iv-sticks-stones/

2 Notable exceptions are the first few deployments to Cyprus, the early days of RAMSI and the transition mission in East Timor known as UNTAET. Occasionally police deployed internationally do so armed for their own self-protection rather than law enforcement. This is often as the request of allies such as the United States and includes deployments to Haiti and Afghanistan.

3 Copeland, D. (2011). *Guerrilla Diplomacy*. Viva Books, New Delhi, p. 207

4 Meyer, C. (2009). *Getting Our Way: 500 Years of Adventure and Intrigue: The Inside Story of British Diplomacy*. Weidenfeld and Nicholson. Orion Books, London

5 Spinoza's Political Philosophy. Stanford Encyclopaedia of Philosophy. First published April 2008, re-published October 2013 https://plato.stanford.edu. Einstein, A. cited in Vesilind, A. (2005) Peace Engineering: When Personal Values and Engineering Careers Converge. Lakeshore Press, p. 43. George Washington quoted in Sparks, J. (1853) The Life of George Washington, Little, Brown and Company Boston, Massachusetts, p. 53

6 Reiner, R. (2010). *The Politics of the Police*. Oxford: Oxford University Press, p. 1

7 Please see Greenwood, N, (1999), *For the Sovereignty of the People*.

8 Chappell, D. and Evans, J. (1997). *The Role, Preparation and Performance of Civilian Police in United Nations Peacekeeping Operations*, Sydney.

9 http://www.ediplomat.com/nd/diplomaticimmunity.htm

10 Bayley, D. and Perito, R. (2010). *The Police in War. Fighting Insurgency, Terrorism and Violent Crime*. Lynne Rienner Publishers, London, pp. 76–7

11 Sieghart, P. (1978). *Harmless weapons a threat to liberty?* New Scientist, 30 March 1978, p. 841

12 It should be noted that if, as some posit, we are in the foothills of a new Cold War, proxy inter-state conflict has again become a feature of international relations. Local and limited conflicts in places like Ukraine, Gaza and Yemen and the Red Sea have the potential to escalate and spread. The implications for international police cooperation and the roles police play domestically in such an event as a major global conflict are profound. In his book, The Next Major War, Ross Babbage, a retired senior Australian intelligence officer identifies 15 credible indicators of preparations for war by the People's Republic of China, and outlines how poorly prepared the West is in the face of this potential catastrophe.

13 AFP International Deployment Group 2010

14 Please see Appendix B: Police Capacity Development and the Rule of Law, for an explanation of the connection between police capacity development and the rule of law.

15 Parliamentary Paper No.47/1978. Report to the Minister for Administrative Services on the Organisation of Police Resources in the Commonwealth Area and Other

Related Matters. https://parlinfo.aph.gov.au/parlInfo/search/display/display.w3p;query=Id%3A%22publications%2Ftabledpapers%2FHPP052016005700%22

16 https://www.afp.gov.au/about-us/our-agency/values#:~:text=We%20value%20fairness%2C%20trust%2C%20respect,why%20not%20join%20our%20team%3F&text=Integrity%20is%20a%20core%20requirement%20of%20ours.

Overview

1 The term 'peacekeeping' is a rather generic one and has evolved over time since the United Nations was established in 1945. Australia has a long and distinguished history of involvement in such missions in the furtherance of peace, prosperity, stability and security under the rule of law. The first Australian peacekeepers deployed to the Netherlands East Indies (now Indonesia) in 1947. Since then, there has never been a year when Australian peacekeepers were not serving somewhere in the world. In over 70 operations in troubled areas in 60 different countries, around 66,000 Australians have served as peacekeepers. Sixteen Australians have died on peacekeeping missions. Peacekeeping roles include both military and police elements and both have been well represented by Australians. In the current era, peacekeeping operations and missions are tasked with not only maintaining peace and security in a traditional sense, but also to facilitating political processes, protecting civilians, supporting the conduct of elections and other ballots, protecting and promoting human rights and assisting in the restoration of the rule of law, in post-conflict environments.

Part I: The Cold War and the Great Peace 1964–1998

1 The Commonwealth Police was one of three independent police agencies that were amalgamated in 1979 to form the Australian Federal Police. The others were the Australian Capital Territory Police and the Federal Narcotics Bureau.

2 Malaya in this case refers to peninsula Malaya, which combined with two former British possessions in North Borneo (Sabah and Sarawak) to become the present state of Malaysia following the Confrontation with Indonesia.

3 Kwan, E. (2006), p. 154

4 Thompson, S. (2014). Fifty years of Australian civilian police involvement in international peacekeeping. Australian Strategic Policy Institute, Canberra.

5 The spectre of inter-state conflict, potentially involving nuclear armed powers is again looming as a possible future. This is discussed in this book in relation to the rise of China and regional expansion in the SW Pacific.

6 The acronym UNCIVPOL (UN Civilian Police) is used throughout this book, there are numerous other terms used in various literature.

7 UN Security Council Resolution 186 (1964). https://unficyp.unmissions.org/unficyp-mandate

8 A1838: 913/5/1 pt 1 Patrick Shaw to Minister 20 Apr 1964. [SECRET] now declassified

9 Chappell and Evans (1997), Ch 1

10 https://www.britannica.com/biography/Norodom-Sihanouk, para 3. For a detailed explanation of this bombing campaign please see *Sideshow: Kissinger, Nixon, and the*

Destruction of Cambodia, Shawcross, W. Simon and Schuster, 1978

11 Estimates range from 1.5 to 3 million people having died at the hands of the Khmer Rouge, with the consensus being approximately 2 million.

12 ASEAN was established in Thailand on 8 Aug 1967. The six original members were: Indonesia, Malaysia, Philippines, Singapore and Thailand. It was largely a cooperative association and a bulwark against communist expansion into the SE Asian region. It has since expanded to incorporate former combatant nation in the region.

13 Frost, F. (2016), p. 68

14 Frost, F. (2016), p. 61

15 Hawke, R. quoted in Frost, F. (2016), p. 69

16 Haydon, W. quoted in Frost, F. (2016), p. 380

17 Frost, F. (2016), pp. 70–1

18 Frost, F. (2016), p. 72

19 Frost, F. (2016), p. 73

20 Frost, F. (2016), p. 75

21 It is now UN policy that all civilian police detachments will be multinational. No national detachments with designated sectors will be employed in the future. Apparently, this is an attempt to balance the quality of the available civilian police officers. See McFarlane and Maley *United Nations Peacekeeping Operations: Ad Hoc Missions, Permanent Engagement* Ramesh Thakur and Albrecht Schnabel (eds). United Nations University Press, New York 2001

22 Whiddett cited in Maley Sampford, C and Thakur, R *Civil Strife to Civil Society*, p. 333

23 Sanderson in Thakur, R. and Maley, W. (2015). *Theorising the Responsibility to Protect.* Cambridge: Cambridge University Press, p. 334

24 AFP UNCIVPOL deployed unarmed but had firearms in a locked container available if required. They did not wear their firearms openly.

25 Mozambique was followed by Rwanda and Togo as members of the British Commonwealth of Nations.

26 Meisler, S. (1995). *United Nations: The First Fifty Years.* Atlantic Monthly Press, p. 309

27 The Bougainville Referendum and Beyond: Institutional Options and Issues for Transition. https://law.unimelb.edu.au/constitutional-transformations/projects/completed-projects/the-bougainville-referendum-and-beyond. See also Dziedzic, A. and Saunder, C. (2019) Research Report: Greater Autonomy and Independence for Bougainville. Institutional Options and Issues for Transition. The National Research Institute, Papua New Guinea.

Part II: Democracy, Violence and the New Security Paradigm 1999–2007

1 UNAMET was the UN acronym for the United Nations Mission to East Timor. The letter 'A' does not stand for anything, but avoids the unfortunate acronym UNMET.

2 In 1999, Paul Dibb used the concept of an 'arc of instability' to describe the security challenges facing the Pacific. Wallis, J. (2012) *The Pacific: from 'arc of instability' to 'arc of*

opportunity'? The Strategist ASPI, Canberra

3 Patrick Shaw to Minister for External Affairs Sir Garfield Barwick 20 Apr 1964: *UN Force in Cyprus-Request for Australian Police*

4 The resolutions were carried 69 to 11, with 38 abstentions. Australia and New Guinea voted in favour of the resolution, as did Singapore. The remainder of the ASEAN nations voted against it, probably related to the non-interventionist foundations of ASEAN as a Zone of Peace Freedom and Neutrality: ZOPFAN. The US, Britain and other 'Western' powers abstained, arguably for more strategic reasons related to the Cold War, which was at a high risk of turning into expansionism through Southeast Asia following the fall of Saigon to North Vietnamese communist forces in Apr 1975.

5 Braithwaite, J., Charlesworth, H. and Soares, A. (2012). *Networked Governance of Freedom and Tyranny: Peace in Timor-Leste.* ANU E Press, Canberra, p. 65

6 Kingsbury, D. (1998). *The Politics of Indonesia.* Oxford University Press. Melbourne, p. 181

7 Braithwaite, J. et al. (2012), p. 65

8 Braithwaite et al. (2012), pp. 79–80

9 Wise (2006) pp. 110–1 cited in Braithwaite (2012), p. 83

10 Braithwaite et al. (2012), p. 64

11 Pilger, J. (1994), p. 314 cited in Braithwaite (2012), p. 84

12 Collaery, B. (2020). *Oil Under Troubled Waters: Australia's Timor Sea Intrigue.* Melbourne University Press, p. 176

13 Diplomatic privileges and immunities – Demonstrations outside diplomatic missions – Vienna Convention on Diplomatic Relations – Impairment of dignity of mission – Amendments to Diplomatic and Consular Privileges and Immunities Regulations. [http://138.25.65.17/au/journals/AUYrBkIntLaw/1992/20.pdf]

14 On 17 Jan 1992, Olney J. granted temporary injunctive relief restraining the Minister, the Commissioner of the AFP and the Commonwealth of Australia from removing the crosses until 23 Jan 1992 or further order. On 20 Jan 1992, Magno and Almeida filed an application in this Court naming those persons as respondents. By that application, they sought declarations that the Diplomatic Privileges and Immunities Regulations (Amendment) 1992 and the Minister's certificate were invalid. On 23 Jan 1992, the temporary injunction was extended to 24 Jan 1992 by Ryan J., but on 24 Jan 1992, his Honour dissolved the injunction.

15 Joint Standing Committee on the National Capital and External Territories: Inquiry into the right to legitimately protest or demonstrate on National Land and in the Parliamentary Zone in particular.

16 In mid-2019, Ms Inês Maria de Almeida was proposed by the government as the new East Timorese Ambassador to Australia, but the official appointment was not made until 28 Jan 2020. On 19 Feb 2020, Almeida presented her accreditation to David Hurley in Canberra. [https://tlembassy.net/ambassador/]

17 Collaery op. cit. pp. 177–8

18 General policing in the Australian Capital Territory is a function of the Australian Federal Police.

19 This came from a remark Indonesian Foreign Minister Alatas once made to a Portuguese journalist who had asked him how he felt about the international stigma over East Timor. He had responded by saying that it was a problem for Indonesia 'but only as bothersome as a pebble in a shoe…' He later wrote a book with the same title: Alatas, A. (2006). *The Pebble in the Shoe: The Diplomatic Struggle for East Timor*. Aksara Karunia, Jakarta

20 Braithwaite et al. (2012), p. 72

21 Cotton, J. interviewed in PM, *A look behind the 'Jakarta Lobby'*, Australian Broadcasting Corporation 15 Apr 2004.

22 Braithwaite et al. (2012), p. 72

23 Braithwaite et al. (2012), p. 72

24 Toohey, B. (1999), *'Hunt on for Indonesian Spy'*, Australian Financial Review, 18 Sep 1999 in Collins, L. and Reed, W. (2005), *Plunging Point: Intelligence Failures, Cover-ups and Consequences*, 4th Estate/Harper Collins, Sydney, p. 50.

25 Connery, D. (2010). *Crisis Policymaking: Australia and the East Timor Crisis of 1999*. Canberra papers on strategy and defence, no. 176 Griffin Press 2010 [https://press-files.anu.edu.au/downloads/press/p501/pdf/book.pdf]

26 There is also evidence that this policy originated from Habibie's Coordinating Minister for Political and Security Affairs, General Feisal Tanjung in Jakarta.

27 John Dauth was the Australian Consul-General in New Caledonia from 1986–7 before being declared persona non grata by the French government after Paris complained that he was too close to the Kanak pro-independence movement.

28 The Matignon Agreements (1988) were agreements signed in Jun 1988 between loyalists who wanted to keep New Caledonia as a part of the French Fifth Republic, and separatists, who did not. They allowed for a delayed period between a decision to hold a referendum and the actual referendum itself.

29 Mules, N., Merrifield, S., Bull, C., Chan, M. and Hooper, S. (2001). *East Timor in Transition, 1998-2000: An Australian Policy Challenge*. Canberra: Department of Foreign Affairs and Trade, Commonwealth of Australia, Canberra, pp. 181–2.

30 Blaxland, J. (ed) (2015). *East Timor intervention: A Retrospective on INTERFET*. Melbourne University Press, Carlton, Victoria, Australia, p. 32.

31 The Indonesian National Police, the INP, more officially known as POLRI (Police of the Republic of Indonesia), had only separated from the Indonesian military (ABRI) in early Apr 1999. What remained became the TNI (Tentara Nasional Indonesia)

32 Mules, et al. (2001), p. 15

33 Mules et al. (2001), p. 50

34 [https://nsarchive.gwu.edu/project/indonesia-documentation-project]

35 White, H. (2008). *The Road to INTERFET: Reflections on Australian Strategic Decisions Concerning East Timor*, Dec 1998-Sept 1999. Security Challenges Vol. 4, No. 1 (2008), pp. 78–80. [https://www.regionalsecurity.org.au/Resources/Files/vol4no1White.pdf]

36 The Gada Paksi was created as a legitimate civil defence group in 1994 but was eventually co-opted into a larger, less legitimate anti-independence militia structure

orchestrated by the Indonesian Kopassus special forces.

37 Hidayat Djajamihardja in Kingbury, D. Guns and Ballot Boxes. (2000), pp. 106–7

38 Alatas, A. (2006). *The Pebble in the Shoe: The Diplomatic Struggle for East Timor.* Aksara Karuna Jakarta 2006. p. 152

39 Kingsbury, D. (ed) (2000). *Guns and Ballot Boxes: East Timor's Vote for Independence.* Monash Asia Institute, Melbourne, p. 72

40 Cronau, P. (2004). *Intelligence Wars:Behind the Lance Collins Affair.* ABC Background Briefing, [http://www.abc.net.au/radionational/programs/backgroundbriefing/intelligence-wars-behind-the-lance-collins-affair/3418864]

41 Cotton, J. (1999). *East Timor and Australia. AIIH Contributions to the Policy Debate.* Australian Defence Studies Centre, Canberra, pp. 15–6

42 Mules et al. (2001), pp. 79–80

43 Michelle Grattan, 'Australia ready to join UN election team in Timor', The Sydney Morning Herald, 15 Mar 1999

44 Paul Daley, 'Downer sets out Timor troops plan', The Age, 1 Apr 1999

45 Australia, House of Representatives, Debates, 11 May 1999, p. 4111

46 The AFP had provided a liaison officer to join discussions with DFAT and Defence from as early as Jan 1999. This member states that a comprehensive highly classified document re: security was compiled which was submitted to AFP HQ and was never seen again.

47 United Nations Peacekeeping Force in East Timor (UNCPIT). The name UN-AMET was to emerge with the signing of the May 5 Agreements.

48 The notion of risk was raised with Mr Howard by journalists and 28 Apr 1999 in Canberra. Mr Howard stated 'there is always an element of risk when anybody goes into an unsettled area, an area where hostilities have recently occurred and are likely to occur in the future. There is always an element of risk and it would be foolhardy of me and wrong of me to pretend that there's never any element of risk.' Transcript of the Prime Minister The Hon John Howard MP Press Conference Parliament House 28APR99. [https://pmtranscripts.pmc.gov.au/release/transcript-11140]. There was no formal Risk Assessment conducted prior to the deployment of UNAMET. Given contemporary Risk Analysis used by the AFP the Risk Assessment would have been Catastrophic. The Likelihood of violence resulting in death or serious injury to UNAMET members was not just Almost certain, it actually occurred. Combined with the Consequences of Severe, place the UNAMET mission in the Critical category and as such place it beyond the AFP Risk Threshold and Risk Tolerance. Both the Risk Control rating and Risk Control Effectiveness were weak to non-existent.

49 The AFP provided a local Canberra solicitor for the taking of wills from UNAMET members. This was unprecedented.

50 UN Security Council Resolution 1246 (1999) Established the United Nations Mission in East Timor (UNAMET) to organise and conduct the East Timor Special Autonomy Referendum on the future status of East Timor. S/RES/1246/ (1999)

51 Mules et al. (2001), pp. 91–2

52 The militia was not part of the military per se but military proxies in an attempt to

keep plausible deniability. There is also strong evidence to indicate that those directing the Kopassus were former Kopassus operators in the political system in Jakarta, including at least one at the ministerial level.

53 The two-hour timing assumes that any victim could reach Dili from remote and isolated regions. This was difficult in daylight hours and lethal in the hours of darkness, as the Indonesian soldiers had orders to fire upon any aircraft flying at night. Travel by road at night was prohibited.

54 Mules et al. (2001), p. 92

55 Mills, A. (2001). *Civilian Police as Peacekeepers*. International Policing Conference, 2001, p. 10

56 Mules et al. (2001), p. 102

57 Mules et al. (2001), p. 83

58 The acronyms INP (Indonesian National Police) and POLRI (Police of the Republic of Indonesia refer to the same organisation and are interchangeable.

59 Mules et al. (2001), p. 124

60 Braithwaite (2012), p. 61

61 Kingsbury (2000), p. 72

62 ABC Background Briefing, 30 May 2004 *Intelligence Wars: Behind the Lance Collins Affair* p.10 [http://parlinfo.aph.gov.au/parlInfo/search/display/display.w3p;query=Id%3A%22media%2Fradioprm%2F2YQC6%22;src1=sm1] Australian Intelligence Corps' former principal analyst for East Timor, Major Clinton Fernandes declined to comment on the report, but Background Briefing extracted the above comment from his contribution to a university discussion list.
[http://www.abc.net.au/radionational/programs/backgroundbriefing/intelligence-wars-behind-the-lance-collins-affair/3418864]

63 Mules et al. (2001), pp. 127–8

64 The follow-on UN mission (UN Transition Authority East Timor (UNTAET) raised a Serious Crimes Unit (SCU), which investigated the post-ballot violence. The UNTAET SCU found 1293 confirmed murders and filed 431 indictments plus 8 national indictments. Most of those indicted fled to Indonesia, and very few have ever been held accountable for their actions. This includes a number of senior Indonesian officials. Unfortunately, the UN, Australia and Timor-Leste gradually lost interest in pursuing these indictments for various reasons.

65 Robinson extensively documented the extent of the carnage and the damage. Please see Robinson, G, (2003) *East Timor 1999: Crimes against Humanity: A Report Commissioned by the United Nations Office of the High Commissioner for Human Rights (OHCHR)*. University of California Los Angeles, Jul 2003, Ch 3

66 A note concerning the casualty numbers: The UN Serious Crimes Unit prioritised investigations and indictments resulted in only verifiable figures being reported and tabulated. There were many additional murders reported but as they cannot be verified they are not included in the official figures.

67 East Timor Militias: People's war: militias in East Timor and Indonesia, Geoffrey Robinson, South East Asia Research, School of Oriental and African Studies (SOAS),

University of London, Vol. 9, Issue 3, pp. 271–318, Issue published: 1 Nov 2001 [https://journals.sagepub.com/doi/10.5367/000000001101297414] pp. 276–7; 303

68 Chega! The Report of the Commission for Reception, Truth and Reconciliation in Timor Leste (CAVR), Executive Summary 2005, The systematic programme of violations in 1999

69 Chega! The Report of the Commission for Reception, Truth and Reconciliation in Timor Leste (CAVR), Executive Summary 2005, The systematic programme of violations in 1999

70 UNTAET Special Crime Unit Report, 21 Jul 2001

71 Robinson, G. (2003). *East Timor 1999: Crimes Against Humanity. Report Commissioned by the United Nations Office of the High Commissioner for Human Rights (OCHHR)*. University of California Los Angeles, Jul 2003. Hak Association & Elsam Dili and Jakarta [https://www.history.ucla.edu/sites/default/files/u184/robinson/robinson_east_timor_1999_english.pdf]

72 Robinson G (2003). *East Timor 1999: Crimes Against Humanity. Report Commissioned by the United Nations Office of the High Commissioner for Human Rights (OCHHR)*. University of California Los Angeles, Jul 2003, Ch 2. Hak Association & Elsam Dili and Jakarta [https://www.history.ucla.edu/sites/default/files/u184/robinson/robinson_east_timor_1999_english.pdf]

73 See the case of U.S. UNCIVPOL member Earl Candler in Liquica on the 4 Sept 1999.

74 Robinson. (2003), Ch 3

75 Hess, M. (2020) in Frame, T. (2020) *INTERFET: Lessons and Legacies from East Timor 20 Years on*. Connor Court Publishing Pty Ltd (12 May 2020)

76 Tanter, R. *Practical Justice in Doe v Lumintang: The Successful Use of Civil Remedies against 'an Enemy of All Mankind'*. Masters of Terror: Indonesia's Military and Violence in East Timor in 1999 (Op. Cit.) Ch 7, p. 224

77 Tanter, R. *Practical Justice in Doe v Lumintang: The Successful Use of Civil Remedies against 'an Enemy of All Mankind'*. Masters of Terror: Indonesia's Military and Violence in East Timor in 1999 (Op. Cit.) Ch 7, p. 227

78 Tanter, R. *Practical Justice in Doe v Lumintang: The Successful Use of Civil Remedies against 'an Enemy of All Mankind'*. Masters of Terror: Indonesia's Military and Violence in East Timor in 1999 (Op. Cit.) Ch 7, p 233

79 U.S. Court of Alien Tort Statute/Torture Victim Protection Act [https://cja.org/what-we-do/litigation/doe-v-lumintang/uscourt-ats-tvpa/]

80 Deputy Secretary-General pays tribute to UN staff as she accepts Elie Wiesal Ethics Award on behalf of UNAMET

12 Oct 2000 Press Release DSG/SM/19 [http://www.etan.org/et2000c/october/9-14/12award.htm]

81 Supplementary Submission to the Senate Foreign Affairs, Defence and Trade References Committee: Allegations Concerning the Propriety of the East Timor Consultation Ballot, Australian Electoral Commission, Canberra, 16 Dec 1999

82 63 'Federal Police members awarded for service in East Timor Police', AAP, 8 Aug

2000

83 East Timor Final Report of the Senate Foreign Affairs, Defence and Trade References Committee, Dec 2000

84 Senator Marise Payne, East Timor, Hansard, 29 Aug 2000 [https://parlinfo.aph.gov.au/parlInfo/search/display/display.w3p;db=CHAMBER;id=chamber/hansards/2000-08-29/0111;query=Id:%22chamber/hansards/2000-08-29/0000%22] ParlInfo - ADJOURNMENT: East Timor: Independence]

85 Hess, M, in Blaxland, J. (ed) (2015), p. 67

86 Gusmao, in Blaxland. (ed) (2015), pp. 258–9

87 White, H. (2008). *The Road to INTERFET: Reflections on Australian Strategic Decisions Concerning East Timor.* Dec 1998-Sept 1999, Security Challenges, Vol. 4, No. 1 (2008) [https://www.regionalsecurity.org.au/Resources/Files/vol4no1White.pdf]

88 Fernandes, C. (2008). *The Road to INTERFET: Bringing the Politics Back In.* Security Challenges, Vol. 4, No. 3 (Spring 2008), pp. 83–98 [https://www.jstor.org/stable/26459192?seq=1#metadata_info_tab_contents] pp. 23–24

89 Ball, D. (2002) in Ch 8 *Silent Witness: Australian Intelligence and East Timor in Masters of Terror: Indonesia's Military and Violence in East Timor in 1999.* Canberra Papers on Strategy and Defence, No. 145, Strategic and Defence Studies Centre, ANU Canberra 2002, p. 253

90 Henry, I. (2013). *Playing Second Fiddle on the Road to INTERFET: Australia's East Timor Policy Throughout 1999.* Security Challenges, Vol. 9, No. 1 (2013), pp. 87–111 [https://www.regionalsecurity.org.au/Resources/Files/SC9-1Henry.pdf] pp. 87–8;109

91 Fernandes, C. (2005). *Reluctant Saviour: Australia, Indonesia and The Independence of East Timor.* Scribe Publications Pty Ltd, p. 5

92 Fernandes, C. (2021). *Indonesia's War of Terror East Timor*: Small Wars and Insurgencies. Routledge, 18 Mar 2021

93 *Transcript of the Prime Minister The Hon. John Howard MP Address to Joint Meeting of the U.S. Congress.* 12 Jun 2002. [https://pmtranscripts.pmc.gov.au/release/transcript-12906]

94 The AFP was instrumental in the East Timor situation in 1999 and onwards in various capacities for almost two decades. The AFP became involved in assisting with the Iraq effort by providing police trainers to a US-led facility in Jordan. The AFP also became involved in the troubled nation of Afghanistan between 2007 and 2014.

95 President George, W. Bush. (2001). *Address to a Joint Session of Congress and the American People,* 20 Sept 2001 [https://georgewbush-whitehouse.archives.gov/news/releases/2001/09/20010920-8.html]

96 AFP. (1997). Platypus Magazine, No. 57, 1997, p. 5

97 Connery, D. Sambhi, N. and McKenzie, M. (2014). *A return on investment: The future of police cooperation between Australia and Indonesia.* Australian Strategic Policy Institute, p. 2 [https://www.aspi.org.au/report/return-investment-future-police-cooperation-between-australia-and-indonesia.]

98 BBC. (2001). *Bin Laden rails against Crusaders and UN*. 3 Nov 2001. [http://news.bbc.co.uk/2/hi/world/monitoring/media_reports/1636782.stm]

99 McFarlane, J. (2007). *The Thin Blue Line: The Strategic Role of the Australian Federal Police*. Security Challenges, Vol. 3, No. 3 (Aug 2007). I Madi Pastika was also officer in charge of BRIMOB in East Timor during UNAMET.

100 Connery and Sambhi. (2014), p. 4

101 Australian National Security website [https://www.nationalsecurity.gov.au/what-australia-is-doing/terrorist-organisations/listed-terrorist-organisations/jemaah-islamiyah-(ji)]

102 Australian National Security website [https://www.nationalsecurity.gov.au/Listed-terroristorganisations/Pages/JemaahIslamiyahJI.aspx]

103 Neighbour, S. (2005). *In the Shadow of Swords: On the Trail of Terrorism from Afghanistan to Australia*. Harper Collins Publishers, Australia, p. 2

104 Australian Federal Police. (2002). *Paradise Lost-Terror on our Doorstep*. Commissioner Keelty. AFP Platypus Magazine, No. 77, Dec 2002

105 Federal Agent Paul McEwan was a member of the 1st AFP deployment to UNAMET in 1999.

106 Australian Federal Police. (2002). *Paradise Lost-Terror on our Doorstep*. Commissioner Keelty. AFP Platypus Magazine, No. 77, Dec 2002, p. 4

107 Australian Federal Police. (2002). *Paradise Lost-Terror on our Doorstep*. Commissioner Keelty. AFP Platypus Magazine, No. 77, Dec 2002, p. 4

108 Australian Federal Police. (2003). *Building Success of Professionalism*. Commissioner Mick Keelty. Platypus Magazine, No. 78, Mar 2003, Operation Alliance, Bali, p. 14

109 Ashton quoted in Connery and Sambhi. (2014).

110 Australian Federal Police. (2003). *Building Success of Professionalism*. Commissioner Mick Keelty. Platypus Magazine, No. 78, Mar 2003, Operation Alliance, Bali, p. 14

111 McDevitt in Australian Federal Police (2003). *Building Success of Professionalism*. Platypus Magazine, No. 78, Mar 2003, Operation Alliance, Bali, p. 6

112 Australian Federal Police. (2003). *Building Success of Professionalism*. Platypus Magazine, No. 78, Mar 2003, Operation Alliance, Bali, p. 6

113 Australian Federal Police. (2003). *Building Success of Professionalism*. Platypus Magazine, No. 78, Mar 2003, Operation Alliance, Bali, p. 14

114 Colvin, A. (2017). *Address to the National Press Club*. 31 May 2017 [https://www.npc.org.au/speaker/2017/398-commissioner-andrew-colvin/]

115 Connery, D. Sambhi, N. and McKenzie, M. (2014). *A return on investment: The future of police cooperation between Australia and Indonesia*. Australian Strategic Policy Institute. [https://www.aspi.org.au/report/return-investment-future-police-cooperation-between-australia-and-indonesia] p. 8

116 *Report of the UN Secretary General on the Protection of Civilians in Armed Conflict*. S/1999/957

117 UNIS/SG/2360; 13 Sept 1999. *Transcript of Press Conference of Secretary-General Kofi Annan*. At Headquarters, 10 Sept. [https://unis.unvienna.org/unis/en/press-

rels/1999/sg2360.html]

118 S/RES/1265 (1999). 17 Sept 1999 [https://documents-dds-ny.un.org/doc/UN-DOC/GEN/N99/267/94/PDF/N9926794.pdf?OpenElement]; 17SEP99 1265 1999 re PoC. Cited S/PRST/1999/6 from 12FEB99.

119 *Report of the Panel on United Nations Peace Operations.* A/55/305–S/2000/809. 21 Aug 2000. [https://peacekeeping.un.org/en/report-of-panel-united-nations-peace-operations-brahimi-report-a55305]

120 2014 UN Security Council Resolution 2151: Security Sector Reform; Resolution S/RES/2151 (2014)

121 Resolution 2185 United Nations peacekeeping operations S/RES/2185 (2014). UN Security Council Resolution 2185: Policing an Essential part of Peacekeeping – 2014 [S/RES/2185 (2014)]

122 Australian Guidelines on the Protection of Civilians, Australian Civil Military Centre (ACMC), [https://www.acmc.gov.au/sites/default/files/2018-08/Australian_Guidelines_for_the_Protection_of_Civilians.pdf]

Part III: Capacity-building and the New Security Paradigm 2003–2014

1 Byrnes, J. quoted in Frame, T (ed). (2017). *The Long Road: Australia's Train, Advise and Assist Missions.* University of New South Wales Press, Sydney

2 Braithwaite, J, Dinnen, S., Allen, M., Braithwaite, V and Charlesworth, H. (2010) *Pillars and Shadows: Statebuilding as Peacebuilding in Solomon Islands.* ANU E Press, Canberra, pp. 49–50

3 Breen, B. (2016). *The Good Neighbour.* Cambridge University Press, Cambridge, p. 361

4 Wainwright, E. (2003) *Our Failing Neighbour: Australia and the Future of Solomon Islands.* Australian Strategic Policy Institute, Canberra

5 More (2005), in Breen (2016), p. 363

6 Breen, B. (2016), p. 364

7 Breen. (2016), p. 365

8 Downer, A. (2003) 'Neighbours cannot be recolonised', The Australian, 8 Jan 2003 in Koorey, S. (2015), Australia and Solomon Islands: what next after 14 years of regional assistance?, p.50 [http://www.defence.gov.au/adc/adfj/Documents/issue_198/Koorey_Nov_2015.pdf]

9 Breen. (2016), p. 365

10 Breen. (2016), p. 366

11 Breen. (2016), p. 367–8

12 *Brief on defence relations with Solomon Islands.* 7 Jun 2000, NAA: A11502, 2000/17014, in Breen (2016).

13 Braithwaite. (2012), p. 50

14 Breen. (2016), p. 361

15 Breen. (2016), p. 369

16 Warner, N. (2004). *Operation Helpem Fren: Rebuilding the Nation of Solomon Islands: Speech to National Security Conference*, Special Coordinator Nick Warner, Canberra,

Australia, 23 Mar 2004

17 Braithwaite. (2010), pp. 51–2

18 RAMSI was led by DFAT. The security aspect was led by the AFP with the ADF in a support role. The show of force was deliberately intended as a demonstration of the capability available should malign actors continue their violence.

19 Warner, N. (2003). *Message to the people of Solomon Islands*. Special Coordinator Nick Warner Henderson Airport, Honiara, Solomon Islands, 24 Jul 2003

20 This is an aphorism attributed to Theador Roosevelt, then the Governor of New York. He first used the phrase 'I have always been fond of the West African proverb: "speak softly and carry a big stick; you will go far"' in a letter to Henry L. Sprague dated 26 Jan 1900. This kind of diplomacy is sometimes referred to as 'big stick ideology'.

21 For a comprehensive and detailed explanation of the conflict in the Solomon Islands please see: Solomon Islands Truth and Reconciliation Commission Final Report Honiara Feb 2012
[https://truthcommissions.humanities.mcmaster.ca/wp-content/uploads/2021/02/Solomon-Islands-Truth-and-Reconciliation-Commission_TRC_Final-Report_Vol1.pdf]

22 McDevitt, B. in Australian Federal Police (2013). *On the Road to Transition*. AFP Platypus Magazine, Oct 2013

23 Murray, J. (2005). *The Minnows of Triton: policing, politics, crime and corruption in the South Pacific Islands*. Fadden, A.C.T., p. 92

24 Warner, N. (2004). *Operation Helpem Fren: Rebuilding the Nation of Solomon Islands: Speech to National Security Conference*, Special Coordinator Nick Warner, Canberra, Australia, 23 Mar 2004

25 Murray, J. (2005), p. 9

26 Murray. (2005), p. 93

27 Murray. (2005), pp. 93–4

28 Keke quoted by Fraenkel, J. (2004), *The Manipulation of Custom. From Uprising to Intervention in the Solomon Islands*, Australian National University, Pandanus Books, Canberra, p. 168, in Braithwaite, J. (2010), p. 53

29 Plunkett, M. (2003), *Stress-Testing Solomon Islands Peace Operations Scenarios*, Griffith University, Queensland, p. 12 in Braithwaite, J. (2010), p. 53

30 Fraenkel, J. (2004), *The Manipulation of Custom. From Uprising to Intervention in the Solomon Islands*, Australian National University, Pandanus Books, Canberra, p.168 in Braithwaite, J (2010), p. 53

31 McDevitt, B. in Australian Federal Police (2013), *It all Hinged on Harold*, AFP Platypus Magazine, Oct 2013, pp.12–3

32 Breen. (2016), p. 389

33 Braithwaite et al. (2010), p. 53

34 Warner, N. (2004). *Operation Helpem Fren: Rebuilding the Nation of Solomon Islands: Speech to National Security Conference*, Special Coordinator Nick Warner, Canberra, Australia, 23 Mar 2004

35 Braithwaite et al. (2010), p. 51

36 Australian Federal Police. (2013). *It all Hinged on Harold*. AFP Platypus Magazine, Oct 2013, p.13

37 Warner. (2004).

38 Murray. (2005), p.95

39 Australian Federal Police. (2013). *On the Road to Transition*. AFP Platypus Magazine, Oct 2013

40 RSIPF Commissioner Varley quoted in Australian Federal Police (2013), *On the Road to Transition*, AFP Platypus Magazine, Oct 2013

41 Mayfield, T. (2009) *AFP in the Solomon Islands* Tim Mayfield AUSPOL 2/2009.

42 [http://www.ramsi.org/media/peoples-survey/]

43 [http://www.ramsi.org/media/peoples-survey/]

44 [http://www.ramsi.org/media/peoples-survey/]

45 Australian Federal Police. (2013). *It all Hinged on Harold*. AFP Platypus Magazine, Oct 2013

46 Coppel, N. (2011). *Building the Capacity to Protect: The work of the Regional Assistance Mission to Solomon Islands*. Special Coordinator Nicholas Coppel, 22 Jun 2011

47 *Report of the Panel on United Nations Peace Operations*. (2000). A/55/305–S/2000/809.
[http://www.un.org/en/events/pastevents/brahimi_report.shtml]

48 Breen. (2016), p. 411

49 Breen. (2016), p. 454

50 Howard, 27 Sept 1999, p. 10517, Parliament of Australia. [http://parlinfo.aph.gov.au/parlInfo/search/display/display.w3p;db=CHAMBER;id=chamber%2Fhansardr%2F1999-09-27%2F0034;query=Id%3A%22chamber%2Fhansardr%2F1999-09-27%2F0000%22]

51 Nugent, 28 Sept 1999, p. 10759, Parliament of Australia. [http://parlinfo.aph.gov.au/parlInfo/search/display/display.w3p;db=CHAMBER;id=chamber%2Fhansardr%2F1999-09-28%2F0028;query=Id%3A%22chamber%2Fhansardr%2F1999-09-28%2F0000%22]

52 It was German influence in the Pacific region in the late 19th Century, particularly New Guinea, which was one of the driving influences which provided the impetus for the federation of the Australian colonies in 1901.

53 Crawford, R. (1943). *Ourselves and the Pacific*. Melbourne University Press, p. 39

54 *The Berlin Conference of 1884–85 (The General Act of the Berlin Conference)*. [http://originalpeople.org/berlin-conference-1884-85/]

55 PNG prime minister rejects claim he ordered Moti flight. Radio NX. 15FEB07. [https://www.rnz.co.nz/international/pacific-news/167889/png-prime-minister-rejects-claim-he-ordered-moti-flight]

56 Merrell, S. (2016). *The PNG Judiciary – The power and the glory* – Part two. Dr Susan Merrell PNG Echo, 30 Mar 2016. [http://www.pngecho.com/category/uncategorized/page/2]

57 [http://www.abc.net.au/news/2006-12-27/*solomons-shuts-out-police-chief*/2162076]

58 *AFP refutes claims made about Solomon Islands police commissioner.* AFP Media release, 12 Jan 2007

59 Media interview, Prime Minister Kevin Rudd, Bali, 13 Dec 2007. [pmtranscripts.pmc.gov.au/release/transcript-15706]

60 *Moti case thrown out as judge slams AFP over witness payments.* Michael McKenna, Sarah Elks. The Australian, 16 Dec 2009

61 [http://www.theaustralian.com.au/news/moti-case-thrown-out-as-judge-slams-afp-over-witness-payments/news-story/52ec288e974a08572d883e147bfb9607]

62 Mullins, J. in Moti v The Queen. (2012). 283 ALR 393

63 A petition by soldiers from Timor's army F-FDTL in Jan 2006 resulted in protests in Mar 2006 when 594 petitioners were dismissed from the army. A rebel group of soldiers led by Lieutenant Gastao Salsinha later joined by Major Alfredo Reinado led a rebellion. The crisis erupted into armed violence in Apr-May. Initial joint operations by the F-FDTL and police (PNTL) soon descended into armed clashes between the police, army, rebel soldiers and urban youth, with over 100 people being killed in 2006. This escalated beyond the capacity of the security forces and resulted in the fall of the Alkatiri Government. The impact continued in Timor-Leste politics and in Feb 2008 there were armed attacks on President Ramos Horta and Prime Minister Gusmao, and the death of Major Reinado.

64 Australian Federal Police. (2007). AFP Platypus Magazine, No 94, p. 16

65 Australian Federal Police. (2007). AFP Platypus Magazine, No 94, p. 16

66 [https://www.mfat.govt.nz/assets/Aid-Prog-docs/Evaluations/backup_from_uat/Mid-term-Review-Pacific-Regional-Policing-Initiative.pdf]

67 With large Exclusive Economic Zones (EEZ), and a minimal capacity to patrol and enforce them, these nations are subject to illegal exploitation of fishing mainly by vessels based in Asia. The AFP in tandem with the ADF Pacific Patrol Boat Program, provides tuition on how to prosecute offenders and seize their vessels under the rule of law, and helps to protect their resources.

68 Cybersafety Pasifika pamphlet-AFP 2017. This program is based on another AFP cyber safety program called ThinkUKnow, targeted at school-aged children and their parents in the ACT.

69 [http://www.naa.gov.au/collection/snapshots/find-of-the-month/september-2010.aspx]

70 Recruitment advertisement: Australian Department of Territories in 1959. (NAA: A452, 1959/4654) [http://www.naa.gov.au/collection/snapshots/find-of-the-month/september-2010.aspx]

71 Connery, D. and Claxton, K. (2014). *Shared interests, enduring cooperation: The future of Australia-PNG police engagement.* ASPI Special Report, Oct 2014

72 [https://www.transparency.org/country/PNG]

73 Connery and Claxton. (2014), p. 3

74 Connery and Claxton. (2014), p. 6

75 Wallis, J. (2014). *Is Australia's influence over Papua New Guinea declining?* The Strategist, Australian Strategic Policy Institute, 20 Oct 2014.

76 In the case of the ECP the purpose of applying 'privileges' and 'immunities' was to ensure that members of the deployment could perform their assigned functions effectively, efficiently and independently. 'Privileges' generally refer to exemptions from the host state's laws and regulations, for example immigration and customs requirements and the application of duties and taxation. 'Immunities' generally refer to protection from the application of legal process, including criminal and civil procedures. In the Wenge decision, any such 'privileges' and 'immunities' were deemed to be inconsistent with the PNG Constitution.

77 AFP Legal Risk Report 2012 Papua New Guinea-Australia Police Partnership, pp. 14–5

78 Australian police may return to PNG – Government says. Oct 21, 2011. [http://www.news.com.au/breaking-news/australian-police-may-return-to-png-government-says/news-story/0902d7abc5b16e0601ef7e5334768abb]

79 Rudd announces deal to send all asylum boat arrivals to Papua New Guinea, The Guardian, 19 Jul 2013. [https://www.theguardian.com/world/2013/jul/19/kevin-rudd-asylum-boats-png]

80 The Regional resettlement arrangement between Australia and PNG was signed in Brisbane 19 Jul 2013. It had as its intention '…encouraging sub-regional and bilateral arrangements to create disincentives for irregular travel, including through possible transfer and readmission arrangements.…Existing cooperation between Australia and Papua New Guinea, in particular through the Manus Island Regional Processing Centre, represents a significant element of the regional response to people smuggling. Australia warmly welcomes Papua New Guinea's offer to adopt additional measures which build on the Manus Island Regional Processing Centre. These measures will make a significant further contribution to encouraging potential unauthorized arrivals to avail themselves of lawful channels to seek asylum and to abandon the practice of perilous sea journeys which has led to the deaths of so many.' Regional Resettlement Arrangement, 19 Jul 2013.

81 Connery, D. and Claxton, K. Shared interests, enduring cooperation: the future of Australia–PNG police engagement. ASPI, Oct 2014. [https://www.aspi.org.au/report/shared-interests-enduring-cooperation-future-australia-png-police-engagement]

82 Wallis, J. (2014)

83 Wallis, J. (2014)

84 Carter, G and Firth, S. (2015). *The Mood in Melanesia after the Regional Assistance Mission to Solomon Islands, Asia and the Pacific.* Policy Studies. [http://onlinelibrary.wiley.com/journal/10.1002/(ISSN)2050-2680]

Part IV: Applying The Rule of Law in Challenging Environments Further Afield 2007–2014

1 See Breen. (2016), p. 411

2 In a somewhat arbitrary division of responsibilities at an early meeting in Bonn the division of responsibilities was allocated as follow: Afghan military: United States; Law and Justice: Italy; Police; Germany; Narcotics: Britain. As one senior British diplomat commented to the author: 'these responsibilities were worked out on the back of a fag

packet.'

3 Rashid, A. (2006), p. 13

4 Rashid, A. (2006). p. 15

5 CIA Briefing to U.S. President Bush quoted in Rashid, A. (2006), p. 59

6 Australian Federal Police. (2014). *Identity Unknown: Identity Crime*. AFP Platypus Magazine, No. 115, Jan-Jun 2014

7 Bush, G. (2001). *Selected Speeches of President George W. Bush 2001–2008*. [https://georgewbush-whitehouse.archives.gov/infocus/bushrecord/documents/Selected_Speeches_George_W_Bush.pdf]

8 Rashid. (2006). pp. 19–20

9 Rashid, A. (2006). p. 120

10 Rashid, A. (2006). p. 265

11 For a comprehensive review of Australian engagement in Afghanistan, including military engagement see Afghanistan: Lessons from Australia's Whole-of-Government Mission (2016) [https://www.acmc.gov.au/resources/publications/afghanistan-lessons-australias-whole-of-government-mission]

12 Adrian Morrice was an ACMC Consultant in 2013. *Security Sector Reform Trends: Conflict Affected States and International Responses: Background Paper*. The epitome of the lineal thinking in traditional SSR is contained in the following sentence: 'Through… multi-year periods civilian leadership of the security sector was often split in power-sharing arrangements, all the while with a transition of authority from the army to the police. As one Australian government interviewee put it, the question is 'when do the blue take over'?', 7

13 For an explanation of SSR see Morrice, A. (2013). *Security Sector Reform Trends: Conflict Affected States and International Responses: Background Paper*.

14 Dodd, M. (2007). *Australian help sought for drug fight*. The Australian, 20 Feb 2007

15 Khosa, R. (2008). *Making it Count: Australia's involvement in Afghanistan*. Australian Strategic Policy Institute, May 2008, p. 12

16 The author deployed to Kandahar Airfield with AFP Op Illuminate in 2010–11. One of the roles he was involved in was with the U.S. Dept of State led Counter Assassinations Working Group. It became patently clear from first-hand observations that justice sector actors such as police, judges, police stations and court buildings were easy targets for insurgents and were specifically targeted by the Taliban both to adversely impact the justice efforts of ISAF and also to demonstrate to the local population that the ISAF-based justice system was ineffective.

17 The term 'outside the wire' refers to the fact that, based on risk assessment, AFP members were specifically prohibited from engaging in operations outside the secured bases in Kandahar and Uruzgan. The 'wire' in this case being the perimeters of the respective bases. Members in Kabul lived in a secure base but travelled in public areas of Kabul for work-related reasons.

18 In a direct parallel, former AFP member David Savage, who joined DFAT/AUSAID after leaving the AFP and serving as a War Crimes investigator with the UN, was targeted by the 12 yo suicide bomber in Uruzgan Province in 2012. His injuries were

near fatal and he was confined to a wheelchair for several years. He still had several pieces of shrapnel in his body and has a brain injury. Unlike military 'veterans' he was left to fend for himself as his own department, DFAT and the Defence Department basically abandoned him. He finally took legal action and the matter was settled by an 'Act of Grace' compensation payment. It should be noted that non-Defence members, including DFAT, AFP and others, who deployed after the Military Rehabilitation and Compensation Act (MRCA) was passed in 2004 are not covered by any specific Act whilst serving in hazardous environments such as Afghanistan. Prior to 2004 they were covered by the Veteran's Entitlement Act (VEA) 1986. Thus, post-2004, if an AFP member was killed or seriously injured on deployment they would be covered under the same Act, the Safety Rehabilitation and Safety Act (SRCA), which covers office workers in Australia. Thus the AFP Commissioner, despite urging by various quarters, including the Prime Minister, to deploy AFP members 'outside the wire' in Afghanistan, steadfastly refused to do so. Mr Savage's experience could well have been any member of the AFP in Afghanistan or elsewhere.

19 Kilcullen, D. (2009). *The Accidental Guerrilla: Fighting Small Wars in the Midst of a Big One*. Scribe Publications, Melbourne, p. 58

20 Woodward, B. (2010). *Obama's Wars*. Simon & Schuster, New York, p. 349

21 Prime Minister Howard's words in 2004, from Breen (2016, p. 411), should be borne in mind that 'the purpose of this group (the AFP IDG) will be for deployment in the region. Nobody should construe from the formation of this group that we have in mind deployment further afield.'

22 Kilcullen, D. (2009), p. 61

23 *NATO's Counterterrorism and Counterinsurgency Experience in Afghanistan: Lessons Learned Workshop Report*. NATO Centre of Excellence-Defence Against Terrorism, Ankara, 18–20 Nov 2014. [https://www.exop-group.com/src/Frontend/Files/userfiles/files/DE/MediaCentre/News/150929_NATO_AfghanistanLessonsLearnedBooklet.pdf.] (*AAP-6 NATO Glossary of Terms and Definitions (Edition 2014)*)

24 *Afghanistan: Lessons Learned from Australia's Whole of Government Mission*. (2016). Australian Civil Military Centre, pp. 24–5 [https://www.acmc.gov.au/afghanistan/]

25 Woodward, B. (2011), p. 17

26 Smith, F. (2016). *The Dust of Uruzgan*. Allen & Unwin, Sydney, p. 300

27 SBS News 26MAR09 [http://www.sbs.com.au/news/article/2009/03/26/obama-didnt-ask-more-troops-rudd]

28 Rudd, K. (2009). *Rudd commits more troops to Afghanistan*. Michael Brissenden, 7.30 Report ABC, 2009

29 Dorling, P. and McKenzie, N. (2010). Rudd: 'Scared as hell' and Afghanistan: our secret fears, Sydney Morning Herald, 10 Dec 2010.

30 Woodward. (2011), pp. 385–6

31 Kilcullen. (2009), p. 60

32 *Afghanistan: Lessons Learned from Australia's Whole of Government Mission*. (2016). Australian Civil Military Centre, p. 4 [https://www.acmc.gov.au/afghanistan/]

33 The SW Pacific, although conflict- affected, did not involve open military combat

involving insurgency bombings, rockets and firearms, countered by Coalition capabilities involving aviation assets and fully operational combat troops. East Timor during UNAMET in 1999 was an exception where unarmed UNCIVPOL including AFP were exposed to active combat operations at the hands of the Indonesian military and its militia proxies.

34 Rashid, A. (2009). *Descent into Chaos: The U.S. and the Disaster in Pakistan, Afghanistan, and Central Asia*. Penguin, London, pp. 319–20

35 Rashid, A. (2006), p. 330

36 Hess, M. et al. (2014). *The Future of Afghanistan in South West Asia: Influences and Challenges. Summary Report*. Asia Pacific College of Diplomacy, ANU, Feb 2014, p. 6

37 Source: confidential

38 According to the Joint Investigation Team (JIT), flight MH17 was shot down by a Buk missile from the 9M38 series originated from the 53rd Anti-Aircraft Missile Brigade, a unit of the Russian armed forces from Kursk in the Russian Federation. The missile was launched by a Buk TELAR installation that was transported from the Russian Federation to a farm field near Pervomaiskyi in Eastern Ukraine. At that time, that area was controlled by the separatists. After firing, the installation was transported back to the Russian Federation with a missing missile.

39 Brown, J. (2016). *Firing Line*. Quarterly Essay, p. 50 [https://www.quarterlyessay.com.au/essay/2016/06/firing-line]

40 Brown, J. (2016). *Firing Line*. Quarterly Essay, pp. 50–1 [https://www.quarterlyessay.com.au/essay/2016/06/firing-line]

41 Toohey, P. (2015). *Former Air Chief Marshal Angus Houston believes those responsible for the MH17 disaster will face justice*. Paul Toohey, New Corp, Australia Network, 14 July 2015

42 AFP Commander Buchhorn Op Arew presentation, Russell Defence Complex, 22 Jul 2015

43 United Nations Security Council Resolution 2166 (United Nations S/RES/2166 (2014)) states inter alia:

> 1. Reaffirming the rules of international law that prohibit acts of violence that pose a threat to the safety of international civil aviation and emphasising the importance of holding those responsible for violations of these rules to account,
>
> 2. Stressing the need for a full, thorough and independent international investigation into the incident in accordance with international civil aviation guidelines…
>
> 3. Supports efforts to establish a full, thorough and independent international investigation into the incident in accordance with international civil aviation guidelines;
> 4. …States who have lost nationals on MH17, to institute an international investigation of the incident, and calls on all States to provide any requested assistance to civil and criminal investigations related to this incident; 9. Calls on all States and actors in the region to cooperate fully in relation to the international investigation of the incident;
>
> 11. Demands that those responsible for this incident be held to account and that all States co-operate fully with efforts to establish accountability. (UNSCR 2166, 2014)

44 DFAT. (2015). An MH17 tribunal: why it is necessary and timely: Media release, Foreign Minister The Hon. Julie Bishop, 21 Jul 2015

45 UN.org. (2017). *Security Council Fails to Adopt Resolution on Tribunal for Malaysia Airlines Crash in Ukraine, Amid Calls for Accountability, Justice for Victims*. Meetings Coverage and Press Releases, online. Available at: [http://www.un.org/press/en/2015/sc11990.doc.htm]

46 UN.org. (2017). *Security Council Fails to Adopt Resolution on Tribunal for Malaysia Airlines Crash in Ukraine, Amid Calls for Accountability, Justice for Victims*. Meetings Coverage and Press Releases, online. Available at: [http://www.un.org/press/en/2015/sc11990.doc.htm]

47 UN.org. (2017). *Security Council Fails to Adopt Resolution on Tribunal for Malaysia Airlines Crash in Ukraine, Amid Calls for Accountability, Justice for Victims*. Meetings Coverage and Press Releases, online. Available at: [http://www.un.org/press/en/2015/sc11990.doc.htm]

48 *Pursuing the Truth*, AFP Platypus Magazine, ed. 120, 2016, p. 18

49 Bellingcat, (2017). Pre-MH17 Photograph of Buk 332 Discovered, 5 Jun 2017. Bellingcat Investigation Team. [https://www.bellingcat.com/news/uk-and-europe/2017/06/05/pre-mh17-photograph-buk-332-discovered/]

50 Concerns about the integrity of the UN Security Council, due primarily to two of its Permanent (P5) members, is discussed more fully below.

51 Colvin, A. (2015). Lowy Institute Address, 5 Mar 2015. [https://www.afp.gov.au/news-media/national-speeches/lowy-institute-address]

52 For more detail see the Netherlands Public Prosecution Service website both [https://www.prosecutionservice.nl/topics/mh17-plane-crash/criminal-investigation-jit-mh17] and [https://www.prosecutionservice.nl/topics/mh17-plane-crash/prosecution-and-trial].

Part V: Australian Security and Sovereignty in the Asian Century 2014–2024

1 See: Babbage, R. (2023). Xi Jinping repeatedly asserts China's superiority with statement that 'there is a vivid contrast between the order of China and the chaos of the West...the East is rising and the West is declining.' 5. *The Next Major War: Can the U.S. and Its Allies Win Against China?* Also Phillips, A. (2023)...the recess of Western power in Asia is unlikely to see a...diminution of the region's survivalist ethos. For this reason, Australia-as a declining middle power-will need to calibrate its diplomacy-in acknowledgment of this reality. 639. Phillips, A. (2024). *Indigenous Foreign Policy: The Challenges of Survivalism Before and After the Era of Western Dominance* in Australian Journal of International Affairs: Special Issue: *Towards Indigenous Diplomacy: Relational Challenges to International Relations and Foreign Policy Survivalism*. Vol. 77, Issue 6, Dec 2023, Guest eds: Morgan Briggs and Mary Graham. See also: *Girt by China: Power Play in the Pacific*, Australian Foreign Affairs, 17 Feb 2023; *We Need to Talk about America: An Alliance in Flux*, Australian Foreign Affairs, 18 Jul 2023; *Our Unstable Neighbourhood: The Contest for South-East Asia*, Australian Foreign Affairs, 7 Jul 2022

2 For an outline of the significance of Sea Lines of Communication see *The trade routes vital to Australia's economic security*, David Uren, ASPI Special report, Mar 2024. [https://

www.aspi.org.au/report/trade-routes-vital-australias-economic-security]

3 Dziedzic, S., Seke, S. and Wasuka, E. (2024). *Solomon Islands Election Sees China Critic Win Seat*. ABC Pacific Beat, 19 Apr 2024. [https://www.abc.net.au/news/2024-04-19/solomon-islands-election-sees-china-critic-win-seat/103740032]

4 *Solomon Islands pro-China PM Manasseh Sogavare fails to secure majority: Sogavare vies with opposition parties to form governing coalition after inconclusive election.* [https://www.aljazeera.com/news/2024/4/24/solomon-islands-pro-china-pm-manasseh-sogavare-fails-to-secure-majority]

5 Wood. T. (2024). *Solomon Islands elections: who won on the night and why?* Devpolicy Blog, Development Policy Centre, 29 Apr 2024, [https://devpolicy.org/solomon-islands-elections-who-won-on-the-night-and-why-20240429/]

6 *Solomon Islands PM Manasseh Sogavare to stand down after poor election result*. The Guardian, 30 Apr 2024 [https://www.theguardian.com/world/2024/apr/29/solomon-islands-pm-manasseh-sogavare-to-stand-down-after-poor-election-result]

7 Aumanu-Leong , C., Dziedzic, S. Dingwall, D. and Wasuak E. *Former diplomat Jeremiah Manele elected as new Solomon Islands prime minister*. ABC Online. [https://www.abc.net.au/news/2024-05-02/solomon-islands-new-prime-minister-election-jeremiah-manele/103791138]

8 Glover, D. (2023). *History Lesson: The World Still Needs a Mighty USA*. Australian Foreign Affairs, Issue 18, Jul 2023, p. 71

9 Varrall, M. (2023). *Shaky Ground: Are We Getting China Right?* In *The New Domino Theory: Does China Really Want to Attack Australia?* Australian Foreign Affairs, Issue 19, Oct 2023, p. 28

10 Jiang, Y. (2023). *Usual Suspects: Our China-obsessed approach to foreign interference is self-defeating*. In *The New Domino Theory: Does China Really Want to Attack Australia?* Australian Foreign Affairs, Issue 19, Oct 2023, p. 75

11 Curran, J. (2023). *Excess Baggage: Is China a Genuine Threat to Australia?* In *The New Domino Theory: Does China Really Want to Attack Australia?* Australian Foreign Affairs, Issue 19, Oct 2023, p. 9.

12 Molan, J. (2022). *Danger On Our Doorstep*. Harper Collins, p. 194

13 Molan, J. (2022). *Danger on Our Doorstep*. Harper Collins, p. 250

14 Green, M. (2023). *The View From America: We're Still Your Best Bet*. In *We Need to Talk About America: An Alliance in Flux*. Australian Foreign Affairs, Issue 18, Jul 2023, p. 60

15 Molan, J. (2022). *Danger On Our Doorstep*. Harper Collins, pp. 279–80

16 Varrall, M. (2023). *Shaky Ground: Are We Getting China Right?* In *The New Domino Theory: Does China Really Want to Attack Australia?* Australian Foreign Affairs, Issue 19, Oct 2023, p. 39

17 Curran, J. (2023). *Excess Baggage: Is China a Genuine Threat to Australia?* In *The New Domino Theory: Does China Really Want to Attack Australia?* Australian Foreign Affairs, Issue 19, Oct 2023, p. 10

18 Davidson, P. (2021). *Statement of Admiral Philp S. Davidson, U.S. Navy Commander, U.S. Indo-Pacific Command before the Senate Armed Services Committee in U.S. Indo-Pacific Command Posture*, pp. 34–5

19 See Babbage, R. (2023). *The Next Major War: Can the U.S. and Its Allies Win Against China?*

China and Russia share an interests in undermining and weakening the U.S. and its allies. Indeed, the two authoritarian regimes have exchanged views and have probably already cooperated in some political warfare operations. Hence, in the event of a developing crisis between China and the US, some Russian involvement should be anticipated. A small number of other authoritarian regimes could also be expected to contribute to the campaign. North Korea and Iran could view participation to be in their interests. 131. See also: Mar 2021, The Iranian and Chinese foreign ministers signed a 25-year cooperation agreement that had been proposed by Xi Jinping in 2016 and detailed in 2020. The document vowed to strengthen military ties through joint training and exercises, joint research, and weapons development [Iran & China: Military Ties, The Iran Primer, United States Institute of Peace 28 Jun 2023] [https://iranprimer.usip.org/blog/2023/jun/28/iran-china-military-ties#:~:text=March%202021%3A%20The%20Iranian%20and,joint%20research%2C%20and%20weapons%20development.]See also: The Diplomat [https://thediplomat.com/tag/china-iran-military-relations/] and China to strengthen military cooperation with Iran, MEMO Middle East Monitor, 16 Aug 2023. [https://www.middleeastmonitor.com/20230816-china-to-strengthen-military-cooperation-with-iran/]

20 Novak, P. (2023). *Timor-Leste's uncertain future*. Lowy Institute. 29 Nov 2023 [https://www.lowyinstitute.org/publications/timor-leste-s-uncertain-future]

21 *'Playing the China card' or a serious regional threat? Timor-Leste's new deal with Beijing*. Guardian, 28 Sept 2023 [https://www.theguardian.com/world/2023/sep/28/playing-the-china-card-or-a-serious-regional-threat-timor-lestes-new-deal-with-beijing-australia]

22 See Island Business website [https://islandsbusiness.com/partner-advertorials/msg-marks-35th-anniversary-melanesia-storian-blo-yumi/]

23 It should be noted that of the five member countries of the MSG, four are independent nations. Only New Caledonia remains under French Government administration. Fiji became independent in 1970, Papua New Guinea in 1975, the Solomon Islands in 1978 and Vanuatu in in 1980.

24 *MSG Secretariat looks to China*. 13 Mar 2023. [https://islandsbusiness.com/news-break/msg-china/]

25 Movono, L. and Dziedzic, S. Fiji PM orders Chinese police out of country, saying no need for them in Pacific police force. ABC Online, 28 Mar 2024. [https://www.abc.net.au/news/2024-03-28/fiji-orders-chinese-police-to-leave-the-country/103640992]

26 *Unpacking Solomon Islands' security pact with China: The tide is turning on the security of Solomon Islands as several ANU experts unpack the security pact with China*. 6 May 2022. [https://www.anu.edu.au/news/all-news/unpacking-solomon-islands%E2%80%99-security-pact-with-china]

27 Barkhausen, B. (2023). *Papua New Guinea: Friend to all, enemy to none*. Foreign and Security Policy, 15 Jun 2023. [https://www.ips-journal.eu/topics/foreign-and-securi-

ty-policy/papua-new-guinea-friend-to-all-enemy-to-none-6774/]

28 Australian Federal Police budget 2023–24

29 The long-term diplomatic effect of UN efforts in Mozambique moved that country to transition from a Marxist past to willingly joining the Commonwealth of Nations in 1995.

30 *Standing Committee on Foreign Affairs, Defence and Trade, Australia's involvement in peacekeeping operations*. The Senate, Commonwealth of Australia, Aug 2008.

31 It should be noted that the Bali bombings followed the al Qaeda attacks in the United States on 11 Sept 2001. There were 2977 people killed in these attacks, including 10 Australians. [https://www.911memorial.org/connect/commemoration]

32 *Defence White Paper 2013*. Commonwealth of Australia, 2013

33 [https://www.afp.gov.au/news-centre/media-release/christmas-message-afp-commissioner-and-overseas-members-keeping. 2021]

34 Smith, R. and Hickman, A. (2021). *Cost of Serious and Organised Crime in Australia 2002–21*. Statistical Report 38, Australian Institute of Criminology. [https://www.aic.gov.au/sites/default/files/2022-04/sr38_estimating_the_costs_of_serious_and_organised_crime_v2.pdf]

Conclusion

1 *War on Corruption: An Indonesian Experience: Todung Mulya Lubis* (MUP), Book Review in *The New Domino Theory: Does China Really Want to Attack Australia?* Australian Foreign Affairs, Issue 19, Oct 2023, p. 101

2 Sen Gen Jim Molan AO CSC (rtd RIP) *The Final Interview. Sky News Special Report*. Jan 2023. See also *Are We Ready for War. Sky News*. Feb 2023 [https://www.youtube.com/watch?v=UUD-sCvtDE0]

[https://www.skynews.com.au/australia-news/defence-and-foreign-affairs/australias-freedom-and-prosperity-should-never-be-taken-for-granted-jim-molan/video/c31cc8ab7c2a5908e9e57a45e5a29462]

Appendix 1: Police Capacity Development

1 (United Nations Rule of Law (S/2004/616) Report to the Secretary-General on the Rule of Law and Transitional Justice in Conflict and Post-Conflict Societies. [http://www.in.org/en/ruleoflaw/]

Appendix 3: Roles of the Military and the Civilian Police

1 From A.E. Hills 'The policing of fragmenting states', *Low Intensity Conflict and Law Enforcement*, Vol. 5, No. 3, Winter 1996, pp. 334–354 at pp. 334–335 included in a chapter by McFarlane and Maley in a chapter titled 'Civilian Police in UN peace operations: Some lessons from recent Australian experience', in *United Nations Peacekeeping Operations: Ad Hoc Missions, Permanent Engagement*, Ramesh Thakur and Albrecht Schnabel (eds), United Nations University Press, New York, 2001, p. 187

Appendix 6: Melanesian Wantok system

1 [https://www.u4.no/publications/reciprocity-networks-service-delivery-and-corruption-the-wantok-system-in-papua-new-guinea] [https://indopacificimages.com/pap-

ua-new-guinea/guide-to-diving-papua-new-guinea/understanding-papua-new-guinea/papua-new-guinea-the-wantok-system/] [https://www.in-formality.com/wiki/index.php?title=Wantoks_and_Kastom_(Solomon_Islands_and_Melanesia)#:~:text=Wantok%20is%20an%20identity%20perception,a%20shared%20attachment%20to%20locality.]

References

ABC Background Briefing, 30 May 2004, 'Intelligence Wars: Behind the Lance Collins Affair' [http://parlinfo.aph.gov.au/parlInfo/search/display/display.w3p;query=Id%3A%22media%2Fradioprm%2F2YQC6%22;src1=sm1]

ABC Online, 28 March 2024, 'Fiji PM orders Chinese police out of country, saying no need for them in Pacific police force', Dziedzic, S. & Movono, L. [https://www.abc.net.au/news/2024-03-28/fiji-orders-chinese-police-to-leave-the-country/103640992]

ABC Online, 19 April 2024, 'Solomon Islands election sees prominent China critic regain seat as counting continues', Dziedzic, S., Seke, S. & Wasuka, E. [https://www.abc.net.au/news/2024-04-19/solomon-islands-election-sees-china-critic-win-seat/103740032]

Alatas, A. (2006), *The Pebble in the Shoe: The Diplomatic Struggle for East Timor*, Aksara Karunia, Jakarta

Al Jazeera, *Solomon Islands pro-China PM Manasseh Sogavare fails to secure majority: Sogavare vies with opposition parties to form governing coalition after inconclusive election* [https://www.aljazeera.com/news/2024/4/24/solomon-islands-pro-china-pm-manasseh-sogavare-fails-to-secure-majority]

Aumanu-Leong, C., Dziedzic, S., Dingwall, D. & Wasuak E., 'Former diplomat Jeremiah Manele elected as new Solomon Islands prime minister', ABC Online [https://www.abc.net.au/news/2024-05-02/solomon-islands-new-prime-minister-election-jeremiah-manele/103791138]

Australian Civil Military Centre, 'Afghanistan Lessons from Australia's Whole-of-Government Mission Report', ACMC November 2016 [http://apo.org.au/system/files/71004/apo-nid71004-15836.pdf]

Australian Federal Police (2012), *Legal Risk Report Papua New Guinea-Australia Police Partnership*

Australian Federal Police (1997), *Platypus Magazine*, no. 57, 1997

Australian Federal Police (2002), 'Paradise Lost – Terror on our Doorstep', Commissioner Mick Keelty, *Platypus Magazine*, no. 77, December 2002

Australian Federal Police (2003), 'Building Success of Professionalism', Commissioner Mick Keelty, *Platypus Magazine*, no. 78, March 2003, Operation Alliance, Bali

Australian Federal Police (2007), *Platypus Magazine*, no. 94

Australian Federal Police (2013), 'On the Road to Transition', *Platypus Magazine*, October 2013

Australian Federal Police (2013), 'It all Hinged on Harold', *Platypus Magazine*, October 2013

Australian Federal Police (2014), 'Identity Unknown; Identity Crime', *Platypus Magazine*, no. 115, Jan–Jun 2014

Australian Federal Police (2017), *International Engagement Strategy: 2020 and Beyond*, Commonwealth of Australia

Australian National Security [https://www.nationalsecurity.gov.au/Listedterroristorganisations/Pages/JemaahIslamiyahJI.aspx]

Australian Strategic Policy Institute, 'Making it Count: Australia's Involvement in Afghanistan', Raspal Khosa, 15 May 2008 [https://s3-ap-southeast2.amazonaws.com/adaspi/import/SI40_Afghanistan.pdf?958l61G_r8RDjeEJd67jsjkLN.DFv3sK]

Babbage, R. (2023), *The Next Major War: Can the U.S. and It's Allies Win Against China*, Cambria Press, New York

Bayley, D. & Perito, R. (2010), *The Police in War. Fighting Insurgency, Terrorism and Violent Crime*, Lynne Rienner Publishers, London

BBC (3 November 2001), 'Bin Laden rails against Crusaders and UN' [http://news.bbc.co.uk/2/hi/world/monitoring/media_reports/1636782.stm]

Bellamy, A. (2009), *Responsibility to Protect: The Global Effort to End Mass Atrocities*, Polity Press, Cambridge

Bellingcat Investigation Team, (June 5, 2017), 'Pre-MH17 Photograph of Buk 332 Discovered' [https://www.bellingcat.com/news/uk-and-europe/2017/06/05/pre-mh17-photograph-buk-332-discovered/]

Birmingham, J. (2001), *The Brave Ones: East Timor 1999*, Black Inc., Melbourne

Blaxland, J. (ed.) (2015), *East Timor intervention: A Retrospective on INTERFET*, Melbourne University Press, Carlton, Victoria

Brahimi, L. (2000), *Report of the Panel on United Nations Peace Operations*, A/55/305–S/2000/809 [http://www.un.org/en/events/pastevents/brahimi_report.shtml]

Braithwaite, J., Charlesworth, H. & Soares, A. (2012), *Networked Governance of Freedom and Tyranny: Peace in Timor-Leste*, ANU E-Press, Canberra

Braithwaite, J., Dinnen, S., Allen, M., Braithwaite, V. & Charlesworth, H. (2010), *Pillars and Shadows: State-building as Peace-building in Solomon Islands*, ANU E-Press, Canberra

Breen, B. (2016), *The Good Neighbour*, Cambridge University Press

Brown, J. (2017), *Firing Line*, Quarterly Essay [https://www.quarterlyessay.com.au/essay/2016/06/firing-line (Accessed 9 Sep. 2017)]

Brown, M. Stiernbald, H. & Durch, W. (2014), *Principles of International Police Command Background Paper for the SGF Thematic Meeting on Police Command*, p. 15 [http://trainingforpeace.org/wpcontent/uploads/2014/12/SGF-Principles-of-International-Police-Command.pdf]

Bush, G., 'Selected Speeches of President George W. Bush 2001–2008' [https://georgewbushwhitehouse.archives.gov/infocus/bushrecord/documents/Selected_Speeches_George_W_Bush.pdf]

Caparini, M. & Osland, K., 'As Police Roles Grow in UN Peace Operations, Clearer Guidelines Needed', March 19, 2014 [https://theglobalobservatory.org/2014/03/as-un-police-become-part-of-peacebuilding-clearer-guidelines-are-needed/]

Carter, G. & Firth, S. (2015), *The Mood in Melanesia after the Regional Assistance Mission to Solomon Islands*, Asia and the Pacific Policy Studies [http://onlinelibrary.wiley.com/journal/10.1002/(ISSN)2050-2680]

Chappell, D. & Evans, J. (1997), *The Role, Preparation and Performance of Civilian Police in United Nations Peacekeeping Operations*, Sydney

Clinton, W. (1999), *Clinton tells Indonesia: stop the killing or become pariah, Independent*, 9 September 1999 [http://www.independent.co.uk/news/clinton-tells-indonesia-stop-the-killing-or-become-pariah-1117450.html]

Coll, S. (2005), *The Secret History of the CIA, Afghanistan, and Bin Laden, from the Soviet Invasion to September 10, 2001*, Penguin Books, New York

Colvin, A. (2015), Lowy Institute Address, 5 March 2015 [https://www.afp.gov.au/news-media/national-speeches/lowy-institute-address]

Colvin, A. (2017), Address to the National Press Club, 31 May 2017 [https://www.afp.gov.au/news-media/media-releases/commissioner-colvin%E2%80%99s-national-press-club-address]

Connery, D. Sambhi, N. & McKenzie, M. (2014), *A return on investment: The future of police cooperation between Australia and Indonesia*, Australian Strategic Policy Institute [https://www.aspi.org.au/report/return-investment-future-police-cooperation-between-australia-and-indonesia]

Connery, D. & Claxton, K. (2014), *Shared interests, enduring cooperation: The future of Australia–PNG police engagement*, ASPI Special Report, October 2014

Copeland, D. (2011), *Guerrilla Diplomacy*, Viva Books, New Delhi

Coppel, N. (2011), *Building the Capacity to Protect: The work of the Regional Assistance Mission to Solomon Islands*, per Special Coordinator Nicholas Coppel, 22 June 2011

Coronation Oath: Her Majesty Queen Elizabeth the Second [https://www.royal.uk/coronation-oath-2-june-1953]

Cotton, J. (1999), *East Timor and Australia: AIIH Contributions to the Policy Debate*, Australian Defence Studies Centre, Canberra

Curran, J. (2023), 'Excess Baggage: Is China a Genuine Threat to Australia?' in 'The New Domino Theory: Does China Really Want to Attack Australia?', *Australian Foreign Affairs*, issue 19, October 2023

Czerny, V. (2017), 'Peelers Alias: "The Blue Devils", "The Raw Lobsters", "The Bludgeon Men": The Police Force under the reign of Queen Victoria', The Ragged Victorians Living History Society. www.raggedvictorians.co.uk, May 2017

Davidson, P., Statement of Admiral Philp S. Davidson, U.S. Navy Commander, U.S. Indo-Pacific Command before the Senate Armed Services Committee in U.S., *Indo-Pacific Command Posture Defence White Paper 2013*, Commonwealth of Australia

Dorling, P. & McKenzie, N. (2010), 'Rudd: "Scared as hell" and Afghanistan: our secret fears', *Sydney Morning Herald*, 10 December 2010

Dziedzic, S., Seke, S. & Wasuka, E., *Solomon Islands Election Sees China Critic Win Seat*, ABC Pacific Beat 19APR24 [https://www.abc.net.au/news/2024-04-19/solomon-islands-election-sees-china-critic-win-seat/103740032]

Einstein, A., quoted [https://www.snopes.com/fact-check/einstein-world-war-iv-sticks-stones/]

Essential Research Poll January 2017 [http://www.essentialvision.com.au/wp-content/uploads/2017/01/Essential-Report_170124.pdf]

Evans, R. (1988), *The Red Flag Riots: A Study of Intolerance*, University of Queensland Press

Fernandes, C. (Spring 2008), 'The Road to INTERFET: Bringing the Politics Back', in *Security Challenges*, vol. 4, no. 3 [https://www.jstor.org/stable/26459192?seq=1#metadata_info_tab_contents]

Finnane, M. (1994), *Police and government*, Oxford University Press, Melbourne

Fraenkel, J. (2004), *The Manipulation of Custom: From Uprising to Intervention in the Solomon Islands*, Australian National University: Pandanus Books, Canberra

Frame, T. (ed.) (2017), *The Long Road: Australia's Train, Advise and Assist Missions*, University of New South Wales Press

Frost, F. (2016), *Engaging the Neighbours: Australia and ASEAN since 1974*, Australian National University: ANU Press

Glover, D. (2023), 'History Lesson: The World Still Needs a Mighty USA' in 'We Need to Talk About America: An Alliance in Flux', *Australian Foreign Affairs*, issue 18, July 2023

Goldstein, H., *Policing a Free Society Cambridge*, Ballinger Publishing Company, Mass., 1977, p. 1

Grabosky, P. (2009), *Community Policing and Peacekeeping*, CRC Press, Boca Raton

Green, M. (2023), 'The View From America: We're Still Your Best Bet', in 'We Need to Talk About America: An Alliance in Flux', *Australian Foreign Affairs*, issue 18, July 2023

Greenwood, N. (1999), *For the Sovereignty of the People*, Australian Academic Press, Brisbane

Guardian, The (30 April 2024), 'Solomon Islands PM Manasseh Sogavare to stand down after poor election result' [https://www.theguardian.com/world/2024/apr/29/solomon-islands-pm-manasseh-sogavare-to-stand-down-after-poor-election-result]

Habu, P. Middleby, S., Naupa, A., Tarai, J. & Taylor, M., 'Perspectives from Melanesia: Aboriginal Relationism and Australian Foreign Policy', in Briggs, M. and Graham, M. (eds), *Towards Indigenous Diplomacy: Relational Challenges to International Relations and Foreign Policy Survivalism*, Australian Journal of International Affairs special Issue, vol. 77, 6 December 2023 (chapter 11, p. 650)

Harbottle, M. (1970), *The Impartial Soldier*, Oxford University Press

Henry, I. (2013), *Playing Second Fiddle on the Road to INTERFET: Australia's East Timor Policy Throughout 1999* [https://www.regionalsecurity.org.au/Resources/Files/SC9-1Henry.pdf]

Hess, M. *et al.* (March 2012), *Preparing for Elections in Afghanistan Prospects and Challenges*: Summary Report, Asia Pacific College of Diplomacy, Australian National University

Hess, M. et al. (February 2014), *The Future of Afghanistan in South-West Asia: Influences and Challenges*: Summary Report, Asia Pacific College of Diplomacy, Australian National University

Hess, M. in Blaxland (2015), *East Timor Intervention: A retrospective on INTERFET*, Melbourne University Press

Hess, M. in Frame, T. (2020), *Interfet, Lessons and legacies from East Timor 20 years on*, Connor Court Publishing

Hilton, J., 'Instructions to the New Police 1977' [https://journals.sagepub.com/doi/abs/10.1177/0032258X7705000103?journalCode=pjxa]

Horner, D., Londey, P. & Bou, J. (2009), *Australian Peacekeeping*, Cambridge University Press, Melbourne

Jennings, P. & Bergin, A. (10 October 2010), 'An Australian agenda for the UN Security Council', *The Strategist*, Australian Strategic Policy Institute [https://www.aspistrategist.org.au/an-australian-agenda-for-the-un-security-council/]

Jonsson, C. & Hall, M. (2005), *The Essence of Diplomacy: Studies in Diplomacy and International Relations*, Palgrave Macmillan

Khosa, R. (May 2008), *Making it Count: Australia's involvement in Afghanistan*, Australian Strategic Policy Institute

Kilcullen, D. (2009), *The Accidental Guerrilla: Fighting Small Wars in the Midst of a Big One*, Scribe Publications, Melbourne

Kingsbury, D. (1998), *The Politics of Indonesia*, Oxford University Press, Melbourne

Kingsbury, D. (ed.) (2000), *Guns and Ballot Boxes: East Timor's vote for Independence*, Monash Asia Institute, Melbourne

Koorey, S. (2015*)*, *Australia and Solomon Islands: what next after 14 years of regional assistance?*, p. 50 [http://www.defence.gov.au/adc/adfj/Documents/issue_198/Koorey_Nov_2015.pdf]

Maitland, F. (1885), *Justice and Police*, Macmillan, London

Maley, W. (2000), 'Australia and the East Timor Crisis: Some Critical Comments', *Australian Journal of International Affairs*, vol. 54, no. 2, 2000

Maley, W., Sampford, C. & Thakur, R. (2003), *From Civil Strife to Civil Society*, Tokyo: United Nations University Press

Mayfield, T. (2009), *AFP in the Solomon Islands*, AUSPOL 2/2009

McFarlane, J. (August 2007), 'The Thin Blue Line: The Strategic Role of the Australian Federal Police', *Security Challenges*, vol. 3, no. 3

McFarlane, J., and Maley, W. (2001), 'Civilian Police in United Nations Peace Operations: Some Lessons from Recent Australian Experience', in Thakur, R. & Schnabel, A. (eds), *United Nations Peacekeeping Operations: Ad Hoc Missions, Permanent Engagement*, Tokyo: United Nations University Press, pp.182–211

Meisler, S. (1995), *United Nations: The First Fifty Years*, Atlantic Monthly Press

Merrell, S. (30 March 2016), 'The PNG Judiciary – The power and the glory – Part two', *PNG Echo* [http://www.pngecho.com/category/uncategorized/page/2]

Meyer, C. (2009), *Getting Our Way: 500 Years of Adventure and Intrigue: the Inside Story of British Diplomacy*, Weidenfeld and Nicholson, Orion Books, London

Mills, A. (2001), *Civilian Police as Peacekeepers*, International Policing Conference

Molan, J. (2022), *Danger On Our Doorstep*, Harper Collins, Australia

Mules, N., Merrifield, S., Bull, C., Chan, M. & Hooper, S. (2001), *East Timor in transition, 1998–2000: An Australian Policy Challenge*, Canberra: Department of Foreign Affairs and Trade, Commonwealth of Australia

Murray, J. (2005), *The Minnows of Triton : policing, politics, crime and corruption in the South Pacific Islands*, Fadden, A.C.T., Australia

NATO's Counterterrorism and Counterinsurgency Experience in Afghanistan: Lessons Learned Workshop Report, NATO Centre of Excellence – Defence Against Terrorism, Ankara 18–20 November 2014 [https://www.exopgroup.com/src/Frontend/Files/userfiles/files/DE/MediaCentre/News/150929_NATO_AfghanistanLessonsLearned-Booklet.pdf]

Neighbour, S. (2005), *In the Shadow of Swords: On the Trail of Terrorism from Afghanistan to Australia*, Harper Collins Publishers, Australia

Newton, M. (2014), 'Role of the private sector in promoting economic growth and reducing poverty in the Indo-Pacific region', Joint Standing Committee on Foreign Affairs, Defence and Trade, Commonwealth of Australia [22/09/2014http://parlinfo.aph.gov.au/parlInfo/search/display/display.w3p;query=Id%3A%22committees%2F-commjnt%2F0e712173-ec81-47ca-907b-138dd027f315%2F0001%22]

Novak, P. (2023), *Timor-Leste's uncertain future*, Lowy Institute, 29 November 2023 [https://www.lowyinstitute.org/publications/timor-leste-s-uncertain-future]

Plunkett, M. (2003), *Stress-Testing Solomon Islands Peace Operations Scenarios*, Griffith University, Queensland

Principles of Good Policing, Civitas, London [https://www.civitas.org.uk/research/crime/facts-comments/principles-of-good-policing/]

Police Service of Northern Ireland [https://www.psni.police.uk/about-us/our-history/history-policing-ireland]

Rashid, A. (2009), *Descent into Chaos: The U.S. and the Disaster in Pakistan, Afghanistan, and Central Asia*, Penguin Books, London

Reiner, R. (2010), *The Politics of the Police*, Oxford: Oxford University Press

Reith, C. (1956), *A New Study of Police History*, Oliver and Boyd, London

Robinson, G, (2003), *East Timor 1999: Crimes against Humanity: A Report Commissioned by the United Nations Office of the High Commissioner for Human Rights*, OHCHR, University of California, Los Angeles

Roggeveen, S. (2023), 'Target Australia: Is the Alliance Making us Less Safe' in 'We Need to Talk About America: An Alliance in Flux', *Australian Foreign Affairs*, issue 18, July 2023

Rudd, K. (2009), 'Rudd commits more troops to Afghanistan', Interview with Michael Brissenden, 7.30 Report ABC, 2009

Ryan A. (29 November 2016), 'Delivering "joined-up" government: achieving the integrated approach to offshore crisis management', *The Strategist*, ASPI

Savage, D. (2002), *Dancing with the Devil*, Clayton: Monash Asia Institute

Sieghart, P. (1978), 'Harmless weapons a threat to liberty?' *New Scientist*, 30 March 1978, p. 841

Slaughter, A. (2009), *A New World Order*, Princeton: Princeton University Press

Smith, F. (2016), *The Dust of Uruzgan*, Allen & Unwin, Sydney

Standing Committee on Foreign Affairs, Defence and Trade, 'Australia's involvement in peacekeeping operations', The Senate, Commonwealth of Australia, August 2008.

Stock, J. (2017) *INTERPOL National Central Bureaus essential in enhancing global security* Secretary General Jürgen Stock 08 March 2017. https://www.interpol.int/

Thakur, R. & Maley, W. (2015), *Theorising the Responsibility to Protect*, Cambridge: Cambridge University Press

Thakur, R. & Schnabel, A. (2002), *United Nations Peacekeeping Operations*, Shibuya-ku: United Nations University Press

Thompson, S. (2014), 'Fifty years of Australian Civilian Police Involvement in International Peacekeeping', *The Strategist*, Australian Strategic Policy Institute, Canberra

Toohey, B. (1999), 'Hunt on for Indonesian Spy', *Australian Financial Review*, 18 September 1999

Toohey, P. (2015), 'Former Air Chief Marshal Angus Houston believes those responsible for the MH17 disaster will face justice', News Corp., Australia Network, July 14, 2015

Todd, M. (2007), 'Australian help sought for drug fight', *The Australian*, 20 February 2007

United Nations Declaration on Principles of International Law concerning Friendly Relations and Co-operation among States in accordance with the Charter of the United Nations, 24 October 1970 [http://www.un-documents.net/a25r2625.htm]

United Nations Rule of Law (S/2004/616), Report to the Secretary-General on the Rule of Law and Transitional Justice in Conflict and Post-Conflict Societies [http://www.in.org/en/ruleoflaw/]

United Nations (2017), 'Security Council Fails to Adopt Resolution on Tribunal for Malaysia Airlines Crash in Ukraine, Amid Calls for Accountability, Justice for Victims', Meetings Coverage and Press Releases [http://www.un.org/press/en/2015/sc11990.doc.htm; accessed 9 September 2017]

UN Security Council Resolution 186 (1964), 'The Cyprus Question: creation of a Peace-keeping Force in the interest of preserving international peace and to prevent a recurrence of fighting' [S/RES/186 (1964)]

UN Security Council Resolution 193 (1964), 'Appeal to Turkey, to cease bombarding the island, and to Cyprus, ordering all her armed forces to cease firing'. The Council called upon all to co-operate fully with the Commander of the United Nations Peacekeeping Force in Cyprus and to refrain from any action that might exacerbate or broaden the hostilities. [S/RES/193 (1964)]

UN Security Council Resolution 745 (1992), 'United Nations Transitional Authority Cambodia (UNTAC)' [S/RES/745/ (1992)]

UN Security Council Resolution 916 (1994), 'United Nations Operation in Mozambique (ONUMOZ)' [S/RES/916/ (1994)]

UN Security Council Resolution 353 (1974): demanded an immediate end to foreign military intervention in the Republic of Cyprus; requested the withdrawal without delay from the Republic of Cyprus of foreign military personnel present otherwise than under the authority of international agreements; called upon Greece, Turkey and the United Kingdom of Great Britain and Northern Ireland to enter into negotiations without delay for the restoration of peace in the area and constitutional government in Cyprus; called upon all parties to co-operate fully with the United Nations Peace-Keeping Force in Cyprus to enable it to carry out its mandate. [S/RES/353/ (1974)]

UN Security Council Resolution 384 (1975): recognized the right of the people of East Timor to self-determination and independence in accordance with the Charter; called upon the Government of Indonesia to withdraw all its forces from the territory without delay; called on the Government of Portugal, as administering Power, to co-operate fully with the UN and urged all states and other parties to co-operate fully with the UN's efforts to achieve a peaceful solution to the situation and to facilitate the decolonization of the territory. [S/RES/384/(1975)]

UN Security Council Resolution 389 (1976): reaffirmed the right of the people of East Timor to self-determination. The Council called upon all states to respect the territorial integrity of East Timor and upon the Government of Indonesia to withdraw all of its forces from the Territory. [S/RES/389/ (1976)]

UN Security Council Resolution 1236 (1999): agreement between Indonesia and Portugal on the future of East Timor and a proposed United Nations presence to assist with the East Timor Special Autonomy Referendum scheduled for August 1999. [S/RES/1236/ (1999)]

UN Security Council Resolution 1246: established the United Nations Mission in East Timor (UNAMET) to organise and conduct the East Timor Special Autonomy Referendum on the future status of East Timor. [S/RES/1246/ (1999)]

UN Security Council Resolution 1264: established the multinational International Force for East Timor (INTERFET) to restore peace and security in the territory. [S/RES/1264/ (1999)]

UN Security Council Resolution 2151: 'Security Sector Reform: 2014' [S/RES/2151 (2014)]

UN Security Council Resolution 2185: 'Policing an Essential Part of Peacekeeping: 2014' [S/RES/2185 (2014)]

UN Security Council Resolution 2166: 'Malaysia Airlines Flight MH17' [S/RES/2166 (2014)]

Varrall, M. (2023), 'Shaky Ground: Are We Getting China Right?' in 'The New Domino Theory: Does China Really Want to Attack Australia?', *Australian Foreign Affairs*, issue 19, October 2023

Wallis, J. (2012), 'The Pacific: from "arc of instability" to "arc of opportunity"?', *The Strategist*, Australian Strategic Policy Institute, Canberra

Wallis, J. (2014), 'Is Australia's influence over Papua New Guinea declining?', *The Strategist*, Australian Strategic Policy Institute, 20 October 2014

Wallis, J. & Carr, A. (2016), *Asia-Pacific Security*, Washington: Georgetown University Press

Warner, N. (2003), 'Message to the people of Solomon Islands', Special Coordinator Nick Warner, Henderson Airport, Honiara, Solomon Islands 24 July 2003

Warner, N. (2004), 'Operation Helpem Fren: Rebuilding the Nation of Solomon Islands', speech to National Security Conference by Special Coordinator Nick Warner, Canberra, Australia, 23 March 2004

White, H. (2003), 'Not hard cop, not soft cop, but still firmly into PNG', *Sydney Morning Herald*, 23 September 2003

White, H. (2008), 'The Road to INTERFET: Reflections on Australian Strategic Decisions Concerning East Timor, December 1998–September 1999' [https://www.regionalsecurity.org.au/Resources/Files/vol4no1White.pdf]

Woods. T., 'Solomon Islands elections: who won on the night and why?', Devpolicy Blog, Development Policy Centre, 29 April 2024 [https://devpolicy.org/solomon-islands-elections-who-won-on-the-night-and-why-20240429/]

Woodward, B. (2010), *Obama's Wars*, New York: Simon & Schuster

Yun Jiang (2023), 'Usual Suspects: Our China-obsessed approach to foreign interference is self-defeating', in 'The New Domino Theory: Does China Really Want to Attack Australia?', *Australian Foreign Affairs*, issue 19, October 2023

About the Author

Dr Martin Hess retired from the Australian Federal Police in 2021 after serving for 33 years as a sworn member. He is a designated detective and has worked throughout Australia in various capacities. He has also served internationally, with the United Nations in Cyprus (UNFICYP) in 1996 and with the first United Nations mission to East Timor (UNAMET) in 1999 which oversaw the ballot which eventually led to the independence of Timor Leste in 2002. He served in Afghanistan with AFP Operation Illuminate in 2010–11.

Martin worked with the International Deployment Group leading mission support desks for Afghanistan and Cambodia as well as Papua New Guinea and the Pacific. Following this, he worked as an AFP advisor and liaison officer to the Australian Civil Military Centre and to the Australian Defence Force HQ Joint Operations Command, just prior to his retirement.

Martin also served for 25 years as a member of the Australian Army Reserve and served with Melbourne University Regiment and 51 Bn The Far North Queensland Regiment, a Regional Force Surveillance Unit responsible for land and estuarine military surveillance in north-eastern Australia.

Martin joined the AFP in 1988 with a Bachelor of Economics which he followed with a Master of Defence Studies and a Master of Leadership and Management. In 2018 he was awarded a Doctor of Philosophy from the Australian National University. His thesis topic was The Australian Federal Police as an International Actor: Diplomacy by Default.